BLOOD
LEGACY

Also by Alex Renton

*Stiff Upper Lip: Secrets, Crimes and the
Schooling of a Ruling Class*

Planet Carnivore

BLOOD LEGACY

RECKONING WITH A FAMILY'S STORY OF SLAVERY

ALEX RENTON

CANONGATE

First published in Great Britain, the USA and Canada in 2021
by Canongate Books Ltd, 14 High Street, Edinburgh EH1 1TE

Distributed in the USA by Publishers Group West
and in Canada by Publishers Group Canada

canongate.co.uk

1

For image credits please see p. 379

British Library Cataloguing-in-Publication Data
A catalogue record for this book is available on
request from the British Library

ISBN 978 1 78689 886 9

Typeset by Palimpsest Book Production Ltd, Falkirk, Stirlingshire

Printed and bound in Great Britain by Clays Ltd, Elcograf S.p.A.

To Elizabeth Delaroche,
born in Jamaica in 1761,
and her mother Mary, whose African
birth name is unknown

CONTENTS

NOTES

Language

As the history of transatlantic and plantation enslavement has been re-examined, a debate has begun over the language used to discuss slavery, the associated industries and the millions of people whose lives were ended or altered by it. The point has been made that some words traditionally employed tend to dehumanise: for example, 'slave' defines a person by the role forced on them by their exploiters. For many, 'slavery' itself is an outmoded and unsatisfactory term. This discussion is still evolving: I have attempted to reflect current thinking, as far as I am aware of it, in the language used in this book.

Sources

The Fergusson of Kilkerran papers, the main archive on which this book is based, are owned by Sir Charles Fergusson. A catalogue is available from the National Records of Scotland (NRAS 3572). More information and further notes on sources at bloodlegacybook.com.

Relative value

My distant great-uncle James Fergusson had two dairy cows at his plantation in Tobago in the year 1777. They were valued at £15 each – so what would they be worth today?

There is little consensus on how to calculate this. The simplest method is to use 'relative price worth' (RPW), which uses the average prices of a range of goods and services as they were in the base year and compares with the same today: it is how we measure inflation. But as time passes RPW gets less meaningful, not least because the things we commonly buy change, as do production methods and availability.

For academic historians wage growth and income 'worth' are more useful. The 'relative wealth index' (RWI) calculates change in prices according to change in purchasing power, using data on average earnings for all workers or 'labour/income value'. A third, 'relative output worth' (ROW), calculates sums according to the gross domestic product of a country in the base year, and then adjusts according to the change in GDP per capita between then and the target year. It is most useful for national economies.

Each system gives very different results. That £15 cow in 1777 is worth £1,950 today according to RPW, £24,760 according to RWI and £28,800 using ROW. In August 2020 the average price of a newly calved heifer in Britain was in fact £1,524, so RPW looks like a good indicator. However, the real price of farm animals and of food has dropped immensely since the eighteenth century, with the industrialisation of agriculture. So RWI may be the better indicator.

RWI seems to work for larger sums, especially in property. An Edinburgh town house is reported to have cost £1,000 in 1800: that equates to £81,300 using RPW, but a more realistic £1.1 million using RWI. The Hunter Blair family, who owned a plantation and enslaved people with the Fergussons, spent £34,000 in 1798 buying Blairquhan Castle and 12,000 acres of land, some of it moor and woodland but also pasture and farms. Using RPW that £34,000 equates to £3.3 million, but using RWI it comes to £42.1 million. In 2012 Blairquhan Castle and 675 acres were sold for £4.85 million. The other 10,000 acres of mixed farm and forest land in Scotland today might cost around £40 million.[1]

Unless indicated otherwise, this book follows most academic practice in using RWI. More information can be found at measuringworth. com, whose calculators I have used. 'Today' is the year 2020.

Reparations and this book

Some members of my family are donating to educational and youth welfare projects in the Caribbean and in the UK. While recognising that the damage done by slavery cannot be repaired, nor the descendants of the people who were enslaved adequately compensated, there is still an opportunity for people who have benefited from this past to do what they are able to change the continuing consequences of it. More details at bloodlegacybook.com.

Any profits from this book will be given to similar causes.

The Caricom group of nations is seeking to begin discussions about reparation with Europe's former slaving nations. This is discussed in Chapter 18, 'Jamaica today'. More information can be found at caricomreparations.org.

INTRODUCTION

It is a privilege to learn about racism instead of experiencing it your whole life.

Sign at a Black Lives Matter rally,
June 2020

I AM AN HEIR OF Britain's slavery past. It marks my mind, my culture, my DNA. I am a descendant of the owners of enslaved people, and of traders in them; of a campaigner for the abolition of slavery and of an enslaved African woman. Like me, the Britain in which I grew up is a place shaped, in no small way, by transatlantic and plantation slavery and the many industries that thrived on them. I am part of the legacy that lives on, economically and culturally, visible not just in grand houses and old statues, but in the systemic and street-level racism that afflicts our country today.

Like most of us, I am a mess of differing inheritances, but the person I present to the world is pretty much the one formed by the wealthy people of my ancestry. As a white, middle-class Briton I am so shielded from everyday racism I rarely notice it. While most of the wealth my ancestors accrued was long ago spent, the privilege garnered from it still protects and supports me. The history of Britain and slavery, worked and glossed to make it distant and irrelevant, is the foundation of my comfortable, liberal life.

My family keeps archives. When I read the papers there that documented our forebears' activities in the Caribbean, most of them carefully annotated by my historian grandfather, I knew that the story they contained had to be brought to the light. I felt it wrong to keep the history from the descendants of the enslaved people who had worked and died on our plantations. Most of the wider family, including my own children, knew nothing of this past. So, with the agreement of the owners of the archive, there began a job of photographing and transcribing the papers. What I discovered profoundly challenged my assumptions about who I was, about the history I had been taught, and about Britain today.

The papers make it possible to untangle some of what happened in Tobago and Jamaica. But a huge hole will always remain where the accounts of the 950 or so people who were enslaved by my ancestors should sit.[2] We have the direct testimony of just one of them. That fact renders this only half a narrative, one that hardly deserves to be called history. So, it is the story of my mother's family, the Fergussons, their partners the Hunter Blairs and the Britain that, not so long ago, tolerated the enslaving of human beings for profit. It is also about the legacy, still toxic, still harming people, 180 years after emancipation in the British Caribbean.

The Fergussons were wealthy, well-educated and influential. They were connected to some of the most powerful in the land, including the politicians on either side of the forty-year-long public debate over abolition of slavery and the slave trade. The individuals who I have come to know through their letters were humane and generous in their dealings in Britain. It is more than uncomfortable to realise that, were it possible to erase their West Indian business ventures, and the great moral disaster that enabled those, you might find some likeable, even admirable people.

As slave plantation owners, the Fergussons were ordinary. They only emerge from the mass of people who invested in this way because of the survival of these records. Like many, my ancestors were absentee owners, with one brief exception. They did not make any great fortune by the standards of the time. The profits they accrued from sugar did not build grand houses or finance a nineteenth-century industrial empire. The British government made more in taxes on the Fergusson West Indies business than the family did in profits.

When the Fergussons invested in land and enslaved people in the West Indies they were doing something ordinary, for people with money, or the means to borrow it, at that time. The compensation records of 1834 list 46,000 slave owners who were rewarded for giving up their 'property' at abolition. Among those are thirty-seven other Fergusons or Fergussons who owned enslaved people: some of them got much richer. Much of what happened at Rozelle, the Jamaica plantation my family co-owned from 1769 to 1848 (and then owned alone till 1875), is average too. The family papers provide some explanations for what happened there and in Tobago: ignorance, bad managers, financial and social pressures, the normalisation of the racist brutality of the plantations, the exigencies of familial duty. Horrified and ashamed of what our ancestors did, we cling to these excuses. But they are not of much use to anyone.

Tens of thousands of Britons profited directly from transatlantic and plantation slavery: many of them ordinary people who did something extraordinarily wrong, understood now as a crime against humanity. Clearly they thought of it differently. But they were not so different. As I got to know my ancestors, I had to acknowledge that the choices they made were ones I might have made too had I lived then. This book attempts to show how that came to be and why the wrong they and the others like them did is downplayed and misunderstood – a history abused by those who did best out of it and a legacy still blighting our society today.

* * *

The many industries dependent on the trade in enslaved people and slavery-run plantations accounted for 12 per cent of British GDP at the start of the nineteenth century.[3] Yet the enslaving side of this was an offshore enterprise, kept 5,000 miles away in the Americas: by the 1770s it was becoming impossible to own or be an enslaved person in Britain itself.* But even if the plantations had been in Perthshire and Sussex, I suspect many white Britons would still find a way to deny the relevance of what was done, to discount the lives of 3.25 million Africans[4] and their uncounted descendants that we squandered for profit. The story is too recent, its legacy too awful, for us to accept it for what it was – an inexcusable crime, the 'original sin' of the British Empire, as the historian Simon Schama puts it. The enslavement of Africans, he continues, was a necessary condition of the success of the Empire – the stain left, 'no amount of self-congratulation at its eventual abolition can altogether wash away'.[5]

....
* The *Somerset* v *Stewart* case in England in 1772 ruled that an owner could not forcibly transport black people back to chattel slavery, though it did not make slavery illegal. The Joseph Knight case in Scotland of 1778 went further, deciding that slavery was inconsistent with Scots law.

I grew up, like most white British people of my age, ignorant of Britain's history of slavery. Why wasn't this crucial period in the forming of modern Britain part of the knowledge we were given to address the world? We learnt a lot about the origins of the First World War. There was just a great empty space around the 250 years of exploitation in the British American and Caribbean colonies. This hole was not just in my mind, but in all of mainstream British culture, from literature and art to film. Why? American twentieth-century literature addressed slavery and its legacy, yet the United States emancipated its enslaved people hardly three decades after we did.[6]

The enslaving of Africans laid the foundations – political, economic, cultural – of the Britain in which I grew up, and which my family played a part in ruling. Yet all I knew by the end of my expensive education was that William Wilberforce inspired the British govern-ment to abolish the slave trade in 1807, and that that was something of which we could all be very proud. This triumph, it was implied, cancelled out all that we had done with and to the people we enslaved. Even more, 1807 was the birth-year of the notion of morally excep-tional Britain, the best-intentioned imperial power that the world has ever known. As the great Caribbean historian of empire, Eric Williams, wrote in 1964: 'The British historians wrote almost as if Britain had introduced Negro slavery solely for the satisfaction of abolishing it.'[7]

The fact that I had no idea of the date when Britain actually did abolish slavery in its Caribbean colonies says much. I knew even less about what happened in those colonies after slavery was ended – another blank that carries on right through to the arrival of West Indians, as we called them, in the great whiteness of the English home counties where I grew up in the 1960s and 1970s. Like most young, middle-class Britons of that time, I did not really know anything at all until Bob Marley and Burning Spear entered my consciousness.

This great ignorance was a product of both shame and pride, I believe. The generations that went before us shaped and moulded the history into something they could live with. They offered them-selves many consolations and reassurances. When historians writing in the mid-twentieth century briefly mention transatlantic slavery and Britain they often quote the then-fashionable philosopher Walter Benjamin: 'There is no document of civilization which is not at the same time a document of barbarism.' Intellectualism, just like patriotism, was and remains quick at providing mitigations and alibis for the unforgivable.

Debates about the morality of forcibly removing people from Africa were – as they still are – dissembled into discussions about the blame that might be shouldered instead by Africans for selling each other to the Europeans. Slavery's role in financing Britain's subsequent industrial growth was discounted. And what the historians could not swallow, they buried. The details of the massacre of the Africans on trading ships like the *Zong* were known, as was the account of the decades of rape by the respectable planter Thomas Thistlewood. There is much more in the records on the gross injustices that led to Samuel Sharpe's 'rebellion'* in Jamaica in 1831 and the insanely brutal retribution that followed the 'West Indian Mutiny' – the uprising of labourers and smallholders around Jamaica's Morant Bay in 1865. But most mainstream, white twentieth-century historians skipped over these.

The British government's failings in Jamaica and other colonies after 1838 – the true date of the end of slavery in the British Caribbean – are perhaps the least told story of all. The history of Britain's Caribbean colonies after emancipation is a story of decades of gross neglect, careless and deliberate. It is not the benevolent imperialism about which we were taught. The colonial period perpetuated the injustice that went before and ensured that the racism of slavery would continue to blight lives today. We did know: missionaries wrote reports, economists visited and deplored the situation. Joseph Chamberlain, Secretary of State for the Colonies, looked at the desperate poverty of the Caribbean colonies in 1898 and promised action to alleviate 'the Empire's darkest slum'. But though people of those islands came to fight in our wars, and do our most menial jobs, we did not act to help them as fellow-Britons, or fellow-human beings.

* * *

Until June 2020 and the rise in mainstream media coverage of the Black Lives Matter movement, most white Britons, however educated, have hardly thought for a moment about this history. 'Why can't they just get over it, move on, live in the twenty-first century?' is a

....
* Accounts from Britain's colonial era frequently use words like 'rebellion' or 'mutiny' for a civil uprising or insurrection.

complaint I heard a lot that year. We know we are ignorant, but we reject with ease the notion that racism against black people is itself born of the transatlantic slavery era, of the beliefs we acquired to make the enslavement of people on the grounds of their colour morally acceptable. If you sift through the eighteenth-century arguments, philosophical and theological, over slavery you will come up with an inescapable conclusion. As Christian people who believed in the rights of man, my ancestors and many like them could not have owned actual human beings. They had to believe their 'property' was something less than human in order to justify the act.

In many ways, the class that rules Britain today is not so different from the one that profited from slavery and delayed its abolition. The political descendants of those who defended slavery now deny or discount its continuing legacy. This mindset refuses, too, to accept that the modern problems of peoples and nations that endured slavery under European colonisers might be caused by that traumatic history. It rejects the health and mental health statistics, the arrest and imprisonment rates, the evidence of barriers in education and work: any excuse will be found for all these except that of racially based inequality. One hard fact illustrates a lot of what goes wrong in our systems: while young white British men are more likely than any other group to report suicidal thoughts, the group most likely to actually kill themselves are young black men.[8]

Any explicatory narrative other than slavery and its legacy of racism and poverty will do, it seems. In June 2020 Britain's prime minister Boris Johnson called for a 'change of narrative', for black people to lose their 'sense of discrimination and victimisation'.[9] That seems both naïve and cruel to people who have clearly been discriminated against and victimised. Johnson's statement came just as the Office for National Statistics revealed that four times as many British people of 'black ethnicity' were dying of Covid-19 as white people.[10] (In the United States, 24 per cent of deaths by August 2020 had been black people, who make up 13 per cent of the population.[11]) While some of the British, from bus drivers to doctors and nurses, were infected as they did their jobs, most appear to have died because of previous poor health or lack of resources: because of structural racism.*

....
* No genetic factor explaining a higher susceptibility to Covid-19 among people with African origins had been identified by the time this book went to press.

The ignorance and the cover-up of racism today are crimes as notable in their way as slavery itself, and their effects on our modern world seem as pernicious. They start with the denial of black people's access to the materials of their own history as well as the interpretation of it, which has allowed the racist slurs of the slavery period to survive and flourish. Modern racism thrives on those ideas: while researching this book I heard every slur and falsehood put about by the pro-slavery lobby during the abolition debates two centuries ago repeated by people in Britain today.

During and after slavery, the British empire used racism as a key organising mechanism. Today, among the poisonous detritus of that empire, is the fact that skin colour is still used to predetermine a human being's honesty, ability and intelligence – their value to society. All you can do with such nonsense and bigotry is take it as proof that those who say that British transatlantic slavery is an era concluded are wrong. We who took possession of the story continue to perpetuate a slavery of the mind that is as powerful and damaging to the victims of it today as it has ever been.

* * *

'Silence is violence'. In June 2020 I saw a poster that said that, made for a Black Lives Matter rally held in Holyrood Park, in Edinburgh. This was a peaceful, well-tempered event addressed by, among others, Sir Geoff Palmer, a retired professor of brewing science. Sir Geoff came to Britain in 1954, aged fourteen, to join his mother, who had arrived on the *Windrush* to help fill the need for workers as the country recovered from the war.

Now aged eighty, Sir Geoff is well known in Scotland for his personal campaign for his country to recognise how much of its wealth comes from slavery. He has spent his retirement touring the country and explaining, with patience and good humour, the history that is in fact in front of Scottish people's noses. A re-plaquer, not a statue-breaker, he puts better than anyone else why it is worth telling this story truthfully. 'You can't change the past,' he says, 'but you can change its consequences.'

Is silence violence? The challenge is that merely not being, or not considering oneself, racist actually props up racism. That notion was enraging some people during the summer of 2020.

Their contention was that being passive was a human right, to call their stance collusion was an aggression. For my part, I feel that, having found out what was in the family archive, silence would have been wrong, a complicity. If my family can admit our history, we can do a right. We can change a consequence; even, in a small way, help steer the long story of transatlantic slavery onto a different path. As the historian David Olusoga said in late 2020, acknowledging slavery and the violence of a part of our past is not 'almost treasonous' – as some people have indicated to him – but constructive and mature. 'Britain is a wonderful country. But like every country that ever existed it did some good and it did some bad and if we only focus on the good we delude ourselves . . . We need a history that functions for a country that's 14 per cent BAME.'[12]

When I first started thinking about this book I spoke to many people about what they would like to read. How could I, a stereotype of a white liberal journalist, ripe with post-imperial guilt, best exploit my privilege – and my access to these papers? 'No more slavery porn!' said one interviewee of African-Caribbean origin. She had had enough of reading about deaths on plantations and slave ships; she had had enough of white liberal breast-beating too. 'What I'm interested in is how you – your family – are going to heal yourselves. That is what is needed: for the white people to work out what they are going to do and be for the future.'

The Fergussons of Kilkerran

Sir James Fergusson, 2nd baronet and Lord Kilkerran m. Jean Maitland, daughter of Earl of Sutherland
(1687–1759)

Sir Adam Fergusson, 3rd baronet (1733–1813)   Charles   **George, Lord Hermand**   Jean   Helen m. **Sir David Dalrymple, Lord Hailes**   James (died Tobago, 1777)

Sir James Fergusson, 4th baronet (Charles's son) m. **Jean Dalrymple**, daughter of Lord Hailes and Helen Fergusson above
(1765–1838)   m. 2nd, **Henrietta Duncan**, daughter of Admiral Lord Duncan of Camperdown

Sir Charles Dalrymple Fergusson, 5th baronet m. Helen Boyle, daughter of David Boyle, Lord Boyle
(1800–1849)

Sir James Fergusson, 6th baronet m. Lady Edith Broun-Ramsay, daughter of 1st Marquess of Dalhousie (and two further marriages)
(1832–1907)

Major General **Sir Charles Fergusson**, 7th baronet m. Lady Alice Boyle, daughter of 7th Earl of Glasgow
(1865–1951)

Sir James Fergusson, 8th baronet m. Frances Dugdale, daughter of Edgar Dugdale
(1904–1973)

Sir Charles Fergusson, 9th baronet m. Amanda Noel-Paton, daughter of Baron Ferrier   Alice m. Tim Renton, Lord Renton of Mount Harry
(1931–

Alex Renton

Offspring that are not relevant have been omitted; names in bold appear in this story.

CHAPTER I

IN THE FAMILY PAPERS

WHEN I WAS A CHILD we spent many holidays at my mother's family home, a grand but decaying old house in the Girvan valley of Ayrshire, south-west Scotland. Her family, the Fergussons, had lived in the valley for more than 500 years: the house, Kilkerran, was a living museum of the preceding generations and of their adventures. The Fergussons had roamed far, 'serving the Empire': soldiers and politicians stared down from their portraits at us, their books were on the library shelves. The rooms where we played – there were more empty and disused than actually lived in – were full of their trophies: medals, uniforms, swords (ceremonial and real), stuffed animals, strange hats all jumbled up with the toys of long-ago childhoods. We were steeped in the family history; we learnt to revere it and those serious-faced ancestors. They did not seem very distant: the adults talked of them and their feats and faults as though they had just departed.

The attic floor was servants' rooms, from the days when the house had a dozen or more of them. In the early 1940s it housed evacuees from the German bombing of Glasgow and Clydeside. Now it was abandoned, a continual battle being waged against the dry rot that threatened the roof. Heaps of junk and broken furniture were piled inside the damp rooms. One rainy day we discovered two half-length coats of chain mail in a former maid's room. We tried to put them on. They were incredibly heavy – it was impossible to pull them over your head. The only way was to crawl into the tunnel of rusty links and then try to stand up.

My grandfather laughed when we told him we'd found suits of armour from the Crusades. He was a gentle and kind person, a historian and journalist – not very like his soldiering forebears. We did not see him much; during the week he was in Edinburgh, where he ran Scotland's national records office. At home he was often shut away in his cigarette smoke-filled study 'working on the family papers'. These were a vast trove. The most important, dating from the seventeenth century, were kept in a thick-walled room at the house's ancient heart. Being shown round the strong-room by my grandfather – who told a good ghost story – was a holiday treat.

No, he told us, it was not armour but chain mail, and not from the Crusades but much more recent – 1839, sixty-five years before he was born. The suits had been made for the Eglinton Tournament. It was a huge fancy-dress party, he said, where families from around Ayrshire, and from all over Britain, came together to pretend to be medieval knights and joust at each other on horseback as in the olden days.

'With real spears?' we asked.

'Oh yes,' he said, 'it was dangerous. And very expensive. Sadly it was not a success: it rained for the whole weekend.'

Years later I found an old paperback book about the tournament titled *The Knight and the Umbrella*, by Ian Anstruther. Quotes from my grandfather's enthusiastic review for *The Bookman* magazine fill the back cover. Anstruther tells how, at the dawn of the industrial age, a group of wealthy aristocrats met at Eglinton Castle in Ayrshire to re-stage a spectacle of the height of feudal times. The novels of Sir Walter Scott, full of chivalry and romance, were an inspiration.

The tournament was the idea of Archibald Montgomerie, 13th Earl of Eglinton, a spoilt twenty-seven-year-old aesthete from an ancient Ayrshire family. He had been infuriated at the lack of traditional ceremony at the coronation of Queen Victoria the previous year. He resolved to put all that right, to remind a swiftly modernising Britain of the greatness of its past and the splendour of its nobility. This fancy was to cost him £40,000, perhaps the equivalent of £3.5 million today.[1]

The knights, some of the best-known playboys of the era, bought horses, trained them and practised jousting with lances. They spent fortunes on outfits for themselves, their horses and their wives. Meanwhile a great medieval fairground, with grandstands, encampments for the knights and their retainers, pavilions, marquees, lists and tiltyards, was set up outside Eglinton's brand new Gothic castle. Rehearsals were held and all was set for a weekend in August 1839.

The new-fangled railways laid on special trains and a crowd of more than 100,000 turned up. To get a ticket for the grandstand you had to promise you were a supporter of the Conservative Party. Queen Victoria expressed regret that she could not attend.

Lord Eglinton, 'Lord of the Tournament', wearing armour that was gold-plated, or gold-painted, was escorted by a troop of halberdiers. Prince Louis Napoleon (later Emperor Napoleon III) and the Duchess of Somerset ('The Queen of Beauty') dressed up to join the opening procession. Prince Louis's presence was particularly pleasing to Archie Eglinton. As he liked to point out, his ancestor Gabriel Montgomerie had managed to kill King Henri II of France – by mistake – in a joust at a tournament in 1559. Montgomerie, who was captain of King Henri's Scots Guards, skewered him through the eye when a splinter from his lance entered the king's helmet.

Archibald, 13th Earl of Eglinton, dressed as the Lord of the Tournament, Henry Corbould c. 1840.

Nineteen knights made themselves ready, each of them attended by esquires, pages and men-at-arms. My grandfather's great-uncle, John Fergusson, acted as esquire to 'The Knight of the Ram', who, under the armour, was the Hon. Captain Henry Gage. It was nineteen-year-old John's chain mail hauberk into which we had been trying to clamber.

Interest was intense: the newspapers covered the preparations, reported the worries of the police over crowds and the possibility someone might be killed, and then mocked mercilessly when it all went wrong, in the most traditionally Scottish way. 'The lists in the park of Eglinton Castle at this time exhibit the appearance of a pond,' reported *The Times* as the tournament weekend began. The visitors had to wade through mud for a mile or more to get to the site.

A gale of bitterly cold rain drenched the vast crowd, flooding the royal box and the grandstand and knocking down the banqueting tent. The spectacle of men on horses charging at each other turned out to be quite dull, so much did the mud slow the action down. There was just one injury to the knights: Lord Stafford's son, Edward Jerningham, sprained his wrist. The whole event was a disaster. The *Spectator* magazine titled its report 'Eglintoun Emasculated Mopstick Middle Age Recovery Society'.[2] Queen Victoria pronounced the tournament 'the greatest absurdity'.[3] The age of chivalry had had its last blast.

The Knight and the Umbrella, published in 1963, sets the story well in the time; it laughs kindly at Eglinton and his friends' quixotic crusade against the dullness of modern, democratising Britain. Ian Anstruther, the author, reprints the invoices from the one man who did well out of the tournament, Britain's last remaining armourer, Samuel Pratt. Just the hire of a suit of armour from him cost £60 – £5,300 today.[4]

Anstruther never questions the source of all the money spent on the three-day wash-out. The answer to that was in part in the papers on which my grandfather worked. Our family, and most of the neighbours, cousins and friends who took part in the tournament – Lords Glenlyon, Cassilis and Airlie, the families of Hamilton, Dallas, Fairlie,[5] Johnstone, Crawford, Montgomerie, Montgomery, Kennedy, Oswald, Cunningham, Balfour, Dundas, Campbell, Balcarres Lindsay, Hunter Blair, Wemyss – had made or added to their fortunes quite recently through an industry that was not at all romantic or honourable.

The same was true for the families of many of the English knights and esquires – Kents, Gages, de la Poer Beresfords, Howard de Waldens, Staffords and Seymours – who performed that day. The 250-year-old enterprise that was the source of some of their money, plantation slavery in the British Caribbean, had finally ended just a year before the tournament's opening day.

Some of the families, like the Fergussons, Hamiltons and Hunter Blairs, still had slave plantations when the Act abolishing slavery was passed in 1833. They had got a windfall as a result. The British government had brought about the end of slavery in the Caribbean colonies by the simple expedient of buying off the 46,000 slave-owners: paying them a sum per person owned by way of compensation 'for loss of property'. The enslaved people received nothing,

The Hunter Blairs and the Fergussons, who jointly owned 198 enslaved people on their Jamaica plantation, received a compensation payout in 1836 of £3,591, eight shillings and eightpence: a little over £3 million today.[6] The total cost to the British taxpayer was £20 million, perhaps £17 billion today, though some analyses put it much higher.[7]

In the Caribbean, even now, people who are the descendants of the enslaved Africans the British imported ask what was actually done with the profits their ancestors laboured and died to make? Did any good things come about? The Eglinton Tournament, gilt armour, velvet caparisons, trained horses and twelve-foot lances designed to shatter in a way that would not injure the jousters, is a part of the answer.

* * *

In the old servants' hall

The history is kept down in the guts of the house. Only three of the five floors of Kilkerran are lived in now, the basement and the huge attics essentially abandoned. In the old servants' dining hall tiers of shelves rise from dust and pigeon droppings. On them are boxes, ledgers and files containing the paperwork of four centuries of the family's business affairs, political machinations, imperial appointments and military exploits.

There are diaries of campaigning aunts and grandmothers (suffragism and Zionism), of grandfathers and great-uncles who were subalterns and generals during the imperial wars in Crimea, Sudan, South Africa, Flanders and Burma. There are photo albums, commonplace books, letters from children at boarding school and notes from prime ministers. There are a lot of bills too.

My grandfather was the last man with deep knowledge of what the shelves contained. He died in 1973. He was Sir James Fergusson, an eminent journalist and historian who was for twenty years in charge, as Keeper of the Records, of all Scotland's historical archive. His own family's archive was his chief hobby, and the source of several of his published books.

In the family, the achievements and adventures of the forebears were much discussed. The Carribean history was not. 'It never came up when we were young,' my mother says now. Much later, when planning to visit Jamaica and the Rozelle plantation, my grandfather discussed the slave-owning past. He told his children that though, like many families in Scotland we had owned people as slaves, it was only briefly and we had made no money. My generation knew nothing about it at all.

My grandfather was a good and kind man and a meticulous, old-fashioned scholar. There was deep shame in the papers, and it called to question the origins of the family's narrative of itself as philanthropic, disinterested servants of Britain and the Empire, champions of liberal causes. I think my grandfather believed that full knowledge of this past was not a burden his heirs should carry. The story was close to him: his grandfather had sold the Jamaica plantation and died while on a visit to the island, a victim of the earthquake of 1907. As eighth baronet of Kilkerran, my grandfather and others in the family still carried the names of the eighteenth-century ancestors – James, Alexander, George, Adam and Charles.

* * *

The papers don't give up their secrets easily. Heavy foolscap sheets of deeds and contracts unfold with a creak, resisting any attempt to scan them. The lighter paper used for letters and notes may crack into fragments that will blow away on a breath. Water blurs a sentence just as it seems about to give up some meaning – tropical or sea damp, or spray from the hoses of the firefighters who saved the papers and the house from a fire some decades ago. The outside of some bundles is black from the smoke of that misfortune.

The cursive italic is often crammed on the page, as though paper was a hideous expense. But that cannot have been the problem, because the sentences go on and on and round in circles. Full stops are rare things. And while my ancestors and their correspondents turn their phrases with elegant, ecclesiastical rhythms they are averse to saying anything briefly. Squeezing meaning from the script can be eye-aching, brain-numbing work.

Some of the documents are more plain. A few tell you things with all the clarity of a punch in the stomach. None more so than the plantation accounts books, with their cold lists of the 'increase' and 'decrease' in human beings. More detail comes in the inventories periodically made of all the sellable assets on the plantations. The first of these I saw was in a bundle that my ancestral uncle Sir Adam Fergusson filed away in January 1781, with this covering note:

> The Within Letters are my only Apology for engaging in that unfortunate business of Tobago. Those who do not know what it is to be anxious to procure an establishment for a beloved Brother will think them none. Those who do, though they may not think them a sufficient Excuse for the Folly, will perhaps allow that they extenuate it.

Inside, among the letters, is a formal document titled 'Inventory and appraisement of Carrick Plantation in the Parish of St John, the property of Sir Adam Fergusson Baronet' and dated 8 November 1777. Eleven foolscap pages follow, bound with thread and laid out as an accounts book. It has been drawn up by a professional and signed by other Tobago landowners, all Scots. It lists everything of any value, from the rooms of the house Sir Adam's brother James had built in Tobago down to the carpentry tools, James's clothing, cutlery and the teapot. But the most valuable things are listed on the first page, starting with the land and its crop. Next comes 'Buildings' and then 'Slaves'.

That section begins with the title 'House' and five names: Emoinda, Rachael, Monimia, Sophia and Peggy. The last three have their roles stated: washerwoman, cook and sick nurse. Emoinda and Rachael were maids, perhaps. In the next column these humans' value is estimated: Emoinda at £65, Rachael at £57 and Peggy, the nurse, £90.

Peggy is nearly the most valuable person on the plantation – valued higher than Scotland, the carpenter (£80) or Solomon, one of the watchmen (£81). Quashie, listed as one of the two 'drivers' – field team leaders, or bosses – is priced at £108. The inventory lists a total of 79 people, most of them under the heading 'Field'. Their total value is £4,198 – nearly £7 million today. They have no surnames and only a few names sound remotely West African, though most of them would have been born there. Many are given plain Scottish names – the Fergusson family's first names are there – or borrowings from literature: Romeo, Polydore, Daphne, Nero, Hamlet and Othello. You imagine the white men were aware of the ironies of renaming an enslaved African Othello: not a proud Moorish general but a field-hand picking cotton, his body and life valued at £80.

When I read this list I felt nauseous. The last heading is 'Children' – just five of them, judged too young to work until over six years old: Billy, Johney, Colin, Jeanie and Flora. Billy has a value of £25, Colin just £8 and the others £10. Immediately below their names on the page the next category gives a context, some evidence of how a child's life in that world was measured. It is of the animals: '1 horse – £40, 2 mules – £58, 2 cows – £30, 3 calves – £12'.

* * *

And so, in the papers in the old dining hall, I realised that my ancestors were indeed plantation owners in the British slave colonies: farmers of human beings. As the abolitionists of the 1790s pointed out, their profits were directly related to the levels of misery they imposed on the people they owned. My ancestors cannot be called murderers: what they and their paid managers did was legal then.* However we view them today, they were, by the standards of their class and the time, considered moral and progressive men. My grandfather, while clearly affected by the details in the letters he had read, considered Sir Adam Fergusson, who for nearly fifty years ran the family's plantations in Tobago and Jamaica from Britain, an ideal figure from a supremely civilised time.

The Fergussons were Christians, liberal-minded politicians, friends

....

* Murder, mutilation or rape of an enslaved person by a free one was not an offence in Jamaica until 1788, though a suit for damage to property might be brought. In 1811 Arthur Hodge, a planter in the British Virgin Islands, was prosecuted and executed for torturing and killing Prosper, an enslaved man he owned, but the case is unique.

of the philosophers and economists of the 'Scottish Enlightenment'. But they enslaved people, traded in them and their children and opposed the end of slavery. When full abolition came at last to the British Empire in 1838, they became wealthier as a result. This story is about how that happened, and what it means for us – me, my family and all of us who profited from the transatlantic slavery industry – today.

TOBAGO – 1773–1785

CHAPTER 2

A PROSPECT OF ACQUIRING
A FORTUNE

The first object is a sufficient and comfortable Subsistance for
James . . . [and] a Prospect in time of acquiring a Fortune.

Sir Adam Fergusson to Charles Fergusson,
16 June 1774

THE FERGUSSONS CAME LATE TO the gold rush. Some of the families
they knew in Ayrshire had been sending sons out to the Caribbean
to purchase sugar plantations and enslaved Africans to work them
for two generations. The wealth they had acquired was plain to see:
old family houses and decrepit castles were being turned into neo-
classical mansions all over the county. But it was not until April 1773
that James Fergusson, my six-times-great-uncle, set off. His older
brothers, who sponsored the trip, hoped that Jamie – as they called
him – would find something to do with his life, and perhaps make
them all wealthier.

James was twenty-six years old, well-read and expensively educated.
His family were lawyers, soldiers and politicians, well-connected in
eighteenth-century Scotland and in London too. Lord Kilkerran,
James's father, had been one of the most famous advocates – a lawyer
in Scotland – of his age. The title comes from his having been made
a Lord of the Court of Session, the Scottish supreme court. The
Kilkerran Fergussons had been firmly on the side of the crown during
Bonnie Prince Charlie's rebellion of 1745–6: they were part of the
ruling elite of what was becoming known as 'North Britain'.

Sir Adam Fergusson, James's eldest brother, was also an advocate.

He would become a Member of Parliament, as his father had briefly been, and rector of Glasgow University, but his main employment was the running of Kilkerran and other family estates in southwest Scotland. That provided the bulk of his income: during his lifetime agricultural rents in Scotland quadrupled. But he also had 'West Indian interests'. With his brother Charles, Sir Adam had since 1769 been owner of half of a thriving sugar estate in eastern Jamaica. It had on it 150 enslaved people, most of them first-generation arrivals from Africa.

James was the youngest child of fourteen, only seven of whom reached adulthood. Though the Fergussons' estates in Ayrshire and elsewhere in Scotland made the family wealthy, there was not much spare for a youngest son.

By 1770 most of the children had made their way in the world. George was an advocate and became a Lord of Session like his father. Charles was a banker and wine importer, John a soldier who left school to enrol, aged sixteen, against the Jacobite forces in 1746. Helen married the historian and advocate Lord Hailes, of another ancient Scottish family, the Dalrymples. So Jamie, much-loved and indulged – notes of his debts from his playboy's life in London in the 1760s still survive in the archive – had a lot to live up to.

Fatherless at thirteen, he had lived on with his sisters in the family home, Kilkerran. James's oldest brother – now known as Sir Adam to all the family – took on the role of paterfamilias. Lord Kilkerran had left his youngest a small annual income; with school complete, a profession had to be found. James tried the sea, as a young naval officer, but by the early 1770s Britain was – inconveniently – at peace and the Navy had a surplus of young men.

Many of the Fergussons' wealthy neighbours in Ayrshire were busy investing in the Caribbean sugar islands. Some, like the Hamiltons, had already banked the returns in land and by building grand new houses. Sir Adam and Charles Fergusson were excited by the cash flowing from their share of Rozelle in Jamaica, a former Hamilton property. There was more to be had.

One idea the brothers discussed was to buy the other half of Rozelle – it would cost them some £10,000 (perhaps £18 million today) but it would be 'a good bargain and would besides afford Jamie a comfortable Estate',[1] according to Charles. However, they decided to encourage Jamie to head for the islands further south in the West Indies that France had ceded to Britain in the 1763 Treaty of Paris (the same deal got Britain Florida, half of Louisiana and several other Caribbean islands). Some of these islands had only just been parcelled for sale, which meant there was still land available where an entrepreneur might start from scratch. Many Scottish families were sending back encouraging reports. And so Jamie took a ship to cross the Atlantic.

The path was well-trodden. Many young Scots of James's time, rich and poor, had gone off to the 'new worlds' of Asia and the Americas seeking to improve themselves and their families. Among them were the Fergussons' neighbours and cousins – one, a Dalrymple, was a passenger on the ship that James took to the Caribbean. A Fergusson uncle had also been part of the disastrous attempt to begin a Scottish merchant colony in Panama, at Darien, in the 1690s.

The opening of fresh lands and peoples to trade and exploitation by the British promised adventure as well as riches. The prospect must have been enticing. These were warmer places than Scottish country houses and freer of the rules of religion, duty and morality that must have irked a young gentleman. Family connections helped the young men decide whether they went to the West or the East Indies: sons of the Fergussons tried both.

Romanticism, the brand new fashion of taking delight in the beauties of the wilderness, excited some of this generation: William Beckford of Somerley, arriving in Jamaica the same month that James Fergusson bought the land in Tobago, gushed over the 'wonders' of his new home: 'no less romantic than the most wild and beautiful situation of Frescati, Tivoli, and Albano'.[2] James is less of an aesthete – he had not been to see Italy, for a start, unlike his brother Sir Adam – but his bubbling excitement at the prospect of the islands is clear in his first letters. The story of his 'adventure' in the West Indies was, however, like Beckford's, to end in a very different mood.*

* * *

* Beckford's attempt to run his Jamaican estates more humanely led him to debtor's prison in England. He is a cousin of the much wealthier William Beckford, builder of Fonthill Abbey in Wiltshire, whose father owned thirteen Jamaican plantations and some 3,000 enslaved people.

Eastern Caribbean, 1775

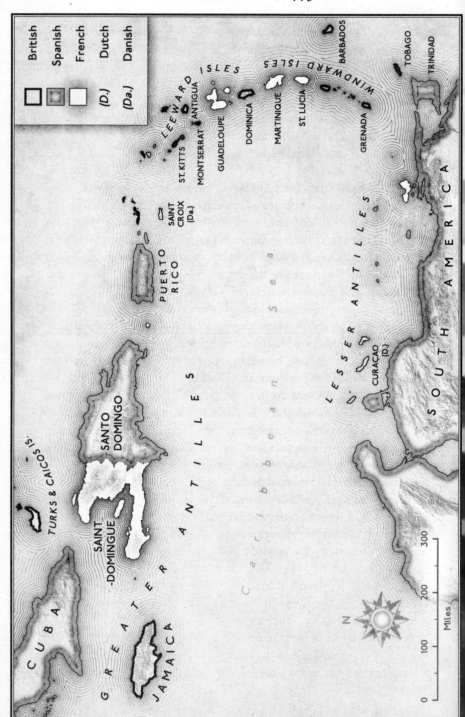

James's ship from Britain was bound for Grenada, but its first stop was the Portuguese island of Madeira, halfway through the journey. He wrote to Charles in high spirits:

> I was never more pleased than with any place . . . if the country was but a little smoother and the Shepherdesses a good deal fairer I should take this to be *Arcadia felix* – for wherever I go I meet with plenty, ease, and good humour – no stiff forms nor stupefying ceremony – everyone does as he pleases . . .

James says he is 'even fond of the Portuguese'.

It becomes clear as you get to know him that my uncle James likes a bit of fun. He is delighted by the novel, gently impatient with the formal and orthodox. He is eager to entertain Charles, six years his senior. Sir Adam, another seven years ahead, is more soberly informed. The two elder brothers are the source of the large sums of money James will need, so he must convince them he is up to the job. But he wants to amuse too. Later in the letter to Charles, James tells how the nuns of Madeira, at whose convent he has signed up for lessons in Portuguese, are not 'demure, meek and modest' as one might expect, but 'as lascivious, brawling, rapacious a set of devils as ever existed'.[3] The Catholic priests are apparently no better.

The next letters come from Grenada. This was a usual Caribbean landfall for ships crossing the Atlantic and a favourite island among the Scottish planters and speculators who had bought land there in large numbers after Grenada was ceded to Britain by France. Scottish entrepreneurs and adventurers had always been at the forefront of these colonial forays, spurred perhaps by lack of opportunity at home. The new colonial possessions could be put to use: tobacco in the seventeenth century and then sugar in the eighteenth were the most successful crops. When slavery was abolished in the Caribbean in the nineteenth century, the records of slave owners showed far more Scots were involved – per head of population – than the English, Welsh or Irish.[4] Not all started as plantation owners: 34,000 Scots went to work in the West Indies between 1750 and 1834,[5] many as merchants, artisans or bookkeepers.

So it is no surprise that the first thing James encounters in Grenada is more Scotsmen. But not the ones he prefers. There is a 'swarm of locusts' on the island, he writes to Sir Adam, a fortnight after he has landed. They are lawyers, attracted by the land boom on the island: they can be seen everywhere in the capital, St George's, clutching their papers. Meanwhile James finds that illness has 'carried off many of the people I heard the best characters of': the last year was 'the most sickly season that has been known since the English had possession of the island'.[6]

Dying as a result of the diseases and 'miasmas' of the Caribbean islands is a constant theme in James's letters, as in those of his contemporaries. Some accounts of the Caribbean in the eighteenth and early nineteenth century suggest the average immigrant white man survived for less than five years after arrival, only a year more than the average enslaved African.* Conscious, perhaps, that he may not see Scotland again, in his next letter to Sir Adam James encloses loving messages for each of his brothers and sisters.

James finds friends and lodgings among the Scots of St George's. A McSween whom he shipped with introduces him to several Campbells and others; they invite him to visit their plantations on Grenada and elsewhere.[7] These new friends are among one of the Caribbean's largest British populations: in 1773 Grenada had 1,661 white people and 26,000 enslaved Africans.[8] It is the hub of the boom that began with handover of the 'South Caribee Islands' under the Treaty of Paris.

In a late June letter to his oldest brother, James is excited and ripe with ideas. Having been on the island three weeks, talking to his new acquaintances, he is already convinced of what he must do to survive and prosper:

> The principal qualifications in my opinion, necessary to constitute a good planter are, first, sobriety – otherwise he will not live long enough in this country to put his schemes into execution – a tolerably sound head, and a good heart. Economy is absolutely necessary – but it requires some judgement to know what is real, and what fictitious economy, for instance, a Planter who is sparing of food and clothing to his slaves, will most certainly save money

....
* Half the white men who settled in the Caribbean 'died in the undertaking': 100 per cent of the black people did, of course. Richard Ligon, who spent two years as a planter on Barbados in the 1640s, wrote that the white population had turned over completely in fifteen years before his arrival – 'Black ribbon for mourning is much worn here'.[6B]

on these articles, but it is equally certain he will lose by it in the long run, and grossly mistakes his true interest.

Besides, farming here is 'not near as intricate' as in Scotland: the weather being 'more steady and regular'. With equal confidence, James goes on to share an enlightened view, for the time, on the other key element of the enterprise: the enslaved humans.

Negroes are not the brutes they are often represented, and I do affirm that there may be more made of them, by well timed kind-nesses and mercy – than by the most severe usage and blows – one would think that self interest (allowing this doctrine to be just) should induce all men to act in this way, but without a higher and better principle of action, there can be no steadiness – therefore, I say a good heart is as necessary as a good head to constitute a good Planter or a good anything else.[9]

These sentiments will have pleased his elder brother. But they come from a beginner. The novels of plantation life popular a few decades later often feature a naïve, liberal-minded newcomer who learns the brutal realities pretty quickly, much to the old hands' delight.[10] But James is confident in his contrary opinions. That the islands are unhealthy, he dismisses as 'a great mistake':

To be sure if people go constantly to bed drunk, and rise muddled, they will die here, and there is no great matter for they are not fit to live any where, but I firmly believe, that a man that will live, as reason and nature dictates, and chuse a situation for his house clear of swamps, will he be as healthy here as in England.[11]

James's research continues over the next four months. He travels up and down the chain of islands, visiting Carriacou, Montserrat, St Christopher's, Nevis, Antigua, Tobago, Dominica and 'Martinica' (now Martinique). He briefly considers buying a coffee estate at Gouyave in Grenada for £16,000.[12] In the same letter, of October 1773, he complains that though he has been away six months he has not received a single communication from anyone at home.

* * *

In January 1774, nine months after leaving home, James at last receives a packet of correspondence from Scotland. Soon after, he writes to Sir Adam to say he is at last decided. Tobago is the right island for him to buy land and make a life, the place for his brothers to invest their money.

It is coffee and indigo he wants to plant. With his usual brash certainty James dismisses the 'sugar-mad' planters of other islands who have so inflated land prices in irrational pursuit of a difficult though fashionable crop. (He turns out to be wrong, and not for the last time: sugar prices will continue rising for the rest of the century, with the ceded islands particularly profitable.) Besides, James continues, the frequent rain and rich soil he has found in Tobago is more suitable for these lesser-known crops. He has even found a parcel of undeveloped land for sale on the little-exploited northwest coast.

The land is offered by a consortium led by a Mr Wilson of Glasgow. James has a new friend, a distant cousin, George Ferguson of Pitfour, who with his soldier brother Patrick is an established sugar planter at the little settlement of Castara on the same side of the island.[13] The pair are to go and judge the merits of Wilson's plot, in a place with the ominous name of Bloody Bay.

A few days later George and James make the boat trip up the rocky coast from Castara. They land in the surf on Bloody Bay's little beach, having navigated through coral heads and small islands. Clambering up to the first rise, they inspect the lot of land, number 12 on the great map of Tobago drawn up in 1767 by a surveyor for the British governor-general in Grenada. It is a parcel of 300 acres, though only ten or so of those are on flat land – the swampy bank of the Bloody River, a stream that descends by waterfalls through forest from the mountain ridge that is Tobago's central spine.

The rest of the parcel takes in steep slopes and narrow valleys, the crumple of the land as it draws up to the main ridge. On the map it is a rigid rectangle: the surveyor has set it out as though it were pastureland in Ayrshire, without any reference to these natural features, other than the river which forms one boundary. A corner of the lot meets the beach and the Caribbean sea. Beautiful and strange the land is still, the forest huge and dominant: it doesn't look like an obvious site for a settlement. It is wild, and even today humans have only scratched its surface.

Nonetheless, the visit with George and conversations at Castara with George's elder brother Patrick convince James that this untamed place is where his plantation should be. On 7 February 1774 he sends Sir Adam a very hasty letter; you can sense his excitement in the scrawled and blotchy copperplate. There is little description of Bloody Bay. But the important thing that his brother needs to know is the deal he has done with Mr Wilson. The previous day, James promised the Glaswegian rather a lot of Fergusson money.

> . . . it consists of six acres of as good land as any in the West Indies, for which I am to pay two thousand pounds sterling in bills at 3, 6, 9, & 12 months and 2000£ to pay four years at 5% interest for which I have likewise granted to him bills drawn upon you, and 250£ that is still to pay to the King [owed by Mr Wilson from his original purchase] + which I shall be obliged to pay in a few months. So the whole price comes to four thousand two hundred and fifty pounds sterling. I hope you will excuse this freedom and honour these bills. I will write by the first opportunity and explain the whole of my plan to you. I assure you it will not be an expensive one.[14]

Sir Adam and Charles must have been perplexed by this note, rushed in order to catch a ship just leaving for Britain. Six acres for £4,250? The sum was vast – £500 a year was the income of a wealthy man in the 1770s, when a skilled servant earned about £25. But the outlay had been planned for. Securing a job for Jamie as the captain of an East India trading ship – another career his older brothers had discussed – would have cost £6,000.

In a longer letter written twelve days later James makes it clear to Sir Adam that the lot is in fact 300 acres, though that is all heavily wooded jungle and only a small part will be readily usable. But he declares it cheap at the price. There are ten acres of 'rich bottom' – riverbank – ideal for planting indigo, a plant that produces a valuable blue dye and needs less investment than sugar cane demands. This would have made sense back home: Sir Adam was a student of agricultural science, among his many interests, and his library had books on crop types and modern techniques. James apologises for rushing into the deal without Sir Adam's advice and reassures him that 'I do not relie intirely on my own judgment in an affair of this consequence'. Cousin George, of Castara, is one of several who have given a thumbs-up: 'His opinion is that it is a great bargain'. Besides, James's haste is fuelled by his desire to get busy, ' . . . for this is the season of falling and clearing wood[,] that I may be in time for the season of planting provisions'. Finally, he says he hopes Sir Adam or Charles will be his partner in the plantation.[15]

James has already signed a contract, on 8 February, in front of witnesses in Tobago's capital Scarborough. The deeds still exist: four heavy sheets of parchment the size of pillow slips. They tell a little of the plot's previous history. In November 1770 the lots of land seen as suitable for plantations on Tobago had been sold at a government auction. The Wilson consortium had bought this and another lot at Bloody Bay from the governor-general of Grenada, acting for the British Crown. They got 'all edifices, woods, underwoods, ways, waters', everything except for rights to any 'mines of Gold and Silver'. The section of beach was Crown property, but the owner could use it. There is no mention of Tobago's first inhabitants, known as Caribs, some of whom were still surviving in these hills.[16]

Wilson and his co-investors had promised the Crown £585 for Lot 12 at Bloody Bay, payable over five years, and a little less for Lot 11 – it is the final part of that sum that James says is owed to the King. Writing to his brothers about the bargain, James doesn't point out that Wilson and friends have multiplied their money by nine times in less than four years. This property boom was much more significant as a generator of wealth than any profits made from planting crops on the island. Tobagan landowners were already notorious in Britain for their wealth: 'as rich as a Tobago planter' was a common phrase in the late eighteenth century. But the Fergussons were late: land values on the island would never rise so high again.

* * *

The bundle of old papers concerning 'the unfortunate business of Tobago' that Sir Adam collected and filed away seven years later mainly contains James's letters. Apart from a few first drafts, there is little that reflects what Sir Adam or Charles thought. But there is a brief exchange of notes between the older brothers at this time. They are hopeful, pleased that George Ferguson of Castara approved James's plan, and they accept that the deal may make sense. Sir Adam says he will 'suspend any further observations' about indigo as a crop until he has consulted others who have visited the island. Charles, who knows something of the shipping business from his trading in Madeira wine, agrees to deal with the shopping list that his brother, the pioneer planter, sends him just four days after signing the contract.

The list goes on for two close-written pages. It is a window on the scale of the enterprise out in a wilderness at least two days' journey from any sizable settlement. It tells, too, of the disparate needs of both James and the men and women he hopes to hire and buy. He wants barrels of beef, herring, tripe and pigs' heads, kegs of oatmeal and barley, casks of Madeira and port wines. He needs '12 Negroe jackets (blue) of different sizes, half Mens half Womens, two dozen Mens and two doz. Womens shirts, two dozen brown petticoats, 2 dozen Killmarnock caps, 2 dozen negroe blankets . . . 2 dozn. coarse earthen ware bowls for the Negroes . . . 1 gross Negroe pipes'. There are long lists of tools – hoes, hand-saws, hammers and nails, cutlery, scissors, pots, fishhooks, a harpoon and a dozen cutlasses. The pipes, you assume, are clay ones for tobacco-smoking.

He needs to provide for the house he intends to build for himself. He lists bed-linen and furniture: '18 Windsor chairs painted green and with back and arms', wine glasses, a table set of stoneware, cheese, corks, candles and three pounds of fine tea. There are all the necessaries of an eighteenth-century physician's store, all with amounts precisely listed. For administering the many medicines, from 'Peruvian bark' to saltpetre, he asks for mortar and pestle, syringes, lint and 'blistering plaisters'.

All these materials will last twelve months and save money, because the stores in Scarborough charge a premium of 100 per cent on British prices. Charles should 'direct the goods to be landed at Bloody Bay'. There is a little in the list that tells about James's own vision of life as a planter. But there is a little: 2 dozn. green handled knives and forks' are there, as are glasses and tumblers. He wants a 'speaking trumpet' and a 'good spy glass'. The Bloody Bay estate was still primeval jungle, but James could already picture himself in a green Windsor armchair on his verandah, watching the workers through a telescope, issuing orders through his megaphone.

There are other items on the shopping list that make it clear this enterprise was more than some elaborate gentleman's camping trip. '2 sets steel Negroe collars with strong padlocks and chain' are asked for, along with four pairs of handcuffs.[17] Three and a half years later, in November 1777, when an inventory of James's possessions and everything else at Bloody Bay, down to the last tablecloth, boiling pot and hoe is made, there are no whips listed, though other accounts of plantations at the time suggest whipping the enslaved workers was habitual. Ninian Jefferys, a Royal Navy ship's master who visited Tobago in 1774, saw the drivers, black and white, 'keeping the whip constantly cracking over their heads while at work, and sometimes lashing them with it'. The usual whip was made of plaited or twisted cow hide: 'when dry it becomes exceeding hard'.[18] Jefferys reported to a parliamentary committee on the slave trade in 1789 that the floggings he saw in Tobago and Jamaica were far harsher than those usually inflicted on a Royal Navy man o'war.

The inventory does list three 'Negroe iron collars', valued at six shillings each, and 'Negroe iron chain', valued at two shillings and sixpence. The collars would have been for control and punishment. Museums of slavery have examples of them, from different eras: hinged hoops of heavy old metal, some with spikes turned in towards the neck, others with long arms or hooks poking out to prevent the wearer moving freely. There are also guns: two brass-barrelled blunderbusses, 'a large soldier's musquet', two fowling pieces and a pair of brass pistols.

* * *

None of the letters say anything about the dangers, for the free and the enslaved, of a place like Bloody Bay. In Tobago disease and violence took lives with a frequency that seems inconceivable today. The valley was remote: an hour or more by horse from any well-organised neighbours, perhaps half a day by boat from James's friends the Fergusons at Castara, or Gilbert Petrie at Englishman's Bay. Should anything go wrong – and it will, given fellow planters' recent experiences on Tobago – there is little chance of friends coming swiftly to help.[19]

The enslaved people outnumber the white planters by twenty to one. In 1775 a census conducted for the lieutenant-governor found that Tobago held 393 white people, 8,611 enslaved people and an unknown number of Amerindians. In remote St John's parish, where Bloody Bay is located, there are 35 whites and 763 enslaved. This imbalance is risky, so the buyers of Tobagan lots from the Crown are penalised unless they keep up the ratio of white people to black. Similar rules exist in all the older colonies.

Uprisings of enslaved people were frequent events in Tobago in these years. There were seven significant ones between 1769 and 1774: so many that William Young, a Scot from Dumfriesshire who was serving as the lieutenant-governor of the island,[20] wrote to London complaining that the unrest was putting off settlers. Money-lenders expressed doubts about financing Tobagan estates. A few of the African people involved in these events escaped by boat to Trinidad, but the risings always failed. Most of the 'rebels' were killed in the fighting or put to death, usually in barbaric ways designed to discourage others from opposing the whites.

James knows of the risings. One resulting in what Young called two weeks of 'bloody and obstinate' fighting was going on in late 1773, across the island, when he first arrived. While prospecting with George Ferguson at Bloody Bay, he would have learnt that there had been a revolt at a plantation at the bay just two years before, in June 1771: George's brother, Captain Patrick Ferguson, had led the volunteers and regular army troops who put down the insurrection.[21]

There are only a few details: Tobago's history of the period is less than sketchy, not least because all government records were destroyed when Scarborough was burnt to the ground in 1781. But we know that in the Bloody Bay incident ten years earlier, thirty-eight of the forty-two enslaved people there rose up, killing one unnamed white man, an overseer. The enslaved were recaptured in September after the militia hunted them down in the woods above the bay, finding a camp and seven houses inhabited by other runaways. There's no information on what punishments were exacted then, but James was very soon to find out how savage were the penalties for runaways and rebels.

The uprising at Bloody Bay happened on a plantation operating with just two white men alongside the Africans enslaved there. One, the owner John Fowke, was away at the time. The bay was only accessible by sea, or a narrow track up and over Tobago's spinal mountain ridge. The risks to white owners were greatest in remote places on the northeast coast, like Bloody Bay, but the whole island was clearly vulnerable. A further uprising happened at Parlatuvier, just a mile from Bloody Bay, in August 1771: five of the 'rebels' were executed and two sold to a Spanish colony. This was a time of uprisings of enslaved people across the Caribbean, news of which passed quickly from island to island. The enslaved people were well-informed about goings-on in the other islands and back in Britain.[22]

In April 1774 Tobago's council (of white property-owners) petitions the King to send financial assistance to the island, pointing out the number of uprisings and stating that the colony was in danger because of 'overstocking' of enslaved people and insufficient numbers of whites due to deaths by disease. Churches, roads, a courthouse, a prison and more troops are needed; the garrison of soldiers of the 48th Regiment of Foot is only seventy men strong, and many of them are sick with malaria and dysentery.[23] The petition gets no reply:[24] another is sent in 1775. It is not until 1779, after the fall of Grenada to the French, that the 48th is supplied with more men.[25]

On 10 March 1774, just as James is getting ready to take possession of his land at Bloody Bay, a serious uprising begins five miles away, across the island at the Queen's Bay estate of Betsy's Hope owned by the lieutenant-governor, William Young, and a Robert Stewart. The fullest account comes from the Royal Navy officer, Ninian Jefferys, who gave evidence to the British parliament's inquiry into the slave trade in 1789. Forty-eight Africans rose, led by a man named Sampson. They killed three of the eight white men at Betsy's Hope and destroyed the buildings. The Africans took six firearms, shot and powder, and went into the woods. The island's militia, along with regular soldiers, went in pursuit. After a week the rising was over. Thirty of the 'rebels' were captured, four had been killed in the fighting and two had hanged themselves rather than be taken. Then the punishments began.

There was a token trial, under military law. The Africans were charged with murder and damage to property but not allowed – as enslaved people – to give evidence. Eight of the leaders of the revolt were found guilty. Fifteen years later, Ninian Jefferys told the House of Commons inquiry what he had seen after the verdicts. Seven of the men had their right arm cut off before being taken to stakes, where fires were lit and they were slowly burnt to death. Sampson was hung alive in chains: he took seven days to die.

At the inquiry, Jefferys was eager to express how brave Sampson and the other men had been. One, Chubb, rolled his sleeve up and laid out his arm for the axe-blow, and then insisted on walking by himself to the stake where he would be burnt. '[They] shewed no marks of concern or dismay that I could observe; a stronger instance of human fortitude I never saw.'[26] Just four of the rebels managed to escape the island.

The reprisals after uprisings were always brutal, but they never seem to have done much to deter the liberty-seeking enslaved people on Tobago or other islands. Later in April 1774 the Tobago planters complained that 'the idea of gaining freedom' had spread to all parts of the island – this after seven Africans at the Bon Accord estate at the island's western end daringly seized a ship and sailed for Trinidad, then still ruled by Spain. Enslaved people believed they could hope for better treatment under Spanish law and practice.[27]

As a landowner, James is elected to the island's General Assembly in November 1774.[28] He has to sit as a juror in criminal cases heard in Scarborough – a distraction he complains about a lot. One of the cases is the trial of Peter Franklyn, who in 1777 shot and killed the lieutenant-governor, William Young, in a duel. But jury duty does have social pleasures. James is able to meet with 'the Gentlemen of the island'.[29]

Despite his early beliefs about kindness and humanity being the preferable tools for the management of the enslaved, James is one of the assembly members who pass the Act for the Good Order and the Government of Slaves in 1775. This broadly copies the law as it is in other islands. It confirms the death penalty as the ultimate sanction for any enslaved person who strikes or wounds a white person, or who has even 'contrived' or 'imagined' his death. Those who run away for more than six weeks are liable to death as well. The enslaved people are valuable property, but in practice most of the people captured after uprisings are executed with the standard savagery.

Buying a workforce

Despite the risks, James plans to start working at Bloody Bay as the only free person living there. His next act is to acquire his first African workers – '10 seasoned Eboe',[30] he tells his brothers. Plantation owners bought what they believed were different 'breeds' of African according to the work required, just as they might have chosen different types of horse: contemporary literature is full of digressions on the relative physical characteristics and psychology of Africans from different places on the continent. It is part of a strategy of deliberate dehumanisation.

Eboe people were considered more civilised than other West Africans; useful as house servants, though 'melancholy' and liable to suicide. (The term Eboe – Igbo today – appears to have been used for anyone taken from the west and southwestern Nigeria area.) There was another consideration, too: 'Eboe is the country to buy women off to breed', was the Jamaican planters' belief.[31] Meanwhile Mandingo people and the Los islanders were considered prone to disease and Mina people weakly and meek.

Kromantis from the Gold Coast, now part of southern Ghana, were seen as 'haughty, ferocious and stubborn'.[32] Accounts of a 1770 Tobago rebellion led by a man called Sandy emphasise that all the twenty-two people who rose up were newly arrived 'Coromantees'. In the aftermath of the uprisings of the 1760s in Jamaica, the island's assembly proposed a higher tax on 'all Fantin, Akim, and Ashantee Negroes, and all others commonly called Coromantins imported . . . to the island' because of the danger they were thought to pose.[33] Yet they were prized: the only Africans judged intelligent enough to labour in the dangerous boiling houses of the sugar works.

Racial stereotypes like these – and the attitudes that make them – persisted. Stories of the 'dangerous Koromantis' were still being repeated by popular historians nearly 200 years later. In his book *Freedom from Fear* (1959), O. A. Sherrard wrote that reports of the cruelty of 'brave' British planters to newly arrived enslaved people are unfair. The critics, he said, fail to understand the harsh means necessary to break the spirits of 'savage and intractable' Kromantis who are 'black panthers . . . powerful brutes, snarling, restless and strong'.[34]

Planters of James's time sought out these men because of that famed strength, believing that after the person's spirit had been broken in 'seasoning', an enslaved Kromanti would make a courageous and faithful servant.[35] Later James Fergusson buys ten people described as Kromantis.

These people and many others of the humans he purchased in Tobago he describes as 'seasoned'.[36] This, in its basic sense, says that they have survived their first six months in the Caribbean. During it they would suffer a first bout of malaria and might begin to recover – if that were possible – from the traumas of the voyage across the Atlantic, during which they would have watched many of their fellow captives die.[37] It could mean more. There are accounts of 'seasoning camps' on some larger islands where Africans were methodically

brutalised to make them more amenable: horse-breaking is the meta-
phor used, as in taming the animal's spirit to make it do its owner's
bidding. There is no record of such camps on Tobago, but the enslaved
people sold there may have been brought first to Grenada, 'seasoned'
and then shipped on to where demand and prices were highest. The
buyer could make a choice. In 1778 Sir Adam Fergusson is advised
that if he buys 160 newly arrived Africans for the family's Jamaica
plantation, he should expect nearly 20 per cent to die during the first
months. For this reason a 'seasoned' African costs more than a 'salt-
water' one, straight off a ship. Within a couple of years, and after the
deaths of seven Africans on his plantation, James declares that it is
only worth buying 'fully seasoned' people.

By May 1774 James has dispatched the bill for ten Eboe men
bought from a Mr McNable to Sir Adam. The price was £757.
Seventy-five pounds is the price of two horses, or a year's salary for
a skilled tradesman back in Scotland: buying an enslaved African was
equivalent, financially, to buying a new estate car today. James appears
to have been taken advantage of by the traders; the price is very high
even for 'seasoned' people, compared with other contemporary
reports. He has also hired six more enslaved labourers, at three shillings a day, from a Mr Fullerton. To sustain them and himself, James
pays a ship's captain £50 for provisions.

* * *

'I long most ardently for a letter', James writes in late June 1774.[38]
He still has not heard a word back from Charles or Sir Adam – the
last letter from home came in January, and that was dated September
1773. Often letters go missing on the voyage from Britain, unpredictable even in peacetime: important ones are copied and sent by
three or four different ships. But in the ten months since the last
communication James has picked an island and bought a plot of land
along with sixteen enslaved Africans, in all spending or promising
more than £5,000 of his brothers' money – a sum approaching £9
million at today's values.

His letters in these months are upbeat, but you sense nervousness
that Charles and Sir Adam may be shocked that James has gone so
far without their approval. He repeats how great a bargain Lot 12 at
Bloody Bay is, according to everyone. But after watching other

planters, he remains sure that coffee, cotton and indigo should be his crops. Sugar, which is making everyone else rich, as his brothers know, is never part of Jamie's plans.

He reports that he has at last left Scarborough, to his relief, and got down to work. Sometime in April he sets off to claim his lot, by boat from the other side of the island. He carries the provisions and the sixteen Africans – there's no report of his having hired any free person in 1774. The first job is felling and clearing land to build houses and prepare fields for the Africans' provisions. This needs to be done quickly before the rainy season begins in August.

Too much water, James has already realised, may be fatal to his plans. Indigo and cotton cannot be picked when wet. But 'this is a fault that will mend dayly, as the more of the country is cleared [of forest] the less rain we shall have'.[39] So, he can tell the family, the Bloody Bay plantation is begun and letters to him should be addressed there. He suggests a change of name is needed, though he never offers an explanation of why it is so named. How about 'Carrick Fergus' – Carrick being a name for the Fergussons' part of Ayrshire. James has started to make his mark on the land. He has still received no word from home.

When James planned the plantation, making 'provision grounds' was on his list of initial jobs, after the felling of the trees and before planting the indigo, his planned first cash crop. After all, these expensive workers needed to be fed, a lot. Shipping food in was a major cost: better that they could grow their own. Plantain, yams and corn were the staples. Providing the protein was a harder job. He laments that none of the Africans knows how to fish, and over the coming years continually asks his brothers to send him fish-hooks, line and – eventually – a fisherman.

When communications are re-established Sir Adam recruits a fisherman named James Dyker in Scotland and dispatches him to Tobago to teach the skills. Paid £70 a year, about the price of an adult enslaved African, Dyker would probably have been indentured, his work bought in advance for a fixed number of years: not much freer than the enslaved people with whom he worked, he would still have retained a Briton's basic rights. Their indentures complete, these men were free to work as they wished: some became wealthy as owners of plantations or merchant businesses. But not Dyker. He is listed as deceased in the estate accounts for 1785.

James doesn't mention the local fauna as food, though his armoury of guns shows he must easily have been able to kill for the table. The wild animals of the Tobagan forests, including armadillo and iguana, are a delicacy on the island today. Like the other planters, he imports much of the protein his workforce needs. Many of his letters home, from 1774 onwards, contain requests for salted herrings, along with 'a few barrels of beef and pork to give them by way of change'. For himself and the white workers, he asks for better fare: casks of 'the best Mess beef and pork, tongues and cheese and anything of that kind'.[40]

Preserved herring are shipped out to him, as to other plantations throughout the West Indies. This was the trade that transformed the economies of coastal Scotland and parts of Ireland: there remain harbours, like that at Isle Ornsay on Skye, built specifically to load herring in barrels onto ships for the West Indies trade. A herring was a normal planters' breakfast. Today in Tobago supermarkets still sell a smoked, dried 'red herring' from northern Europe, much saltier and tougher than a British kipper: hotels that do a 'Caribbean breakfast' offer the chopped herring fried into a mush with onions and peppers.

* * *

In July 1774 James at last hears from Charles Fergusson. The letter has not survived, but James's terse reply to it shows that his elder brother delivered a severe reprimand for the younger's expenditure on people, land and indeed half a pipe – 225 litres – of port wine. Bills have been arriving at home, amounting to more than £2,000.[41] James's annoyance at this rebuke is understandable. After all he has written several times over the last six months to explain his plans. He points out that he had to sign the deal for Bloody Bay without his elder brothers' approval because, had he waited, they would have missed the bargain. James's letters to Charles are usually chattier than those to Sir Adam. Sometimes he includes jokes he has heard. But this one is stiff. It ends:

Pray excuse me to Sir Adam for not writing to him by this opportunity. I could not write another word on this subject had [it] be to save my life and I can think on no other – Your letter has struck such a damp on my spirit that renders me totaly unfit to write to him at present.[42]

All must have been resolved because Sir Adam soon after decides to take a 50 per cent share in James's venture at Bloody Bay. He says to Charles that if the total expense of turning the land into a productive plantation can be kept to £6,000, the enterprise is 'practicable'.[43] And so the new planter gets busy. Lots of work is done at Carrick, as James now calls the 'settlement', over the rest of the year. In December he writes to Sir Adam 'as a partner in . . . one of the finest lots in the West Indies'.[44] Everyone who has seen it is agreed on that, he reports. Since May the Africans have built a house for James and two more capable of containing forty enslaved workers.

The house is two storeys and quite grand: it includes a hall, gallery and three bedrooms upstairs. There's a store, medicine shop and a shed for a kitchen.[45] It is of local wood, probably from the trees felled in the clearing of the plantation. By 1777 there are also eight 'Negroe Houses'.

In December, James says that he and his workers and a hired logging gang have now cleared eighty acres at Bloody Bay, the equivalent of about sixty football pitches. It is an immense undertaking, since all the land appears to have been mature, thickly treed jungle. James says that he will soon plant fifty of these acres with cotton and thirty more with food plants. This was swift work: an account of the founding of a new Tobago plantation in 1771, the Bartlet & Campbell company's Friendship estate, says it took two years for twenty-one enslaved workers to clear forty acres and build the dwelling houses.[46]

Meanwhile the enslaved workforce is increasing. James reports he has bought '10 new Eboe negroes', the bill for whom Sir Adam must expect soon. The letter is short, though it includes the usual protest about a lack of news from home. James is in a hurry. A schooner is about to leave Scarborough's port; he must sign off so he can board it 'with the Negroes to take them home' – home, that is, to Carrick.

> The Negroes are all in high health and spirits. Of course I am so too. Every thing seems to prosper and if this estate does not answer me none in Tobago will or it must be my fault. For there can be no objection made either to soil or situation.
>
> James Fergusson to Sir Adam Fergusson,
> 17 August 1775

By early 1775, James is settled on the plantation and his routine established. If all have survived, there are thirty-six bought Africans living alongside him at Carrick, with Dyker, the white Scottish fisherman, and a newly hired white overseer, George Gordon, sharing the dwelling house. James tells Sir Adam he has further bought 'ten prime Mandingo Slaves from Messrs. Bruce and Miller' for £430, and a further four from Crother and Fullerton. A gang has been hired from the latter to clear fifty more acres of land.[47]

In April James tells Sir Adam that more bills are on their way for payment, including £114 to Messrs. Ian and Alex Campbell and Co. for provisions and lumber.[48] Expansion is on his mind, as is the task of getting more white workers at Carrick, as the law requires. In July he asks Sir Adam to look in Ayrshire for a 'good young fellow' as a carpenter to dispatch to Tobago and 'indent' for three years, at £30 a year, meaning that the man's three years of labour, and his freedom, is sold for the period. But he is not 'owned', and neither are his children.

As ever, the name of every white person he deals with seems to be Scottish. His nearest neighbours are a Campbell and a Petrie at Englishman's Bay, not to mention the Fergusons at Castara. Today the Trinidad and Tobago phone book is full of Scottish names, with Campbell, along with Stewart, more frequent than any other (there are 350 Campbells and 90 or so Fergussons and Fergusons). The last surviving victim of the slave trade in Tobago bore the name Campbell – William 'Panchoo' Campbell.[49] He had been taken by the Portuguese from the Congo in 1849 or 1850. En route for Brazil, where slavery continued to be legal until 1888, the ship was intercepted by the British Royal Navy, by then actively working to stop the trade in people. The enslaved people were taken to the island of St Helena and then to Tobago along with many other freed Africans to work as hired labour. He probably took – or was given – the surname of his first employer. William died on the island in 1938, a father, grandfather and respected smallholder. He still bore, according to the local newspaper, 'the scars of the terrible branding iron put to his skin'.

CHAPTER 3

PEOPLE AS PROPERTY

Disagreeable I had long found it, but I think I should have quitted it sooner, had I considered it as I now do, to be unlawful and wrong. But I never had a scruple upon this head at the time; nor was such a thought once suggested to me by a friend. What I did I did ignorantly; considering it as the line of life to which Divine Providence had allotted me, and having no concern, in point of conscience, but to treat the slaves, while under my care, with as much humanity as a regard for my own safety would admit.

John Newton, former slave ship captain,
Thoughts upon the African Slave Trade, 1788[1]

IN EARLY 1775 CHARLES FERGUSSON in London receives a letter from a Mr Grant, an old acquaintance in the wine shipping business and now an established planter in Tobago. It is the first news Charles and Sir Adam have had of Jamie's progress in Tobago from anyone other than their brother himself. Grant has previously written saying that he does not think James's idea of buying jungled land on Tobago is a good one.

Charles takes that view, worries to excess about it, and decides that Jamie should immediately sell up the Tobago plot. He tells Sir Adam that he has heard of an indebted estate with 200 enslaved people on the island of St Vincent. It is producing 264 hogsheads of sugar a year: he thinks it could be bought with a down payment of six or seven thousand pounds.[2] But Mr Grant's latest letter, of May 1775, has a report that delights both the brothers.

I have neither seen nor heard from your brother Jamie but I have heard of him what has given me a great deal of pleasure and what I am sure will surprise you which is that he has turn'd an Arrant Miser, would you believe it! I am sure I would not if I had it not from the best authority . . . He is situated in the heart of the woods without any method of going to him but by Sea; He has not a Creature with him but an overseer he has 50 new Negroes that he feeds and attends to like his Children, he dresses all their Sores with his own hands. He turns out with them before day and labours till it is dark; He is happy I am informed beyond measure with his Situation & cannot think of leaving it for a day, all this will surprise you more than it does me but cannot give you more pleasure for I am sure that this attention will overcome all difficultys.[3]

Charles comments in a letter to Sir Adam: 'This is a picture of worth and integrity which I am sure will please you'. The brothers are able to compare Grant's account with one from James, written to Charles in April in the happiest of moods (and enclosing notice of bills on their way for a further £2,700). He thanks Charles's wife for a waist-coat she has sent and jokes about the 'rappsoddys' he tries to write to the family about life in Tobago. He reports he is 'becoming a perfect negroe' and 'an honest Savage of Bloody-bay'.

James's desk is full of half-finished letters to various members of the family – 'my usual entertainment of a rainy day'. He is continually interrupted by work. 'The Gentleman who lives with me as manager is not at home and I am constantly called away, either to administer Physic or advice; I have actually since I sat down to write given two injections and one emetic, and dressed about twenty sores.' He adds that Charles need not fear that this letter is polluted: James washed his hands in soap and warm water before taking up the pen again.

He has employed a doctor, who visits once a week for a payment of £15 a year. At other times 'I help of them all male and female with my own hands'. He has just completed 'one of the darkest offices of a surgeon on one of them'. An amputation, perhaps? Mostly, though, his medical work is less demanding. It often involves fooling his patients.

My method is when any of my negroes complain to me of being sick, and if I cannot find out the nature of their disorder yet am convinced that they really are sick, putting on a very sagacious face

I rub their temples with spirits of Hartshorn [ammonia], I send them to sleep. I have performed several very notable cures this way, assisted by the strength of imagination; for as I never seem at a loss for a remedy for any kind of disorder, they think me a capital Physician.[4]

Sir Adam is certainly impressed by this, along with the account from Grant. From Harrogate – where stomach pains have sent him to take the waters – he writes back to Tobago. The bulk of the letter deals with the paperwork necessary to formalise their joint ownership of Carrick. Then, in paternal tones, Sir Adam congratulates James on the 'kindness and Humanity' he is showing to the enslaved Africans. This kindness is, of course, entirely practical. James lays that plainly out in a letter of July 1775.

I have got very little Cotton planted yet owing to the extreme wetness of the season – and most of the slaves not being thoroughly seasoned I dare not work them much in such weather both for the sake of Humanity and Interest as the life of a slave or two would be considerable deduction from the profits of our Crop.[5]

There is another consideration beyond these. James, his manager George Gordon and the fisherman James Dyker are living in extraordinary circumstances. Carrick and the two other plantations in Bloody Bay are among the most remote on the island, most easily accessible by sea. Among some seventy enslaved Africans – James bought the contractor Fullerton's gang of twenty-eight 'very fine young people, healthy and thoroughly seasoned' at around this time – the three men must have felt outnumbered and at risk in the event of an uprising.

As John Newton wrote, a modicum of kindness to enslaved people was part of ensuring a white man's safety. There are many accounts of enslaved people who rose up and spared white people on plantations from whom they had received justice or kindness, while killing others. 'Do pray be sure of his character', James writes to Sir Adam in July 1775, when asking for a carpenter to be sent out from Scotland. 'A bad man on a plantation is not only very disagreeable but actually dangerous.'

When James buys Fullerton's gang of seasoned men – whom he knows from having hired them twice to help with the jungle clearing at Bloody Bay – Fullerton (who is selling up and returning to Scotland) lets him have the Africans at a good price. James explains: 'his people were all very desirous of coming to me on which [account] he gave up these advantages. This looks a little romantic but it is the case notwithstanding.'[6]

In early 1776 Fullerton changes his mind about returning home. He has bought more land and wants his gang back. But James has decided against, though the deal Fullerton offers is very good.

'Such a step would have very much hurt the rest of our gang as it would plainly have shown them that their staying or going did not depend on their own behaviour but on my caprice or interest which would be a certain means of preventing them having any attachment to me or the place on which more depends than many wise planters seem to think'.[7]

Health and death

In most of his letters James mentions the mood and health of the enslaved people at Carrick. They are, of course, his and Sir Adam's biggest single investment. The brothers spent more than £5,000 purchasing humans between 1774 and 1777, more than they had paid for the land and more than £8 million today. The people, however, are a fast-depreciating asset, despite the birth of a few children. Buying new Africans is the only practical way of replacing the dead. In 1777 James and his neighbour Gilbert Petrie share the purchase of a group of twenty-eight enslaved people from the Los islands, off Conakry in modern Guinea. They cost £38 each.[8]

These people, Petrie later told Sir Adam Fergusson, 'were apparently as fine slaves as never I saw, but turned out to be cadavrous wretches': typical, he says, of people from the Los.[9] Most were dead by 1780, mainly from yaws, a nasty bacterial disease which initially leaves lesions on the skin. Untreated – and until penicillin there was no treatment – yaws can cause blindness and eventual death. Many eighteenth-century doctors confused it with syphilis.

Neverthless, in May 1776 James writes that his bought workforce is now in 'high health and spirits': 'tho we have lost seven since the beginning of the settlement yet I think the gang now remaining worth considerably more than their original cost – the difference of value between a thoroughly seasoned Negroe and a new one – is in general estimated much too low. But besides all our Negroes being now seasoned – consequently less subject to sickness – they are vastly improved in every respect.'[10]

We know that James bought at least seventy-nine African people between February 1774 and May 1777: eleven of those were dead by November 1777. It is a terrible toll, though below the average. Two nearby Tobago plantations, Castara and Englishman's Bay, had death rates of 10.3 to 12.5 per cent each year during the 1770s. At Gilbert Petrie's much larger Englishman's Bay estate seventy-three adults died between 1772 and 1780. So did fifteen of the thirty-one children born.[11] Disease accounted for all the Englishman's Bay deaths except for three: one was 'killed by runaways', one 'shot by accident' and the last 'lost presumed drowned'.

These precisely worked figures appear in neat tables among Sir Adam Fergusson's correspondence; they must have been sent to him by Gilbert Petrie and George Ferguson, owners of Englishman's Bay and Castara respectively. When in 1778 Sir Adam was considering investing to expand the Bloody Bay estate into an indigo and cotton plantation with 200 enslaved workers, Petrie calculated the 'Mortality of Slaves' at a very optimistic 6 per cent. That would mean twelve deaths a year. But he also advised that 160 newly arrived Africans would have to be bought to add to the 79 already at Bloody Bay, to be certain of increasing the numbers to 200.

One of the reasons James had given two years earlier for planting cotton and indigo was that it would be less hard on the Africans than sugar and it does seem that the workers were slightly more likely to die at Castara or Englishman's Bay – both of them sugar-growing estates – than at Bloody Bay. But life was precarious for enslaved people; bear in mind, too, that these were healthy times, free of hunger and serious epidemics. This was not to last. Famine lay ahead for Tobago.

Scruples

Carrick, Tobago
2nd December 1774

My Dear Brother

. . . I long most ardently to hear from you, allowing me the honor of writing to you as a partner in (I do affirm) one of the finest lots in the West Indies. It has opened out beyond my most sanguine expectation and I have not the least doubt of its turning out a most advantageous bargain and I do assure you this is the sentiments of every one who has seen it since I came upon it. I have purchased ten new Eboe Negroes for which I have drawn on you as by advice but shall not mark them till you give me your sanction for putting on J. &. A. F.* than which, nothing would give me greater pleasure as I am certain in a few years I should have the pleasure of adding very considerably to your income . . .

My most affect. Compl. to all our friends and believe me to be
My Dear Brother
Yours most affect.
J. Fergusson[12]

For all my combing of the letters to understand how my ancestors squared their consciences with the acts of murder and cruelty done on their behalf, I have found only a few crumbs. They serve to make the Fergusson brothers' morality more inexplicable, and the men more alien. Clearly James believed there was regard or even affection for him among the Africans at Bloody Bay, but it appears to be what he might expect from a faithful horse or a dog. These 'possessions' were capable of killing him, as he well knew: the only thing that says his relationship with the enslaved workers may have been different from that of the usual white planter is that he felt safe enough to live, at times, as the only free person on the plantation.

There is no idealising James's relationship with the African people he bought, and no ignoring the fact that the 'Negroe collars' and chains were there to be used. He jokes about his hard work alongside the enslaved people and is proud that they trust him, but, obviously enough, he exploits that trust. Though the neighbour Mr Grant says James 'feeds and attends to [the Africans] like his Children',[13] the relationship is more that between master and animals that can talk. But you do not take a red hot iron and burn your initials into children or pets.

So, in James's mind, are the enslaved Africans intelligent stock animals which you might brand? He does not believe they have much mental capacity. He writes of the house he has built for his and the manager's residence, on the flat hill that rises immediately behind

---

* 'Marking' the slaves is branding them – J. & A. F. are the brothers' initials.

the beach of Bloody Bay (today the site of a government-built picnic area and a disused toilet-block):

> From this situation I not only command the bay but also the whole estate which I assure you contributes not a little to the despatch of the work, as I took some pains with the most knowing of my negroes to shew them that with my glass I could at any time tell who was idle altho' I was not with them.[14]

When James is feeling fanciful he says 'my people' but more often they are 'my negroes' – a possession that is named for the way it collectively looks, not what it is. Only once in all the correspondence between the brothers is there any discussion of relative humanity. It reveals what Sir Adam – who appears to be the best-educated and most religiously-minded of the three brothers – believes are essential differences between the races. Towards the end of a letter full of talk of money and title deeds, Sir Adam turns fatherly to his younger brother. He says he wishes to address a matter in their correspondence that 'were it new to me, would give me much more pleasure than even the immediate prospect of your acquiring a large Estate':

> I mean the strong marks of a good heart which they [James's letters] contain. I had by a paragraph of a letter from Mr. Grant to Charles been informed of your Kindness & humanity to your negroes – which I could easily have believed without being told of it from my knowledge of you. Difference of Colour I knew would be no reason with you not to feel for them & I cannot doubt that Gratitude & Affection for those who treat them kindly is natural to them as to the rest of Mankind.[15]

This seems significant. Here Sir Adam, friend to philosophers, MP and former rector of Glasgow University, states that African people are as emotionally capable as other humans, and that perceived racial difference is no reason for any lack of empathy. He implies that he considers them as much members of humankind as any white – in which case the treatment of them is surely intolerable to the God in whom he believes. It is certainly illegal in Britain, where – as a series of court cases were resolving at just this time – a black person has the same rights under the law as a white one.

But for all this talk of kindness oblivious of skin colour, only seven months earlier James had written speaking of the pleasure he would feel if Sir Adam approved a design made of their intertwined initials as the mark to be burnt into the chests of the ten newly acquired Eboe men. (The logo must have been agreed, since a branding iron made of silver was ordered from Barbados.[16]) As we will see, Sir Adam approved other, even more brutal ways of treating enslaved Africans in Jamaica. He appears to have been a thoughtful and fair landlord in Scotland, but his commercial enterprises outside Scotland show very little feeling for fellow humans – the enslaved Africans – at all.

Several writers who were owners of Caribbean plantations explored their feelings about the business of slavery, and the suffering of the enslaved people. Robert Dallas arrived in Jamaica from Scotland in 1779[17] to take charge of his dead father's debt-laden estate. Initially the twenty-five-year-old found the whole business, and the 'rapacious . . . inhuman . . . ignorant and cruel' white people in charge of it, revolting. On his first day he saw an enslaved servant punched in the face by his master because a fly had landed on the butter. 'My blood rebelled against the blow.' In a memoir published in 1790 he lists the punishments and tortures he sees, and pronounces himself 'daily sicken'd'.

As time went on, though, Dallas felt he was becoming inured to the 'tyranny, cruelty, murder' that he saw. 'There is a kind of intoxication. I have not lost my natural abhorrence to cruelty, yet I see it practised with much less impatience than I did, and I have only to pray that I may not feel an inclination to turn [slave] driver myself.' By the time he was middle-aged, he had abandoned much of his anti-slavery ardour. He held on to the plantation till 1810: 'I was young and intoxicated with the Utopian ideas of liberty',[18] he wrote to excuse his early qualms. What was the point, he asked, in questioning a system that makes people so rich?

* * *

James never writes directly of any cruelties he may see or inflict, and very little about his feelings. But then there is a lot wanting in his letters. One abiding puzzle is the lack of any mention whatsoever of the uprisings of the enslaved people, events that must have dominated island gossip among black and white. James does mention some political events and, from 1775, he is concerned about the rebellion in North America against Britain. This is a matter that materially affects the planters' lives and prospects: the end of trade with the American colonies is a disaster. Yet we hear nothing of the dissent in Tobago that was a threat to the white men's existence.

James was in the final stages of preparing his move to Bloody Bay in March 1774 when the enslaved Africans at Betsy's Hope plantation in Queen's Bay, just five miles away, rose up against the owners. There's no letter from him to his brothers in March that year, but there are in April, May and June. None contain any mention of an issue you would imagine was pressing: the deaths of ten near-neighbours, the three whites murdered and seven Africans subsequently grotesquely tortured and executed.

Did James play a role in this? The island's militia is mentioned in the account of the quashing of the Queen's Bay revolt. It was formed in 1772, and by 1776 numbered 330 men, not including officers. Given that there were only 391 white people on the island,[19] it seems reasonable to assume that James, with his Royal Navy experience, was a member of it. He had bought a 'militia rifle' and bayonet from his neighbour Gilbert Petrie. But there is no mention of the bloody week-long fight and its aftermath in his letters.

I wonder, not for the first time, if there has been some censorship done in the archive. My grandfather read all these letters, as his inked notes make clear. He transcribed parts of some, typing them up – perhaps about 10 per cent of all. But, more than once, he passes over the more unpleasant details. His transcript of the letter of December 1774 has some interesting remarks about the housing Jamie has built and the progress of felling the jungle. However, it leaves out the paragraph where he asks Sir Adam to approve the design of a brand to mark 'the ten new Eboe Negroes'. But I believe my grandfather was too dedicated a historian and archivist to destroy a letter. If there was censorship, perhaps it was done long before, by Sir Adam.

A triangular trade

In May 1776 James tells Sir Adam he now can supply about half the plantation's food needs with Carrick's own crops. More plantains and corn are being grown, and he is increasing the amount of land for the Africans to grow their own provisions, the usual Sunday activity on all plantations. He is expecting the imminent arrival of a ship bearing everything he ordered via Charles two years earlier. Clothing cannot be got in Tobago at the stores, but he will make do: when the 'Americans . . . return to their duty they will find they have lost some of their very best customers',[20] he says sharply. Is he becoming more nervous? Bills are mounting, and the first cotton crop has proved much smaller than he had hoped.

Until this point the British West Indies were dependent on the American colonies for most of their pigs, horses, poultry and cattle as well as staple foods like cheese, butter, oats, peas, onions and beans. Soap, candles and most of the timber for building came from the mainland, as did half the supply of enslaved people.[21] So the British government's banning of trade with America from the end of 1775, a measure intended to bring the rebels to heel, had devastating consequences in the British Caribbean, though it turned out to be lucrative for Britain.

The loss of the American market for sugar and rum caused prices for those to fall. An economic slump began. Though imports of food from Britain and particularly Glasgow increased massively to compensate, prices of essential foods rose by between 35 and 300 per cent in 1776. In several islands there were soon reports of both white and black starving: in Barbados 5,000 enslaved people died in a year because of food shortages.

The Caribbean historian (and first prime minister of independent Trinidad and Tobago) Eric Williams made the point in his *Capitalism and Slavery* (1944) that the British slavery colonies farmed in order to produce crops for export, not to support their populations. They were from 1775 almost entirely dependent on supplies from Britain, and indeed it was as consumers that the colonies were so valuable a cog in the global British economic machine. For Williams, and some other economic historians, the economic and political damage done by the American Revolution was the beginning of the end of British plantation slavery.[22] But it also began an economic boom in Britain and Ireland, as these stepped up to supply everything from clothing and ironware to grain and pickled herring for the plantation islands. This benefited landowners, farmers and workers across the nation. Millions of British people were to become a key part of the slavery-based economy by producing the things it needed to function.

James, though obviously unaware of the wider implications, could see the problems he and his fellow plantation owners faced. 'Most of the old settled Estates are absolutely in a starving condition,' he writes in June 1776, 'their Negroes absolutely dying of putrid fluxes [dysentery] for want of proper food, owing to the American Rebellion and their not keeping provided w/. ground provisions.'[23] But because he has addressed that last problem, his estate is better off.

In the same letter he attaches another shopping list. It begins with requests for cotton and linen, thread, buttons, needles and other clothing items for the enslaved people. He also wants 'iron work' and fittings to make twenty gin traps, and a dozen 'small locks and hinges for Negroe boxes', presumably for the enslaved people to keep possessions in. At the end he lists his personal wants: candles, oil, vinegar, mustard, spices, tongues, hams, cheese, beer, oatmeal, barley, cloths, towels and china – bowls, cups and saucers.

These items all arrive eleven months later[24] on a ship called the *Charming Nancy*[25] captained by a man named King. This was a feat, given that American privateer ships – licensed pirates, the British called them – were by then stopping almost all vessels to and from Tobago. Another effect of the American war was an interruption in supply of the one commodity without which all the planters' schemes would come to a halt: enslaved Africans. Even if the slave ships did get past the privateers, prices would certainly rise. But in July 1776 James is brought into a plan being cooked up by some of the planters to address this problem. He writes to his brother Charles, full of enthusiasm.

> What forces me to write at present is a scheme I have entered into (w/. some of the principal and most intelligent Gentlemen of this Country) of sending a vessel to the Coast of Guinea [West Africa] with Rum to purchase slaves: this scheme was planned by Mr. Petrie who was many years a Governor on the Coast[26] and is perfectly acquainted w/. all the steps necessary to be taken for insuring success . . . there is not a planter in the island that did not make a push to be admitted a partner in this adventure so high is the general opinion both of the scheme and the Conditions of it.[27]

Trading rum for African people makes sense. The spirit is liquid currency, easily produced from by-products of the sugar-refining process. It is usually sold to visiting ships who use it as part of their crew's pay. White workers in Tobago expect to be given a pint of rum each a day;[28] at Carrick the Africans receive a mug-full if they have had to work in the rain. James goes on to tell Charles that he has taken a half-share in Petrie's scheme.

He ends the letter requesting more supplies including two decanters, Madeira wine and 'a cask of second [cheaper] wine for the sick'. He signs off with curlicues, a Carrick with a comically enormous 'C' and a chirpy postscript asking Charles how he likes his florid new signature, 'J.F.' – 'I think my F is something like yours'. The letter also tells for the first time that James's health is no longer the reliable asset reported in all his previous correspondence. He has been seriously, perhaps dangerously, ill with a 'bilious flux'[29] – probably dysentery.

> I have had a severe brush since I wrote to you and Sir Adam last [a month earlier] but am now perfectly recovered but still very weak: now it is over, I think it the best thing that could have happened me, as a good hearty fit at once insures one against these little qualms and sicknesses that are so frequent in this Country and plague one more than enough, but I have now paid my fine and am entering in a new lease of good health.

It is an optimistic prognosis, given the known life expectancy of both black people and white. James has been in the Caribbean for three years: after four he will be battling the averages. The letter goes on in boisterous good humour, though as he ends it James comments that his head aches 'consumely': 'this Climate is by no means a promoter of writing, even in perfect health it is disagreeable – but when one is at all out of order it becomes painful.'[30]

The brigantine *Christie* – trading rum for Africans

James's 'Adventure to Africa', first mentioned to his brother Charles in the letter of 29 July 1776, is a sensible plan, given the pressures of the American war on supply of African people and the huge profits to be made from slave trading. But it is a leap into a deeper moral darkness. This excited James is hard to reconcile with the young man who just two years earlier stated that he would set out to treat Africans well, not just because he thought they would work better but because of his belief that they should be treated like any other member of humankind. There was no kindness on the Guinea ships. The appalling toll the voyage took on the African people packed inside the holds like cutlery in a drawer was well known: it is not something you can imagine anyone claiming to be a morally sensitive man tolerating.

Although it is still seven years before the first petitions calling for an end to the slave trade were delivered to Parliament, in eighteenth-century Britain and in the Americas a strong moral distinction was made between being a slave owner and a slave trader. Though the first North American states began outlawing slavery from 1777, owning a plantation in the Americas – and the necessary enslaved Africans to work it – remained a respectable occupation until the abolitionist movement began to dominate the discourse in the early 1790s.

But even before first-hand accounts of the Middle Passage became widely distributed in the 1780s, the trade was known to be inhuman. Quite apart from the buying or capturing of African men, women and children, the voyage was a murderous event, as even the most business-minded of British traders would have been aware. The statistics are stark. On average, one in every seven Africans put aboard British ships would die before they arrived in the Caribbean, their bodies thrown overboard without ceremony.[31] On some voyages more than half the Africans who left West Africa died. At least 5 per cent of those surviving died almost immediately after arrival.[32]

James and his brothers would have known of all this. Many Scots were involved in transatlantic shipping. They made up the majority of ships' surgeons, and many of the captains, and they were telling the stories of the barbarity they had seen on those voyages.

Despite the rising clamour against the trade, when Sir Adam found out about his brother's investment in the rum-for-Africans syndicate and its chosen ship, the brigantine *Christie*, he made no objection. He may have wished he had: of all James's enterprises this turned out to be most ill-starred. A 'tedious affair' Sir Adam called it, when the legal arguments over the *Christie* and its disastrous voyage were finally completed half a decade later.

The *Christie* was a brig, or brigantine. There's a subtle difference in the sail plan, but this is a two-masted sailing ship, probably armed with a few cannon. It was 110 tons, making it small for an ocean-crossing merchant ship, though it would still have carried at least

190 enslaved people. The great East Indiamen were anything between 500 and 1,200 tons.[33] The brig *Zong*, infamous because of a notoriously disastrous voyage in 1781 that shocked the British public and gave great energy to the abolitionist movement, was the same size as the *Christie* but carried 442 Africans. It was too many. When the *Zong* reached Jamaica only 208 were left. The crew admitted that, because of fear of disease and a lack of water, many of the Africans were thrown overboard while still alive.

George Craik was the *Christie*'s captain, an experienced skipper who had been working the transatlantic trade since 1770.[34] He and the brig were caught up in the war with America: the *Christie* was captured in Savannah River, Georgia, and then released by the Royal Navy after the Battle of the Rice Boats in early March 1776. From there Craik and *Christie* made their way to Tobago.

The 'intelligent gentlemen' of the island who made up the syndicate are listed in the British government's records as James Fergusson, Gilbert Petrie, Peter Campbell (who became Tobago's lieutenant-governor the following year), Edmund Lincoln and Craig Caldwell. James in fact had a tenth-share, having sold the other half of his fifth to a friend called Robertson, who in turn shared his with a Balfour. Captain Craik also had a share of Petrie's three-tenths of the whole, and the syndicate bought the ship.[35] James's investment was £93 sterling (£153,000 today), for which he gave Craik a bond.

The *Christie* set off from Tobago for the Gold Coast in October 1776: the syndicate had insured it and its cargo at the end of September. A large quantity of medicines were on board and 140 puncheons – 318-litre barrels – of Tobagan rum, worth £1,175 sterling[36] in London. The price of an enslaved African adult was about £17.50 sterling on the West African coast around this time (though most trades were done in guns, tools, trinkets or even cutlery).[37] Back in the Caribbean the enslaved people would sell for at least £40 each.

Captain Craik and the *Christie* arrived at Cape Coast Castle, now in Ghana, in February 1777. He spent three months buying Africans there and at nearby Anomabu. Craik set sail on 16 May for the West Indies[38] with 139 enslaved people aboard. If he followed normal practice – some 850 Africans were being shipped to the Caribbean every week at this time – he would have bought an equal number of men and women. A quarter of the total would have been children.

All the Africans would have been packed below decks in chains, head to toe.

Craik must have been pleased as he weighed anchor for the voyage west: the price of Africans back in the West Indies was at an all-time high, and he and the syndicate could expect to receive 130 per cent profit on their investment in each human.[39] The next news of the ship was that the *Christie* had sprung a leak near the island of St Thomas, far up the chain of islands that fringe the Caribbean. The ship was towed in 'with difficulty' and condemned as unfit to go further. In St Thomas Captain Craik sold twelve of the Africans to the Portuguese to pay for the rescue and maintenance of the rest. Some others died: we do not know how many.

Then, according to his account to Gilbert Petrie, Craik tried to ship seventeen more of the Africans as 'freight' back to Tobago. But this ship was seized by an American privateer and taken to Martinique. Captain Craik finally reappeared in Tobago in March 1778, eighteen months after leaving for West Africa. He had been via Barbados all the way to Liverpool and then back to the Caribbean along with the sixty-five of the remaining Africans – a voyage that cost £4 a head. Yet, for the syndicate, there was good news. The Africans were sold at the slave market in Scarborough, Tobago, 'at the enormous price of £50 a head' – because, writes Petrie, of their 'Remarkable quality'.[40]

All the detail that remains of this nightmarish drama is dry and financial: a contested insurance claim. We know no more of the fate of the Africans involved beyond the fact that fewer than half of those who left West Africa made it to Tobago. In 1782 Sir Adam and others had George Craik arrested in London for debts he owed the syndicate as a result of the sale of some of the Africans after the wreck; the Captain countersued for the cost of his stay in Tobago, the recovery of his health and damages for his unfair arrest. Eventually there was a settlement with Craik and an insurance payout to all the syndicate for the *Christie*'s cargo,[41] which can only refer to the African people lost. Ultimately, Sir Adam and Charles Fergusson appear to have got about £500 through various payments. Tedious it may have been, but the brothers appear to have made a profit.

CHAPTER 4

MANY WAYS TO DIE: PIRATES, FAMINE AND THE FLUX

My complaint was a bilious flux but I am now perfectly clear of it and the Drs assure me that it has given me a new lease of life – for which I have paid pretty handsomly – this is a most extravagant Country either to live or dye in.

James Fergusson to Sir Adam Fergusson,
8 January 1777

IN 1773 JAMES FERGUSSON PROMISED his brothers and himself that he would make a success of the plantation at Bloody Bay within four years. By early 1777 he is close to fulfilling that pledge. In January he says half the 300 acres are now cleared for cultivation and he hopes to start picking this year's cotton within a month. 'Barring accidents' he will ship ten or twelve thousandweight. (That would have sold for between £666 and £800 in Britain.[1]) Once the cotton is in, he will turn his efforts to the indigo crop. He has even higher hopes of that.

But there are all sorts of accidents that can and often do befall. Unpredictable weather is always a problem; more troublesome now is the war with the American states. By the middle of 1777 American ships have not only succeeded in scaring off or seizing most transatlantic shipping – only three letters from James reach Scotland during the year – but they have also taken almost every Tobagan coastal boat, the only means for supplying the outlying plantations.

Five miles up the coast from Bloody Bay towards Tobago's north-eastern tip, near the little town of Charlotteville, there is a sheltered cove still known as Pirate's Bay. Today's tourists are told that all the famous Caribbean buccaneers used it as a base for attacking Spanish treasure ships. That makes strategic sense: a good harbour at the windward tip of the island, with 360-degree views from the ridge above, is an ideal jumping-off point for predators on shipping. The British Navy valued this bit of coast too. The larger bay off Charlotteville was surveyed in 1770 for navy use: hence its name, Man o'War Bay.

Pirate attacks were a danger in the islands well into the nineteenth century. James and other planters on the northeast side of Tobago were acutely aware of the threat. Royal Navy ships based down the coast could find it hard to move promptly against the prevailing wind to protect the more easterly settlements. In any case, surprise raiders might be long gone before a man travelling on horseback over the hills could raise the alarm at Fort King George in Scarborough.

With open war between the American colonies and Britain, both sides were at liberty to raid each other's possessions, on land or at sea. A fleet of armed American merchant ships was already well used to navigating the islands to trade. From March 1776 the Americans started issuing letters of marque permitting their merchant captains to attack the enemy. In January 1777 James writes saying that since the small ship he is sending his letter by is not going in a convoy, 'it is probable she will fall into the hands of buccaneers'.[2]

By 1777 there are said to be 175 ships of this licensed American wolf pack active around the sugar islands. In March Tobago's new lieutenant-governor, Peter Campbell, writes in despair to Whitehall saying that merchants do not dare ship any crops and the colony will soon be 'ruined' without more warships.[3] The plantations on Tobago's more remote, hilly northeastern coast are easy targets, and Bloody Bay is one of the remotest and most vulnerable of all. James has firearms at home, but not much to deter determined attackers.

In 1776 a 40-pounder cannon was installed to protect the bay. Either James bought it himself, or he prevailed on the lieutenant-governor to send it round by ship. A copy of a contemporary map is in the museum at Fort King George, showing where each 18- and 9-pounder was positioned on headlands around the coast. James would have had to pay, one way or another: the authorities were strict about making the planters contribute to their protection. Each time the military put down the uprisings of those times, an instant tax was imposed upon the planters to cover the costs.

In early July 1777 one of the most famous of the American privateer captains, David McCullough, sailed his schooner the *Rattle-Snake* round the rocky headland and into Bloody Bay. The American ship, two-masted with 150 men aboard and eighteen 6-pound cannon, would have looked vast and terrifying in the small bay. The *Rattle-Snake* is well known at this time, and Captain McCullough a celebrity. He has taken at least eight ships already in 1777, working the chain of the Windward Islands. Among his prizes were an important transport from London and several ships on their way from Africa. One of those was carrying 511 enslaved people, and another was laden with ivory. Most of the captured ships went to the French island of Martinique, where they and their cargo – humans and goods – would have been sold. A contemporary account from Barbados of the *Rattle-Snake* calls Captain McCullough the 'boldest fellow':

> Bets used to be often laid at Martinico, relative to the captures the above little vessel would bring into any of the respective harbours. People would be looking out for her; and on her appearance with a prize, the joyful alarm was, *Le Serpent a Sonnettes!* — The beach would then be crowded with spectators, and the *Rattlesnake* enter the harbor in triumph.[4]

Only once had the British navy come close to her. In May 1777 HM sloop *Beaver* chased the *Rattle-Snake* between the islands of St Lucia and St Vincent, but the famously speedy privateer got away.

James was not scared off by this reputation, if an account printed later in the year in the Edinburgh paper *Caledonian Mercury* is to be believed. He and the Carrick workers had just finished unloading the long-awaited supplies brought across the Atlantic by the *Charming Nancy*. The two small coastal vessels loaded with that cargo – the last two in Tobago, according to the paper – were just leaving Bloody Bay when the *Rattle-Snake* appeared. They fled back to the shallows below the Carrick plantation.

> Mr Ferguson saw the chance, and immediately, with his overseer, Mr Gordon, and another white man belonging to his estate went armed with their muskets to the assistance of the small vessels. In one of these there was two guns two pounders, and two swivels,

which, with the crews of both, consisting of seven men, he brought onshore, after taking down the running rigging, to make it as difficult as possible for the privateer's people to get off the vessel; the guns they planted among the cotton bushes, that they might be as much out of view of the enemy as possible . . .

By making his men go through the bushes, sometimes to the right, and sometimes to the left, Mr Ferguson made them seem more numerous than they were, and by his spirit and good conduct prevented the enemy from attempting to land.[5]

The newspaper says that the Carrick men shot at least five of the *Rattle-Snake's* musket-men out of the rigging.

There is no mention of this drama in James's letters to his brothers, an omission probably explained by the usual interruptions to the transatlantic mail. Clearly the threat was grave. James must have assumed that the *Rattle-Snake* intended to raid his house, which was only a couple of minutes' walk from the beach and clearly visible from the sea. After that, the Americans would have looted the plantation stores and captured as many people as they could. (Many of the *Rattle-Snake's* crew were black, according to one account, but the privateers habitually took enslaved Africans from the ships they captured and sold them as they did other plunder.) Upmost in James's mind was the 8,000 pounds of newly harvested cotton,[6] his first crop, ready at last to send home to pay something back to his brothers. Nonetheless, he took the risk of trying to save the Messrs Campbells' boats.

The brief letter that James does write at the end of July tells us very little. He bemoans the lack of ships to send what is now a 'small crop' of cotton and rages at the failure of the British admirals to provide the protection the island needs – 'entirely neglect'd', even though Tobago is, he feels, more important than St Vincent or St Lucia. He has sent Mr Gordon, the manager, with half the cotton to the more accessible Courland Bay, in the hope that he can sell it 'at £8 sterling' or get it on board a ship with a Captain Bing. If not, it will have to be stored until the next convoyed fleet appears.

The letter is short and panicky, it must be dispatched 'twenty miles through a most wretched road' in half an hour since Bing is due to sail tomorrow. 'I hope what I have there said will convince you that it is not my fault that our small crop is not sent home or not that I did not write for insurance.'[7] This is the last we hear from James Fergusson: three months later he is dead.

William Bruce, a plantation owner in the flatlands of west Tobago and a close friend of James, writes to tell the Fergussons the news. The death came on 27 October, 'after a long & painful illness, which he bore with the same good temper & spirits, which was usual to him in good health'. James had been recuperating at the Bruce estate, Shirvan, where he had stayed to get over his previous bout of dysentery. Bruce explains that the air at Shirvan is 'drier' than that at Bloody Bay, and the best doctors live nearby. These had seen him, prescribed opium and advised a voyage to Bermuda to 'restablish him'. He had resolved to do this.

> But about 2 o'clock the following morning, he was suddenly sieged with a very great weakness, and died seeming without pain or struggle, about two hours afterwards, nature being quite exhausted.[8]

James was thirty-one. He had been in the Caribbean for just four years and four months. He was probably buried immediately near William Bruce's house at Shirvan – the climate dictates the haste, and Tobago then had no minister, no church or formal cemeteries. The most likely site for the grave is now a shopping mall on Shirvan Road, near to Tobago's international airport.

* * *

How do you sum up James's time in Tobago? The deaths, first: we know that at least eleven Africans bought by him died in the three years that the Carrick estate operated, along with an unrecorded number of children. These people's only memorial is the names we have for them, many of which were forced on them by their captors. It may be the case that James treated the Africans better than did the average planter. He certainly set out with that intention. But he still put their lives at enormous risk. The suffering of the seventy-eight men, women and children remaining at Carrick when James died would only increase over the following years.

These are their names, as totted up in the inventory made for James's heirs – his four siblings – in November 1777. Their total value was put at £4,198.

Ann
Emoinda (house servant)
Rachael (house servant)

Monimia (washerwoman)
Sophia (cook)
Peggy (sick nurse)

Solomon (watchman)
Offa (watchman)
Scotland (carpenter)

Quashie (driver)
Bob (driver)
Pollydore (stockkeeper)

'Field men and boys'

Achilles	Frank	Lyon	Quamie
Adam	Glasgow	Jock	Quamino
Arthur	George	Lincoln	Romeo
Billy	Hill	Monday	Tom Senior
Cato	Hamlet	Mooza	Tom Junior
Caesar	Hector	Nero	Trim
Coffie	Hercules	Ned	Wooma
Creole Lara	Joe	Othello	York
Danda	Jack	Peter	Zara
Edinburgh	Kusurie	Paddy	Manza

'Field women and girls'

Amanda	Hawa	Maud	Pennie
Charlotte	Janet	Maria	Rose
Caabo	Kelly	Musundie	Tickie
Coomba	Koolakoo	Nancy	Tachitiba
Daphne	Kamiza	Peggy	
Fatima	Katharine	Polly	

Children

Billy	Colin	Flora
Johney	Jeanie	

After Jamie

In 1777, before he became ill, James Fergusson was close to financial success at Bloody Bay. The Carrick estate harvested a significant amount – three and a half tons – of cotton that year, though the £800 it might have fetched (on £11,000 or more invested in the four years) in London was not as impressive as the returns from sugar investments. But there was one consolation for James's backers, his brothers: the land which had cost £4,250 in early 1774 as jungle was now judged worth £7,244, six shillings and eightpence, and the new buildings a further £471.[9]

As so often in the Caribbean colonies in this period, the rise in land value eclipses the profit from the crops. But 1777 was to prove the highpoint of the Fergusson adventure in Tobago. According to Sir Adam's own notes, at his death James owed him more than £6,500,[10] nearly £11 million in 2020. Sir Adam was to recover virtually nothing of that sum.

Sir Adam and the Fergussons mourn Jamie. 'One of the best fellows that ever lived, or that ever will live', their brother George writes to Sir Adam, adding, 'Would to God he had been spared to make some return [from the Tobago estate]'.[11] Sir Adam's papers contain many more letters of condolence from friends and relations. George and the rest of the siblings – Jean, Charles and Helen – agree that Sir Adam's 'kindness' to Jamie should be repaid, and they sign over their dead brother's remaining cash – £867 – to him. As his heirs, they agree to share the Carrick estate equally.

George Fergusson is dubious the plantation will ever succeed. Sir Adam, nonetheless, presses on. He makes an agreement with Gilbert Petrie, Jamie's friend and neighbour at nearby Englishman's Bay. Petrie will oversee the management of the plantation and advise on the strategy, along with George Ferguson at Castara. The other important job is the settling of Jamie's many debts, which include bills for enslaved people acquired in 1777. In total the Carrick estate owes nearly £4,000 to merchants, traders and to the Castara Fergusons. Petrie produces a seven-year plan to increase the numbers of enslaved workers to 200, and to clear much more of the 150 or so acres at Carrick that are still untouched forest. Petrie is doing just the same on his property at Englishman's Bay.

By the end of 1777, 113 of the Fergussons' 300 acres at Bloody

Bay are planted with cotton, which should produce 70,000 pounds of harvested fibre. But Petrie's ambitious plan will involve buying 160 enslaved people in addition to the 76 now remaining at Carrick. He estimates that if they buy newly arrived Africans, thirty will die in 'seasoning'. But, with cocoa and coffee planted between the cotton rows, in seven years he hopes for a net profit of £2,310 a year – against the £550 the current set-up ought to realise.

Nothing approaching this will ever happen: the Fergussons never made any profit from Tobago. Petrie's letters to Scotland over the next months carry bad news followed by worse. A severe hurricane hits Tobago, and then pirates attack Carrick again. When an American sloop – a single-masted ship – sails into Bloody Bay on the morning of 30 December 1777, no alarm is raised; the Carrick staff think the ship is the vessel they had been expecting to take away the last of Jamie's one and only cotton crop. It sits ready in bags in the store he had built above the tide-line. There are four white men at Carrick now: the manager George Gordon, a new overseer called John Livingstone, James Dyker the fisherman, and an unnamed carpenter. But there is no time to organise a defence.

The sloop lands forty armed men, who quickly take possession of the 40-pounder cannon. Gordon rounds up as many of the workers as he can; they are, after all, the most valuable property on the plantation. Petrie tells the story in a letter to Sir Adam:

> Except one who was stationed as a Watchman at the Bay and an old Blindman who was with him, they were all conveyed into the woods before the Pirates Reached the House; and afterwards, one only who had strolled from the rest was taken. The house & Store were not burnt, but plundered of everything worth carrying off which yr. house Negroes had not been able to convey into the woods. All the Plantation Stores and Provisions were lost, together with yr. Cotton, the Gunpowder and Stores belonging to the Great Gun, which they spiked but in so superficial a manner that it was easily cleared Afterwards. Upon an adjoining Plantation, the Invaders were more successful; there they got Eight Negroes of which Six belonged to a poor unfortunate man whose Plantation had some months before been destroyed by Runaway Slaves.[12]

Petrie goes on in some anger, complaining that four Royal Navy warships were at anchor ten miles down the coast in Courland Bay, but as usual they failed to come up to the windward – the eastern end – of the island to protect it. This despite the series of privateer attacks that northeast Tobago has seen: at least three in the last year. In addition to the cotton and a huge amount of food, tools, clothing and other stores, three of the enslaved people were taken by the Americans: Solomon the watchman, the old and blind Hamlet and a woman named Creole Lara ('Creole' means that she was born in the Caribbean). Petrie assesses the total loss at £328 and fourteen shillings.[13] Now, he says, the army has posted three soldiers and another cannon to guard Bloody Bay and all its three plantations. He pleads with Sir Adam as a Member of Parliament to intercede with the government or the Navy to get further military help.

Worse follows. In 1780 the cotton plants are devastated by the chenille worm and several acres of planted land are washed away when the Bloody River rises after a hurricane. Then, in May the following year, the French invade Tobago. Despite a resistance effort led by James's old friend George Ferguson, commanding a force including many enslaved men, a French administration gains the island and takes control of government. The white Scottish planters are allowed to continue in business, but they have lost Britain as a market and the French soon start squeezing them for taxes.

By 1783 the Carrick farming enterprises seem to have been more or less abandoned, apart from the growing of food for those who live there. The cotton produced barely covers costs. Petrie is renting out the Carrick workforce as jobbing labour to other plantations. Sir Adam Fergusson vacillates about the future: he proposes to sell Carrick, then retracts because he thinks prices will rise when the British re-take the island, as the government has pledged.[14] He considers dispatching the remaining enslaved workers to Rozelle, the Jamaica plantation of which he is co-owner. Petrie does not approve. He tells Sir Adam why, showing some attempt to understand the psychology of an uprooted person:

> Untill a Negroe forms an attachment to a Plantation, he is never seasoned, and when he does, a separation from the Objects of his Attachment breaks his heart, he becomes indifferent to good or bad treatment, careless of his food, Clothing and Person; and if he

does not hang himself he falls into a lingering disease and dies. It is that attachment to their country in Africa, that renders it so difficult and tedious a matter to season new negroes, by reconciling their minds to the Change of food accomodation & Habits. The same cause destroys almost all the Negroes brought from an Old to a Newly Settled Island . . . by taking them from their Houses Gardens ground, and other little possessions which habit had insensibly let them to consider as their Own Property.

In November 1784 Petrie has another inventory of the estate done for Sir Adam, in preparation for a sale. As he says, it shows that the Carrick workers are unusually sickly; the toll, Sir Adam agrees, has been 'dreadful'.[15] Seventeen adults have died in the seven years since James's death,[16] along with, again, an unknown number of children. More children have been born but of the five listed in 1777 only two, Billy and Jeanie, have survived. Billy is listed as 'mulatto' and is now a house servant, but 'lame from sciatica'.

Rachael, 'mulatto', a house servant and seamstress from James's time, still survives, as does Peggy, now named the cook. One of the newly acquired enslaved people – Petrie bought fourteen Africans for Sir Adam in 1778 – has been given the name 'Jammie', perhaps in memory of James Fergusson. Twenty-five are listed as 'sickly', 'incurable' or 'unserviceable', most of them because of yaws. Two have been blinded by the disease. Petrie has ordered the carpenter to build 'a yaws house' to isolate the sufferers. Next come the deaths of Carrick's manager John Livingstone, who replaced Gordon in 1780, and James Dyker, the fisherman shipped out from Ayrshire. He has, at least, taught three of the Africans enslaved at Carrick to catch the local fish.

Tobago's governor, Comte Arthur Dillon – an Irish aristocrat in the French Army – issues an edict on all the failing plantations across the island. Unless cultivated they will be forfeit, he declares, under the existing British law that says land plots sold by royal grant must remain in use. Petrie warns Sir Adam that Dillon's friend the Marquis de Bouillé, conqueror of Tobago, has his eye on Bloody Bay, which he will be able to snap up if it is 'condemned'.[17] The French claim Sir Adam is in default on his taxes – which they have increased – and also the payments for the initial purchase of the lot by the Wilsons twenty years earlier. They tell him that he must come in person to cultivate the land or lose it.

Sir Adam gives up. Losing the land, he says bitterly, would be better than having to move to Tobago.[18] So in early 1785 he sells the remaining seventy-nine enslaved Africans and everything moveable at Carrick to Gilbert Petrie and his brother John, a planter in India.[19] The land and houses are put on the market, for sale or rent. Advertisements for it are sent to be printed in the government gazettes. in Grenada, Martinique and St Vincent.

However, Sir Adam is too slow. By May 1787 20,000 acres of Tobago plantations have been seized by the French authorities[20] and de Bouillé's managers have taken possession of Carrick. Over the coming years Sir Adam remains busy petitioning Paris for the return of the Tobago land, while the revolution in France exiles de Bouillé and sends Dillon to the guillotine. He enlists a friend, the powerful politician Henry Dundas, to try to get his case settled through diplomatic channels. Another attempt seeking compensation for the family would be made by the Dalrymples of Newhailes after the fall of Napoleon in 1813.

Of the enslaved Africans we know nothing more. If they ended up at one of the Petrie plantations at Englishman's Bay, they were at least situated somewhere prosperous and settled, run by a man who, from his letters, might appear more sensitive than most to his enslaved workers' well-being. Gilbert Petrie died in 1807, leaving sums in his will to many of the enslaved people who worked for him. One of them is named Quamino (who got £50): this is one of the names on the list of enslaved people that Petrie bought from the Fergussons. He also left £500, a huge sum, to each of three freed 'mulatto' men. They may well have been his children.[21] But of these people's voices nothing remains.

The long battle to gain compensation for the loss of Carrick generated a pile of paperwork, much of it in French, far larger than all the correspondence in the years that Jamie ran the plantation. It was to no avail. The Tobago plantation, a little bit of Fergusson land at the world's edge, was lost. It soon reverted to jungle. It had indeed been, as Sir Adam described it in a note to Gilbert Petrie in 1785, altogether 'an unfortunate Undertaking'.[22]

CHAPTER 5

TOBAGO TODAY

I Come From

I come from borrowed names, given names, names
    of dis-possession
Hawker, Harris, Princess Margaret waving her white-gloved
    hand
from the motor cavalcade.
I come from faces, earth & sun faces, tamarind faces,
    watermelon teeth.
From hands: rough carpenter's hands, smooth Nivea-creamed
    hands, blue-veined & cutexed, hands that reached for the
    cane.
I come from skin & bone, Portuguese skin, African bones,
    buried in forgotten oceans

from the ringing of bells, the clapping of hands
from foreday morning drums over a Pentecostal backyard
from cutlasses and ships
from red bauxite pyramids of barges
from that name, Captain, cutting through those rivers
they charted, navigated, christened, 'Home'

Maggie Harris, born in Guyana in 1954[1]

The little village is far from today's tourist routes.

To Bloody Bay

The rain has lightened, at last, though heavy dark clouds are still rolling down from Main Ridge. The gorge of the Bloody River seems to funnel them at us like bowls down an alley. Ruth and Lulu, my wife and daughter, want to go back to the guesthouse at Castara, to swim and sleep off the jetlag. We are just one night away from Edinburgh. But I have signed us up for a tour of a little dasheen plantation, the only farming now on the site of Carrick, James and Sir Adam Fergusson's Tobago estate. The rest of the land is regrown scrub, rainforest and an incongruous municipal playing field, neatly laid out on the flat land beside the river.

The tour's ticket price comes with a bowl of hot callaloo stew – dasheen leaves and armadillo meat – and the use of a pair of wellington boots. Junior Thomas is the guide: there are the three of us and five tourists over from Trinidad for Tobago's annual Blue Food Festival, happening today on the Bloody Bay sports field. Blue food is the island's heritage meal: yams, stews and mash-ups of wild animal meat all coloured by dasheen (the taro plant), the roots and leaves of which gives food a strange bluey-purple tint.

'Why has this place got this terrible name?' asks one of the Trinidadians as we set off. 'Bloody Bay?'

Junior explains: 'There was a pirate battle here, so fierce the water in the sea turned red from all the blood that was spilt.'* Everyone likes this story. There's a cove a few miles on up the coast that's known to have been a base for Captain Kidd and Captain Morgan, he of the rum brand – it is Pirate's Bay. There's supposed to be treasure hidden there.

We squelch away down a narrow path beside the rushing brown river. I've no idea what we may find. The crumbling remains of a plantation house with faded white columns and fretworked balconies losing a battle against the forest? But Fresh Greens Farm turns out to be just two shaky-looking tin-sided shacks. The smaller one is a long-drop toilet.

The farm is run by two big men, Lindsay Edwards and his father, Sherwin. Lindsay is round and smiling, Sherwin lean and grey-bearded: they're both wearing T-shirts so lacquered with layers of hardened filth down the front that my daughter can't stop staring at them. It is dasheen juice: when the men cut the leafy plants and lift them, the sticky sap runs down their chests.

Dasheen is the new farm's only crop so far, Lindsay explains. Fresh Greens comes from a government-funded initiative to restart small-scale agriculture in the poorer parts of the island: the Tobago House of Assembly has leased the Edwardses an acre and a half of land and given them a grant. Before, Lindsay says, there was nothing here.

We wander along the embankments between the watery dasheen fields: they remind me of rice paddy. The crop grows tall and shiny green, like monster spinach plants. Lulu finds a dead snake, orange-yellow. The urban Trinidadians are fascinated and the motor-driven Nikon that one of them has chatters on. 'Dasheen is our culture, our roots,' one of the visitors tells me. 'It's like the Irish are with potatoes.' The enslaved brought dasheen and yam with them on the ships from Africa, she says. Does she like eating it? Yes, but only the leaves, she says, stewed with spices. They are much more interesting than the bland blue root.

Sherwin says that after a life working in the construction business, getting his own place and working with his son is the fulfilment of

---

* There are other explanations. One is that the bay got its name after a seventeenth-century naval battle between the British and the Dutch; another is that a tree with a red sap was harvested by early settlers who floated the bleeding logs down the river.

a dream. 'I'm working hard: that's my joy, God be praised. When I was growing up I was taught nobody owes me anything: I got to work for what I want. And I wanted a farm of my own, I wanted to be self-sufficient.'

'Do you know,' I offer, 'that my great-great-great-great-great-great-uncle was a farmer here too?' I realise as I say it how inadequate this is.

'He was?'

'Yes. His name was Fergusson.'

He widens his eyes, nods. 'So, you're telling me this farmer, Fergusson . . . he was a white man? In the slavery time?'

I nod. 'He owned a plantation. In the 1770s.'

'Your uncle, way back . . . Weys! Interesting, that.'

'Are your family from here?'

'Yes – well, one of my granddaddies, his father came from Grenada. But my mammy's family are from here, all the way back. Since . . . well, since they were brought to Tobago.'

Junior, the tour guide, is beckoning us on – though since the plantation is just the Edwardses' one and a half acres, there cannot be much more to see. The boom of the sound system at the food festival reverberates through the misty drizzle.

'Do you know any Fergussons?' I wonder.

'Yeah, there's Fergussons.' Sherwin thinks for a moment. 'Not in Bloody Bay. But there's definitely some of that name around. Charlotteville, maybe? In Castara, there's a man with a convenience store there – he's Fergusson.'

Castara is five miles away: it's where we're staying. I thank him. He tells me to come back any time.

'I'll see you, boy.'

I've already learnt that 'boy' is friendly here, though I'm not going to use it back at anyone. But I am cheered – first contact achieved.

We struggle back up the narrow embankment. As we leave the fields I see two of the Edwardses' workers knee-deep in muddy water, harvesting the dasheen. Sherwin tells me they're 'schoolboys', here on a work experience scheme. They work steadily, clutching the leaves of the shoulder-high plants to their chest with one arm while the other arm brings a long machete down at the stalks. Here the machete is called a cutlass: it is the basic work tool on a plantation.

I want to take a photograph of them, the dull grey steel rising and falling, the virulent green under the lead sky. One of them sees me framing him with my camera: he stops and scowls. Stupid: I should have asked. I raise an arm to say sorry.

Main Ridge

Early in the morning, I meet Junior Thomas at the crossroads in Bloody Bay township. This is a straggle of low buildings along the ridge enclosing the west side of the valley: the usual sprawl of breeze-block villas and tin-roofed shacks. Some of the largest houses look unoccupied, weeds growing up at the gates, black mould staining the fretted wooden eaves. The smallest houses are the busiest. Some are just a basic box on concrete stilts, hung with washing that looks unlikely to dry in the steamy warmth. Tethered goats graze underneath the stilts, or along the road's verge. On a few dwellings the walls are sheets of chipboard, unvarnished and unpainted: there is no glass in the window holes.

Junior pulls up in his truck. He lives in Bloody Bay, further up the hill. I liked him when we met at the dasheen farm, a man who enjoys his job, with a rumbling laugh that shakes his whole frame. So I asked if he could help me explore a bit further. I haven't told Junior any more than that I'm a writer, and I have some papers that describe what one of the first Scottish planters did when he came here in the eighteenth century. He was interested – 'I have got to see those letters. The village needs to see them.' I have some photo-copies with me, but I am nervous, uncertain how much I should reveal of my own history. Is the name Carrick used here? I wonder. Never heard that, Junior says.

We drive up to the forested Main Ridge, the backbone of Tobago, nearly 2,000 feet high. Then we start the walk down through the steep glens all the way to the bay. It's green and brilliant today in the hills, the air full of bright birdsong; it seems a pity to dive into the dark of the forest. Junior finds a hole in the tree-wall. It gives onto a muddy path: the Gilpin Trail, named not for a Scottish planter, but for the manufacturer of a brand of vegetation-clearing cutlass. It is ancient: 'This is how the people carried their goods and crops to Roxborough, to market, before the roads were built,' Junior says.

Junior's grandfather used to take his dasheen crop over the ridge on a mule. When Junior was a child he walked the lower miles of the trail every day after school, carrying containers up to the first clear waterfall to get water for the family home. Mains water did not arrive in Bloody Bay until the 1980s, and electricity even later. When we stop at the fall to drink, the water is cold and delicious, clear despite the startling streak of golden mud underneath from which it roars. The gold is the iron oxide in the mountain: people used to collect the mud to decorate their faces for Carnival.

For four hours we stumble through the cathedral of the forest, vast and green, full of alien things. I wonder how much of it my distant uncle James would now recognise. He must have walked this way himself, showered under the same waterfalls. It would have made him remember the haul up the Toddy Burn above Kilkerran, the family's standard Sunday afternoon walk, through old beeches and bracken and onto the Carrick moors.

The smells – fresh water, rotting undergrowth – are not so different, until something fetid and tropical shocks us, trumping all other odours. A termite's nest, fallen just nearby, says Junior. Around us on the vines hang the nests, football-sized balls of mud constructed out of reach of the grub-seeking armadillos. Eventually, like any overbuilt city, they reach terminal point and crash down. The stink is like rotten fruit and stale urine: it advertises a feast for insect-eaters.

We are in the heart of what Tobago's tourist literature calls the 'world's oldest nature reserve' – a huge area ordained in 1776, the year before James Fergusson died. It was a decision made by the lieutenant-governor and his council, of which James was a member. The planters said, with surprising percipience, that without the forest the rain would fail and the land become useless, and so felling of trees in this last, most inaccessible area – some 10,000 acres – was forbidden.

James doesn't mention this radical environmental decision in his letters: but the rain, its violence and its infuriating failure to stick to a logical pattern is a repeating bass note in his accounts. With it come, as the years pass, a sense of his exhaustion and growing malaise. Gilbert Petrie reckoned this micro-climate was to blame for the appalling death rate among the enslaved African workers, worse than on the plantations on Tobago's western flatlands.

Few of my family have visited Bloody Bay in the 230-odd years since James died. My great-uncle Bernard, his wife Laura and their son, George, tried to do so in 1965. They came on a government launch (Bernard Fergusson was then governor-general of New Zealand), and landed in the surf on the beach. But they had to abandon their attempt to venture inland because of a downpour too dense to see through. I'm lucky to be here in sunshine.

I mention James's weather reports to Junior. 'Yes, Bloody Bay – lots of rain. The most in the island.' He rolls his eyes. 'Unpredictable! They say here you only know it's gonna rain when it rains.' Only once during our trek down from the ridge does the rain arrive. It is heralded by a shiver in the air. Then comes a blast of cool wind that startles the parrots in the canopy above into bitter complaint; a few seconds later we hear noise building, a whisper, a rumble and then a roar. Junior quickly stuffs his binoculars and laser pointer into a waterproof pocket in his rucksack.

When it comes, the rain seems to fill the greater part of the space usually occupied by air. It is as if you'd been thrown into water from a capsized boat. I wonder if you can drown in it. When the shower passes, we're left breathless, refreshed, humbled: the forest fills with vapour as the sun starts to suck the water back up to the clouds again. Hummingbirds in petrol-green and -blue appear, hovering as stable as drones to inspect the flower buds and dip their curved beaks. James must have been amazed by the birds on his first encounter. Only the herons that watch the pools in the lower reaches of the Bloody River would have been anything like what he knew in Scotland.

James told little of the wonders, though he was not unaware of them. He is 'no botanist', he writes in 1775, but there is 'the greatest variety of plants and shrubs of perhaps any island in the world' . . .

> I never go into the woods without seeing a new kind [of bird] but I am no sportsman tho there is more game in this island than in any island I ever was in before there is I believe a greater fund of amusement here, for a naturalist, than on any piece of land of the same extent in the world.[2]

Junior talks of how the forest might have changed since the 1770s. 'There would be more then. Wild pigs: very dangerous, territorial. More big trees, much bigger. Most of these are new growth – the hurricane of 1963 took out 90 per cent of the old trees. There would have been no bamboo' – he gestures at the huge fans of the plant, some stalks as thick as my arm, that spread out from a single base and reach halfway to the canopy – 'that was introduced later by the Europeans.'

I tell Junior of James's accounts of trees in the virgin forest four feet or more in diameter and '80 feet in length to the first branch'.[3] He nods. 'There's a few like those at the top of the ridge.' He recognises a few of the names James mentions: greenheart, locust, angeline, gregory, marlick and iron wood. James's house was built of greenheart – 'Very strong, lasts for ever – but there's none left on this side of the ridge.'

Muddy and light-headed with the heat, I am startled when we reach a ribbon of tarmac. I pay Junior his fee and say goodbye. I promise to email him some of the detail of the Scotsman's letters. Then a thought pops up. There was a risk of pirates attacking the plantation, I say. Junior nods. I ask if he ever heard of a big cannon. Yes, he says, he knew one in the woods when he was a child. But he has to go – a cruise ship is due in and he wants to be on the dock to tout his services as a wildlife guide. We agree to have a look later in the week.

The Bloody Bay beach, scene of pirate attacks and James's first landing, is a hundred yards or so below the cleared land where, a few days before, had been the tents of the Blue Food Festival. Now the expanse of gravel and grass is empty and tidy, strangely tame amid the clamour of the forest all around it. From up on the ridge, the old plantation is a strip of tropical paradise straight from a travel brochure, green lawns giving way to palm trees that bow to sweep a golden strand. Or it would be if the day was sun-filled and the sea limpid and blue. But this is the rainy season.

Just above the sand is a row of concrete buildings, government-built, painted in purple. Hopeful signs promise an art gallery and the 'Baywatch Bar'– both locked up, they look as though they have not been used for years. There are a couple of bored lifeguards. Don't swim, they say. Too much debris in the water from the past days' storms.

I stand in the surf in my flip-flops, letting the rough sand suck till I am buried to my ankles. Looking out to sea, to the Sisters Rocks, I think that the view cannot have changed. To my right there's a long sandbar, with one of the island's strange miniature herons stalking it. The swollen Bloody River pours out, spreading a mushroom cloud of brown into the green of the sea. More clouds are gathering over the ridge behind and a grey gloom fills the still, humid heat.

Just above the beach, a concrete arch painted lime and orange straddles the tarmac road. 'Bloody Bay Beach Facility' is painted across an arch. Beside this are a couple of concrete gazebos in the same livery, with tables for picnickers. The only old thing is a vast mango tree, knotted and gnarled and standing in the centre of a small car park. I am convincing myself that this is where James built his house of greenheart, cabbage palm and crabwood shingles.

It is the obvious vantage point: from here you can see both to the flat land where the first planting must have been, and to the beach, and out to sea. James wrote to his brother to tell how he showed one of the Africans that he could see everything that was happening from his house. I try to picture James in his green armchair, spyglass and speaking trumpet to hand. But his ghost is feeble. His years here seem a very long time ago indeed.

The museum

Scarborough is Tobago's capital, home to fewer than 20,000 people. It is scruffy, low-rise and unassuming. But lack of modern development leaves its history plain to see. Where a grand town centre plaza might be in a richer place, there is a free car park for shoppers. This was Market Square: it is overhung by a row of vast cotton trees, the same trees, or their offspring, that shielded James Fergusson and other plantation owners when they came to see enslaved people newly arrived from Africa or Antigua for auction under the sun. There is also a saman tree, a fat trunk holding up a great green parasol. From its, or a predecessor's, branches Africans were executed by hanging.

On the hill above this are the limestone-block buildings of Fort King George. Pragmatic and symmetrical, it was started by the British as their military headquarters the year James died, in 1777, and finished just in time for the French to take it over in 1781. Glossy black cannon push out over the walls at the sea towards Trinidad. In the former officers' quarters is the Tobago Museum.

The little museum is underfunded and unloved. T'keiah Alleyne is the only academic on the site, though paid only as an intern. She is a recent history graduate, just twenty-two, having studied at the University of the West Indies. T'keiah is a generous, knowledgeable guide who is thinking of applying for a postgraduate degree in Europe, though she questions her motivation: 'I have so many issues with European countries, and what they have done to mine, and still do.' Besides, when she first visited the UK she says she only saw the sun five times.

The museum's best collections are its Amerindian artefacts and folk-history displays. But there are some costumes and furniture from the early colonial period, the slavery era too. Hung on a wall are a couple of satirical coloured prints, published in London in 1808, a time when British people had begun to question the habits of the West Indies' tycoons. One shows a planter, Mr Newcome, and a vast black woman, 'Mimbo, Queen of the Harem', and their children. 'West India Luxury!!' shows various scenes of white people being helped do simple jobs – like take a boot off – by absurd numbers of black people.

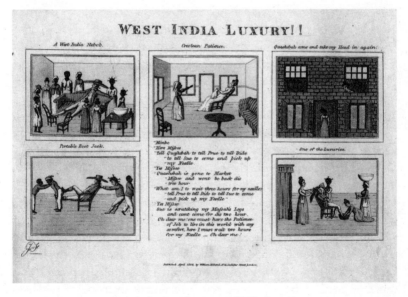

Popular satirical print, published 1808.

Under the headline 'Creolean Patience' there's a picture of a white lady sewing a sampler; 'Mimbo!' she says, 'Tell Quashebah to tell Prue to tell Dido to tell Sue to come and pick up my needle!' Mimbo replies that Sue is busy, 'scratching Massah's legs and cant come for dis two hour'. Another of the drawings shows a white man leaning his head out of a window and shouting to a black female servant: 'Quashebah! Come here and take my head in again.'

'The schoolchildren love that,' says T'keiah.

We look through the few documents that the museum holds on the late eighteenth century, mainly lists of plantation owners and their holdings. Most of the names are Scottish. T'keiah finds a map that shows the distribution of cannon round the island at the time of the privateer threat: it marks two stationed at Bloody Bay, and one at Castara, to protect George Ferguson. (Later I find it, built into the foundations of a wooden house on the hill above the bay.) I've given her the summary of the Fergusson letters about Bloody Bay and the short life of the Carrick plantation. She is excited by them: 'We have absolutely nothing like this.'

How does the slavery period affect ordinary lives most now, here? I ask.

T'Keiah doesn't hesitate. 'The core ideology still exists – and that's seen in the negativity about people of African descent. Even if the shackles are not there physically they are there mentally, sometimes they are there emotionally. They can torment an entire community.

'Under slavery, if you had a lighter skin, you got a better job. Mulattos worked in the house, full black-skinned people in the fields. You were seen as more intelligent, less animal [if your skin was lighter]. You were not quite so alien – all because a white man had had sex with your mother or your grandmother.

'And those beliefs have not changed, all these years later. Natural hair is bad: it's not right for being in an office. It's "soft", it must be straight. Black is bad. Black people are idle: here and in the States, that's what we get.

'I'm, like, my ancestors worked for you for free for hundreds of years. Don't call us names! The people you see as "lazy", that is the legacy of colonialism. Poverty as a result of it excludes people, if you don't get any help. The way the British government treated the Caribbean islands! Healthcare is bad, the education is bad. Even though slavery ends, colonialism doesn't end. And though colonialism officially ended nearly sixty years ago, economically it still continues.'

* * *

T'keiah is not the only person I meet who points out that the slavery-era practice of assessing people's value by their colour did not end with emancipation. Nor did the harm. Trinidad, Tobago's dominant neighbour, has particularly complex and tragic problems today with discrimination over class and colour as a result of the British rulers' policy of importing South Asians as labour to replace workers of African origin after emancipation. This happened all over the British Caribbean, but more Asians came to Trinidad and British Guiana than anywhere else. This addition of another people, ethnically different, exacerbated the multiple problems of 'colourism'.

As a Trinidadian friend, the journalist Judy Raymond, explains to me, on that island shade gradation is now a verbal and social maze. 'If you ask someone to describe somebody, they will say "Oh, she's Trini white", or "She's kind of Spanishy-looking". European features but brown skin. "People from Venezuela" – a code for not entirely African. She's a dugla, half-Indian, half-African.' Judy goes on, half laughing, half exasperated. 'People mixed with Chinese are called haquai – which means a half-breed, which is derogatory in Mandarin. Some people would describe me as mixed, some people would describe me as "red". Red women are the worst, vocal and domineering. Red men are seen as lascivious. They can fool around, because they are much in demand. They are high-status [among people with African origins].'

Meanwhile, Judy says, any suspicion that someone might have a 'secret' black African among their forebears is a matter for malicious gossip. 'It is shocking, but that is an acceptable attitude here.' I had read in a Trinidad newsblog of complaints in the island about a 'brown tax': the extra money a paler-skinned person must pay to market vendors or odd-job men because their skin colour says they are wealthy. All of this seems risible. But it is no joke at all if you have to live with it.

'At school there was a rhyme the kids used to chant,' T'keiah Alleyne tells me, grimacing.

If you're white, you're all right.
If you're brown, stick around.
If you're black, get back.
Go back, go back, go back.

Back in Britain, friends tell me they heard the same at school.

T'Keiah continues. 'When I was much younger I really wanted to be fairer. I have an elder sister who resembles a lot more my mother's side, that sort of Spanish thing; she's very fair in complexion. In a lot of ways she could pass in Trinidad and Tobago society as white. Oh God, I wanted so much to look like her. Even though my father is dark, he has grey eyes. I used to think, "Oh, why didn't I get grey eyes too?" Because of slavery, it's so hard being dark. I'm already a female, I already have issues when it comes just to womanhood, and now I have to add blackness on top of it?' T'Keiah laughs. 'Oh, I feel tired of it every day. My experience as a young woman of darker complexion is completely different from my sister's, where they would treat her better than me. Look at adverts: if you see a black family, you never see a dark one. TV shows use fair black people. Colourism is an evil; it's the biggest problem within the black community.'

Did your sister know how you felt, I ask?

'She did. She does. She completely understands because she knows she gets treated better. And I cope by negotiating my blackness. You see, I compensated. I read a lot. I thought, "I didn't get the complexion. Or the eyes. But I have the brains – and the hair [T'keiah's is straight]." When I lived in Trinidad, I thought, "Come on, you're not all the way black," and so I was able to negotiate that, because of my hair and the way I spoke. And how well-read I was. Though you can't know I'm well-read just by looking at me.

'So some people are completely surprised by me. And that's kind of a double-edged sword. Because it shows what they still think of my community. They are thinking: "Oh, she's one of the good blacks."'

Who thinks that? I ask.

'Other races. And all races.'

The gun above Bloody Bay

Huge rainstorms have come in, lashing the whole country. New landslides have ridden onto old along the thin road that winds between the bays of the northeastern end of the island. There are floods in towns across the strait in Trinidad. On the phone, Junior has a hacking cough. He doesn't want to go out to look for the cannon until the rain stops. Which will be when? 'In Bloody Bay?' He laughs. No one knows, right? I reply. 'Yeah, boy.'

I'm thrilled therefore that at last a day has dawned still and clear. The rivers have stopped disgorging mud into the blue. The clear water reveals the stingrays behind the breakers in Castara Bay, black shapes like spread overcoats patrolling the sunlit shallows.

Below Bloody Bay village, on the last headland before the site of the Carrick plantation, are a set of wrought-iron gates belonging to a villa built by an Englishman. They see him every six months or so. Leonard Quashie, a neighbour of Junior's from up the ridge, looks after the garden; he lets Junior and me in. We descend flights of wooden steps down through a tidied-up version of the forest, and then, in a lawn-mowered clearing on a little headland almost above the beach, we find it. James's gun.

It is a trunk of iron some eight feet long. It points out at the blue sea between the coconut palms; if you fired it now, you might just bounce a cannon ball all the way to the green-topped shards that are the Sisters Rocks, just off the point.

A 40-pounder naval cannon at Bloody Bay where it was installed to deter pirates in 1777.

I feel breathless. It has been a long haul from the old servants' hall at Kilkerran to this nugget of land off the coast of South America. Here, at last, is a link – you could hardly choose one more solid – to my ancestor. It is just five minutes' walk from where I think his house was. I run my hand down the gun's warm brown flank. There's hardly a flake of rust; iron was made to last in those days. On its rump, as clear as when it was cast, is the royal insignia – 'G R' and a '3' in a cursive script under a crown. Georgius Rex: King George the Third. Cruder are the scratched numbers near the firing hole – '39 – 2' – which designates the ideal size of the cannon's load.

Leonard says he's always known about it. He points to a small pile of ancient bricks off to the side. 'There they're keeping the bullets. We used to pick them up, from in the ground.' He circles thumb and forefinger. 'Heavy, they were. Twenty or so of them.' Grapeshot, perhaps? More useful than a single forty-pound cannon ball for causing devastation to the rigging of a privateer, and to the limbs of its crew. Maybe, the men nod. Leonard doesn't know what happened to the bullets they dug up. Junior is beaming: delighted that I've found what I wanted and that he has another string to his tour-guiding bow. 'You're gonna have to write this all up for me, boy,' he says. 'It's important. People want to know.'

On the verandah of Fred's empty guesthouse I spread out my photocopies of the inventory of James Fergusson's Bloody Bay estate, made for his heirs. 'This is what was on the land of Bloody Bay, on the patch this side of the river, 240 years ago,' I say. I show Leonard and Junior the pen-and-ink sketch of Bloody Bay's Lot 12, done in 1768 by the surveyors, commissioned by Lord Melville on behalf of the British government. It's pretty clear that the river, which forms one of Lot 12's boundaries, hasn't moved at all in the intervening years. It still curves along the bluffs that are the valley's northeastern wall. So we can say with confidence where James's land was.

The eighteenth-century cursive isn't easy for anyone at first go, so I read the lists out, starting with the land: '"12 acres Bottom in Plantains worth £55. 10 ditto, viz, in Plantains 6 Months old. 2 ditto of Negroe grounds, hilly" – that's for the slaves to plant their own crops. "56 acres planted Cotton, all hill land. 30 ditto, part & part Bottom and very foul. 15 ditto Rattoon, Bottom."'

A rattoon is the new shoots of sugar cane or cotton, Leonard says.

There's lots more lists of land, some of it 'broken, very mountainous'. I move on to the buildings: '"One Dwelling House, with a Gallery containing a small Hall, & 3 small bedchambers floored with Pine Boards above stairs, a store and a Medicine shop below. The

Frame all of Green Heart covered with Boards of Cabbage Trees, the Roof of Crab wood Shingled, with a very small out Room & Shed for a Kitchen." It's valued at £250. "1 Cotton House, Thatched . . . 8 Negroe houses. 1 store at the Bay, Walls pallisadoe and Thatched.'"

'That might be the place we called the depot,' says Junior. 'Above the beach, when we were kids.' Leonard nods. 'It's gone now.'

'The workers' houses – well, there's nearly eighty of them at this stage. So that must have meant twelve or so people to a house,' I say. There's polite interest, only: both men want to get on with their days. I point to the next item. 'And this is the list of slaves . . .' I start to read the names, and their occupations. The list begins with the most important, and valuable. 'House servant, Emoinda, Rachael, Monimia – she's a washerwoman. Sophia, the cook, Peggy the sick nurse. Solomon, Offa – both watchmen. Scotland – it says "carpr." – carpenter?'

'What's this number beside it – their age?' asks Leonard.

'No, that's their value. In British pounds. So Solomon the watchman, and Scotland – they're the most valuable men. Worth £80. But the cook, even more – £90. Ordinary field hands – see the next page – mostly £50 or £60. As little as £25 for some of the women.'

The air has become still between us.

'How much is £60 today?'

'Today, well – hard to say. A lot. It might buy you a good car? Look, here, under the slave children, there's a list of the stock. A horse was valued at £40 and – well, £60 then would buy you four cows, at £15 each.' The smallest children, Colin, Jeanie and Flora, are listed above the horse and cows at just £8 and £10 each. 'How much would you pay for a cow in Tobago today?' Neither of them answer. I go on, reading the list of slaves and jobs. I suddenly realise what's coming next. 'Quashie – driver.'

'Your surname,' I say to Leonard. He raises his eyebrows, and nods. 'What do you think?'

He is quiet for a long moment. 'Things were like that. Back then. That was the olden days.' He looks away, out to sea.

I go on. 'I've heard it said that Quashie is a name from what's now Ghana, in West Africa. It would be Kwasi there . . . Most Africans were given English names when they were taken to a plantation from the ships. But Quashie, maybe . . .'

The jungle is loud all around us.

'What do you feel?' I ask. What do I want them to feel? The silence continues. It's a familiar pause, one that any journalist waiting for a quote knows well, but that doesn't make it comfortable, or fair. I wish I hadn't asked: it is time to come clean. 'Well, it feels pretty strange to me. Here I am, the great-great-great-great-great-grandchild of a family who made themselves rich here. You see, James Fergusson and his brothers were my uncles and my grandfather . . . seven generations back.'

Leonard and Junior look at me. What am I getting at? I plough on. 'Men who made money out of exploiting this land and enslaving Africans . . . How do you feel about me?'

There's a little smile now in Junior's eyes. 'It's good to move on in life,' he says, after a moment. 'You can't hold things to ransom all your days . . . Shit happens. If you sit down and think about what happened before, you could go nowhere. For me, it's happened. It's a new page.'

I look at Leonard. He nods and then pats me gently on the shoulder. He turns and we leave the verandah, head off back up the hill. I feel an important moment slipping away. 'So what should we do now?' I say to their backs as we go back up the path into the trees. It's steep. 'Do you think we should pay reparations? Give what we British gained back to you?'

I think they are going to ignore me. But then Junior stops, turns to me. 'Nothing wrong with that, we need a bit of dough. It's not a bad idea. Move the country on a bit. That's feasible. The British government can pay their dues. The English people who come now and enjoy the country are going to benefit too.'

He starts again up the steps, and I scurry behind with Leonard, trying to scribble down every word. 'It's good to have the history of your country. If it means understanding, that means more unity.' He thinks for a moment. 'Y'know, even this can bring black and white together, have a better relationship. We need it – because life is short, yeah?'

He stops and looks at us. Leonard and I both nod. 'At the end of the day, when you give, you get,' says Junior, to conclude. He does his great big chuckle – a little embarrassed at his speech – and puts up his fist for a bump. I tell him I like his philosophy, and his generosity. Is there anything that can I do for him? Yes, says Junior, there is. Let's go to his house.

We say goodbye and thank you to Leonard Quashie, and Junior drives me back up the ridge to his house, high above the Bloody River valley. It's where his family farmed. Now Junior lives there with his teenage son and his brother. He is building a humming bird sanctuary there for the tourists. I have a six-pack of Carib beer in the car, so we sit outside in the slight breeze and watch the little birds, garish as costume jewellery, flit between the feeders he's hung. They hover to dip their beaks into the sugared water. Junior reels off their luminous names: the tufted coquette, the ruby topaz, the white-tailed sabre-wing.

The favour Junior wants is simple: an interview to place on his business's Facebook page. So he arrays his certificates, his binoculars and the guide books around him on the verandah table. I hold his smartphone, press the video button and record him talking about how much he loves this place and his work, while the hummingbirds flit and hover behind his head.

I walk to the ruined breeze-block house on the first ridge above the beach at Bloody Bay, an enlarged dune, really, where James's two-storey dwelling might have stood looking over the plantation and over the cove. I poke through the damp books in a broken-windowed room – they're all workmen's logs, presumably from the time the government built the beach buildings below.

The place is entirely different in the bright sun, after the days of storm and downpour. Finding the gun has brought James Fergusson closer. My hand has rested where his did. While James's ghost is a little more present I want to explore the land he owned. Leaving the house and the old mango tree that gives it a little shade, I walk down and across the expanse being improved as the Bloody Bay sports ground. Council workers are refurbishing a shed for a changing room. The mown green turf squelches underfoot. I head for the river and what looks like the easiest route into the thick growth. It's midday, the sun is high and I can feel my bald head cooking.

A few steps up the river, as I pause to take a photograph, there's a tickle and a sting on my calf. I look down to see a giant horse-fly, a Scottish cleg on steroids. I swat it away and then slip into the mud by the river, nearly dunking my camera. I've lost my hat, drunk all my water, I'm in flip-flops, and as I knot a handkerchief to shield my scalp I feel more white and silly than ever. 'The place hates me,' I think. I have to keep moving – as soon as I stop the insects settle on my pale legs, ready to snack.

I head up the river, lulled by the peace of it and the cool breeze that comes off the water. It is much quieter in the midday heat: few birds call and even the cicadas' tinnitus-drone has subsided. There seems little life, just a humming bird darting down to drink from the brown water. Then there's a flurry of motion on the riverbank – I've startled an iguana. But it doesn't turn to confront me: it doesn't even wait for its portrait shot.

A quarter of a mile or so up, I seem to be at the end of the wider flood plain: the ridges are looming closer and the growth is so thick there's nowhere to walk between the jungle and the river. The bright water streams faster and louder: the only way to proceed is in it, but I'm risking a fall. Then, over the bushes, I see a gap and a clearing: a fence and a high pole like a flagstaff. Feeling foolish – wishing I was better-dressed – I push through overgrown plantains to see what civilisation is there. It is just an electrical substation, presumably for the floodlights for the sports ground.

I set off back downstream. Among the flat shingles of the riverbed, I spot something larger, paler, out of place. A stone with a perfectly curved half-moon edge and a grip on the other side. I pull it out and heft what seems a perfect hand-axe. It looks like those in the dusty display cases of the Scarborough museum. Caribs used these. They were wiped out in the eighteenth century: by 1810, there was one family of twenty left, near Charlotteville, a few miles further up the coast.[4] The others died, or fled the Scotsmen and their tree-felling and went over the sea to Trinidad. James must have known of them, though there is no mention in the letters.

On a hill high above Tobago's capital, Scarborough, Dr Susan Craig-James pours thick mango juice pressed from the fruit of the tree that shades her yard. Her father planted the tree and he was proud of it. An unusual variety, Buxton Spice from Guyana, it is known for a rich and complex flavour. The name is a memorial to the hopes of the Africans after full emancipation came in 1838. In the early 1840s, in what was then British Guiana, some of the newly freed people pooled their money to buy two former plantations: they founded a village (it still exists) and named it Buxton-Friendship, after the British MP and anti-slavery campaigner Thomas Fowell Buxton. That is the story behind this mango.

We toast Thomas Buxton and the abolitionists as we drink the juice. Susan is in her seventies and widowed; there's no one around to eat the fruit of the trees. The house is white and breeze-filled but it is strangely empty. Retired, selling copies of her books is important to her finances. They are wonderful: profound, deeply researched works that reflect the neo-Marxist debates about society current when she studied at Edinburgh University in the late 1960s (and subsequently at the London School of Economics, where she got her doctorate).[5] In the UK her massive two-volume social history of Tobago from 1838 to 1938 fetches £200 for a second-hand copy. 'I'd better get over there with my big suitcase full,' she chuckles.

We discuss the names of Tobago. There's echoes of Scotland everywhere – places called Speyside, Montrose, Merchiston, Auchenskeoch, Culloden and Glencoe. Then, all the surnames, including hers. The formerly enslaved people of Tobago began to take surnames in the 1840s. But having a Scottish name does not mean the existence of a Scottish male ancestor: it may be borrowed from a place or a plantation owner. A family named Craig, as in her surname, owned the Les Coteaux plantation, the site of a famous Tobagan folk tale of escape from bondage by flying back to Africa. But Susan has no knowledge of any other link.

'My father looked for the history, after my mother died. But the old people who might have known had no memory any more. His father was called Pinker Craig or Pinker Joseph Craig. Who were Pinker's parents? There's a Virgil somewhere, I know. I've found Virgils, in baptism and birth records, but I can't be sure of the connection. In this country the records are not always complete: it's much easier with prominent people. But we were at the bottom of the heap.'

Susan's own emergence from Tobago's twentieth-century poverty is an extraordinary story. Its hero, for her, is her father. Lionel Craig was a small farmer, born in the 1920s. He was very different, Susan emphasises, from some of the young men she sees around the rural parts of the island today.

'He was a black man from a poor, dirt poor, family. From the age of nine he had to work for a living. My mother too, both of them.

They'd get up and go and do whatever work there was and after that they would go to school. Up at three to get the water from the river to the house to wash. Part of his work was to carry the headmaster's lunch: so, he could not be at school after eleven-thirty, because he had to wait for the lunch to be ready, and then carry it, barefoot, down the hot roads to school. When he did get to school, he was often too tired to learn.

'But he always wanted to. In his eighties he went and bought a grammar book. I said, "Pappy, where are you going with this?" At seventy-eight, he was going to seminars on agricultural improvement. He was a life-long learner. He didn't fritter away his time, waste his substance and not mind his children.'

Lionel encouraged his studious daughter. At the age of twelve she passed the exams to get a scholarship at Trinidad and Tobago's best girls' high school, the Bishop Anstey in Port of Spain: the first in her family to do such a thing, and an extraordinary feat in the late 1950s for someone of her background and colour.

Susan sets her parents' story of diligence and hard work in context. The freed Africans of Tobago in the later nineteenth century managed, slowly, to earn enough through fishing and farming to buy land. On richer islands like Jamaica, with larger plantations, the white owner class clung on to their way of life, often by importing indentured labour to replace those of African origin who would not work in conditions so like slavery. All the same, as she writes, by 1882, 70 per cent of Tobago's adults were still landless.[6]

'The one thing the black people in Tobago accomplished was not to become a proletariat,' Susan says. 'They were not wage labour, in the way Marx meant. They worked to get away from slavery. The first thing you had to do was a build a house, that was the first rung on the ladder. You see so clearly the hunger for freedom was tied up with one for land, and how the planters denied land, and tried to curtail the options of the freed people. That went on until the sugar price crashed.' This final disaster for the planter class, in 1884, also brought down the institutions that lent them money. Land prices collapsed. That was an opportunity for the rural poor. 'A strong, rugged, hard-working peasantry emerged in Tobago – by 1938 they were the prominent rural class.'

Do you hold with the view that the traumas of slavery and the poverty that followed it hold this society back now? I ask. Susan sighs.

'It bothers me. I know this goes against current trend, but when I look at people who got out of slavery, walked into emancipation, I'm seeing how hard these people worked. In education, in building houses, in small farming. And walking out of emancipation they didn't say, "I was a slave, I can't do anything." History shows they were getting up and doing stuff.'

I hear similar from other older people here and in Jamaica. What went wrong, they ask, as do senior citizens everywhere: why are the young people not like we were? But of course in countries like Trinidad and Tobago, where levels of youth crime, social and mental health problems are pushing world records, the question is very pertinent.

There is a view, I say, from sociologists and psychologists, that the normal role of a father was destroyed in the plantation system. A male was only there for breeding: all the other jobs of fatherhood, like protecting and providing for family, were deleted. Generations of that experience must leave a mark.

Susan shakes her head. 'But look at my father. There is such variation in all these people descended from slavery: some go one way, some people another. We have to explain that rather than lazily say that everything negative comes from slavery. This is the problem. Slavery will always be an item in the past, and it did circumscribe how far black people could go: racial prejudice in society was rampant. But when are we going to take responsibility for our time and for all future generations? Are there any other factors that help to explain the variations we see? Or are we going to blame everything on slavery for ever?'

One of the problems for Susan and other historians of Tobago – there are not many – is the lack of historical records. Birth, marriage and death records from the slavery period are sparse: the island did not even have a church minister until the 1780s, and baptism – which in Jamaica provides the best records of ordinary lives – of African people started very late compared with other plantation colonies.

Tobago's ownership swapped between France and Britain four times between 1779 and 1803. In 1781 a fire started by mutinous French soldiers destroyed all of the town of Scarborough except its tavern. All the governmental records went up too.[7] Having looked through the Fergusson letters about the Bloody Bay plantation, Susan says they are unique – the fullest and most vivid account of the time she's ever seen. So it seems very important to find a way of giving Tobago's historians and students access to them. We talk about how to do that. Then, just as I am saying goodbye, I remember the cannon at Bloody Bay. I tell her about it, and what it meant to me. She is delighted. 'Oh yes! It's all just there. Still with us, that history. It only just happened.'

* * *

Tobago seems cursed by its history. The island's small size and subjugate status – in its union with Trinidad – serve to amplify the problems of previous centuries. The Scottish names that litter the island are a reminder of the colonial regimes, all of them neglectful, at best. Tobago has not been wealthy since those first Scots were exploiting it, when the enslaved population was – at 25,000 in 1813 – more than all of Scarborough today. The poverty was exacerbated by the failure to develop the economy during the British colonial period, along with the usual Caribbean brain-drain that sees so many leave for the UK, Canada or United States. Any interruption to the island's chief income-generating industry, tourism, is a crisis, as it was when coronavirus stopped overseas visitors arriving in 2020.

'Tobagonians are an African society, disciplined, Protestant and indeed almost entirely African, ethnically. There is a small brown middle class. Never more than a handful of whites. And the narrative of Tobagonians is that they are oppressed by Trinidad, far more than by slavery or by Britain,' one eminent Trinidadian academic, who asked not to be named, said to me. With conversations like these I began to understand why so many discussions about reparations for the slavery period in the Caribbean lead to an insistence that any putting right of this history must involve a right of return to Africa. Anywhere in Africa. For many, this place of tragedy and exploitation will never work as a permanent home.

Modern Trinidad has known wealth – chiefly because of an oil boom in the late twentieth century – and it has an economy beyond the big-jet tourism on which so many Caribbean islands depend. But it is tortured by its divides of race and status, as well as record-breaking violence. Alongside Jamaica, Trinidad regularly tops murder-rate tables for the whole world, including some countries that are officially at war. That is not just because of its lethal proximity to the cocaine economies of South America. That fuels crime, but the origins of the violence, most people I talk to believe, are in the deeper traumas that derive from history.

That plays out in complex ways. Gerard Hutchinson, Trinidad-based professor of psychiatry at the University of the West Indies, is on the front line, dealing in his clinical and academic work with a range of psychoses and mental health problems that seem to afflict people in his country worse than almost anywhere else. He tells me that more people from Trinidad than any other country, per head of population, joined Islamic State – the jihadist army that was at the time we spoke successfully running its Islamic caliphate in northern Iraq. Three of them are former clients of his – all people of African origin. Meanwhile, here in Trinidad, more of his clients have died in violence than he can remember.

Hutchinson is a collaborator and former student of one of the most famous names in psychology in the Caribbean region – Professor Frederick Hickling. In 1999 they co-authored a short but celebrated paper which gave rise to a term – 'roast breadfruit psychosis' – to describe the phenomenon of disturbed racial identity in African-Caribbean people.[8] It explored a problem that was troubling social and criminal psychology – the 'epidemic' of schizophrenia and other mental health problems in people of African-Caribbean origin in Britain. The tendency to suffer these is between four and seven times as high in the black British population as in the white one.[9]

Hickling and Hutchinson's paper rejects usual European explanations. Instead it suggests racism as a primary cause: black people were becoming ill because of the impossible stress of trying to fit into a British society that rejected them, of trying to be, like the roast breadfruit, white inside their black skin. They wrote:

> The characteristic features of the [roast breadfruit] syndrome include an overwhelming desire for acceptance by European society, being ashamed of one's indigenous culture with an exaggerated rejection (in language and manners), and attempts to alter skin colour to appear more White. This can be exacerbated to psychosis by experience of social difficulties because of racism, and/or experiencing abuse because of an inability to succeed in European terms . . . the progression from syndrome to psychosis may be

insidious or acute but is likely to be precipitated by recognition that the immutable inferiority lumbered on Black people by European racism is difficult to dislodge.

The psychiatrists pointed out that there was no excess of such psychological illnesses in equivalent populations of the Caribbean, nor was there from a study of white people who moved to predominantly black countries. This was illness caused by white people, whose negative attitudes to black people Hickling had experienced himself during his academic career in the UK. He and Hutchinson went further in the paper, suggesting that the past was a part of the problem too: 'Psychopathology in formerly colonised and oppressed peoples can take a form that reflects continuing problems with their identity arising out of the ambivalence and anomie fostered in their collective and personal history.'

The two were writing long before the rise of epigenetics, the controversial theory that genetic changes in behaviour and physiology can be fast-tracked over one generation, particularly where the first generation has had traumatic experiences. This was conclusively proven in laboratory animals, but that was easy: proving the effect in humans less so. 'Transgenerational epigenetic inheritance' – or 'foetal programming' – is a new area of study and hypothesis, and so a much-debated one. Just as with the initial reaction to Darwin's theory of evolution, the thesis excites and enfuriates scientists, and the journalists who comment on scientists. The reaction often runs along predictable ideological lines.[10]

There is a large constituency that resists any suggestion that the colonial past should be blamed for the problems of today – political, cultural or psychological. There is a more sober one that believes that it is too early to say we know what the epigenetic mechanism does. 'The story that's often told is overblown relative to the results, and too much causality is claimed,' says one eminent American professor of paediatric genetics, John Greally.[11] But other academics, including the historian Timothy Snyder, now conjecture that all African American people descended from enslaved people suffer a form of inherited post-traumatic stress disorder, as do Native Americans.[12]

Naturally the concept of inherited trauma is appealing to people studying the contemporary after-effects of transatlantic slavery, not least in the movement for reparations. And Susan Craig-James, the old sociologist-historian on top of her hill in Tobago, does not dismiss this as another aspect of the blame-dodging she condemns. She says: 'I am a huge believer in ancestral memory and in trans-generational trauma: genetic memory. We need to explore that.'

* * *

In Trinidad Gerry Hutchinson, co-author of the roast breadfruit syndrome paper, was setting up a study to compare black youth in three cities, in West Africa, India and Trinidad, to measure psychosis and mental health in these understudied groups. One interesting factor is that while all these societies have been through exploitative and abusive colonialism, to different degrees, so far the results don't seem to show remarkable differences. Incidence of psychotic illness appears higher in the chosen Trinidadian city, however. Hutchinson's research convinces him of a link between this and the experience of immigrants from ethnic minorities.[13]

In Trinidad and Tobago he sees another strange outlier among the statistics – life expectancy for men is among the lowest in the Caribbean, lower even than Jamaica, with its similar stratospheric homicide rates. In an article titled 'The Brutal Impact of Crime on Public Health', Hutchinson blames a historical lack of faith in govern-ance and institutions: 'The crisis of legitimacy that has facilitated both the growth of crime and its accompanying fear is also compro-mising personal health.'[14]

Hutchinson's former colleague Frederick Hickling died in 2020. He was much lauded internationally and became emeritus professor of psychiatry at the University of the West Indies. His last book, *Owning Our Madness: Facing Reality in Post-colonial Jamaica*,[15] pins the mental health issues of the modern Caribbean firmly on the legacy of colonialism and slavery – the 'psychological ravishment' of Africa and Africans by a European culture that was and is psychotic, duplic-itous and racist. For Hutchinson, at the front line of dealing with violence, crime and a mental health crisis in urban Trinidad, you sense that however much he may agree with Hickling's thesis, it is not of great use in the middle of the storm.

* * *

Many discussions in Trinidad and Tobago lead to Rhoda Bharath. She is a fiction writer, a journalist and political activist: a brave, young voice in a violent and dissatisfied nation. Political corruption and hypocrisy among the country's ruling class are her usual punchbags, and she attacks them with wit and fire. When we meet in her office on the University of the West Indies campus – she lectures in the languages department – Rhoda has just come from a meeting to discuss a specific problem among the undergraduates: how to enable them to be more daring.

'We are not a risk–taking society,' she complains. Students she encounters are diffident, insecure, nervous of their own capacity. 'That pernicious self-doubt,' she says with a sigh. It isn't something she suffers from herself – her bleached blonde crop and her table-top thumping persona tell you that. My hour or so chatting with her is invigorating, more than any discussion I've had in the islands yet. 'I don't have time for white liberal guilt,' she says to me briskly after I explain what I'm doing in her country. 'White awareness – now I'd rather deal up with that.'

Not much self-doubt to see there: so why is Rhoda an atypical Trinibagonian? She considers for a moment. 'I'm not worried about victimisation. I tend to think I have all the resources housed within me to be able to survive whatever comes at me. I don't have that self-doubt; but I'm also aware that if I was to lose my home there's somebody else's home I can crash at – you need to know you have a safety net. And to have been taught risk-taking skills.

'People who pick up themselves, like Christopher Columbus, and jump into boats and cross the ocean and fight for wealth when they can't even plumb: that's a risk-taking society. So I have to ask: how does the culture that you come from, Alex, help us become risk-takers, entrepreneurs, masters of our own destiny? Columbus had patrons. The Caribbean does not.'

How, I wonder, does she think my culture, all the nations that brought the Africans to work enslaved in the Caribbean colonies, could best support them now?

'Any white community that has had a role in colonialism and colonisation ought to feel the need now to acknowledge they have done this and that it has hindered the development of other cultures globally, and ask how do we now unhinder those cultures? It may not be through aid but just, perhaps, something as basic as white cultures leaving our culture alone.

'If I lived in your home, with you, if my life had been impacted by your decisions in your life, you'd now have to find ways to empower me. You could decide "Okay, you know what, there are things your family did to my family which were really shitty" and give me money. And I don't know what to do with that money. I do something really stupid. It needs to go beyond fiscal empowerment.'

The view of liberals in my culture, I say, is that the answer to all this is indeed to transfer some of the money back again. It is the way we have dealt with guilt for more than half a century, since the official end of the colonial era: the Oxfam syndrome.

Rhoda responds briskly. 'It's not just about wealth transfer. Colonialism wasn't just about money. It was reshaping our culture, ordering how we thought about ourselves, how we ruled ourselves. Our laws here are still from the colonial system, holding on to a lot of old colonial ways – still policing our bodies. We still don't think our bodies – in terms of colour, shape, texture – are good enough, because of course good-enough looks like your body.'

Rhoda herself is, as she ruefully explains, a perfect example of the ethnic mix that the nation is still trying to process. For her and other people seeking the route to a post-racial society, the persistent relevance of colonial history holds that enterprise back. Rhoda's mother was from Les Coteaux in Tobago, site of one of the largest plantations, with 500 people enslaved at its height. Her family names are English: Williams and Woods.

'I am black; I'm also mixed. I could also say I'm Indian, because I've grown up around that culture. But though I have Indian ancestry I am not allowed to identify by that group as Indian.' That's a savage form of racism, imposing a one-way gate like that, I say. 'Yes, but I also have white blood in me, but I am not allowed to be white. You can be more than one thing but there's only one thing that will embrace you. Black seems to be far more fluid in terms of allowing for identity – you can be the lightest of skins and say I am black, or the darkest of skins and say I am black. But with other ethnicities purity is the thing. It's not a big deal for a black identity.'

I feel a pressing need to apologise, though I know that that is a useless thing. 'This is my fault. We started this,' I start to say. 'And you built the structures for it . . .' She smiles. 'Complexion is one, having the right connections, education, but the thing that trumps all is generational wealth. Inherited money is the bedrock of safety and confidence. When your family, or the Clan Fergusson, thinks about what it should do to pay back, bear that in mind.'

Like many in Trinidad and Tobago with the space and time to think about their nation, Rhoda seems to have only a little hope. These thinkers sketch out a nation caught up in an ongoing psycho-drama, an endless crisis driven by politics, identity, mistrust and lack of self-belief. And, of course, the echoes of that violent history, now repeating with new violence.

We talk about one of the first things to strike a new visitor: the signs. They are everywhere, advising people, but more often telling them not to do things. You sense an old-fashioned bureaucracy that has little trust in the people it serves. 'Don't put your feet up', 'Don't spit on the floor', 'Don't walk here'. All over the university where we are meeting stairways and individual steps have stencils on them saying 'No sitting'. In any bar you enter, the biggest sign, often emblazoned across a whole wall, says 'No cursing, no blasphemy!' I say I can see that might be an inheritance from British colonialism: but why?

'We're a very forbidding society. Very unsure of our relationship with rules and enforcement of law, with legislation. We are still happy to see how much we can get away with. Our attitude towards changing culture is to legislate it. Which is unfortunate.

'It's all pushing, pulling tensions. Rule by different colonial powers. And our political landscape has never allowed us to settle down, to develop a stability of identity. I visit other countries, I come back here and I always feel unsettled. Anxious. Oh my God, wherever I go, other places are so calm. Here there's this energy, sometimes positive, sometimes frenetic and panicky.' She shakes her head, smiling, nearly despairing.

I remember Susan Craig-James's verdict: 'Everything is tied up. Slavery was in the warp and woof of this society, it was in the interstices of everything, every corner. And now, even now, it is very, very close.'

'Oh yes,' says Rhoda. 'It surely is.'

Genetics

When the friendly customs officer at Piarco International in Trinidad had a look through my bag, one item took a little explaining. It was a buff envelope packed with swabs on sticks, sterile vials, sheets of disclaimers, consent forms and labels for consigning the used kit to a laboratory in Texas. 'Right, understood, DNA testing,' she said. 'I've seen that before. But, hey, man, look at all this! You're come to find a lot of offspring, eh?'

Investigating your genes is popular in Trinidad and Tobago. There are posters advertising services on the billboards lining the highway from the airport into Port of Spain. Paternity is a much discussed issue in the English-speaking Caribbean, as you can see in TV soaps, songs and humour. Increasingly too, the sites with big databases are telling people where ancestors are from, narrowing the possibilities to specific areas of Africa.

A British friend of mine did a mitochondrial DNA test that purportedly told her from which district in Angola her African ancestors had come. My own test via one of the most popular (and cheaper) companies told me I was 1.2 per cent 'Nigerian', with a further fraction from North Africa.

In the US, where DNA testing for ancestry is most popular, people who identify themselves as 'Afro-American' have, on average, 24 per cent white ancestry. The 'white' population average 0.2 per cent African. In a smaller study carried out in Jamaica, the 'black' population is said to have an average 18.9 per cent 'European-derived' chromosomes.[16] The analysis now can make assumptions about when more unexpected strands entered the mix. The more recently they turn up, the longer the strand is.

Thus I'm told that the Nigerian strand joined my more ancient chromosomes during the mid to late eighteenth century. The most recent ancestor who was 100 per cent African was born between 1720 and 1810. This accords with the Jamaican baptism records, which show a woman called Mary, a 'freed negro', having an illegitimate child by a plantation owner named William De La Roche in 1761. Their daughter, Elizabeth Delaroche, a 'free mulatto', had four children with a white Scottish merchant in Jamaica called John Graham.

One of those children was called James: he was my father's mother's great-grandfather. He is listed at baptism as 'non-white', but the fact of his being mixed race is not something my grandmother mentioned, if she knew it. John and Elizabeth did not marry. He had two more children by another woman described in the baptism records as 'mulatto'. John died in 1808 when James was ten.

There is a portrait of James Graham made not long before his death in 1860. There is no trace of his African heritage in it: he is a white-whiskered Victorian gent, with a stick-up collar and black cravat at his throat. He was a respectable and wealthy merchant, dealing with the Caribbean colonies, who lived most of the latter part of his life in Britain. At his death he was living with his second wife and a large family in Rodney Street, Liverpool. It is his grandmother Mary, perhaps born and enslaved in Africa herself, who explains the Nigerian strands in my DNA.

James Graham, 1789–1860.

Large-scale analysis of the data emerging as testing becomes more popular reveals that most white DNA enters 'black' West Indians – and Americans – prior to the end of slavery. It also – as in one study of 3,726 African Americans – shows that the white DNA comes from a white male impregnating a black female. This is what sociologists examining the history shorthand as 'the rape factor' – or, as it was put in a report in the *New York Times* on the research: 'Buried in DNA, the researchers found the marks of slavery's cruelties, including further evidence that white slave owners routinely fathered children with women held as slaves.'[17]

Historians of slavery use the term 'concubinage' for the longer-lasting relationships between enslaved women and plantation owners. But who is to say these women had any kind of freedom to choose?

All I know is that William De La Roche and a woman who appears to have been my five-times-great-grandmother Mary had a child. At some stage she was freed.

* * *

I had not yet found out about Elizabeth and Mary when I looked through the Trinidad and Tobago phone book for Fergussons. I wanted to try sharing DNA test results chiefly because I was attracted by the idea of randomising my interviews: what better way than by choosing one Scottish surname and trying to talk to everyone who owned it? I had not thought through what I would do if I found a genetic cousin through the DNA test. But since the technology existed, it seemed wrong not to have a go with it. I gave a kit to Rhoda Bharath, who felt the same way.*

The chances of James Fergusson having left a child did not seem very high. He was only on the island for four years, and the 1777 list has none under that age. Of course, an African woman might have been pregnant by him when he died. The 'List of Negroes Belonging to Carrick Estate' and a subsequent one made in 1784 name the children, but do not mention their ages: only their potential prices at market. There are five in 1777, while in 1784 the number – it's not clear at what age children were considered adults, though the children were expected to work from six years old – is thirteen. Only Billy – 'a mulatto'[18] – seems to have survived from 1777.

Who was Billy's white father? No mention is made in Petrie or Bruce's letters after James's death of him leaving any offspring, but that might have been concealed in order to spare his Scottish family embarrassment. Though common enough in the slave colonies, especially in Tobago at this stage of its history, such behaviour might upset the mourning family back home. Better that Jamie's boy – if there was one – try his luck in Tobago.

* * *

---

* So far no match has appeared between my DNA and that of any of the people in Trinidad and Tobago who agreed to be tested.

The phone book lists ninety Fergusons and Fergussons. That makes it a fairly common name, though it is easily beaten by Wallace, Young and Bruce. As in Jamaica, Campbell and Stewart are most common of all – 330 and 350 entries each. Campbells owned eight plantations in Tobago and in Trinidad in 1834, claiming compensation for the emancipation of 830 enslaved people. But the only Ferguson or Fergusson claimants were for the two plantations near Bloody Bay at Castara and Parlatuvier, with a total of 299 enslaved people on them.

These plantations were the property of the Fergusons of Pitfour, in Scotland's Perthshire. George Ferguson, James's friend and neighbour, lived on the island for decades. He became lieutenant-governor of Tobago shortly after James's death and had an illegitimate son by an Edinburgh lady. Despite this apparent disadvantage, the son (also called George) became the fifth Laird of Pitfour, inheriting the estates in Tobago and Perthshire and becoming an admiral in the Royal Navy and a Member of Parliament. He was also a notorious gambler. At abolition, he received £5,274 compensation for the 299 enslaved people emancipated in Tobago. This may have helped with the bills at Pitfour, whose grandeur led to its being dubbed the 'Blenheim [Palace] of the North'. There George spent the money on, among other things, a two-mile horse-racing track and a 'Temple of Theseus' where he housed his collection of alligators.[19]

The Pitfour Fergusons may well have fathered children with enslaved Africans. Neither of the men ever married, and there was little or no social stigma attached to such sexual exploitation, especially in Tobago with its lack of churchmen. The slaves emancipated at Castara in 1834 are also likely to have taken the Ferguson name at baptism, or when registering land titles. So it is no surprise when I start looking for Fergusons around the little village of Castara that quite a few turn up. Most people are curious when I knock on their door. Only one did not want to talk at all.

Ancle George, the owner and manager of a little hotel on the beach in Castara, tells me his mother was called Ferguson. She had grown up in Castara, but he was not sure if the connection with this part of the island went further back than her parents.

'But she knew where the Fergusons came from,' he says, smiling. 'Her grandmammy told her that the Fergusons were two brothers who came to Tobago on a visit from Africa. They flew here, over the ocean. But they were stupid, they let their feet touch the salt and so they could never fly back again. They were stuck.' I tell him that there were two Ferguson brothers, George and Patrick, powerful men who owned the Castara and Parlatuvier estate. 'Oh yes,' says Ancle, 'I know that. George was an important man. That's why the castle in Scarborough is called "Fort King George".'

We argue about that, amiably, for a while. There's no doubt, though, that George Ferguson of Pitfour, Ancle's mother's possible ancestor, my distant great-uncle's cousin, friend and neighbour, was an important figure. As lieutenant-governor of the island in 1781, with a scratch army of enslaved Africans and redcoats, he fought the invading French. He survived, and his son used the slavery earnings to build the palace back in Perthshire.

At a bar on the village's outskirts I meet the man known as the village historian. George Wallace presides over a spotless room of concrete, painted a gorgeous pink. A stencilled sign in letters a foot high runs half the length of the longest wall: 'NO OBSCENE LANGUAGE'. There's an off-sales area with bottles of whisky – Johnnie Walker, J&B, Famous Grouse – all far cheaper than they would be in Scotland. He is a heavy-set man, with deep twinkling eyes. We shake hands.

'My great-grandmother, her father was a Scot called Wallace. A white man – he worked on the Castara plantation, as a manager. Yes, she was a slave. He never married her – he had a child with her and one with another woman.' George roars with laughter.

Are you angry? I ask. 'Ehhh, man, that was then . . . it was a long time ago.' George is interested but not much bothered. Sir Christopher Codrington, owner of the Bon Accord and Courland plantations in the 1830s, is, he thinks, another ancestor: George's mother's name was Codrington – a common one in Tobago. 'That man must have got around, eh?'

He certainly did. Sir Christopher Bethell Codrington was one of the West Indies' biggest plantation owners. His family had owned the entire island of Barbuda and several estates in Barbados since the seventeenth century, as well as seven more in Antigua and these two in Tobago. Retired from the Caribbean, he returned to Gloucestershire and took up cricket and land-buying. Sir Christopher was a Member of Parliament in the 1830s, and a bombastic and aggressive player in the abolition debate. He is one of the men who lobbied for the compensation scheme that gave a final sweet to the 46,000 slave owners right at the end of slavery.

In 1832 Codrington published a pamphlet aimed at his electors in Gloucestershire, and the abolitionists.

> I have lived among my Negroes, and seen their comforts, and I will assert (defying all contradiction), that a more happy and contented class of beings never existed, until cursed with the blessings of the Anti-slavery Society . . . I will say that no man can be more desirous of their emancipation than myself, because no man would benefit more by it . . . I have bought my Negroes, and cultivated my land, on the pledged faith of England. Secure me from loss, or give me compensation, and you may offer manumission to the above Negroes tomorrow.[20]

The Codrington family did very well out of the compensation scheme. They got £32,123, about £28 milllion today: the 377 enslaved people they owned in Tobago netted them £7,000. This money was not spent in the Caribbean. Its most obvious legacy is in Gloucestershire. Dodington Park is a palace in 'Regency picturesque' style built at the end of the eighteenth century by the same Sir Christopher at a cost of £120,000. It sits in the Cotswold hills, in three hundred acres of Capability Brown-designed parkland. The Codrington family sold it in 1980: James Dyson, the vacuum cleaner magnate, lives there now.

These details I did not know until after I left Tobago. But I did have one titbit for George Wallace. I told him that I knew a Christopher Codrington, a direct descendant of the Codringtons who owned West Indian plantations and enslaved people. 'Is that right?' said George. 'Well, if you see him, tell cousin Chris to come over to Castara. We can have a beer.'

JAMAICA – 1769–1875

CHAPTER 6

A FINE PROPERTY IN JAMAICA: ROZELLE

One little moment, and we shall arrive
At those bless'd islands, where, from guilt refin'd
By sharp affliction, we no more shall feel
Death's torpid grasp, and agonizing pang!

From *Jamaica, a Descriptive and Didactic Poem*
by plantation owner Bryan Edwards, 1792

THE FERGUSSON BROTHERS STARTED INVESTING in the slavery-powered sugar industry nearly a decade before the youngest, Jamie, set off to the Caribbean. After all, most in their world were doing it: cousins, neighbours, friends and correspondents in Edinburgh and London, colleagues and allies in Parliament, the inns of law, the philosophical societies, the banks and university courts. It was a gold rush: if you had money or the means with which to borrow it, why would you not get involved in something so provenly lucrative?

Business ventures in the West Indies were coming to be seen not just as a daring use of capital, but a patriotic enterprise. An investment in land and enslaved Africans was an act that helped in the construction of a network of interdependent trading colonies, the money-engendering machine that Britons were learning to call an empire. A gentleman spending money on land and people in the West Indies stimulated industrial growth in Britain, not least in the Scottish textile industry, whose mills were clothing many of the 650,000 enslaved people of the British Caribbean. Modern historians believe that the industries that supplied plantation slavery transformed the Scottish economy even more than that of England.[1]

In the library at Kilkerran were books on the new science of economics, including those by Adam Smith. Also on the shelf was John Campbell's *Candid and Impartial Considerations on the Nature of the Sugar Trade*, published in 1763. Campbell demonstrates both how a Briton should invest in the West Indies and why government, supported by Parliament, ought to help in that worthy enterprise by encouraging sugar consumption and lowering taxes.[2] Everyone, at home and in the Caribbean, would benefit – with one category of human being excepted, of course.

The Fergussons were late to the game. They had reason to be more cautious than others in Scotland. They had lost a son, Captain Alexander Fergusson, and family capital in the Darien scheme, the disastrous attempt to build a Scottish colony in Panama two generations earlier. This blow to Scotland's pride, and to its economy, was one factor that led to the union of England and Scotland in 1707. But in 1765 Charles Fergusson, my five-times-great-grandfather, Sir Adam and James's brother, took the first step in the West Indies lottery by lending £4,000[3] at 5 per cent interest to an Ayrshire neighbour, Charles Montgomery. This was to improve the sugar plantation, Rozelle, that Montgomery had just bought in Jamaica from another Ayrshire family, the Hamiltons.

In 1769, after Montgomery's death, Charles Fergusson took over a half-share of his plantation. The other half was taken by the Hunter brothers, friends and neighbours in Ayrshire. William Hunter was an army officer, but both he and his brother James were bankers, soon to start enterprises under their own names which would lend to Scottish plantation owners and other businesses involved in the West Indies.[4]

The Hunters and Charles Fergusson paid £14,200, some £26 million today,* for Rozelle.[5] The price included houses for the workers, a 'works built in stone' for processing the sugar cane, 100 or so steers and cows, and 154 enslaved humans. The land totalled 1,650 acres, 210 of them planted with sugar cane. It lay on the plain below the Blue Mountains, beside the sea, twenty miles east of Jamaica's new capital, Kingston.

....
* In relative labour/income value. According to retail price change, the value today would be just under £2 million. See note on 'Relative value' at the beginning of this book.

It was a perfect package. A small river – useful for powering a sugar mill – ran through it, the main highway to the southeast of the island went across it, and the little town of Morant Bay, with its wharf for small ships, lay just three miles off. St Thomas-in-the-East parish, where Rozelle is, had sixty-six sugar estates at the time. It was bustling with Scottish gentlemen-proprietors,[6] along with managers, book-keepers, overseers, tradesmen and a swiftly growing population of enslaved Africans – perhaps 15,000 by the 1760s.[7] It must have seemed a much safer investment than Jamie's shot-in-the-dark Tobago 'adventure' five years later.

Nevertheless, £14,200 was a vast sum at a time when land in Scotland cost £2 an acre and £500 was considered a sufficient annual income for an aristocratic family.[8] In Jamaica, as in Tobago, there was a boom going on in property: the plantation's previous owner, Charles Montgomery, had paid the Hunter brothers' stepfather, the Ayrshire landowner – and veteran Jamaica sugar baron – Robert Hamilton, just £6,000 for Rozelle and a similar number of enslaved Africans in 1764. So the price of the land with the enslaved people had more than doubled in just five years. Some 60 per cent of the price of Rozelle was accounted for in the value of the workforce.

The Hamiltons were the richest of all the Ayrshire plantocrats, to use the term coined by the nineteenth-century anti-slavery movement.[9] Robert Hamilton, the paterfamilias, had gone out to Jamaica in 1734, soon followed by his brother. By 1754 they were owners of three Jamaican plantations totalling 3,680 acres.[10] In 1769 several Hamilton sons and nephews were still involved in the island, co-owning a successful estate on Jamaica's northeast coast with some of the Hunter family. The Hamiltons had been well-to-do merchants in south Ayrshire, but Robert's initial moment of money-making genius was meeting, and marrying, a rich widow within a few months of his arrival on Jamaica. Jean Mitchell brought with her two estab-lished sugar estates, Pemberton Valley in St Mary's parish and Rozelle.

Robert and his brother John, the first generation of Hamiltons to go to Jamaica, had retired by 1769. They set up home back in south Ayrshire in several large houses, accompanied by African servants brought from Jamaica. Grandest of all was a large estate and buildings outside the town of Ayr, whose house Robert Hamilton remodelled in the fashion-able neo-classical style. He named it Rozelle, after the estate he had sold to Montgomery, a merchant in Kingston and subsequently a neighbour in south Ayrshire. The sale was an easy way of repatriating some of his profit from the rise in land values in Jamaica.[11] Marrying the Hunters' widowed mother, Ann, brought more land and money, but perhaps just as important, it enabled him to climb the social ladder in Scotland. His daughter Eleanor brought estates[12] and money to the Montgomerie/ Eglinton family when she married the 12th Earl of Eglinton.

The Hamilton family continued running the lucrative estate at Pemberton Valley in Jamaica while at home in Scotland they used their new wealth to lever their way into far more valuable money-making ventures such as the banking and insurance industry that made trade with and from the sugar colonies possible. Lending money secured on property to planters was safer and more lucrative than being them.

When Montgomery's heirs ordered the sale of the Rozelle estate, just five years after he had bought it, William Hunter and my great-times-five-grandfather Charles Fergusson acted fast. The latter was wealthy through his London businesses, in wine importing and banking.[13] Sir Adam, his elder brother, also helped finance the deal.[14]

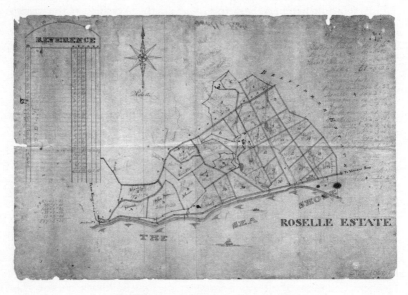

The Fergusson-Hunter estate, c. 1780.
The 'Reference' shows the acreage of each field.

The Rozelle plantation was average-sized, by Jamaican standards, but it was a reliable business, begun over a hundred years earlier.[15] At the time of the purchase it was sending around 100 hogsheads – barrels nearly as tall as a man, containing perhaps 700kg in sugar – back to Britain in most years. It also produced rum, a by-product of sugar-making, and beef for sale on the island and to visiting ships. If nothing untoward happened – and the list of potential hazards was long – the two partners might share £1,000 profit a year or so. That is perhaps £1.8 million today.

Although Charles Fergusson and Major – soon to be Colonel – William Hunter's names ended up on the title deeds, their brothers James Hunter and Sir Adam Fergusson retained a close interest. None of the men, or their heirs, appear ever to have considered visiting Jamaica to see the property. Like many others, they worked through paid managers with oversight from lawyers in Kingston, all Scots too. The Hunters also had a resource in Jamaica-based Hamilton men, their step-relations.

The island was full of other Ayrshire men who owed their jobs to the clique of inter-related land-owning families in the county. These hired their poorer neighbours as artisans, overseers and book-keepers and dispatched them to Jamaica. A few years later they were nearly joined by the twenty-seven-year-old Robert Burns, an educated but impoverished Ayrshire farmer, then down on his luck. Attempting to flee his various romantic difficulties, and his debts, in 1785 the poet signed up to become a 'poor Negro-driver'[16] in Jamaica – by then a known route to a fortune, or a swift death from disease. He wrote a ballad* announcing his departure and booked his passage. But, famously, Burns missed the ship out. The success of his first volume of poems (with James Hunter and other Scots with slavery connections among its subscribers) appears to have put him off the plan.[17]

The Fergusson-Hunter syndicate inherited a manager named John Paterson, another Scot. In 1770 he drew up an ambitious plan for the new owners. Through investing in more enslaved people and some mules he could clear more land for planting. Thus he hoped to increase sugar production until by 1776 he would be producing

----

* 'On a Scotch Bard Gone to the West Indies' is the poem. He was in fact hired as a bookkeeper; his salary was to be £10 or £12 a year.

300 hogsheads of sugar a year, along with 175 puncheons of rum. Those would sell for £8,820 in total.[18]

Against that Paterson calculated 'contingent expences' in Jamaica of £1,740, largely wages of the white men who would have to be employed. There was also a significant outlay on two sets of living things crucial to the business plan: £550 on ten more enslaved Africans each year and £300 on ten mules. These were the minimum needed, in both people and animals, to replace those who would die.

In fact, in 1776 the estate produced not 300 hogsheads but 68. The deficit was blamed on a drought but in fact Paterson's entire plan was madly over-confident, just as were the projections for an expanded Carrick at Bloody Bay after James's death in 1777. The written plan does assume one 'unseasonable' year in the period. As it turned out, the Caribbean climate was at odds with industrial sugar production more frequently than once every seven years: the 1780s saw a historic string of hurricanes. But there were other problems a manager in a colonial backwater could not foresee.

The fall-out between the British colonists in America and the London government seems to have come as a surprise, though even before the American revolution became a full-scale war in 1775 there were trade restrictions and boycotts. Hostilities closed one of the West Indies' most important markets and so the sugar price fell: the market was 'low and dull',[19] as Paterson put it. But even after prices recovered in the 1780s, the Rozelle estate rarely produced even half the amounts of sugar Paterson had so confidently foreseen for his new employers.

A two-page 'Sketch of Produce of Rozelle' written by Sir Adam Fergusson in 1773 drily assesses the estate and its financial prospects. He concludes that 123 hogsheads was the minimum needed for the estate to 'defray its own expence . . . even without any allowance for extraordinaries'. Yet the 123 barrels shipped in 1772 (which were worth £2,000 when sold, before taxes) is 'a quantity fully as large as can be expected from it, one year with another'.[20]

Nonetheless the investment must have looked attractive, in these years before the anti-slavery movement began to intrude on the plantocrats' strategies. A meticulous inventory and valuation of everything at Rozelle – buildings, land, enslaved humans and farm animals – is done in July 1773. It prices the whole business at 40 per cent more than the brothers had paid just four years earlier. It is now worth more than £20,000 sterling: £7,000 of that the value of the 164 enslaved Africans.[21]

The following year the estate produces a mere eighty hogsheads. In 1775 the crop is nearly twice as much, but Paterson warns that the land is 'worn out and exhausted'.[22] And many 'extraordinaries' do befall the estate in the first years of Fergusson and Hunter ownership, including drought and a hurricane.

Between 1772 and 1773 twenty-nine enslaved people are added to the workforce: ten women and ten men newly bought, as Paterson's plan requires, and nine more reclaimed from a Mrs Peyton, the widow of a former owner of the estate who had taken them to work for her in Kingston. Between 1771 and 1775 five children – Prince, Charlotte, Sukey, Jim and Phill – are born and survive their first year. So common were deaths of newborns that their names were usually not entered into plantation rolls until they complete some months.

Meanwhile eleven of the older people die: Duke 'with age', a man called Syley of 'a bloody Flux' (dysentery), and a 'man boy' called Hamlet of a 'Nervous fever' – a term used for typhoid. A woman – or 'wench' – named Luanda dies of 'Lethargy' in 1773, while in the next year Taditha dies of smallpox, Parthia in childbirth, Belinda 'with Asthma and Age', and Juno and Mimba both of 'an inflammation of the bones'.[23] One man, Dick, has been 'transported' – sold and shipped off to another island, the extreme punishment for someone thought to be unmanageable. It was cruel and intended so, because the transported person would be separated for ever from family and friends.

The estate – and its manager, John Paterson – are now run by Sir Adam Fergusson. Charles has become caught up in the domino effect of a banking collapse, a regular event in the overheated economy of the time. Many private banks and money-lending enterprises had popped up in Ayrshire, London and elsewhere. They serviced the immensely complex and lucrative trade with the British colonies, issuing banknotes and guaranteeing promised payments for people and businesses in those far off, near-cashless economies. But the system was little regulated and, obviously enough, unstable.

So in 1772 Sir Adam, with the Fergusson lands to back his finances, bails out his brother, taking Charles's half of the Rozelle estate in return.[24] He agrees with the Hunters to manage it. Colonel Hunter, co-owner of the estate, is often referred to in the letters, but seems to have taken little active interest. His regiment, the 8th Foot, was deployed in Canada and then from 1775 was fighting the rebel American colonists.

Sir Adam Fergusson is a busy man, active in the Edinburgh courts as an advocate and, from 1774, in London with his political career. Managing and improving the Fergusson Scottish estates take up much time too, judging by the extraordinary volume of accounts and correspondence he left behind. He is also occupied publishing his father Lord Kilkerran's legal decisions and dealing with the fall-out of the disastrous collapse of the Douglas, Heron bank, in which he was a shareholder.

A distant tyrant[25]

With Sir Adam's formal, often nit-picking, letters to John Paterson at Rozelle there begins forty years of correspondence between him and his employees, all Scots, in Jamaica. Together with the plantation books and hundreds of pages of administrative paperwork – lists of stores, inventories of enslaved people and stock, accounts and receipts – the archive is an extraordinary record not just of the day-to-day running of a sugar estate, but also of the mentality of a man determined that the 5,000-mile distance should not be any encumbrance to scrupulous and 'proper' – a favourite word – management.

The sheer volume of words is astonishing. Handwritten letters, with a first draft kept for his own files, were sent from his houses in Edinburgh, London or Ayrshire to Rozelle. In addition to Sir Adam's file copy, several more were made so the same letter could travel by different ships, in case of mishap. Other letters were written to banks, to lawyers in Jamaica and in Britain, to Alexander Houston & Co. in Glasgow and William Sibbald of Leith, the merchants who shipped out supplies to the estate and sold the hogsheads of sugar.

Then there were letters to the Hamiltons and the Hunters, seeking their views, discussing news of Jamaica, of the sugar markets, ruminating over the Jamaican employees and candidates for jobs. Discussion of the enslaved people is rare in these or the letters with the Rozelle managers. They usually have more to say on the things produced – sugar, beef and rum – than on those who produce them. The managers may write twice or even three times a month; Adam will respond once in every two or three, unless the matter is urgent.

His writing never contains any expression of emotion beyond mild irritation. Nor, in all his thousands of long, precisely formulated sentences, is there ever any debate – with his peers, or his employees – on the morality of their business, though wider society was increasingly questioning the slave trade and enslavement itself. There are occasional moments of humanity in those long, yellowed pages, but it always goes hand-in-hand with practicality. Kindness is just one of many tools involved in running a profitable business.

Making precise judgements affecting the lives of both the Europeans and the enslaved African people who worked on the plantation was a part of Sir Adam's task too, and he approaches it with lawyerly frigidity. Over the decades the side-effects of some of the grotesque errors he made, in human terms, do become clear to him: in old age the waste of lives seems at last to affect him. But for most of the period his decisions on matters of life and death far off in Jamaica are as a hanging judge's: adamant, self-certain and stony-hearted.

* * *

By 1776 Sir Adam Fergusson is frustrated with John Paterson's management, especially – a particular torment for the meticulous Sir Adam – his haphazard bookkeeping. Paterson also oversees the Hamilton-Hunter estate at Pemberton Valley on the other side of the island. So he is asked to recommend a deputy who could look after Rozelle alone, and Andrew Murdoch is appointed. In March 1777 Murdoch writes to Sir Adam, his new boss, with a first assessment of the estate, the animals and the enslaved Africans. He prefaces all that with a deferential introduction.

> I have a Warm sence of the Good opinion, you are pleased to Entertain of me, through Mr Paterson's friendly Recommendation & could not let slip this opportunity, the first that offered of Embracing your invitation, to a correspondence.
>
> The interest and improvement, of your property under my charge, is what I have near at heart, for that Purpose, you may be assured of my attention & diligence, in managing it, to the best advantage, and it will be a Pleasing satisfaction to me, to make every transaction upon the Estate, appeared to you, in plain a light as possible.[26]

A July letter has just as much bowing and curtseying but it goes into more detail. Rozelle has sufficient planted land and 'a tolerable Strength'²⁷ of enslaved people for it to produce more sugar, though Murdoch warns that this year the crop will be small because of drought. He seems contemptuous of the work done by John Paterson.

In December 1777 – these delays in the correspondence are the norm, with no letter arriving in less than two months and many taking much longer – Sir Adam replies at length from his London address. He puts the new man in no doubt as to how he likes things done.

> Intending to leave Town for some time I could not think of doing so without acknowledging [receipt of your letters] and expressing the Satisfaction it will give me that you should continue to write me as fully and frequently as you can. The Accompt for 1776 with Journal for that Year I have perused and also the Accompts for 1775. The form of the Journal is pretty much what I wished only I should rather chuse that the Books formerly Sent over should be filled up & when filled up returned here rather than that a Copy only Should be sent. The fuller it is Kept the more Satisfactory it will be.
>
> And I have no doubt that you will be attentive to inserting an exact State of the Increase and Decrease of the Stock both of Negroes and Cattles of different kinds so that the precise State of the Plantation may always Appear as far as possible.

The next page goes into more detail on how he prefers matters to be explained. Each cane 'piece' – or field – should be listed by name and number according to the plan of the estate, along with the amounts of rum 'sold and on hand'. There is a steady chunter of complaints. This is a feature of most of Sir Adam's letters, especially after he has received the annual journal or plantation book, in which each day's activities on the estate is noted.

> I observe in Mr Patersons Accompt Credit taken for 12 new Mules whereas the List of Mules contains only 6 new ones . . . I formerly mentioned to Mr Paterson my Surprise at the Sums being paid for Law [legal advice] without any notice being taken of the object of it.

Finally, he writes: 'I need not mention to you how important it is to be careful about the Quality of sugar', before going on to mention it quite a bit. The only good news in the December letter is that there has been a 'great Rise of price of Sugar'[28] – though the Rozelle shipment was sold before that occurred.

Punctilious correctness is the usual tone. Sir Adam is always polite, sometimes threateningly so, when writing to underlings. He is a little easier when writing to the lawyers, and to businessmen like Hugh Hamilton, who were closer to him in social rank. But all the letters are dry and formal, sometimes pernickety. It must have been dispiriting to have been a manager in the sweaty heat of the Rozelle great house waiting long months to get one of Sir Adam's coldly querulous complaints about a failure to number properly this season's rattoons.

I find myself combing the dense prose for indicators of humanity. There are very few. Even the worst news – of hurricanes and the deaths of white and black people – is received with typical calm, the interest lying, for Sir Adam, in the latest disaster's financial implications.

An apology to Murdoch in March 1780 for a delay in answering letters refers to how busy he has been fighting to retain his seat in Parliament. He had first been elected in 1774, for Ayrshire. He stood as a 'democratical' independent, 'a champion of the county against aristocratic influence'[29] – which meant some of the other powerful families in Ayrshire, led by the Cassillis/Kennedy clan, another one enriched by slavery.

That is nearly the only reference in the letters to the managers of any other aspect of Sir Adam's life, private or public, although some of his enthusiasms come through. Sir Adam's library had books on agricultural innovation and he spent much time and money tidying and improving his and his tenants' lands in Ayrshire – hugely increasing, according to contemporary accounts, the income for the tenant farmers and labourers as well as his own revenue. In 1778, after some discussion, Sir Adam sends six ploughs out to Murdoch at Rozelle. The tool is unknown on Jamaican plantations, and so a young Ayrshire man, David Dunbar, is found, indentured at £30 a year, and shipped out to teach the art of 'plowing'. Murdoch dutifully reports back in November 1779:

The plowing will prove a great advantage to the Estate, and I have this Year pusht it as much as I could without injuring the Stock. By it the Labour of the Negroes is not only considerably eased

but the land improved even beyond my expectation. The Negroes
& Stock (thank God) are in grand order, and thrive well, & I do
not think it will be necessary to put You to any Extra expence
uppon Account of the Estate for some time, A few Mules only will
be wanted . . . I shall be glad to have your approval as soon as
possible to Purchase some.[30]

In the same letter Murdoch reports a little of the wider world. In
August Jamaica had feared an invasion by the French under Comte
d'Estaing, who had taken the British islands of St Vincent and Grenada
earlier in the summer. But the threat passed, the Comte and his fleet
sailing off to help the American revolutionaries in Georgia. Murdoch
says the main result of 'the Alarm' is a likely rise in taxes to pay the
Jamaica militia. Disappointingly, nothing more about this tumultuous
time is said by either man.

There is not even a reference to the disasters in Tobago, beginning
with the death of Jamie in 1777, nor of the depredations of American
privateers and the island's capture by the French in 1781. We only
hear of Jamaican ups and downs – the rise in the price of supplies
with the end of American trade, the loss of all the Rozelle estate's
sugar in 1778, when both the ships carrying it to Britain disappeared
at sea.[31] But, as was usual with cargoes, whether human or goods,
insurance had been taken out. The following year, under Murdoch's
meticulous management, the crop is the biggest since the Fergusson-
Hunter regime began at Rozelle: 163 hogsheads – 126 tons of sugar
– which would have made perhaps £5,600 in Britain. Duty, insurance
and shipping costs would take some 45 per cent of this. Nonetheless,
after ten years, and enormous outlay, the West Indies investments
were now producing a significant return.[32]

CHAPTER 7

ENLIGHTENMENT GENTLEMEN AND RUNAWAY SLAVES

But happy ye, who dwell midst Britain's isle,
Thrice happy men! If fortune deigns to smile.
No sighing slave there makes his heedless moan,
No injur'd Afric echoes forth his groan;
No torturing lord ransacks his fruitful mind,
Some unthought woe, some unknown rack to find.

From *Jamaica*, by an anonymous Jamaican planter, 1776

IN 1780 SIR ADAM FERGUSSON turned forty-seven. He was an influential man in Scotland, a member of its overlapping intellectual, legal and political elites. He had already served as rector of Glasgow University and he knew many of the figures of the Scottish Enlightenment – the poet Robert Burns, the writer James Boswell, the economist Adam Smith and the philosopher David Hume (who died in 1776) – along with a useful assortment of lawyers, politicians and aristocrats. Many were newly rich, having invested in the outstanding business of the era: trade with America and the sugar economies of the West Indies.

It was a life lived in ease and confidence at the nation's top table. Sir Adam was equipped to be the ideal of a late eighteenth-century gentleman: educated, well-travelled, brilliantly connected and comfortably wealthy. He had done the 'grand tour' of Europe as a young man with his schoolmate and life-long friend, the landowner and reformist politician George Dempster of Dunnichen. Sir Adam was no wit, but he was busy and gregarious.

Adam Fergusson by Pompeo Batoni, 1757. Adam paid the
fashionable artist £12 and six shillings, adding a little extra
for some later alterations to the ruffles and the book.

His first portrait, painted in Rome when he was twenty-four, shows
a slight youth with an alert, quizzical air and a nose and hairline
familiar to succeeding generations of Fergussons. He is holding – by
way of advertising his interests – a book: the pretty picture is a
contrast to those of other heads of the family who appear not in
embroidered velvet, but armour, broadcloth or military uniform.

In later portraits Sir Adam is grave, a Scots patrician of the
Georgian age. In a time when pleasure-seeking among the upper
class was more acceptable than it would become in the nineteenth
century, he was known to be an ascetic. 'Luxury corrupts a people',
he told Samuel Johnson in a conversation noted down by James
Boswell, and 'it destroys the spirit of liberty'. Samuel Johnson replied
by telling him he was a 'vile Whig'[1] – a little like being called a
tedious liberal today.

Sir Adam's first career was in law, as was his father Lord Kilkerran's, whose title arose from his role as a Scottish judge. Some of the most important advocates of the time were Sir Adam's friends and colleagues while two of Scotland's future senior judges, Lord Hermand and Lord Hailes, were his brother and brother-in-law. The high moments of his long service as a Member of Parliament came through his support of William Pitt. The young prime minister's close ally and senior minister Henry Dundas, later Lord Melville, was a friend and patron to Sir Adam.

Through these links came roles in government, and eventually the offer, in 1797, of the top job in the British imperial structure: governor-general of India. Sir Adam turned it down, with characteristic elegance:

> How far I should, at any time, have been able to acquit myself with honour in a situation in which so many have failed I cannot say. But my time of life is alone an objection insurmountable. A man of sixty-four must be an indifferent calculator who proposes to pass some years in India with the view of spending the remainder of his life more comfortably at home.[2]

All his life, as his vast correspondence reveals, he was a motor in the machinery of Scottish public and intellectual affairs: using his influence to choose a new professor of Moral Philosophy to Edinburgh University, helping found the city's Royal Society, advising a publisher on which books on Italian antiquities were the best, taking part in Edinburgh dining clubs and listening to essays and poetry written by his friends. If not in London or Edinburgh, he might be at the spa at Harrogate in Yorkshire, socialising while taking the waters for a long-lasting stomach complaint.

But much of his time was spent at home in Ayrshire, busying himself with improvements to the farms and roads, dispensing favours to worthy tenants and their relatives – some of whom he dispatched as indentured labour to Rozelle* – and entertaining his wider family and his peers, the titled landowners of Scotland.

....

* Britons who arrived as indentured labour or hired underlings could prosper, if they survived. The overseer Thomas Thistlewood arrived in Jamaica in 1750 with only £15. When he died in 1786 his estate was worth more than £3,000, and he owned thirty-four enslaved people.

People found him attractive. A female guest at Kilkerran saw the young Adam read a sermon to the household on a Sunday when it was too wet to travel to the kirk at Dailly and she gushed at length that evening in her diary about the twenty-five-year-old, recently returned from Europe and 'heir to a great fortune':

> . . . so genteel in his person, easie in his address, totally void of foppery, or affectation, idolized by his parents, admired by every body . . . so obliging and equally affable to his acquaintances, sensible and sedate yet so chearful, upon occasion even gay . . . his sentiments just and refined, and his understanding great and manly . . .[3]

She was Margaret, the daughter of a neighbour, Sir John Hope. Despite her interest in Adam, she was married to a Church of Scotland minister a few months later. There is no trace of romantic involvement in all of Sir Adam's life, despite the pressures to procreate incumbent on the head of such a family: in all his correspondence no hint of his even considering marriage appears. Robert Burns referred to him in a poem about Scottish parliamentarians and taxes on whisky (Burns was against the latter) as 'aith-detesting chaste Kilkerran'.[4] James Boswell, who feuded with Sir Adam and liked to laugh at him, observed: 'there were few people but were mixed characters, like a candle: half wax, half tallow. But Sir Adam Fergusson was all wax, a pure taper, whom you may light and set upon any lady's table.'[5]

It is impossible to find out more about his emotional life. Was there one? His brother Charles appears as a hard-drinking party-goer in one memoir of the time: there's no sense that Sir Adam ever indulged in such a way. He was never alone: his unmarried eldest sister Jean lived with him, and she had many friends and visitors. She was a confidante and companion until she died in 1804, when they were both in their seventies. The Fergusson houses in Ayrshire and Edinburgh were always full of guests.

Politically he was an 'independent Whig' – an unaligned position that allowed him freedom in Parliament, where he was busy on issues domestic and foreign. He generally sat with the reformers, opposing government's attempts to regulate and impose more taxes, and supporting the notion that Parliament should be supreme. He was a unionist, opposed to separate policies for Scotland – he refers to himself as a resident of North Britain – and he supported military action against the rebels in America in 1776. He was an energetic collector of books on all his interests, including religious and political philosophy and novels, not least Smollett's *Roderick Random*, the first fictional account of life as a planter in the West Indies.

On British social issues he seems mostly liberal, by the standards of the time. He spoke up for the rights of 'Dissenters' to the established church, as he did for Scottish fishermen, but he was also, in 1779, a backer of a bill that attempted to make adultery illegal. It was inspired, apparently, by a popular view that sexual licentiousness was on the rise among the rich and fashionable. The bill failed.

* * *

There is no sign at all of any liberalism in the letters to Jamaica. By the 1780s the campaign against slavery was beginning to make noise in Britain and parliamentarians, including the future prime minister William Pitt, were taking notice. Pitt was a Tory allied with Edinburgh friends of Sir Adam such as Henry Dundas, who would become Pitt's most important minister. William Wilberforce, who led the first abolition movement, had been a close friend of Pitt's since childhood, and Pitt encouraged him at the beginning of his campaign.

In Ayrshire and across Scotland, well-known ministers of the kirk and philosophers such as Adam Ferguson of Raith – who moved in the same Edinburgh circles as his near-namesake – were forming arguments against slavery on moral, economic and scriptural grounds.[6] The economist Adam Smith – whom Sir Adam read and may have known – was against it. His grounds were that slavery was inefficient because it did not offer the workforce adequate motivation. Paid labour was twelve times as productive, by Smith's calculation.

But this change in the wind does not seem to have affected Sir Adam Fergusson, either as parliamentarian or as West Indies proprietor, let alone as a reader of moral philosophy and the Bible. The Kilkerran library contains several books from his time on the West Indies and the slave trade, including parliamentary reports and an abolitionist polemic, *The Crisis of the Sugar Colonies* (1802),[7] which demands more support for the planters from government in order to reduce dependence on slavery. There are also works by Smith and

the philosopher Edmund Burke – also, in his way, an opponent of
slavery. But there is nothing in Sir Adam's letters of the 1770s and
1780s on the subject, not even with his life-long friend the radical
MP George Dempster. In the winter of 1780, however, Sir Adam was
to have an astonishing encounter, the only one in which he came
face-to-face with the reality of what he and the Hunters were doing
in Jamaica.

The runaway

In these years Sir Adam spends much of the winter and spring in
London, while Parliament is sitting. He lodges in St James's, the
elegant village of gentlemen's clubs, coffee shops and town houses
set between Piccadilly and the Mall. It is convenient for both the
Houses of Parliament and the royal court at St James's Palace. One
winter day in early 1781 an uninvited visitor arrives at his door in
Charles Street, off St James's Square. The man, well-built and in his
mid-forties, would have stood out – he was black, for a start.

Several thousand people of African origin were then living in
London, among a population of three-quarters of a million. In a
wealthy area like this, most – but not all – black people worked as
servants and wore the livery of their masters. This man probably
wore little more than the clothes in which he had left Jamaica several
months earlier. He called himself Augustus Thomson, but he introduced himself to Sir Adam by the name under which he had been
enslaved, since birth, on the Rozelle plantation: Caesar.

His arrival on Sir Adam's doorstep is the end of an extraordinary
journey that started at Rozelle a year and a half earlier. Thomson
has been on the run, arrested at least once, hidden in caves and rooms
in Jamaica's port towns. He has managed, somehow, to persuade a
ship's captain to take him on board, though it was a serious crime to
harbour a runaway slave.

Caesar/Augustus Thomson's own risk was greater, of course. The
Africa-born Olaudah Equiano's account of his experiences as an
enslaved boy and man on ships and in the islands, published in London
a few years later, tells of the fate of another man who tried the same
escape route as Thomson. In a passage describing various cruel and
inventive punishments he saw in different places, Equiano writes:

While I was in Montserrat I knew a negro man, named Emanuel Sankey, who endeavoured to escape from his miserable bondage, by concealing himself on board of a London ship; but fate did not favour the poor oppressed man; for, being discovered when the vessel was under sail, he was delivered up again to his master. This *Christian master* immediately pinned the wretch down to the ground at each wrist and ancle, and then took some sticks of sealing wax, and lighted them, and dropped it all over his back.[8]

Once aboard, Thomson, who had never been far from the plantation where he was born, would have had to work his passage as a seaman the two months or more of the voyage to London. There he may have found shelter and support. Quakers and other groups had missions in the dock areas that helped indigent sailors, and he would have come across others from the Caribbean among London's immigrant population. Somehow, someone found Sir Adam's address, and helped Thomson get to St James's.

Thomson was forty-three or forty-four years old, tall for the time at five and a half feet: Rozelle's manager Andrew Murdoch described him as 'likely' and 'well made' – of good physique and health. He carried scars and they could be used to identify him: a broad one across the back of a hand from a childhood burn, and another from a cut on his chin. Murdoch describes him as 'Creole', which in that era meant anyone, white or black, who was born in the Caribbean islands.

These details all come from the advertisements Murdoch has been placing in the *Jamaica Mercury & Kingston Weekly Advertiser*, offering a reward of £5 for information leading to the return of a 'run away': 'Caesar', an 'artful fellow' well known in the parishes of St David and St Thomas-in-the-East, who might 'endeavour to pass in the Towns for free'. More money – £10 – was offered for information about who was harbouring him. Caesar left the plantation sometime in September 1779: the first advertisement for his return (along with half a dozen others seeking runaways) appears in the 4 December edition of the weekly paper.[9] Around this time Augustus Thomson rejected 'Caesar', the name given to him at birth by his enslaver.

In all the stories of transatlantic and chattel slavery the people at the heart of them, the enslaved, are well-nigh invisible. You could easily write a book about Sir Adam Fergusson, but no more than a sentence at best on most of the hundreds of people he called his property. One of the bonds of their enslavement is permanent silence, enforced by custom and the denial of education. Stories of those enslaved people are usually written by and for their oppressors. Most of what we know of Augustus Thomson comes from the manager Andrew Murdoch, who had his own reputation to defend, and Thomson's to destroy as he wished, unchallenged and unchallengeable. You need to seek between the lines for the truth.

* * *

The first record of Caesar is in an inventory made on 1 January 1770, an 'Account of the Negroes & Stock, upon Rozell Plantation', for the new owners, the Fergussons and Hunters. He is listed among the 145 enslaved people as 'a black doctor'. Caesar was a common name for an enslaved man or boy: the owners liked to label the Africans using the ancient Greek and Roman stories. Caesar's mother was almost certainly a woman named Fortuna; she was born in 1720, worked as a nurse and was still enslaved at the Rozelle plantation in 1786.[10] Fortuna gave birth to Caesar when she was sixteen or seventeen. His father was an unknown white man, probably a worker at Rozelle.

This Caesar stands out in the list of humans and animals at Rozelle. In January 1773 he is valued at £160 (Jamaican currency) – only two people are put higher. This sum is twice or three times the annual wage of a junior white man on the estate (the manager Murdoch was paid £280), and three times the price of an adult African newly arrived at Kingston market. 'Dr Caesar' is an important asset. Then in his late thirties, he is the man who gelded and shoed the horses and assisted in looking after the sick and injured humans. In the annual lists he is numbered with the other important enslaved workers: carpenter, mason, coopers, the head sugar-boiler, the cook and the washerwoman.

His job meant status way above that of the ordinary field-hand. There were material privileges too: possessions, a hut of one's own and, perhaps, the chance to live as a family with some sort of stability. Of course, should the estate be sold, all that might quickly come to nothing: families could be split at a master's whim. The artisan enslaved had no privileges beyond those they accrued with their usefulness. A trusted senior enslaved person might be injured or fall ill and quickly lose all that hard-won advantage. Or, as in Thomson/ Caesar's case, he could fall out with the white men who ruled everything.

* * *

Only a handful – perhaps five – of testimonies exist that tell, in the first person, the story of being enslaved under the British in the eighteenth century. In the 1780s accounts of former enslaved people became powerful tools of the abolition campaigns. The best-known are polemical and written some time after the events they describe; the most successful was Olaudah Equiano's *Interesting Narrative* (1789), which went through nine editions in five years. Equiano had been enslaved as a child in Benin and purchased by a Royal Navy officer with whom he travelled the Caribbean; though sold twice more, he eventually bought his own freedom in his twenties.

Equiano and eleven other ex-slaves formed what we would now see as the first black activists' group in Britain, the Sons of Africa. They campaigned against the slave trade in the 1780s, addressing meetings and writing to newspapers. Alongside Thomas Clarkson and William Wilberforce they played a major – though poorly recognised – role in the foundation of the parliamentary abolitionist campaign in 1787.

Another member of the Sons of Africa was Quobna Ottobah Cugoano, who was captured and sold aged thirteen in modern Ghana, shipped to Grenada and ultimately freed fifteen years later in England. In 1787 he published his *Thoughts and Sentiments on the Evil and Wicked Traffic of the Commerce of the Human Species*, which called for immediate abolition of the trade and slavery itself. These works, along with the 'African Prince' Ukawsaw Gronniosaw's memoir (1772) and the letters of Ignatius Sancho (1782), were reprinted many times as abolitionism grew to become the liberal cause of the age.[11] The authors were all Christians, as was their intended audience, and divine benevolence plays a role in the narratives.

Augustus Thomson's short account is very different. It is a private appeal to an employer (for that is how he appears to see his 'owner') seeking basic justice against a cruel and corrupt middle management. It is addressed to Charles Fergusson (as the plantation's original co-proprietor). As far as I can tell it was never seen by anyone at the time other than the two Fergusson brothers and the writer to whom Thomson dictated it. My grandfather read it, but this is the first time it has been published.

To Charles Fergusson Esq Scotland

Jamaica Is.

This is to acquaint you that the falling out between the Overseer [Andrew Murdoch] and me was as follows Viz. when he was going to leave the Estate and going to Town, he left every thing to my Charge and there was white people upon the Estate that was little acquainted with, as they are but lately come, and I was to take good Care of every thing upon the Estate as lay in my power. The hog sty was fallen down and the hogs got several times into the canes, The driver then began to find fault and ordered the Negroes then to go & make a New Sty, without any Driver with them. and seeing them Idling away there time, I thought it best to go and push them on to make as good hast as possable which when the Carpenter saw that I was with them he was Angry and said I took too much upon myself. Upon Acct. of I furthering your work, and made a Complaint to the Overseer against me for pushing the Negroes to Work. the Carpenters name is James Moody [a white employee]. After the Overseer hearing him, he without speaking a Word, took & screwed my two thumbs together, and put me in the Stocks, after giving me two hundred Lashes and I begd the People to let me out which they did. I went to Mr Brice to get him to be [illegible] for me and he would not pardon me. after this the Overseer went to Town and as he would not Pardon me, I went in the Hott-house [the place for the unwell] to mind my business as usual and the Book-keeper came and told me he did not want me on the Estate and order'd me off the Estate. when the Overseer Mr Andrew Murdoch came home he told me to go about my Business and never Trouble him at all, which I took him to his word and Accordingly did. & then the Very next day he went he took possession of my [vegetable-growing] Grounds and plantain Walk and put a Watch upon it and Ordered the Watchman not to let my wife Child,

Mother or Sister to come upon it which all Gentlemen that has got property looks upon it to be Very hard. I went afterwards to John Pattison [John Paterson, the former manager of Rozelle Estate, still overseeing Murdoch] to make up matters amicable between us which he would not and said he would punish me to such time as I lost my life, he hit me in such a manner that I spit blood for three days and one of his Acquaintance named James White came and seed me on the Bilbo [an apparatus with iron shackles to hold the legs] spitting blood ordered the Overseer to Employ a Doctor, which he said I might dy and be damd, but at last by much persuasion he was advised by some of the Gentlemen in the House to send for a Doctor and when the Doctor came he blooded me directly, and found I was Very much bruised in the Breast and prepared medicines for me to my relief by the best of his Knowledge and that gave me great relief. By giving me two hundred lashes put book and Chain upon me & Slung my feet to my neck at last I got away by the help of God. after this he Ordered me to the field being a thing I was never brought up to, he gave my wife & Children three hundred lashes each for giving me a little Victuals when inn that Bilbos. I allways was brought up a Doctor & horse farrier and horse Gelder, after yon [?] he ordered the Negroes to eat my Hogs and fowls Goats &c which I thought it very hard. I was very sick and the Doctor told him to Knock off the Chains and he would not. Said if I died I should be buried with them, soon after I gave Sancho 4 bills to let me Out of the Billbo which he did and After that he let me out the people told him that I was gon, he went to some of the neighbours negroes after that acquainting them I was gon. They told him he would be blamd. They then advised him to set fire to my house which he did and said when he went to kill the fire I made my Escape. I hope you'll think upon it Very much for if a Negro set fire to a house he would to a Cain piece. you will think it was no such thing for I Bargaind with him and gave him 4 bills to let me go, there was Strange Negroes at Morant Bay that saw me there when the house was burning. his name is Sancho and that a negroe wench saw him go into the house with [letter torn] sticks of fire when he went to set fire to the house.

I hope You'll have mercy upon me for the Overseer & Moody the Carpenter. The Overseers name is Andrew Murdoch Owes me

Money & they want me out of the World before they pay me. so
that was all there grievance.

I am Your Obe.t Hu.e St, [Obedient Humble Servant]

Doctor Ceasar. his X X mark.

The two Xs are carefully marked between 'Doctor' and 'Ceasar' with
the same pen used by whoever took Thomson's dictation.

The letter – and Augustus Thomson himself – must have amazed
Charles and Sir Adam Fergusson. There is no account anywhere in
the years of correspondence they received from white people at
Rozelle that gives any picture at all of how life was lived there by
the enslaved people, let alone of a dispute between white underlings
and a trusted enslaved artisan. There has been no hint that torture,
starvation and savage punishment – three hundred lashes – were so
freely used, even on bystanders such as Thomson's wife and children.
It is the first and last time the words 'lash', 'stocks' or 'bilbo' appear
in any surviving correspondence.

Today, the other element of Thomson's letter that strikes you is
his understanding of justice – and indeed his expectation of it. These
seem extraordinary in an illiterate person, someone you assume has
no knowledge of any law beyond the great lack of access to it that
enslavement entails. (Enslaved people in this period were sometimes
tried in 'slave courts', presided over by white magistrates, but had no
right to give evidence in their defence.) This must have fascinated
Sir Adam, as a learned man in an age concerned with liberty and the
rights of man. Thomson knows law: he understands that his case
needs evidence, impartial witnesses, alibis, as well as a motive for the
ill-treatment he and his family received at the hands of Murdoch and
the other white men. He provides all these courtroom necessities in
his statement.

Most heartbreaking of all is his belief he will find justice and indeed
'mercy' at the top of the hierarchy: that is what brought him to Sir
Adam Fergusson's door in wintry London, an ocean away from his
family. Thomson was, however, to be disappointed.

The deposition is filed in Sir Adam's papers with a note in his
handwriting: 'Letter & Accnt. from Caesar a runaway Negro of Rozell
1780'. There's no knowing whether he got the pages from his brother

Charles – whom Thomson and other enslaved people must have believed was still co-owner of the plantation – or whether Thomson handed it directly to him in London early in 1781. The 'account' that came with the letter is on two further pages, written in the same hand:

Mr Andrew Murdock which took away from Doctor Ceasar

3 dozn. Plates, 5 dining dishes
A Dozn wine Glasses, ½ dozn Tumblers
which the above was Lawfully bought from Alexander Graham.
one horse Which Bought of Joe Pagan
a pair of Silver Shoe Buckles.
a Silver Hock & Salad Knive ditto
a Claret Coloured Broad Cloath Cloak
a Pale Blue do.
a Case of Doctor's Instruments

The Above was Holt [taken] by Murdock from Doctor Ceasar in his Absence, out of his house.

18 Goats, which he eat with the comerads about the house.
a pair of Shoes @ 15/ [shillings] both from Mrs Comalla

And there are two invoices, apparently written by Andrew Murdoch, acknowledging debts due to 'Ceasar'. One is for two horses, at £80, the other for plantains at £108 and ten shillings, in Jamaican currency.

These are not much as evidence, but they reveal a great amount about the life of Augustus Thomson as Dr Caesar, a senior enslaved worker living with his family on the plantation. Wine glasses and silver knives? Horses? Goats? And the manager is in debt to him for over £135 sterling? Sir Adam must have been surprised.

He would have known that the enslaved people on Rozelle, along with most on other plantations, were encouraged to grow their own food and to trade in it. The plantation diaries show that on most Sundays enslaved people were allowed access to 'their grounds', meaning the plantain walks and provision grounds where they could grow vegetables and, evidently, keep some livestock.

This was no act of kindness on the owners' part, merely a way to reduce the cost of feeding the workforce, a major expense since in most years grain and pickled meat and fish had to be shipped in from Britain or Ireland to supplement the local food. Clearly trusted enslaved people were able to use these markets to acquire the possessions of the middle class, such as horses, houseware and indeed that claret-coloured broadcloth cloak. Thomson may also have been selling his services as a doctor. At Rozelle, as Sir Adam was soon to learn, favoured enslaved people were themselves able to keep others as servants.

But the more important thing the lists say is that Augustus Thomson had tried to make use of what he had, in influence and wealth, to give his family the closest he could to the lives of free people. This ordinary ambition was to prove fatal, as was his excessive confidence in taking on the management of the plantation in Murdoch's absence and illness (the manager told Sir Adam he was 'very weak from fever' at the time). Thomson had stepped over the boundary that separated enslaved and free, white and black. The junior white men on the plantation, the carpenter Moodie and the unnamed bookkeeper, could not tolerate that. Murdoch and Paterson sided with them.

So Thomson ran away, eventually arriving in London to put his life in the hands of the highest power he knew: the men who owned him. What did Sir Adam feel when this man appealed to him? Frustratingly, no trace remains of any correspondence with his brother or the Hunters about the affair. All we have is Sir Adam's letter to Andrew Murdoch, dated London, 18 February 1781. It begins with expressions of satisfaction and relief at Murdoch's reports that the hurricane damage in 1780 was not so very bad – only the plantain walks were severely damaged. Then Sir Adam moves on to Thomson's visit.

The immediate occasion of my writing now is the return of a Negro, who calls himself Dr Caesar, to the Estate. To my surprise, I found him here at my coming to Town [London]. Upon examining him with respect to his Motives for coming away, I find he had been punished for some Misdemeanour. You may suppose that, in such a Situation, his own Account of the Offence would not have a tendency to exaggerate it, nor of the Punishment to represent it as less than it was. But the question was how to get him back to the Estate. I found him not unwilling to return; but apprehensive of the punishments he would probably undergo upon his return. In order to obviate that Difficulty, I have given him my word that he should be pardoned for his coming away, and the fault he had committed overlooked, hoping that he will do his Duty and give no Cause of Complaint in time to come. I therefore beg that, in consideration of my promise, his fault may be forgiven for this Time. I shall be glad to hear of his being returned to the Estate and of your having received this letter.[12]

* * *

I assume from Sir Adam's laconic response that he and Charles Fergusson either did not believe what Thomson said, or, more likely, that they already knew how discipline and punishment were meted out to the people at Rozelle, and had no quarrel with that.

Sir Adam's use of 'duty' is interesting. It appears often in the letters. Here it implies some kind of contract between enslaved and owner, though it is hard to see how, given the lack of freedom on one side, such a thing could be fair. Did Sir Adam really believe that his property had a 'duty' to work for him for ever, in return for food and lodging? What duty, beyond that, did Sir Adam have to Thomson and his family?

The answer lies perhaps in the prevailing notion of the ideal relationship between planter and enslaved African, as set out in the Jamaican landowner Edward Long's highly successful *The History of Jamaica*, published a few years earlier. It takes as unarguable a theory of Africans as the lowest 'species' of humanity – intellectually, physically and morally uncivilised. It is the Fergussons and their like who can rescue them from Africa's barbarity by enslaving them and leading them to what Long calls a 'limited freedom' in the West Indies.

The compact is clear – there is 'a reciprocal obligation', producing 'protection and maintenance on one hand, service and loyalty on the other'. Converting the enslaved people to Christianity, a popular idea at the time, is something Long rules out. Such projects are not feasible because of Africans' 'barbarous stupidity'.[13]

Whether Sir Adam has absorbed this – and Long's arguments were immensely influential as the fight between abolitionists and slavers gathered pace in these decades – we do not know. The racial theorising would not have been remotely strange. David Hume, the pre-eminent

Scottish philosopher of Sir Adam's time, 'consistently' wrote of his belief in the innate inferiority of black people, as a race.[14] This thinking was still dominant in the minds of the ruling whites when the enslaved workers' descendants rose up against injustice at Morant Bay, near Rozelle, eighty-six years later.

Sir Adam must have warmed to Long's picture of a benevolent paternalist utopia on the plantation, based on the 'principle of good-ness'[15] natural to the ruling class. The idea would not have surprised him: such idealised relationships between master and slave appear in Latin and Greek texts. Long had spent twelve years in Jamaica as a plantation owner, giving him his authority. But he surely knew the real nature of ordinary plantation management on the island. He was acquainted with his neighbour in Clarendon, Thomas Thistlewood,[16] who for decades used rape and torture in the running of John Cope's Egypt estate. Yet this is Long's sketch of a benevolent white master holding court over the enslaved people on a plantation:

> His authority over them is like that of an ancient patriarch: concil-iating affection by the mildness of its exertion, and claiming respect by the justice and propriety of its decisions and discipline, it attracts the love of the honest and good; while it awes the worthless into reformation.[17]

* * *

Sir Adam may not have believed in Long's notion of a compact between master and enslaved, but Thomson had to. What was he seeking when he went to London but, in Long's words, the justice and protection owed him in return for his service – even, perhaps, his 'love'? Sir Adam spurns this notion along with the man. He does not – judging by the letter to Murdoch – even consider Thomson's complaints, only the 'misdemeanour' for which he was punished. He ignores all the counter-accusations in the story that strike us as most important: the torture, the whipping of Thomson's wife and children, the theft or burning of his possessions – the coats, the livestock, the wine glasses and the doctor's instruments.

In his response, Sir Adam tells Murdoch that he attaches little value to Thomson's statement. He is not interested: his job is only to ensure 'how to get him back to the Estate', to get this asset functioning again. To that end he gives Thomson his word – a gentleman's promise. Thomson is fooled: he has been misled into believing that a white man in authority has some respect for him and his humanity. The truth appears to be that, to Sir Adam, giving your word to a black man is as meaningful as giving it to a horse. The extraordinarily dishonourable thing Sir Adam does, in making what will turn out to be a false promise to get Thomson to return, is not in his eyes dishonourable at all.

Sir Adam's task in getting Thomson back to Jamaica was not simple. On British soil Thomson is no longer Sir Adam and Colonel Hunter's property. In Scotland and in England the courts have in the last decade delivered rulings that in essence make slavery impossible in either country. The most recent of these judgements had been delivered in Edinburgh three years earlier.

The case concerned Joseph Knight, an enslaved man brought to Scotland from Jamaica by his owner, Sir John Wedderburn of Ballindean, who kept him as a servant. When Knight married a Scots girl and sought to leave the Wedderburns' service, Sir John had him arrested. Backed by Scottish supporters, Knight fought a case that eventually came to Scotland's highest court on appeal. To general surprise the Lords of Session ruled in Knight's favour, comprehensively stating that slavery in itself, along with the violence-enforced laws of Jamaica, were breaches of Scots and British law as well as what we would now call human rights. Lord Kames, one of the judges, said 'we sit here to enforce right, not to enforce wrong'.

Thus Knight could not be forced to work for Wedderburn in Scotland, or be made to return to Jamaica; indeed the court ruled he could not even be subject to Jamaican law since he had been taken there from Africa without his consent.[18] The English ruling – in the Somerset case of 1772 – had been merely that a person could not have another as his or her property in England. As an advocate Sir Adam would have been well aware of all this, not least because one of the Lords of Session who made this judgment was his friend and brother-in-law, Lord Hailes.

While in London Augustus Thomson surely knew he could no more be made to return to Jamaica and his life as Caesar than Sir Adam could order him to jump out of the window in Charles Street. Africans from the Caribbean and elsewhere in eighteenth-century London were well aware of the legal ramifications of their status, and able to challenge them. In 1764 the *Gentleman's Magazine* estimated there were 'near 20,000 Negroe servants' in London. The writer did not think employing one a good idea: 'they cease to consider themselves as slaves in this free country, nor will they put up with an inequality of treatment, nor more willingly perform the laborious offices of servitude than our own people'.[19]

A black middle class was emerging. In the same St James's street as Sir Adam's lodgings was the grocer's shop and home of the family of Ignatius Sancho, born on a transatlantic slave ship, former valet to the Duke of Montagu and a celebrity in literary London. He is said to be the first black person to have had a vote in England. (Sancho died in December 1780, a month or so before Augustus Thomson and Sir Adam Fergusson met.)

Accounts such as Olaudah Equiano's show how terrified black people in Britain were by the prospect of being sent back into slavery.[20] They knew the awful penalties under slave colony law for running away and the likely treatment meted out by overseers to returning enslaved people. There is a well-known story from 1773 of a man, married to an English woman, who was recaptured and then shot himself on the ship, still in the Thames, that was to take him back to the Caribbean.[21]

In Jamaica, indeed anywhere beyond domestic British law, Thomson was not a person, but an owned thing. In 1783 England's solicitor-general, John Lee, was counsel in the famous case over the 122 Africans who were thrown overboard from the ship *Zong* en route from Africa to Jamaica in order to save water rations and claim insurance. Appearing for the *Zong*'s owners, Lee stated the enslaved people were 'goods and commodities' under the laws of trade and property.

But Thomson had further reason to fear a return to Jamaica. In the year since he had left Rozelle he had gained a reputation in Jamaica that would not in any way help him with vengeful whites on the island. This meant he might be punished for crimes much worse than those of arson and running away. Somehow he had become caught up in an uprising whose disputed history was to become one of the most famous folk tales from slavery-era Jamaica.

'Mr Wood as Three-fingered Jack' – one of many nineteenth-century
representations of actors playing Jack Mansong.

Jamaica's Robin Hood – Three-fingered Jack and his gang

We know a little of Augustus Thomson's movements between the end
of 1779, when he ran away from Rozelle, and his extraordinary appearance on Sir Adam Fergusson's doorstep in London in February 1781.
In December 1779 he was 'taken up' – arrested – at the Aeolus Valley
estate in St David parish, about five miles from Rozelle, according to
a further newspaper advertisement placed by Andrew Murdoch. This
says he was sent 'home' to Rozelle but, eight days later, escaped again.
The next information comes from the *Jamaica Mercury & Royal Gazette*
on 5 August 1780. It ran an item about a bandit known as Bristol, or
Three-fingered Jack, calling for the island's government to send an
armed force against him and his gang of highwaymen and women.

> A gang of run-away Negroes of above 40 men, and about 18 women,
> have formed a settlement in the recesses of Four Mile Wood in
> St. David's; are become very formidable to that neighbourhood,
> and have rendered traveling, especially to Mulattoes and Negroes,
> very dangerous; one of the former they have lately killed, belonging
> to Mr Duncan Munro of Montrose, and taken a large quantity of
> linen of his from his slaves on the road: they have also robbed

many other persons' servants, and stolen some cattle, and great numbers of sheep, goats, hogs, poultry, etc., particularly a large herd of hogs from Mr Rial of Tamarind Tree Penn. They are chiefly Congos, and declare they will kill every Mulatto and Creole [Jamaica-born] Negro they can catch. Bristol, alias Three-fingered Jack, is their Captain, and Caesar, who belongs to Rozel estate, is their next officer. This bandittie may soon become dangerous to the Public . . .

As with all reports of uprisings or rebellions by enslaved people, we have only the word of those who felt threatened by them – in this case the reports in the Jamaican newspapers of the hunting down and punishment of the 'bandittie' later in 1780. There is no more detail until the first histories were published twenty years later – and none of it is reliable. The true story of Bristol – later named as Jack Mansong – and the runaways sheltering with him in the caves and woods of the Blue Mountains will never be known. It lasts just a few months, and ends, like all the stories of rebellion in the eighteenth century, in bloody tragedy. But the legend of Three-fingered Jack and his outlaws has had an extraordinary life, turned and reworked to suit every conceivable different interest.

Since the beginning, the Jack story has been spiced with stories of obeah magic and supernatural powers. In Jamaica today he is said to have been a giant, over seven feet tall.[22] The robberies and murders of which he was accused in 1781 are now, to some, justifiable acts in the two centuries of guerrilla war against white tyranny. Abolitionist writers furnished Jack with a back-story: noble parents and an African beginning featuring a cruel and treacherous white slave trader. His story appeared in many forms, on stage and in print, as propaganda to bolster white beliefs of black barbarism (useful for encouraging the authorities to spend more on security), and as a Robin Hood tale.

In today's Jamaica, Jack Mansong and his gang are figures on the roll of black freedom-fighters. They stand with Queen Nanny – a woman who led the free Maroons to victory against the British in the 1740s – and the enslaved Akan man called Tacky, who led the great uprising of 1760, along with the nineteenth-century figures of Sam Sharpe, Paul Bogle and George William Gordon. These are the martyrs and heroes about whom young Jamaicans learn at school today. Nanny and Sharpe are on Jamaican banknotes. It is the nation's founding story, the epic struggle that took its people from slavery to emancipation, enfranchisement and finally independence. Was Augustus Thomson, enslaved doctor at Rozelle, a part of it?

* * *

Less than twenty years after his brutal death, Jack Mansong was a big hit on the London stage. In 1800 a musical 'seriopantomime', *Obi; or Three-Fingered Jack*, opened at the Haymarket Theatre. Its plot features a young white couple finding love as they battle Jack, a terrifying black bandit, in Jamaica. An instant success, the 'magnificent spectacle' was performed in New York, Boston and Philadelphia within a year. In 1801 a novelised version of the story appeared, but that plays more to abolitionist sympathies, with Jack portrayed as an unjustly enslaved former African king.[23]

The play and derivatives of it remained in repertoires for much of the nineteenth century, providing work for black male actors. Caves in Jamaica's Blue Mountains where the gang is supposed to have lived are on tourist routes today, and there is a spring on the side of Mount Lebanus named for Three-fingered Jack.

Caesar's name and his possible role in this was lost until modern historians began to research the Jack legend and draw wider conclusions from it about race and society in slavery-period Jamaica. But their interest in Caesar is based on almost nothing: the line in the *Jamaica Mercury* of August 1780 is the only mention of the runaway from Rozelle anywhere, including in the more trusted histories of Jamaica written around the time.

On balance, there seems little reason to believe that he was involved. The manager Murdoch, who is understandably eager to paint the tell-tale runaway as evil as he can to Sir Adam, never refers to the story in the eight letters to Sir Adam Fergusson and Colonel Hunter during the year that the Jack Mansong group and Caesar/Thomson were at large. Many problems – from sickness among the white workers to low sugar prices – are mentioned, but nothing of the fearsome gang preying on the road to Kingston.

Mansong and his group may have been no more than refugees hiding out after their escape from plantations, stealing to stay alive and living in perpetual fear of recapture. Many runaways lived that life, before and afterwards, and Augustus Thomson may well have hidden with them. They were at risk not just from the white authorities but also from the Maroons, free people of African origin who in the 1730s had made a peace treaty with the British authorities. The Maroons agreed to help catch and return escaped enslaved people in return for money.

It is hard now to tease out truth from the mass of speculation and invention surrounding the climax of the story of Three-fingered Jack and the fugitives with him. We know that in December 1780 the Jamaican House of Assembly issued proclamations offering £100 for Jack's capture and £5 for any other member of his gang, above the usual recompense for an escaped person. A week later this offer was upped to freedom for any enslaved person who turned Jack in or killed him.

Shortly afterwards, the group was surprised and beaten in a fight with bounty-hunters from the Maroon town of Scott's Hall. Only Jack Mansong and a few others escaped. Five members of his gang were convicted of committing robberies on the roads and sentenced to death. Then, on 13 January 1781, the reward for Mansong was increased to £300. Before the end of the month some Maroons led by a man called Jack Reeder surprised and shot him at his mountain hideout. They took off his head and his famous maimed hand, carrying them in a bucket of rum to Morant Bay (going past Rozelle plantation) to claim the reward. Reeder became a hero of the free community in Jamaica, receiving a pension until his death in 1816.

*　*　*

It seems extraordinary that Sir Adam succeeded in persuading Augustus Thomson to return to Jamaica, despite all the dangers that awaited him. Extraordinary, too, that Thomson trusted him. You have to conclude that the lure that took the runaway back, protected only by a letter from the Fergusson brothers asking that their manager forgive him, was his wife, his mother and his children. Rozelle was home.

It is not clear when Thomson saw his family again. We know he did not stay much longer in London: in April, presumably with the aid of the Fergussons, he went to sea on the Royal Navy battleship *Prince George*. By mid-May it had brought him back to Jamaica, according to a letter from Murdoch to Sir Adam.

By the time Thomson returns to Jamaica, the manager's usual deference has taken on a distinct note of grievance. The threat to his authority offered by Thomson's trip to see his employer in London has upset him. On 24 April, not having yet received Adam's February letter with his account of the meeting in London with Thomson/Caesar, Murdoch writes:

> I am informed by my friend Mr Day, in London, that Caesar, who has been long runnaway from the Estate, haveing made shift to get of the Island, was in that Capital, and had been with your brother. He is an artful, sensible, Fellow, & I have no doubt has told a very plauseable Story. In the Journal I transmitted you last year, I made a full remark on this Character & behaveour. I hope a method may be fallen upon, to secure and send him out again, should he be suffered to return to the Islands, & be suffered to escape with impunity, there is no describeing what mischief such a Fellow might be the Cause of. He well knew his Crimes were so flagrant and dangerous to the Community in General that had he been secured here, he ran the risk of his neck.[24]

As the plantation book for 1779 is missing from the archive it is unclear what these 'flagrant and dangerous' crimes were. Were they merely the argument with the overseers and the arson that resulted in the burning down of Thomson and his family's own home? The journal Murdoch refers to was written long before the Three-fingered Jack story became known. In his next letter, on 6 June 1781, Murdoch writes that 'Caesar, (now Augustus Thomson) arrived at Kingston about three weeks ago in the Prince George'.

A few days earlier a Mr Robertson had arrived at Rozelle delivering letters Thomson has carried from England, including one from Charles Fergusson. The manager is appalled by what he reads. He writes to Sir Adam:

> Had your brother [Charles Fergusson] been at all informed of the management in this Country, He might have foreseen the dangerous consequences that would attend my complyence with the terms He mentions in Mr Robertsons letter to have made with Caesar, were it in my power, but Himself and His Crimes are so well known to the Community in general, that the Law must lay Hold of Him. Should He yet come to me, I am under the necessity if I am to excuse Him, but (altho I have endeavoured to keep this

matter as quiet as possible) the general Cry against Him is so great
that I fear He will endeavour a second time to get off the Island.
It would be an object well worth attention if We could get a proof
against the Captain that carried Him off last.[25]

Perhaps fearing that Sir Adam and Charles might blame him for
Thomson's insurrection – they have after all made 'terms' with him
– Murdoch defends himself.

> Severity in the managment of Negroes is what I have allways
> abhorred, Lenient measures and attention, is the conduct I have
> ever pursued, and seen in Others, most successfull, but there is at
> the same time a Steady command, of Authority, necessary to be
> kept up, which if a manager once loses, nothing but neglect, &
> confusion, can be the consequence.

Thomson, presumably in hiding in Morant Bay town or elsewhere
in the parish, aided by this Mr Robertson, clearly thought better of
giving himself up to Murdoch. The next letter from the overseer,
two weeks later, says he has received Sir Adam's letter asking that
Caesar be pardoned:

> I immediately wrote Mr Robertson, begging Him to let Caesar
> know that I should undoubtedly Comply with Your desire, and to
> advise Him to return quietly Home. Mr R wrote me for answer
> that Caesar had been with Him some days before, but He being
> indisposed had not been able to Speak with Him, and He did not
> know where He was since gone. I understand the Fellow has been
> skulking about the Neighbourhood, and so far from repenting of
> his past faults, has been endeavouring to Hurt the Negros Minds.
>   Were not the Negros upon the Estate in general well disposed,
> and I may venture to say, really attached to My Person, Caesars
> practices might give me much disturbance. As it is Your desire, You
> may be assured I would for My own part, look over what was past,
> but I cannot protect Him against the Laws of the Country.[26]

Back in London, Sir Adam has been having second thoughts. His instinct
throughout the forty-year correspondence with Jamaica is to trust and
back his managers until evidence of their failings is undeniable. A black

man's testimony is clearly not sufficient to doubt them. And so he goes back on the promises he and his brother made to Thomson. He gives Murdoch permission to use his own judgement: to do as he will with the runaway. On 30 June, four months since his last letter, he dispatches a lengthy one. Most of it is about the accounts, Colonel Hunter's questions about the possibility of building a water-mill, and compliments on Murdoch's work. And, then, on a matter that has been troubling Sir Adam:

> You may think my writing, as I did about Caesar, a little strange, considering the Note you have Enterd concerning him in the Journal 1779. The Truth is, that I had not then attended to that Note . . . That will I hope, account to you for my writing as I did, about Caesar, and I am now I confess, a good deal uneasy, lest the method I took to get him to go back to the Estate, which, by the bys, was the only one that would answer, may have been attended with rather Loss than Advantage. But what I should be most sorry for, would be, your supposing that my writing as I did, implied any neglect of your opinion or inattention, to what you had written in the Journal. If you think that Man dangerous to be kept on the Estate, or that his Example is like to corrupt the rest, it would be better to get rid of him, than to keep him to do harm.

The letter goes on to discuss crop prices and then:

> . . . I cannot help again adverting to Caesar. Your expressions respecting him in that Letter [of 24 April] are so strong, and your opinion of the Danger arising from his Impunity so positive that I now heartily wish that I had let him remain where he was than sent him back in the manner, & under the Condition, that I did.[27]

Thomson may have wished the same. But we have to wait to hear Murdoch's reaction: his next letters are largely concerned with more pressing problems. There is a famine in Jamaica as a result of the drought of 1781. 'The Negroes upon the Estate, and in the neighbourhood, are at this time so pinch'd for Provisions, that we are oblig'd to keep three of the most lusty field negroes as temprory watchmen to keep them from culling the young Canes,' he writes in July. Then, on 1 August, another hurricane hits. It destroys the plantains and most of the enslaved people's grounds for growing food. There are no deaths, but Murdoch fears famine and 'fluxes' – he asks for supplies of food and clothing to be shipped out.

Simon Taylor, a neighbouring plantation owner, reports the Africans on one of his estates at this time 'crying out very much' from hunger, and too 'weakly' to be able to work on the sugar canes. The famine even affects food supplies for the white sailors and soldiers stationed on the island. A modern estimate is that 24,000 enslaved people died in the aftermath of the extraordinary series of hurricanes and storm surges that hit Jamaica in the 1780s – 10 per cent of all of them.[28] By April 1782 Murdoch at Rozelle reports 'great depredations' in the sugar cane caused by hungry people from other estates. Meanwhile fifty casks of peas, beans and flour sent by Sir Adam from London in response to the previous August's hurricane have arrived.

Around this time Murdoch hears from Sir Adam, still worrying about his management of the Thomson affair and whether the manager received his last letter:

> I shall be sorry however if it has not come safe to hand; especially as it contained my Apology for what I very much regretted, my having written as I did about Caesar, merely from not adverting to the Character you had previously given him in the Journal. I should be very sorry if you were to suppose that I laid so little weight on your opinion as to send him back under the restrictions I did, if what you had previously written of him had not escaped my notice.[29]

The next news of Thomson from Murdoch comes in a letter from May 1782 (which also contains news of Admiral Rodney's defeat, at the Battle of the Saints, of a French and Spanish fleet intending to invade Jamaica). If Thomson did return to Rozelle he left again.

> Caesar is still runnaway, haveing committed several Robberies. He was about two Months ago taken by some of the Free people at Scotch Hall (a Maroon Town). But either from Address or bribery, found means to escape before they brought Him to Spanish Town where, or in this Parish, had He been conducted safe, the Law must have put a speedy period to His life.[30]

The Scotch Hall Maroons continued hunting the last of Jack Mansong's group for most of the 1780s. Only two names remain –

Dagger and Toney – said to be associates of Jack Mansong and leaders of gangs of robbers. Dagger had a £100 reward put on his head. He was eventually captured and sentenced to transportation.[31]

The next reference to Caesar comes ten months later. Incredibly, it implies that he has taken a ship to England once again. Murdoch writes:

> I found Caesar was in London, from a letter I detected he had sent his Mother Here. if the Villain could be secured, & sent back, it would be a service to the Island in General. He getting off twice easily must be an encouragement to other Slaves to make the same attempt. We have lately many instances of it, I believe principally from their being received as Free people on board of Ships of War, without proper examination.[32]

In wartime the Royal Navy was eager for extra hands and not choosy about their provenance. A year later Sir Adam replies, on behalf of himself and Colonel Hunter: 'You give us your reasons for returning Caesar that he may be punished in an Exemplary manner. We have not of late heard of him, but if we do we shall endeavour to comply with your wish.'[33] This of course leaves it unclear whether or not Thomson had indeed been in London.

Murdoch says no more about him. He is busy with the death of his brother William, a merchant in Jamaica. But he is growing record-breaking numbers of 'luxuriant' sugar canes after years of bad weather and disappointing crops. In April 1784 he writes in high spirits predicting a sugar shipment of more than 200 hogsheads. The prospects for trade are looking up, too, with the end of the war with France.

> Now that peace is established I hope it will be agreeable to You to add some strength of Negroes to your Estate, although We are fortunate in keeping up our Numbers, You will observe You have a fine little Gang of Children coming on, but they are long before they are capable of hard labour. Many of the older are getting past their vigour & some must drop of.[34]

On 23 July he writes that the plantation has indeed made 196 hogsheads of sugar, ready for shipping to Britain (ten were sold in Jamaica).

An amazing 100 puncheons of rum – 25,000 litres, or enough to fill
300 baths – have been produced, and there is still molasses to be
processed. But further calamity is approaching. On 31 July another
hurricane hits Jamaica, with St Thomas-in-the-East taking the brunt.
According to the records there were also two earthquakes: every
house in the parish was damaged. At Rozelle the great house was
'strippt' of tiles but still habitable, while 'the Malthouse, Horse Stable,
Stock Houses, and all the Negroe Houses, except two thrown down'.
Most galling of all is the loss of the transatlantic freighter *Eliza*,
which had been lying at anchor just below the Rozelle works. It was
loaded with most of the record crop.

No lives were lost at Rozelle in this storm. But Murdoch had more
to report: 'As an Individual I have Myself suffered very severely, at
my own little Mountain about 7 miles from this Estate, I have not a
building of any kind left standing, three negroes killed and several
dangerously hurt.'[35]

The next hurricane, the fifth since 1780, will kill Murdoch himself.
It hits the plantation on 27 August 1785, and though the damage to
the buildings is less than the year before, the canes and other crops
suffered more. 'Our hopes are totally Blasted', writes Murdoch to Sir
Adam on the 9th of September. He pleads for more shipments of
peas and flour, since no goods can be got from Kingston by land
because all the bridges have gone. The letter done, Murdoch takes
to his bed. The Kingston lawyers Ballantine and Kennedy (both of
them Ayrshire men) report his end to Sir Adam and Colonel Hunter.

> During the late Hurricane he catched a cold, which with the fatigue
> he afterwards had putting things in order, brought on a fever the
> very day he wrote to you last; and notwithstanding every possible
> assistance was given he died on the 12th inst.[36]

Peter Ballantine, who is a business partner of the sugar plantation
tycoon Simon Taylor, offers to manage the estate until a replacement
for Murdoch can be found. A junior overseer, Rob MacDermit, is
put in in charge of the day-to-day matters. The lawyers seem efficient.

> In the first place our principall study must be to keep the Negroes
> easy & contented, the late dreadfull storm in which they lost most
> of their possessions, and immediately on the back of that the loss

of a master in whom they had the greatest confidence, makes such conduct absolutely necessary and it gives us pleasure to be able to inform you, that not withstanding these fatall calamitys, they express themselves well satisfied, and pleased with your appointment of us to take charge of them.[37]

This is the first time anyone reports to the Rozelle proprietors on the feelings of the humans they kept there.

Sir Adam responds approving these measures, noting that the calamity might at least have the benefit of raising sugar prices and – in his dust-dry way – regretting the demise of the man who has toiled for him in Jamaica for eight years.

I do own that the Death of Mr Murdoch has given me much regret. He has given me and Colonel Hunter much satisfaction as an Overseer; regular in his accompts; the produce of the Estate subject to the Variation of Seasons, was improved under his management, and we had every reason to be convinced of his real regard for our Interest. It is impossible not to regret the loss of such an Overseer.[38]

Peter Ballantine's next letter, in December, is sent after a week spent inspecting the property and the hurricane damage. Supplies are urgently needed at Rozelle, he says, and heavy rain means no new canes have been planted since the hurricane. He also addresses the question of Caesar: he was clearly known beyond Rozelle. Murdoch's death might inspire Augustus Thomson to 'come out', presumably from a hiding place on the island. 'If he does you ought to empower your attorney to Ship him off, as from the Character I have heard of him he is too dangerous to remain on the Estate, & I have the pleasure of informing that the people at present behave well.'[39]

'Shipping off' was one step from the ultimate punishment for a recalcitrant enslaved person – it means selling him or her to another island. But though in his next letter, in January 1786, Sir Adam gives his and Colonel Hunter's permission for this to be done, nothing more is heard of Augustus Thomson in the correspondence between the proprietors and Jamaica.

What became of him? There are two possible codas to the story, but no evidence to support either of them. In 1786 there is a black man called Caesar (though not referred to as Augustus Thomson) living in St Paul parish in Deptford, on the Thames downstream of London: this was a place of naval dockyards, and sailors, and it had a black community. He was convicted at the Kent assizes in March 1786 of stealing four shillings and fourpence. Many of the thousands of black people then in London were very poor, according to the historian Cassandra Pybus.[40] In January 1786 a Committee for the Relief of the Black Poor was established, with one of its founders arranging for free bread to be handed out. Public sympathy was gathered by broadcasting that many of the poor Africans had shed blood for Britain with the Navy or as infantry in the American war.

A more likely end to Augustus Thomson's story can be found in the Kingston Workhouse's published list of inmates of 1789. Enslaved people were sent there for punishment, for which the estate where they belonged would pay a fee. But it also contained the homeless and destitute. Many on the list are noted with 'Says he is free'.

CAESAR, alias John Thomas, a creole of this island, and was to be shipped off some years ago by sentence of the court, to Monsieur McLEUR, Hispaniola, both ears crop't,* 5ft 5 in high.[41]

There's no more in the newspapers or the public records. 'Caesar' is listed under 'runaways' in the annual plantation books for Rozelle until 1785, six years after he first left the plantation. But then he disappears. He was replaced, of course: in 1789 a forty-five-year-old enslaved man named Adam is listed as 'doctor'. We know nothing of what happened to Caesar's children and his wife: we do not know their names. Fortuna, his probable mother, died in August 1786, aged sixty-six – 'she has been useless for two years past', wrote Rozelle's new manager, Archibald Cameron.

There were of course more Caesars at Rozelle. Managers liked the name. In 1792 an eighteen-year-old called Caesar was working as a shepherd. He was one of a group of 'boys of the Ebo Country' shipped from Africa and purchased in 1788. The three girls bought at the same time were renamed Grace, Harriet and Agnes – the first two were fourteen years old and Agnes fifteen. In a nod to the owners back in Scotland, the other boys were Fergusson, Hunter, Blair and Colonel.

....
* 'Cropping' or cutting off of the ears was commonly done to mark runaways.

CHAPTER 8

'GOATISH EMBRACES' AND THE BREEDING OF HUMANS

The man must be a prodigy who can retain his manners and his morals undepraved by such circumstances.

Thomas Jefferson on his ownership
of enslaved people, 1781

PLANTATION MANAGERS WERE HARD TO come by in Jamaica; it took nearly a year to replace Andrew Murdoch, dead after the hurricane of 1785. Peter Ballantine and William Kennedy ran the plantation from Kingston in the interim, writing frequently of Rozelle's continual problems. They are lawyers, after all: bad news is good for business. The year 1786 is full of 'calamitys': the ongoing drought is 'dreadfull', half the canes destroyed, the sugar prospects poor and the relief food shipped by Sir Adam from Glasgow inadequate.

In May there are more deaths among the enslaved people: Eve of a fever that 'fell upon her lungs' and Deborah in childbirth. On Colonel Hunter and Sir Adam's instructions, Ballantine and Kennedy buy ten enslaved men, paying £517, and propose buying at least ten more a year for at least three more years. In 1786 just a hundred hogsheads of sugar are sent to Britain.

Another problem the lawyers lay out for Sir Adam and the Colonel is that there are not enough white people employed at Rozelle. In Jamaica, as in Tobago, there is a perpetual fear among the ruling elite of the ratio of white to enslaved people falling so low that the disparity encourages insurrections. At this time the law demanded that 'for every 30 Negroes a white man must be upon the Property'.[1] Rozelle, with 160 or so enslaved people, should have five resident whites: currently there are only four. In a subsequent year, Sir Adam and the Colonel have to pay £26 in 'deficiency fines'.[2]

In August a fifth white man arrives – the new manager. Sir Adam and Colonel Hunter found Archibald Cameron in London; he appears to have been recommended to the banker Sir James Hunter Blair, the Colonel's brother. Cameron has spent considerable time 'in the management of slaves' in Jamaica[3] and he takes charge with a brisk competence. His letters are not as painstakingly frequent as Murdoch's and they are less deferential. After all, he was a member of the aristocracy, the Cameron of Lochiel clan, grand but impoverished after backing the losing side in the Jacobite war forty years earlier.

Cameron writes to give his ideas for the troubled estate, where he finds many of the enslaved people sickly, 'useless' and 'superannuated'. Four of them die in the first two months of his tenure: Cooper Dick, of a putrid fever; two elderly people, Dido and Plato; and one of the newly bought Africans, Jacob. 'He died of a Lethargy he was but very worthless', writes Cameron in October 1786. Perhaps to reassure his new masters, he tempers the callousness of that with his next statement:

> I have the consolation that [the four dead] had all manner of Justice done them well by the Doctors as myself, I do assure you nothing hurts me more than the loss of any of the Nigroes under my care. The rest of the Nigroes are in good Spirits and are well Satisfied [though at least eight have died in ten months]. The neighbouring Estates have lost more in proportion . . .

Then another hurricane hits, and more deaths follow among the enslaved people, including a child fathered by one of the white workers, 'the dropsical mulatto boy Andrew'.

Cameron shows a firm hand. Despite the lack of white men on the estate, he quickly dispenses with the two who have run it since Murdoch's death, Hateley and McDermot,[4] for neglecting their work. In 1787 he starts campaigning to be allowed to sack Moodie, the carpenter who fell out with Augustus Thomson. This act needs permission from the owners, for while white bookkeepers and overseers could be hired in Jamaica, a reliable carpenter would have to be dispatched from Scotland.

Archibald Cameron is an old hand at slave plantation management and he clearly knows how to make himself comfortable. Within a few months he has picked out an enslaved girl for his bed. She is fifteen-year-old Annie, described as 'mulatto', the daughter of the enslaved 'housekeeper', Jeanie, and an unknown white man, probably one of the paid staff. The practice of choosing what were then known as 'concubines' was common among white men on plantations in Jamaica: many accounts of the slave colonies make it clear this was done with little or no social embarrassment. There is no reason to believe that the women had any choice at all in the matter.

* * *

Even married men on the plantations would procure sex with enslaved women, and their children, official and unofficial, often grew up alongside each other. Simon Taylor, the richest Jamaican planter of this era – and by his death in 1813, one of the richest men in the British Empire – had unknown numbers of children and left legacies to many enslaved former 'mistresses' and their offspring, buying some their freedom.[5]* One of them, Grace Donne, lived with him for thirty-six years – when she died in 1804, he said he was 'like a Fish out of the Water by her loss'.[6]

Some planters disapproved of any informal liaisons, less on racial grounds than Christian ones. Edward Long ranted in his 1774 *History of Jamaica* about the frequent incidence of 'flagrant concubinage' with 'white women . . . Negresses and Mulattas'. 'Many are the men, of every rank, quality, and degree here who would much rather riot in goatish embraces, than share the pure and lawful bliss derived from matrimonial, mutual love.' He blames the torrid climate.[7]

On some plantations the white staff raped and impregnated black women at will. Thomas Thistlewood, a correspondent and neighbour of Long, was a senior overseer and subsequently a slave owner in his own right. In the thirty-seven years he was in Jamaica (he died there in 1786) he had sex with every one of the enslaved women under his control, other than the very old and the pre-pubescent.[8]

We know this because Thistlewood left coded diaries, a pile of

----

* In the late 1980s some villagers in St Thomas, Jamaica's poorest parish, took apart Simon Taylor's elaborate tomb, inspired by the rumour of gold hidden there. They found nothing.

books amounting to 10,000 pages comprising almost two million words. He recorded every one of his sexual activities – time, place and person – as meticulously as he did data on the climate, wildflowers, local politics and the punishments he exacted on the enslaved Africans who annoyed him. On a whim, he ordered whippings of hundreds of strokes of the lash three times a month or more. He devised other penalties that seem even worse.

Most of the women he had sex with were given a coin or two afterwards, so long as he had enjoyed the act. But there is no indication of his seeking of consent from them, if any were possible. He writes that his boss, John Cope, the resident owner of Egypt plantation, preferred the youngest females, and would have them whipped if they were reluctant to have sex with him. It was not until 1826 that rape of an enslaved woman became a crime in Jamaica. At the same time sex with a girl under ten was, for the first time, outlawed.[9] Nonetheless it appears no white man was punished for rape in Jamaica during the entire slavery period.

Cope's white wife Molly lived at Egypt and, you assume, had no choice but to tolerate this behaviour: John had at least two children by women enslaved there. There is very little in the historical record about the lives of white women on the plantations, apart from some mockery of the coarse manners and strange accents of Creole (West Indies-born) planters' wives.[10] They 'suffer much, submit to much and lead a life of misery', wrote the planter William Beckford (of Somerley) in 1790.[11]

Thistlewood does on one occasion act to prevent a white colleague from raping a child. But he also blandly recounts the rape by six white men of one enslaved serving girl; the only detail that interests him is how drunk the men were. There were side-effects of such licence. Venereal disease was rife among the white men on the plantation, and of course the enslaved people too. Many diary entries deal with Thistlewood's attempts to cure himself of various 'poxes'.

Many of his sexual partners were whipped in the course of their ordinary lives. Thistlewood could be exceptionally sadistic, in a culture that was well accustomed to elaborate tortures. He details grotesque punishments he devised, for example rubbing pepper, rotten salt and birds' urine into the wounds left after a whipping. At Egypt, as elsewhere, both men and women were whipped equally, though one concession was made for pregnant women: to avoid harm to the baby a hole would be dug in the ground and the mother would be put face down with her swollen belly in the cavity.[12] Thistlewood also invented a punishment he called the 'Derby dose', after the first man on whom he inflicted it. This involved one enslaved person defecating into the mouth of another, after which their jaw would be clamped shut with wire.

Thomas Thistlewood was a man his peers thought unusually civilised – an intellectual. He was an avid consumer of books on science, philosophy and politics, a gardener and a scientist whose studies of meteorology, botany and astronomy in Jamaica were much valued by his scientific correspondents back in England. Though acutely aware that, as a farmer's son, his social status was not high, he dined or took tea with powerful Jamaicans such as the Beckfords and the Vassalls, and he corresponded with Edward Long. But he was not invited to the balls given by the smartest planters.[13]

He is not the only person in this story who is both an Enlightenment man and a monster. Thistlewood's diaries show that he was certainly aware of the notion, increasingly popular among radical thinkers, that the moral corruption of the slavery industry was contaminating Jamaican and British society more generally. In 1778 he read *Jamaica: a Poem in three parts*, a long pamphlet published the year before in London. In a preface the anonymous author – who claims to have spent some months on the island as a planter – says he wishes both to celebrate Jamaica's beauty and condemn 'the cruelty of the planters and the miseries of the slaves'. Thistlewood was struck enough by the poem to copy some of it into his notebook.[14] It concludes:

At each new crime this labours in my breast,
And this each night denies a quiet rest:
Some Afric' chief will rise, who, scorning chains,
Racks, tortures, flames – excruciating pains,
Will send his injur'd friends to bloody fight,
And in the flooded carnage take delight;
Then dear repay us in some vengeful war,
And give us blood for blood, and fear for fear.

Like many of the whites of the time, Thistlewood also had more regular sexual relationships with some of the enslaved women. His longest-lasting 'mistress', a girl called Phibbah who was Mrs Cope's maidservant, bore him a child. When he left Cope's employment to work his own farm he bought her, and she stayed with him until his death. She also gave him a gold ring to remember her by when he was first forced to leave her at Cope's Egypt. In his will Thistlewood left instructions and the necessary money so that John, their child, and Phibbah should be freed and looked after.

There is no knowing if the practices of the Cope plantation and Thistlewood's own farm, where he had twenty-eight slaves, were normal on the Rozelle estate or other ones. But many other accounts from Jamaica and elsewhere in the Caribbean exist to show how common such licence was. By the early nineteenth century popular fiction of plantation life, with a pornographic edge, was emerging in Britain. Books such as the anonymously written *Marly: Or, a Planter's Life in Jamaica* may have encouraged some young men to make the journey to the West Indies.

There is nothing in the historical record to suggest that any slave plantation owner forbade the rape of enslaved people: at the most it seems to have been a nuisance, with the saving fact that any child born was the property of the mother's owner. In all Thistlewood's years in Jamaica only one white man was ever tried for crimes against black people. John Wright, a Scottish doctor, was a serial killer convicted of murdering four of his female partners but allowed to escape sentence on the condition that he left the island.* The normal punishment for a black person, enslaved or free, who raised a hand against a white one was death by maiming, burning, or by being left in a cage on a gibbet until dead.

It may be that on a usually ordered estate, the use of enslaved women for sex would be kept to a number of 'house' servants. These were frequently the children of white men and black women: in the plantation lists they are sometimes referred to as 'house wench' or 'housekeeper'. In January 1791 two women are listed at Rozelle as 'housekeeper' – Jeanie, aged forty-two, who was the 'concubine' of the carpenter John[15] Moodie, and Margaret, who was thirteen.

* * *

---

* The historian Trevor Burnard speculates that Wright was only tried because one of his four victims was of mixed-race: if they had all been black, he would have escaped justice. Wright killed himself on the voyage home.

At the time of Cameron's arrival at Rozelle, we know that at least two other white men there had an enslaved woman as a sexual partner. When David Dunbar, the Ayrshire ploughman, died in 1789, he left 'trinkets' in his will to 'a Mulatto woman'.[16] Moodie and Jeanie had four children together. These alliances, whatever their nature, were common on the estate: of the twenty-five children under ten years old in the 1785 inventory, half are listed as 'mulatto', most of them under five.

Since Sir Adam had never authorised the purchase of children so young in the sixteen years he and Colonel Hunter had owned Rozelle, it must be assumed these were all fathered by the white workers there. Sir Adam does not comment on this undeniable evidence of his employees' behaviour: when he writes about matters sexual it is usually to deplore the 'irregularity' of the black people's relationships, which he believes contributes to the low birth rate.

Annie was fifteen in 1786 when Archibald Cameron took up his post at Rozelle. She was listed as a daughter of Jeanie, the mother of Moodie's children. But her father must have been a different white man, since Moodie only arrived on the estate from Scotland in 1774. She worked as a seamstress, one of the 'house slave' roles. There Cameron must have noticed her. Within eighteen months Annie was pregnant with the first of six children she was to have with the manager. This child was a girl called Jean, like her grandmother. She was born in 1788 and listed as a 'quadroon'.* On 12 December 1789 Annie gave birth to a son, named Archie, presumably after his father.

Archibald Cameron made himself very comfortable in the great house at Rozelle. In his first year there he compiles the annual list of supplies to be sent out: the bill is for £161, which Sir Adam complains is the most ever, and includes such trivialities as a dozen silver spoons. As the new broom, Cameron has run up many bills: on surveyors, on rebuilding the hurricane-damaged houses. He plans to spend even more erecting a wharf so ships can bring supplies and take off sugar from the reef-riddled bay that fronts the plantation. During this period the estate becomes increasingly indebted. More than one telling-off is dispatched from Kilkerran:

....

* The term then used to describe the child of a 'mulatto' and a 'white' person.

You must be sensible that economy is indispensably necessary to
render a plantation such as Roselle of any real value to the
Proprietor . . . the residue that remains to us after defraying all
the Charges annually is very moderate.[17]

Cameron apologises at great length to these reprimands and sends
his employers boxes of 'Sweet Meats' and Jamaican fruits to placate
them. But apart from these and the usual boilerplate pleasantries,
Cameron's letters are most notable for complaints about his health
and his white neighbours. He has a foul temper and a corrosive
paranoia: not unusual in Sir Adam and Colonel Hunter's managers.

Cameron now picks a fight with the nearby planters Dr Peat, Mr
Watts and Captain Gordon about the trespassing of people and
animals. Peat is sacked as doctor to the estate. So are Ballantine and
Fairlie, the lawyers. Meanwhile, Cameron continues lobbying for the
removal of Moodie, the 'indolent and indifferent' carpenter.[18] Sir
Adam agrees to look for a replacement.

Whether Moodie is aware that his days at Rozelle are coming to
an end, we do not know. But shortly after Cameron starts agitating
for his dismissal Moodie makes a request via the manager that surprises
Sir Adam. He has four children, three boys and a girl, Jean, and he
wants to buy the freedom of his daughter. There is no mention of
Jeanie, their enslaved mother, or her other daughter Annie – by now
Cameron's 'concubine'.

This news prompts the only joke from the proprietor in four decades
of correspondence with his employees in Jamaica: '[You] express yourself
as being desirous of getting another Carpenter in the room of Moodie,
whom you considered not well qualified for his business. He seems at
least to have been industrious in another way.' Sir Adam continues:

With regard to his present request, it does seem rather hard to
refuse a Man the Liberty of purchasing his own Child; and therefore Colonel Hunter and I have agreed to it; and for that purpose
written the inclosed letter in the form you wanted it. At the same
time I own, I am so much impressed with the superior value of
Slaves born on the Estate that I am not satisfied that even a prime
new Slave is a good Exchange. You will at least see by this how
much it is our wish to see the Number of Children born on the
Estate multiply, & those born on it live and prosper.[19]

For all the whisper of humanity that meets Moodie's request, the Colonel and Sir Adam have also noticed that selling fathers their children is good business. Sir Adam had asked Cameron what the normal practice was when manumission of an enslaved relative was requested, and what price could be had. Cameron responded:

> It is impossible to say what the Custom is in regard to manumitting or exchanging Mulattoes for Negroes. Some Masters taking Advantage of that Affection so natural to a parent have insisted for two Prime Negroes to be given for one Mulattoe. Others will not dispose or part with their Mulattoes upon any Consideration whatever which is looked upon as a Hardship. But the more common Method is to replace them with a Negroe that is a prime slave. In the present instance I have charged Mr Moodie with £68 [Jamaican currency], the present price of a prime slave which is considerably more than the value of the Child.[20]

Moodie, in no position to argue, has been squeezed. But there is some good news for him. No new carpenter has been found and by September 1789 Cameron has relented. Moodie will stay. Cameron writes explaining his change of heart: Moodie has children on the estate 'and seems attached to the place'. More important: 'There is also some risque in a new Comer particularly a Mechanic too many of that class being rather addicted to liquor and [Moodie] is sober.'[21]

Perhaps Cameron was moved to help Moodie and his family because by now Annie was six months pregnant with their own second child. In 1790 the carpenter does manage to buy the freedom of another child, his eleven-year-old son, James. He thus had to pay the equivalent of three years of his salary to free two of his children, which may explain why he did not do the same for all of them. In any case, the cruelty of the selling of children was to be experienced by Archibald Cameron himself before long.

Sir Adam and, you assume, his partner Colonel Hunter were now increasingly interested in the prospect of using Rozelle not just as a sugar plantation, but as a farm for breeding enslaved humans. The need to produce more babies becomes a theme in the letters in the coming years, to the point of obsession.

The reason behind this is eminently practical: as the West Indies sugar industry boomed, the price of enslaved people soared. By 1800 a male 'able field Negro' in his mid-twenties will be £168 in Jamaican currency (£120 sterling). The other driver of the price was the growing possibility of abolition of the slave trade. The merest rumour of that was likely to push up the prices in the market.

Before the 1790s the notion of making money by producing more enslaved people in the West Indies was not uppermost in the slave owners' minds. Breeding – the word commonly used – was patently inefficient as a method of replacing dead or superannuated workers: it was more cost-effective to buy a new African. Children were expensive to raise, and producing and caring for them took women away from field work. Only at six years old were they of any use; more than half of children born enslaved died before becoming adults and fully capable of the hard labour of sugar plantations.[22] The cargoes of Africans coming to the New World usually held twice as many men as women, and though women generally did the same type of work, men fetched a higher price.

The brutal effects of a high death rate and low birth rate are obvious from the statistics: at least 2.7 million Africans were shipped to the British Caribbean, yet in 1834, at the official end of slavery in those colonies, those of African origin there numbered a mere 800,000 (700,000 enslaved and a little over 100,000 free non-white people).[23] There are no figures for West Africa, but between 1600 and 1830 the population of England tripled.

Thistlewood's diaries show that of the 153 pregnancies he knew of among enslaved women and older girls, over a time-span of thirty-seven years, 121 children were born alive. Of those only fifteen survived beyond the age of seven. The historian Diana Paton writes, 'Enslaved women's experience of pregnancy, birth and motherhood was marked by ill-health and death, pain and grief . . . The everyday loss of children was one of the hidden traumas of slavery.'[24]

But times were changing and the lives of enslaved humans became more important as the prospect of abolition of the trade with Africa loomed. In 1788 the Jamaican assembly introduced financial inducements to encourage childbirth. A twenty-shilling reward for each live birth was to be given by the owner as a bonus to manager or overseer, the Jamaican exchequer returning the money as a rebate on the property tax.[25] In 1792, as the 'gradual' abolition of the slave trade became British policy, the reward was increased to £3, if the birth meant an overall increase in numbers on the plantation. Meanwhile enslaved women who had more than six living children were excused hard labour. On some plantations women were given a cash reward for every child they produced.[26]

In the early 1790s William Wilberforce and the abolitionist campaign adopted what was to be called 'pronatalism'. To silence the planters' lobby, who said that their business – and all the businesses in Britain that were fuelled by it – was dependent on the continual supply of fresh enslaved workers from Africa, Wilberforce said that they could fill the shortfall by breeding. Sir Adam – along with many others – was struck by the notion: it may have seemed to them a humane answer, though of course to us it is just another example of the reduction of enslaved people to the status of farm animals. Sir Adam's friend the politician Henry Dundas was in favour of tax incentives for planters buying young women and 'rearing a sufficient number of native Negroes' on the plantations.

In practice this meant enslaving girls and women between the ages of twelve and twenty-four, when they were thought more likely to have successful pregnancies. The changes elaborately discussed in the British Parliament can hardly have seemed well-intentioned to the young teenagers who were bought in greater numbers in West Africa and marketed as 'fine Wenches' for breeding. On arrival at Simon Taylor's plantations, they were immediately given to a deserving enslaved man as a 'wife'.

Some planters, including Taylor, judged girls under sixteen too risky to purchase for these breeding programmes. 'If girls are bought too young, the fellows play the very devil with them, but after they are 16 or 18 there is no danger,' wrote Taylor. His concern that the girls should be old enough to defend themselves was less a care for their safety than a worry about the spread of venereal disease.[27] Taylor's own white workers on his seven plantations may be among the 'fellows' about whom he was concerned: it appears that some white men would, like John Cope, the owner of Egypt plantation, select children for sex in order to avoid such infections.

Sir Adam must have known that the pressure to end the slave trade was growing. Some neighbours in Ayrshire were outspoken abolitionists. His unbound and well-thumbed copy of the 1789 report of the Privy Council committee on slavery and the slave trade, ordered by William Pitt, is still at Kilkerran: it coldly details practices on the ships and plantations that shocked Britain at the time.[28] There is no record of his reaction in his correspondence. For the moment, Sir Adam's concern was with profit. In a 1789 letter where he outlines Wilberforce's propositions for abolition to Cameron, Sir Adam goes into the practicalities of producing more babies, and then of keeping them alive.

> But it is vain to think that the numbers can be kept up while there is such an Inequality between the Sexes in point of Number; the Males in the list 1787 being 96 and the Females only 70 to which Inequality must be added that of 7 boys being lately purchased and only 3 girls. I wish to have your opinion about this; as well as to recommend to particular Attention the case of the young Children, a considerable proportion of which die everywhere among Mankind; but I believe more among Negroes than anywhere else. I observe, from the evidence of some Surgeons before the House of Commons, that the Mothers have an abominable custom of swathing the Children tight around the body, and even before the Navel has time to heal, which they say breeds filth and corruption, and may be, in part, the cause of the Frequency of the Locked Jaw among them. Be this as it will, cleanliness is certainly of Importance to health.[29]

The surgeons were of course correct about neo-natal hygiene: modern analysis shows tetanus, or lockjaw, killed 25 per cent of newborns in slavery-era Jamaica.[30] Cameron responds, pointing out that the inequality in the sexes was normal because as field workers 'males do a deal more labour than females, even without making a deduction of the time when they are nursing or breeding'. On the new-fangled ideas about hygiene and infants:

> The Doctors' informations relative to the bad practices amongst the Negroe Women are certainly just. It shall be my study to counteract their many evil habits as much as possible. I have fitted up a Room near the Dwelling houses purposely for the lying-in Women. Whenever a Wench is brought to Bed she can be there attended by the Surgeon that attends the Estate.[31]

The 'evil habits' of the women enslaved at Rozelle are to become a recurring theme as owner and manager make it their business to save money by promoting more births. But the accusations of immorality among the women goes beyond concerns about sexual health: it was a line that was to become part of the racist propaganda put about by the lobby against abolishing slavery.

Meanwhile the deaths of older children and adults continued at Rozelle, though it was rare that either man remarked on them. In 1789 there were six births and eight deaths, all of the latter apparently from disease. One hundred and eighty-three enslaved people were alive on Rozelle on 1 January 1789, so in terms of the larger enslaved population of Jamaica at the time, the death rate of 4.3 per cent shows this tragedy to be quite ordinary – 5 or 6 per cent was normal at the time. The reality of this is that in just ten years more than half the older children and adults owned by Sir Adam Fergusson and Colonel Hunter at Rozelle died.

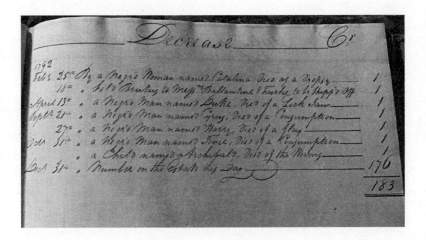

A column in the Rozelle estate plantation book for 1789, detailing that year's deaths.

Abolition in prospect

The letters to the plantation managers rarely mention politics. But Sir Adam was, as a Member of Parliament in Prime Minister William Pitt's wider circle, well placed to see what was happening in the arguments over Britain's ever-growing colonial economy. He did sometimes pass on useful intelligence to his managers. On 20 May 1789 he writes to Cameron with the authority of a well-briefed insider:

You have no doubt observed much in the Newspapers about the Proposition in Parliament for abolishing the Slave trade. I hope this is not so far mistaken in any of the Islands as to have it supposed that it goes to any Emancipation of slaves already in the Islands. The utmost length it is carried by any body is the prevention of any new Importation from Africa. It is far from certain that any so strong a measure as a total Prohibition will take place. What is more probable is a further regulation of the trade without abolishing it. The Proposition however, joined to the Probability of its, one day or other, taking effect, tho' it should not now, makes it very material to look forward to such an event. I mentioned in my letter of Febry. 18th ult. that my wish was to see a number of Children born on the Estate. The circumstances I have now mentioned add much to that wish.

The letter was written just over a week after William Wilberforce, a close friend of the prime minister, made his first speech to Parliament on the slave trade. Sir Adam may have been in the House of Commons to hear it. Wilberforce gave the house a lengthy description of the cruelties of the slave trade and the Atlantic passage. Then he put forward twelve resolutions condemning the trade. In line with the abolitionists' strategy, however, he did not then tackle the larger issue of slavery itself. Instead he insisted that abolishing the trade would help improve the conditions of the enslaved people on the plantations in the British colonies. If replacement slaves were to be bred there, then the women, at least, might be better treated.

Archibald Cameron answered Sir Adam's warning about the Wilberforce propositions on 12 September. It is interesting how familiar the points Cameron makes are. They might and perhaps did come straight from Simon Taylor, the well-connected Jamaica plantation owner whose correspondence with business friends in Britain at this time uses the very same arguments.

The proposition in parliament relative to the Slave Trade no doubt made a considerable noise in this island and caused some alarm and some people were rather apprehensive it might create some Tumult amongst the slaves but I believe few or none ever thought the British Parliament could mean to emancipate the present set of slaves in the Islands we supposed and still hope that this business will end in the mode that you mention. The Late Laws pass'd here for the government of slaves are perfectly adequate to make them as happy as it is possible for people in their present state of Civilisation to be consistent with the Safety of the white Inhabitants, and with any advantage to their owners, and though it will perhaps not be believed by an English Mob or some high flown patriots I will venture to say the slaves in this island live happier than common people of most if not any Country in Europe.

The powerful lobby run by the London Society of West India Planters and Merchants maintained from the beginning that ending the slave trade meant ruin, and for more than just the Britons of the slave colony islands – it would be 'an axe to the root' of the triangular trade[32] and leave a 'wilderness' in the islands.

Taylor, owner of more than 3,000 Africans in Jamaica by the end of his life, was contemptuous of the abolitionists' complaints about the treatment of enslaved people. Inhumane? 'I positively deny it.' Like Cameron, he believes they lived 'infinitely better than the lower class of white people at home'.[33] That liberals should look to the lot of the poor in Britain before they interfered in the West Indies was a favourite line of the pro-slavery lobby in the 1790s. It managed to enlist the radical journalist William Cobbett to enlarge on that theme.

Arguments like these have a long life. The slow pace of the dismantling of Britain's slavery-based economy has long been justified on the grounds that a faster process would have resulted in financial meltdown on both sides of the Atlantic. Meanwhile, the wealth of slavery is still said to have brought great good for Britain and its people. That line remains current, along with the other common eighteenth-century one that enslaving Africans was an act of philanthropy, a rescue from Africa's barbarism to a more civilised life in the West Indies. One of the most influential sugar trade lobbyists, Thomas Hibbert, wrote in 1788 that 'the Removal of the Negroes from their own Country, governed as it is, must, under any Circumstances, be a change for the better'.[34] Only the language changes: one correspondent of mine who is of mixed race himself and also a member of a family who inherited great wealth from slavery was told by a (drunken) relation at a family dinner: 'If it wasn't for us your lot would still be swinging in the trees – but look, you're here.'

The strategies and indeed the characters in this great debate also seem very familiar. The tactics and the arguments of the slavery industry, its overt and covert lobbying and its purchase of politicians and media outlets, mirror the approach taken today by industries that extract fossil fuels and other raw materials from the poorer parts of the world. The power of the lobby associated with the sugar economy and the 'triangular trade' was immense. Parliament had many members who were also planters and West Indies merchants – seventy of them in the years between 1750 and 1775[35] – while many more had connections with the wider industry through family and their own business interests. Lord North, prime minister from 1770 to 1782, famously said that the 'West Indians' were 'the only masters I ever had'.

In the same letter of 1789, Cameron tells his masters about some new legislation – the New Consolidated Slave Laws – recently passed by the Jamaica assembly and sent on for approval in London. The Laws have been seen as a sincere attempt at reform by the planters, an effort to make slavery more humane – and more acceptable to the sceptics back in Britain – by codifying the punishment systems. Use of the whip was restricted to a mere thirty-nine lashes, while rewards to encourage good behaviour on the part of enslaved people were introduced. For the first time mutilation or murder of an enslaved person became felonies.[36]

These reforms must have looked good to ordinary Britons as they became concerned about how their sugar was made. Enslaved people should be given clothing and allowed the land and the time to cultivate their own food crops, the laws stipulated. To anyone who knew even a little about the Caribbean colonies this was a nonsense. Clothing the workers was normal and obviously necessary – they were valuable – and encouraging them to grow their own food saved money. But the amended Slave Laws were ammunition to counter the stories of cruelty and injustice told by the abolitionists in Britain.

The most discernible effect of the legislation at Rozelle is the increasing use of the local magistrates' court to punish workers. Cameron has to buy the horses of the few enslaved men at Rozelle who owned them, as the new laws prevent black people, enslaved or free, from owning them.[37] They also prohibited large gatherings of enslaved people and the use of drums and shell-trumpets – the traditional music of rebellion. Cameron tells Sir Adam the horses will be useful to power the sugar-mill – a job done up till now by humans.

Implementation of the legislation was delayed, in part because of an argument over whether owners should have to promote religious instruction and baptism for enslaved people. Many planters viewed this as a pointless and even dangerous step. But it was likely to appeal to churches in Britain, many of whose congregations were abolitionists.

In 1788 Stephen Fuller, agent for Jamaica in London and chief lobbyist for the planters, said that in his work copies of the Consolidated Laws were the most useful tool of all for 'opening the eyes' of ordinary Britons and arguing against the abolitionist 'Fanaticks'. But this work only went so far. By the following year Fuller had to report to the assembly in Jamaica that it was losing the argument. 'The West India planters [are] stigmatized all over the Kingdom as Brutes', he reported.[38] Abolitionism was becoming a popular campaign: in December 1787, 10,000 people in Manchester, a city that benefited from trade with the West Indies, had signed a petition calling for an end to trading in African people: seventy-four more petitions arrived at the House of Commons by the following Easter.

This was just the beginning. In 1792 alone hundreds of petitions with a total of nearly 400,000 signatures were delivered to Parliament. There had never been a popular movement like this in Britain before, driven by the middle class and, notably, by women. To the ruling elite, the pressure must have seemed irresistible: the change was surely coming.

CHAPTER 9

THE MONEY AND THE POX

AS THE LAST DECADE OF the eighteenth century began, the Fergussons and Hunters (soon to be 'Hunter Blairs'*) had been owners of Rozelle for more than twenty years. It has become a 'tedious' enterprise for Sir Adam Fergusson; his correspondence gives no hint that he finds running a Jamaican sugar plantation rewarding, intellectually or financially. Even in good years, when the crop is large and safely shipped to a market where sugar prices are high, he is dissatisfied. The bulk of his letters to his managers are complaints, and often he seems to be just a few steps away from losing his temper. These are very different from his urbane letters to political allies and friends, and his kind and generous ones to his family.

Managing the Jamaica estate – and dealing with the aftermath of the failed plantation in Tobago – occupies a significant amount of his time. The reports he gets from Jamaica are a ceaseless litany of bad news: hurricanes, shipwrecks, disease, grotesque mistakes of management and of course the endless toll of deaths. The unreliable communications[1] and the parade of unreliable white employees can hardly have soothed him. The Hunter Blairs, as sleeping partners, did not have to deal with the run of crises.

So was it worth it? Were the partners getting rich? There was never a better time to be in the sugar business. Demand for it in Britain was soaring: the price was at an historic high in 1792. Rum had become more profitable, not least because the Royal Navy decided that it would stop issuing its daily ration of a pint of spirits in brandy and use the sugar-alcohol instead. Britain and France were at war

....
* Colonel William Hunter's brother, Sir James, took the new name after marrying the heiress Jean Blair of Dunskey: their son David was William's heir.

until 1783 and then again from 1792 – buying French brandy was unpatriotic. This policy change is one of the successes marked to the lobbying of Jamaica's busy agent, Stephen Fuller.

The wars also put up the costs of shipping and insurance. Rozelle's economics were dependent on what were usually two sea voyages a year to Britain carrying sugar, and an important one back with supplies, ranging from food, clothing and tools to items such as the copper vessels and boiler parts necessary for processing sugar cane. More important, the price of enslaved labour had been rising as well.

Sir Adam's meticulous accounts for all his many enterprises are so voluminous it is not easy to work out what actual profit he and the Hunter Blair family made. Back in the early days of their ownership of the plantation he calculated that unless more than 123 hogsheads of sugar were shipped annually, Rozelle would operate at a loss. But at that time matters were very different. The American colonies were as important a trading partner for Jamaica as Britain, and the price of an adult enslaved African was around £40. By the mid-1790s it was £90 or more; between 1787 and 1801 the partners purchased eighty-two enslaved Africans. Even though the British were consuming four times as much sugar in 1800 as they did in 1700, the inflation-adjusted price of sugar stayed fairly stable through the period.

In only a few years did the estate make more than 123 hogsheads. That was very disappointing for the partners. The rule of thumb in Jamaica was that every acre of sugar cane should produce a hogshead of sugar and by 1792 Rozelle had 256 acres planted. Meanwhile the outgoings often outstripped the income. Quite apart from the costs in food, clothing and hardware, the estate paid thousands of pounds in taxes each year to both the Jamaican authorities and the British Crown. From 1781, £8.70 was payable on each 1,550lb hogshead of sugar imported to Britain. This tax kept rising, as British politicians looked for ways to finance the nation's wars. On an average Rozelle annual shipment of 100 hogsheads of sugar the tax was £1,125 by 1791, and more than £2,000 by 1807 (£2 million today), That year the duty payable was 78 per cent of the market price per hundred-weight of sugar in London.[2]

There were parish and property taxes to pay, and duties on everything imported to Jamaica, from African people through to supplies. Added up, these often amount to more than the profit after expenses. In the eight years between 1776 and 1789 for which there are clear records from bank statements, Sir Adam and Colonel Hunter's annual take, after all expenses had been settled, was an average of £660 a year each: once it was £1,156 and at its lowest (in 1777, during the war with America) it was £413.[3] After 1801, the two men paid an income tax on the estate's profits, on average about £70 (£80,000 today) each a year.

Nevertheless, the profits were substantial sums. In relative wage/income value £660 in 1780 is equivalent to about £1 million today. But these are not so enormous in terms of the wider finances of these wealthy men. Sir Adam ran households in Edinburgh, Ayrshire and London, as well as his tens of thousands of acres of Scottish estates: his outgoings on Kilkerran alone approached £2,000 a year. Generous allowances to family members came to several thousand pounds too.[4]

Sir Adam Fergusson, attributed to Henry Raeburn. Date unknown.

Modest returns and fat cats

Rozelle was a useful investment, but not a wildly profitable one, for the time: it produced an annual return of 6.6 per cent on the £20,000 the business was valued at in 1773. This means Rozelle performed half as well as the average Caribbean sugar estate.[5] Sir Adam knew this. When the sale of 1788's record crop meant a payout of £1,156 to each of the proprietors, he wrote to Archibald Cameron:

> Now if this sum was to be received by us every year, I should be very well satisfied: But when this is the Amount of by far the greatest Crop we have ever had, you will see how well I was founded in saying that the Nett sum that comes to us is very moderate compared to what wd. be supposed when the number and value of the fields is then showed.[6]

The estate becomes much less profitable after the turn of the century. But the Fergussons and the Hunter Blairs do not consider selling up until much later, in the 1840s.

The £1,300 or so in profit produced in an average year by Rozelle's sugar seems tiny in the light of the figures that were bandied about as British people began to gape at the wealth of some of the most successful British-Caribbean planters. Simon Taylor, William Beckford and the Gladstone family were among those with Jamaican holdings, and their immense fortunes – Taylor died in 1813 worth over a million pounds (£778 million today) – lay chiefly in their land, which had risen in value through the second half of the eighteenth century. In 1792, when Rozelle was valued at the orders of the British government, the estate and its assets, including the enslaved people, were worth £33,573.[7] Twenty years earlier, an audit had valued everything at £20,100.

Thus the value of the Fergusson half-share, which cost £10,500 sterling in 1769, had increased by 60 per cent in twenty-three years. Seen in these terms the annual return on sugar from the estate looks pretty paltry. Modern historians point out that most of the great fortunes made out of the West Indies trade during slavery were 'hidden': the money that came from insuring, bank-rolling and mortgaging the planters, merchants and shippers.

On top of that are the fortunes made through supplying the trade and the plantations with British-manufactured goods, from guns to clothing and preserved food. Though the figures are hard to disentangle, the Hunter Blair wealth that enabled the family to buy the Blairquhan estate in Ayrshire and build a neo-Tudor castle there (between 1798 and 1821) was derived not from plantation ownership at Rozelle, but almost entirely from Colonel William Hunter and his brother Sir James Hunter Blair's banking enterprises.[8]

The 1790s, though, saw the last great boom in the West Indies plantation business. Politics and social upheaval elsewhere are the reasons behind that, more than any change in sugar-farming or trading practices. Most important of all was Toussaint L'Ouverture's revolution in St Domingue (renamed Haiti in 1804), which began in August 1791. Inspired by the revolution in France, it was the largest uprising of enslaved people since Spartacus's rebellion in ancient Rome, and the only one ever to succeed.

St Domingue served notice to the nearby white elites of their vulnerability. Sixty-eight thousand free people (two-thirds of them white) had ruled over nearly half a million enslaved in the colony. As fleeing French planters, along with their families and servants, arrived in Jamaica by boat – the islands are just twenty-four hours' sailing apart – they brought stories of anarchy and destruction. The planters had good reason to fear that these events would inspire the enslaved people on Jamaica, and elsewhere.

Songs about the struggle for liberation in St Domingue were being sung in Jamaican cane fields within a month of the revolution beginning. 'I am convinced that Ideas of Liberty have sunk so deep in the minds of all Negroes, that whenever the greatest precautions are not taken they will rise',[9] one planter wrote to Henry Dundas, a senior minister in the British government. Across Jamaica it was believed that an uprising was planned for Christmas 1791.

Of course the abrupt halt of sugar production in St Domingue, then the Caribbean's most productive colony and responsible for 40 per cent of all the sugar going to Europe, had a distinct silver lining. Sir Adam was quick to see what was going to happen. In December 1791 he wrote to Cameron to tell him not to sell sugar in Jamaica: prices had already risen from seventy to eighty-seven shillings a hundredweight in Glasgow, 'owing probably to the effect of the news from St Dominga'.[10]

The Jamaica planters knew when to back a horse, and they seized the opportunity that the St Domingue revolution offered: for all their fears about being 'swamped' by non-whites, in 1793 alone they imported 25,000 new enslaved Africans,[11] four times as many as the annual arrivals in the mid-1780s. Rozelle took part: ten 'young women' and ten men were bought in 1792 and 1793 for the plantation, at more than £80 each.[12] Sir Adam, ever keen on breeding, orders the purchase of ten more enslaved people just as Cameron reports, in

November 1792, that the 'new Negro' price in the Kingston market has reached £90.

* * *

There is no evidence from the letters that the boom brought any joy to Rozelle's owners or to their manager, Archibald Cameron. The latter's mental health seemed to be deteriorating. In 1789 Colonel Hunter had heard worrying reports from a returning Scot, Campbell Douglass, who had lived near Rozelle: 'He did not believe Cameron a planter or understood the business'.[13] Some of this is relayed back to the manager, who is furious and defensive at the suggestion of incompetence. He knows the detractors, he says: 'several Private enemies' and a former bookkeeper whom he sacked for gossiping. This goes with a stream of criticism of his predecessor, Andrew Murdoch, and his decadent 'Bon Vivant' lifestyle.

> In his time this place was a receptacle for all Idlers, and was more like a Tavern than a private House. I am but ill calculated for a Sphere of that sort and if I was I by no means think that it would be conducive to your Interest . . . my sole Attention is the management of your Estate.[14]

Sir Adam, as is usual, retracts and apologises to Cameron, professing that he and the Colonel have complete faith in him as their manager. But the run of problems continues, not all of them Cameron's fault. Sugar production is disappointing because the land is exhausted; fences are inadequate and the cattle fail to thrive because his predecessors allowed the pastures to become 'almost a Wood'. The Kingston lawyer Peter Ballantine, now a business partner of the chief justice, Jamaica's most powerful planter, Simon Taylor, is accused of having cheated the estate with poor supplies. A fire destroys seven of the enslaved workers' houses: they might not all have burnt, says Cameron, if the previous managers had not built them too close together. There is an outbreak of measles, and in 1791 another hurricane.

Cameron never mentions ordinary punishments such as whipping and use of the stocks in his reports, but Sir Adam has to be consulted over a plan to get rid of a troublesome worker. Brutus is his name. He has had a long history of unspecified 'evil Practices', says

Cameron.[15] Now he wants Brutus to be 'shipped off'. Sir Adam enquires what this means, in his lawyerly way:

> I do not understand what is meant by the permission you ask to ship off Brutus. Banishment I understand to be a Punishment for a free Man. But shipping off, which I understand to be banishing a Slave, seems to me to be punishing ourselves by giving away our property. I wish you would explain this more fully, both as to the meaning of shipping off and the circumstances which lead to it. Without this I can give no opinion on it.[16]

Cameron responds:

> When a Negroe will not stay at home without keeping him in Confinement, or do his work without punishment and the constant dread of the Lash, it is customary to transport such a Negroe, to either the French or the Spaniards, and this mode has often a good effect on the rest of the Slaves upon our property, for even Negroes consider Banishment as a very great punishment not only expecting that their treatment will be much worse by French or Spaniards than by Britons, but as they are deprived of their acquantance and friends, and Negroes are very susceptible of friendship and regard to their Relations, amongst whom they consider their Shipmates or even Children of Shipmates through many generations. Those Foreigners are well informed that we sell seasoned Negroes only for their faults, they will not give a high price for them never above £40.[17]

Nevertheless, Brutus is shipped off. In 1794 a runaway named Adam, 'really very dangerous upon the Estate', is tried at Cameron's request by the magistrates' court and sold 'to the Spaniards'. It is an acknowledged cruelty. Cameron writes: 'nothing but necessity could have induced me to ship of a Creol [someone born in Jamaica] who had a numerous connection on the Estate'.[18]

A particular disease

To his July 1790 letter, Cameron attaches a long list of medicines and medical equipment required for the plantation. It includes opium and supposed cures for dysentery, such as Dr James's Fever Powder. There is also mercury oxide, balsam capivi and '1 long beak'd Ivory Penis Syringe',[19] all for treating syphilis and gonorrhoea.[20] Mercury is of course highly toxic, as is the antimony in Dr James's powders, though the latter remained a celebrated cure-all on sale into the twentieth century.

Sexually transmitted diseases were rife on the plantation, as they were at Egypt, the Cope plantation in Jamaica where Thomas Thistlewood and other employees were at liberty to use enslaved people for sex. Thistlewood writes in horrible detail about his own ailments, the rashes, buboes, purulent discharges and agonising erections. He blames the women he has slept with and orders them to be examined by the doctor.

Egypt plantation's Dr Horlock bleeds Thistlewood and prescribes mercury pills, purges and laxatives. There are bleedings, probes and syringings, and Horlock recommends the bathing of the penis twice a day in fresh milk. After forty-four days of treatment Thistlewood doubts he is cured, but goes off to have sex with two women on the plantation, including one, Dido, whom he accused of infecting him.[21]

The decadent lives and sexual habits of the West Indian planters were the subject of many satirical prints of the time. This print, one of a series following the career of a planter, was published in 1808.

But it is clear from Thistlewood's diaries that he had brought gonorrhea and chlamydia (hence the buboes) to Jamaica, having contracted them from sex workers – or perhaps his best friend's wife – back in Britain. This hypocrisy, the shifting of blame to the black population, is common in accounts of the time. As the historian Trevor Burnard and others point out, the diseases and sexual licence rife among the West Indian planters and their employees became a potent tool for the abolitionists. A narrative about how slavery corrupts its white proponents – morally and physically – begins.

By the 1790s medical theorising about the illnesses of the Caribbean had moved on: it was not the place that was at fault but the habits of the people. The amoral lifestyle and the death rate of the sugar growers was taken as both cause and effect. It summed up the evil of the industry for a British population ready to condemn and possibly envious. Satirical cartoons depicting drunken and gluttonous young planters sporting with their 'sable Venuses' (and then expiring), like the one I found in the Scarborough museum in Tobago, were increasingly popular. The planters' wealth was excessive, the means with which they got it distasteful and their licentiousness un-British. So venereal disease becomes a symptom of colonial excess, as Burnard and Richard Follett put it – and one of the factors that turned the planter class from the much envied, most powerful interest group in the empire into objects of derision, 'demonized as despotic tyrants'.[22]

Sir Adam – who is of course no one's idea of a decadent plantocrat – rarely comments on the illnesses or the medical supplies demanded, though he approves of plans to inoculate the Africans against smallpox. He frets at the poor results of the plan to produce babies. By the mid-1790s there is gender parity on the estate because of the buying of more adolescent girls. Yet only eight newborns survive the first months in the years 1796, 1797 and 1798. Annie, the mother of Archibald Cameron's children at Rozelle, lost at least two children in infancy in this period.

Sir Adam frequently uses phrases like the 'wretched morals of these people' when he speculates on the cause of the failure to produce more children, though he tiptoes around quite what moral habits he means. 'If any Degree of Regularity of living could be introduced among them, it would contribute more than anything to an Increase of their Numbers', he writes in a letter of 1791.[23]

The following year he is a little more specific, suggesting Cameron takes care 'to prevent promiscuous use of the women, and to keep them exclusive to their own Husbands'.[24] He may not have been aware yet that Cameron was himself 'using' at least one of them. He does also suggest that they should be cared for properly when pregnant, a novel idea in a society where the enslaved women were supposed to work in the canefield to the point of giving birth and resume two weeks later.

The Jamaican planter Robert Hibbert told the Parliamentary select committee investigating slavery in 1790 that the 'natural indolence' of black women meant they 'took advantage' of being pregnant, when in fact he understood the exercise would be good for them. This contrasted, as ever, with his beliefs about white women. When his own wife was pregnant in 1800 he records that she spent twenty-two days in bed, or on a 'sopha', in the hopes of avoiding a miscarriage.[25]

Historians estimate that a quarter of pregnancies among enslaved women ended in miscarriage: as a result many planters said that the women had a culture of making themselves abort. You can only guess why they should have done this, if it is true. Was it as a result of trauma, including rape? How much Sir Adam knew, or guessed, is hard to discern.

He may have absorbed the racist theories regarding the inherent immorality of black Africans that were becoming increasingly common in essays and pamphlets written by the pro-slavery lobby for the abolition debate. They were not new: Edward Long's *History of Jamaica*, published in 1774, makes exactly this point about African people. Quoting ancient Roman and Greek authors as well as modern travellers, he seeks to show quasi-scientifically that an African species – he uses that word – is distinguished from the rest of humanity by 'bestial manners, stupidity and vices', even a particular 'stink', and 'every species of inherent turpitude that is to be found dispersed at large throughout the rest of human creation'.[26]

Dr John Lindsay, an Anglican priest in St Catherine's, Jamaica, who wrote anti-abolitionist essays, had this to say in 1788: 'The infertility of Negroes [derives from the] state of uncurb'd Nature among them . . . both men and women changing mates as often as Humours and Conveniency shall suit them.'[27] The surgeon (and self-declared expert on venereal disease) Jesse Foot echoes this in his *A Defence of the Planters in the West-Indies*, which ran through three large editions in three weeks when it was published in 1792.

The fact is that it is the libidinous practices of negroes that want reform . . . They are so amply provided for and their toil is so light . . . are so free from the incumbrance of providing for a family . . . that their burthen of life is ever light, and their anxiety for their children is as short as that of a bird whilst its young are fledging . . .[28]

At the root of these writings is a determination to picture black Africans as differently as possible from white Europeans, in both body and mind: it is the key discourse of those seeking to justify slavery. The abolitionists' principal line of attack, since the 1780s, had been to counter this and stress the common humanity of Africans and Europeans, equal in the eyes of God and so – necessarily – under the law. Josiah Wedgwood's famous ceramic medallion of 1787 has, under a relief of a slave in chains, the line 'Am I not a man and a brother?', which became the movement's best-known slogan on both sides of the Atlantic.

The anti-abolitionists' othering of the black African had many forms. One of the criticisms of French plantation slavery was that people of mixed race worked in the fields. British people – pro and anti-slavery – saw this as an outrage: 'mulattos' could not tolerate

Josiah Wedgwood designed the Slave Medallion in 1787. 'Ladies wore them in bracelets, and others had them fitted up in an ornamental manner as pins for their hair. At length the taste for wearing them became general, and thus fashion . . . was seen for once in the honourable office of promoting the cause of justice, humanity and freedom', wrote Thomas Clarkson in his *History of the Abolition of the Slave Trade* (1808).

the harsh labour of the canefield as could those without discernible white ancestry. All this reinforced the view that wholly black people did not qualify for the same rights as did brown or whiter human beings. The echoes of these prejudices continue in the colourism that so hinders T'Keiah Alleyne in Tobago today.

Blame the women

Discussion of a more rational cause for the low birth rate among the enslaved people began eventually to reach Sir Adam. In 1795 he wrote to Cameron about a new doctor who had been hired to visit Rozelle.

> To say a simple word more upon what interests me much, the few Births among the Negroes, I observe from the Accompt opened with Caleb Dickenson, you have employed him for a particular Disease. I have no reason to doubt but this is right. But so many Females, as well as Males, affected with a Disease the most baneful to Propagation, gives a sad view of the manner in which they live, and gives, in part at least, a key to the Cause of their being so unproductive.[29]

A 'particular Disease' is Adam's squeamish way of referring to venereal illness. The hiring of Dickenson to tackle it at Rozelle is interesting: he is a famous figure in Jamaican medical history. Born in Jamaica, into a wealthy plantation-owning family, he was of mixed race – the first mixed race free person we know to have been employed at the plantation. After training as a doctor in England he became famous in Jamaica as a racehorse breeder and a philanthropist.*

The 1795 plantation book records two deaths from 'lues venerea' [plague of Venus], and that 'many have the venereal disease, both Male and Female'[30] – this would mean gonorrhea or syphilis, and was probably information gained from Dickenson's diagnoses, since the plantation books never usually carry this detail. The lesions caused by yaws, which was very common at Rozelle, may also have been mistaken for syphilitic sores, and vice versa.

....

* When Dickenson died in 1821 he left his estate (which included enslaved people) to set up a free school. It is now Munro College in St Elizabeth, Jamaica. The reggae star Protoje went there.

Thistlewood's diaries of life, sex and death at Egypt plantation are the most reliable (thus, still not very) evidence of the prevalence of cases on plantations: in a population of sixty adult enslaved people, twenty-eight women and fifteen men had at least one bout of venereal disease over nine years. But gonorrhea is often symptomless in women, and syphilis is not usually an obvious cause of death, therefore very rarely cited as such.

There is a link, we now know, between some sexual diseases and low fertility. Infected women are less likely to get pregnant and, when they do, more likely to see their babies die. Examination of the skeletal remains of infants who died in the time of slavery in Barbados reveals that 10 per cent show signs of congenital syphilis.[31] The Rozelle estate books, with their lists of mixed race (black and white) children, make it obvious that the white employees were sexually exploiting the enslaved women; they may well have been the carriers of the disease to the plantation in the first place. Another unremarked issue that rebounded on the enslaved women is that mercury poisoning, which was a frequent result of its overuse as a medicine against the pox, can also cause infertility. Venereal disease was indeed, as Sir Adam writes, 'baneful to Propagation'.

Some planters began to realise that the best way to improve the birth rate was to not treat enslaved people like unproductive animals, but rather as people in need of the normal care when having children. This had the added advantage of addressing a key complaint of the Christians in the abolitionist lobby. By 1790 baptism, marriage and edicts prohibiting physical violence against women, especially when pregnant, were being introduced by some planters. Joseph Barham at Mesopotamia in western Jamaica allowed Moravian missionaries on the estate and allotted time for religious observance. In 1807 Barham, as a member of the British parliament, backed the abolition of the slave trade.

In 1800 the Jamaican assembly stated that the way to end the 'immorality of Negroe Mothers' and their 'barbarous and heathenish persuasions many of which tend to the prejudice of natural population' was Christian instruction.[32] Sir Adam, while quick like many others to blame the enslaved women for the low birth rate and the spread of disease, does not suggest this solution. Nor did his more religiously-minded successor, Sir Charles Dalrymple Fergusson, the fifth baronet, though he was a busy church-builder in Scotland in the last decades of Caribbean slavery.

Abolition, gradually

Two events that would greatly affect the people at Rozelle happened back in Britain in 1792. One was the death, aged fifty-two, of Colonel William Hunter, Sir Adam's partner in the plantation.[33] Unmarried, he left his half-share to his brother James's son, David Hunter Blair,[34] along with the rest of his estate. David was then only fourteen. His father had died in 1785, and so a quartet of trustees was set up to manage his affairs, led by his relative, the old Jamaica hand Hugh Hamilton, now running matters from his home back in Ayrshire. Hugh was a co-owner of the Pemberton Valley estate, along with various Hunter and Hamilton relatives, including the Countess of Crawford. He would take much more of an interest in running Rozelle than did Colonel Hunter and knew the workings of sugar plantations much better than did Sir Adam.

The other matter was the peak of the first campaign for abolition of the slave trade. Sir Adam was well aware of the debate, both as an MP for Ayrshire closely allied to Pitt's government (which initially supported William Wilberforce's bill) and as a major landowner in the county. Two local Church of Scotland figures in his circle, the Kilmarnock minister John Russell and William Dalrymple, the moderator of Ayr assembly,[35] had come out as campaigning abolitionists. Petitions to do away with slavery were appearing in the Glasgow and Edinburgh newspapers.

Closer to home, the former business partner of Sir James Hunter Blair had also turned abolitionist. Sir William Forbes helped found the influential Edinburgh Committee for the Abolition of the Slave Trade. It was an interesting position for Sir William to take, given that the success of his and Sir James's bank owed a lot to their financing and servicing of Caribbean plantations and merchants.[36] Sir Adam was one of the bank's clients.

There is no record of Sir Adam speaking in Parliament or lobbying over the Wilberforce bill. But he must have taken an interest. His life-long friend and ally Henry Dundas (later Lord Melville) was home secretary at the time. Dundas is now seen by most historians as the principal villain of the 1792 slave trade abolition battle (though

his descendants hotly dispute this[37]). He was the most important lieu-
tenant of the young British prime minister William Pitt and a source
of patronage and influence so powerful he earned the nickname 'King
Henry the 9th'. He had no interest, unlike Pitt, in ending slavery. It
was an important source of tax revenue as well as the origin of the
wealth of many of his friends and allies: as a good politician his natural
interest would be to derail William Wilberforce's parliamentary
campaign while not tarnishing the reputation of Pitt, his master.

The West Indian planters and merchants formed a powerful lobby;
they are said to have bought a number of members of the British
parliament, while other MPs' own interests made them natural
defenders of slavery. By the 1790s half of Britain's trade was with the
West Indies and Americas. Industries from shipbuilding to iron-
smelting, textile-weaving and gun-making had boomed as a result of
the growth in the British slave trade: the businessmen behind them
were naturally against abolition.

The debate in the House of Commons was one of the most famous
in its history, the culmination of years of petitions, campaigning and
the sitting of a Commons committee to take evidence about the trade.
William Wilberforce, Charles James Fox – the leading star of the
Whig opposition – and Pitt, the prime minister, spoke fervently in
favour of abolition of the trade. The popular mood in Britain clearly
favoured the cause. But Dundas, ever the parliamentary pragmatist,
made an astute intervention. He said he agreed with the prime minister
and deplored the slave trade. But he proposed 'gradually' introducing
abolition, with 1796 mentioned as a possible date.

Dundas's amendment to the bill, which had no timetable attached,
easily passed the Commons, but was rejected by the House of Lords.
Nevertheless his gradualism became government policy, derailing the
abolitionist campaign for a decade. It is estimated that as a result of
Dundas's 'skilful obstructions', as the historian Hugh Thomas put it,
Britain took and shipped 583,000 more enslaved humans from Africa
during the next sixteen years, 300,000 to Jamaica alone.[38] Had the
abolition bill passed, other nations might have been inspired by
Britain's example. Nevertheless, Denmark, which had three small
sugar-producing colonies in the West Indies, abolished the slave trade
in 1792, and by 1799 seven American states had outlawed the trade
and slavery itself.

There is no record of Sir Adam's vote in the Commons in 1792.

But in 1796, when Wilberforce brought a further bill, Sir Adam was one of the MPs who voted against abolition of the trade.[39] This was crucial: the abolition side lost by only four votes. Wilberforce said that if a few of his promised supporters had not decided to go and see a new comic opera at Drury Lane that night instead of voting, the slave trade might well have been ended. He blamed this, and a subsequent defeat of a 1797 bill which merely tried to improve conditions on slave trading ships, on his friend the prime minister and the lobby – 'Pitt and the West Indians'.[40]

* * *

At the beginning of the parliamentary battle, Sir Adam writes to warn Cameron in Jamaica that a new bill is being put forward. He mentions the 'numerous petitions from all Quarters of the Kingdom' and the 'growing unpopularity of the Trade'.[41] As ever, he repeats his desire that more babies be produced. Then on 4 April 1792 he delivers news that must have been very welcome in Jamaica.

> [I] have now to inform you the result of that Proposition was a vote of the House of Commons carried by a great Majority, that the trade should be gradually abolished. The Proposition, as made, went to an immediate abolition: but in these terms, was rejected. The resolution as passt is in general satisfactory; at least to all those, among whom I profess myself to be, and always to have been one, who think that, a reasonable equality between the sexes being established, a proper attention being given to the Relief and ease of Women with child and especially care being taken [to prevent polyamory] there can be no reason to doubt that number may be kept up among the Negroes in the West Indies as among any other Human Creatures on the globe.

Thus using the bodies of enslaved people for breeding purposes becomes a philanthropic act, enabling the end of the slave trade. Sir Adam repeats his request for Murdoch to buy more young women as soon as possible, and notes that, should the trade be abolished in 1796, he does not want to be part of any flouting of the law. He finishes with a thought on the end of slavery itself:

Though I should hope there will be little Danger of Mistake on that head; yet to avoid any possibility of such an idea getting among the Negroes, I think it right to repeat that there is not an individual, either in or out of Parliament, who does not disavow the most distant thought of the enfranchisement of the Negroes already in the Island.

Cameron reports that he has been to Kingston several times to try and buy more female Africans at the market, without success. But more ships are expected and the price per adult is now over £80, excluding the duty to be paid on every African. Wilberforce's bill had the predictable effect of making 1792 a record year for British slave trading: more African people shipped, at a higher price, than ever before.

In mid-May Cameron is at last able to send the news his employer has been demanding:

Last month I purchased ten young women for the Estate, 7 at £83 and 3 at £81. The price is great but I am informed the next sales will even be higher yet as it is the general opinion the trade will soon be abolished, I mean if I can get as good choice to buy ten more.[42]

Cameron's downfall

Cameron's reign at Rozelle becomes more chaotic as the 1790s wear on. Senior enslaved workers, including Ned the head driver and Hugh the watchman, join an ever-growing list of runaways. Cameron accuses them of an arson attack on the cane fields and asks permission to get rid of them by shipping them off the island.[43] Then he does the same to one of the most valuable men on the estate, Cooper Tom, the maker of the barrels for the sugar and rum. The sugar harvest remains disappointing, and the costs of supplies requested from Scotland continues to rise.

The statistics reveal in plain terms the usual brutal cost in black human lives: two of the adolescent girls bought in 1792 are dead by 1794, while the annual birth rate stays the same, at just two surviving infants. Cameron is often ill and the estate is short of white staff – indeed the whole island is. He reports that the salaries of bookkeepers

– the usual entry job for young white men – have risen from £40 to £80. Hugh Hamilton and Sir Adam undertake to recruit three young men and ship them out.

Amidst this comes another security crisis. The free Maroons have risen up in arms, and all white men have to report to fight them with the militia. Cameron says he has no idea when the 'war' with them will end, though the governor has imported fifty Spaniards and a hundred bloodhounds from Cuba to hunt the rebels in the woods.[44] All this, but particularly his attacks of fever, combine to persuade Cameron that he wishes to give up the job. It is agreed that he will leave in 1797, after he has got the sugar crop done and the new white recruits 'settled in'.

Three young Scottish men – John Dick, William Campbell and James Cassels[45] – arrive, Cameron reports, in June 1797. He writes the letter a day after the death at fourteen months 'in consequence of teething' of Mary, his youngest child with Annie – though this is not a matter he mentions to the proprietors. But within two months the 'well recommended' Dick has been sacked. Why, we – and Sir Adam – don't know. Cameron is often hazy on the details: 'Suffice it to say he is a dangerous man.'[46]

You can almost hear Sir Adam's groans at this news, which is swiftly followed by the information that another of the young men, Campbell, has died. Sir Adam writes:

> You cannot be doubted to have good reasons for dismissing Dick; but their having been upon the whole of so little advantage to the Estate is vexatious . . . But there is no help for it. Where there is no neglect, there ought to be no regret.[47]

However, Sir Adam clearly suspects there is neglect, and that Cameron must shoulder some blame. John Dick was indeed to be 'dangerous', to Cameron. He had gone from Rozelle to Kingston, where he joined Ballantine's merchant and lawyering business. Ballantine was no friend of Cameron's and so it is no surprise that Dick wrote a damning report of his manager for Sir Adam and Hugh Hamilton. It must have arrived at the same time as the news that James Cassels, the third of the young men sent out, was also dead, with no cause given – 'a most discouraging circumstance',[48] comments Sir Adam. (Cameron merely writes asking for two more youths.) Meanwhile the crop again is poor. That turns out not to matter too much since the ship, the *Chance*, onto which it was loaded caught fire and sank.

Quite what the final straw was is unclear, but Cameron's time is over before his planned departure. Hugh Hamilton, David Hunter Blair's trustee, steps in: the suggested replacement is a twenty-one-year-old relative, George Hamilton, who has been working at the family's Pemberton Valley estate. The lawyer Ballantine, back in Ayrshire, persuades Sir Adam that, though 'he thought Mr Cameron to be an honest man, he thought the Estate very ill managed'.[49] Indeed, Rozelle 'is going to the Devil' and will be almost the only estate in the parish 'to make a bad crop this year'. Sir Adam writes to Hamilton giving his approval for the sacking of Cameron – 'notwithstanding my general Aversion to changes'. He cites Cameron's 'changeable Disposition' and, unusually, a suspicion that an enslaved worker has been unjustly treated.

> One Instance which took me with surprise in his letter dated Decr 22nd 1798 in which he writes that he had shipped off Cooper Tom on account of running away and other faults not specified. This shipping off, which I understand to mean selling him to a much harder Slavery, besides its loss to the Proprietors, would seem to require a high Degree of Guilt to justify the doing it. Yet this Cooper, Tom, I have all along understood to be one of the steadiest Men on the Estate and Mr Ballantine gives him an exceeding good character. This proceeding I cannot but reprobate, without some better apology than I have seen given for it.[50]

On taking over, the new manager George Hamilton finds a mess – the new men always do. But this seems grave. Buildings are still wrecked from the hurricanes of the 1780s, there are overgrown pastures, no 'hot house' (hospital), and the workforce is sick with sores and ulcers. Many of the enslaved people are 'superannuated'. Hamilton proposes more purchases, to bring numbers to 200.

The shipping-off of Tom clearly weighs on Sir Adam's mind. Eight months later he writes to Hamilton asking for news of the cooper:

I wish this poor man have not met with hard Usage, and should really be glad to know if he deserved what I understand to be a hard fate. I am affraid that, be the Answer to this Inquiry what it will, is too late to be of any use to him.[51]

'Poor man'? 'Hard fate'? These are terms not seen before. Is Sir Adam developing a concern for the well-being of his enslaved people that goes beyond the practical?

CHAPTER 10

SLAVERY MODERNISED

Children for sale

During Archibald Cameron's fourteen years at Rozelle he presided over some eighty deaths, far fewer births and – of most importance back in Scotland – little improvement in the size of the sugar crop.[1] The 1790s were the last great boom years of the British sugar industry in the West Indies. Yet by the standards of most Jamaican plantations, Rozelle underperformed. Cameron's tenure was not a success.

However, while running the plantation Cameron did accomplish one thing his proprietors continually demanded: he personally increased the birth rate. By the time of his sacking in 1799, the teenage house slave Annie had become the twenty-nine-year-old mother of four children by Cameron. They are Jean (sometimes called Jane), who is eleven, John (eight), Betsy (five), and Anna, who is two. Two more, Archie and Mary, died in infancy.[2] Annie's ostensible job, in the plantation rolls, is 'seamstress taking care of young children'. If accounts of other estates are anything to go by, she would have been as empowered as any enslaved woman could be. Her mother Jeanie was in a similar situation, as the 'favourite' of the estate carpenter John Moodie, and mother of several of his children.

While Cameron was in charge, Annie had a servant for herself: an enslaved man called Jack. She would have had money, possessions and some control over her and her children's existence. However, like any woman who had had to trade her body for safety and protection, her position was far from secure. She was totally dependent on the white men with whom all the real power rested. As she said goodbye, for ever, to Archibald Cameron in October of 1799, Annie was, for the seventh time that we know of, pregnant with his child.

The 'quadroon' (as they appear in the lists) children and their 'mulatto' mother were of course the property of the proprietors, Sir Adam Fergusson and (as he became in 1800) Sir David Hunter Blair.[3] No one knew that better than Archibald Cameron, who only a few years earlier had mediated John Moodie's purchase of two of his five children by Jeanie at Rozelle. It was Cameron who had told his proprietors that the custom was to ask the price of an adult male for each child, no matter how young.

In the meantime, that price had risen by more than 40 per cent,[4] and a woman with Annie's skills would be judged to be worth much more than an ordinary worker. Just before his sacking Cameron had bought nine 'new' African people for £100, while the price of a 'good seasoned slave' had risen to as much as £140 sterling. He could expect that freeing his family would cost at least £500[5] – nearly four times what his annual salary had been as manager, and equivalent today to around £600,000.[6]

Annie can only have been in terror at the prospects for her and the children when Cameron left. As the de facto wife of the most senior white man on the estate, she would have had privileges and security unknown to the other women, especially those who worked in the fields. Clearly that bred resentment. She had some hope of freedom for herself: although Moodie did not free the mother of his children, many white men did, either at retirement or at their deaths, buy manumission for their long-term 'concubines'. Even Thistlewood, the most monstrous of all the white overseers we know, purchased Phibbah, mother of his child, after he left Egypt estate, leaving money in his will to free both of them after his death.

Cameron could simply have gone to Kingston, taken ship for Britain and forgotten his Jamaican family. Many men like him did: the planter and author Robert Dallas wrote of the typical white father parting 'for life' from his enslaved offspring 'with as much indifference as with a pair of old shoes'.[7] But shortly after his return to Britain Cameron paid a visit to Sir Adam at Kilkerran, bringing with him various books and papers from Rozelle. This is the only record of Sir Adam ever meeting one of his Jamaica managers, but the encounter at the Fergusson family home is not so surprising. Archibald Cameron was what Sir Adam would have termed a gentleman, a cousin of the chief of the Clan Cameron, and so a social equal.

Sir Adam's meeting with Cameron was cordial. 'If hurt at being removed, [he] was guarded in his expressions about it', Sir Adam wrote to George Hamilton. More important, the sacked manager made an offer for all his Jamaican family: £100 each for Annie and the oldest child, Jean, and £50 for the younger three. He also offered £10 for the unborn child, should it live. According to Sir Adam's notes, he offers cash, paid in Ayr or Edinburgh. This total of £360 was certainly less than the market value, but a significant sum for the owners. Sir Adam agreed to put the proposal to Sir David Hunter Blair's trustees.

In May Sir Adam writes to Cameron with Hugh Hamilton's answer, as a trustee: 'Five prime Slaves will have to be delivered to the satisfaction of the manager at Roselle, for the Mother and the four Children.' He adds that the £10 offered for the unborn child will be accepted. Sir Adam gives half an apology: Hugh is 'so much more acquainted with the subject'.[8] A reply swiftly comes back from Cameron, who is now at his father's house, Fassfern in Lochiel.

> I would with pleasure agree to what Mr Hamilton proposes (in giving five prime slaves for the Mother and four Children) was it not that my circumstances is such that I cannot nearly aford it. I am much obliged for your kind intention and trouble.[9]

Adam passes this rejection of the deal on to Hugh Hamilton, with his own thoughts:

> Now I own it is not desireable to part with Slaves from an Estate underpeopled, I confess I should be much inclined to gratify a Man with respect to his own children and their Mother; especially as I suppose the Mother at least will never be of much use by her work upon the Estate. But in this I shall acquiesce in what you and the other Gentlemen who act for Mr Hunter shall determine. Let me know if I shall say any more to Mr Cameron, or let the matter drop.

Hamilton replies saying that there is a Mr Alexander in Maybole[10] (five miles from Kilkerran) who was permitted to liberate his daughter for £50 when he left Jamaica; 'Mr Ballantine and myself think it would be cruel to prevent Mr Cameron from getting his family and are willing to second Your humane intentions towards him and shall agree to what You think proper.'[11] So Sir Adam writes 'with pleasure' to tell Cameron he can have his family on the terms he proposed.[12]

But no more is heard from Cameron, for the moment. After waiting for a response, Sir Adam tells George Hamilton at Rozelle that the Cameron family will remain on the plantation after all, explaining that their father finds it 'inconvenient' to spare the money.

> Whether this is a matter to be pleased with or regretted I know not. The children may be useful upon the Estate, and probably will be so. But as to the Mother, I doubt if any woman who has been in the situation in which she was with Mr Cameron can be of much use to an Estate.[13]

The new manager George Hamilton writes back in September 1800 saying it would be better all round if Cameron's children were sold, since they will prove of little use.

> People of their description are by no means as valuable in my opinion to a property as negroes, they are in general Soft & only fit for House Servants, some of the Men answer tolerable well for Tradesmen but I would always prefer a good Negroe to any of them. Annie has done nothing since I came here, she begged very hard when I first took charge to allow her to hire herself & that she would pay any hire I might ask which I agreed to in consideration of the situation she had been so long in with Mr C. provided, she would get an able field Negro to work in her place . . .[14]

You cannot but ache for Annie, especially if, as seems likely, Cameron had assured her that she and their children would be rescued. George Hamilton's arrangement for her, which allows her to keep a little dignity and some freedom, does not last long. The reign at Rozelle of this unusually competent manager ends within months.

In June 1801, Hamilton announces that he is leaving to go to America. After several fevers his health is too precarious for him to risk it further in Jamaica. Sir Adam is very disappointed. From the beginning he has found the young manager much more acceptable than his predecessors – 'a man of business and a man of sense'.[15] Hamilton does indeed seem able to get a lot done with little fuss. He writes clear, concise letters too.

One feat of Hamilton's was the tracking down of Tom the Cooper. He had not yet been shipped off the island but was languishing in the Port Royal workhouse with another Rozelle worker also called Tom, the head carpenter. Despite Cameron having told him they 'led the other Negroes very much astray', Hamilton brought both Toms back to the plantation and their families – Tom the Cooper had seven children – where they did very well. 'I perceive there was almost a general disaffection' among the enslaved people in Cameron's time, says Hamilton mildly, adding he has decided to take no notice of what is past.[16] Tom's stint in the workhouse cost the Rozelle proprietors £16 and eight shillings.

Hamilton has also helped John Moodie conclude a deal to liberate the rest of his children, Sandy (nineteen), John (fifteen) and Nancy (ten). Again, the deal is good for the proprietors: 'four prime Negroes' – at a likely cost of £340 – for the three. It is fourteen years since Moodie first tried to free his offspring, but could then only afford to buy two of them. The price per child has now doubled. But the manumission of Jeanie, the children's mother, is not discussed and she is in effect abandoned, as we see the following year. In order to help Moodie, George Hamilton raises his 'very low' salary to £100 in Jamaican currency (£71 sterling).[17]

Sir Adam and Sir David will have good cause to miss George Hamilton, as will Annie and her children. His replacement is yet another of the Hamiltons' team in Jamaica. The outgoing George Hamilton sets off for Philadelphia with a cordial goodbye letter, though he notes that Sir Adam should be aware that the salary he has been paid is 'very low': 'most of the Overseers upon good Estates have £200 Currency [£142.85 sterling] & some Properties give more'.[18]

Bad overseer

The new man, John Ferguson – who spells his surname with a single 's' – must have looked ideal. An experienced Jamaica hand originally from Ayrshire, he has all the right family connections. He is the nephew of a distant cousin of the Kilkerran Fergussons, Captain Hugh Fergusson of Castlehill, who holds a military post in the town of Ayr and is an acquaintance of Sir Adam. These Fergussons are also linked by marriage to the Ballantine and Hamilton families. All most encouraging in the nepotistic world of Ayrshire-Jamaica plantation management.

Captain Hugh Fergusson writes from the Ayr barracks to Sir Adam to recommend his nephew, John: 'He is industrious and not without Capacity, and for his Integrity I would pawn my Existence on it.'[19] John is seeking plantation work because his merchant business in Kingston has gone bust. He has had six years' previous experience running his brother's stock farm near Bath, seven miles from Rozelle.

Sir Adam acquiesces on account of the general enthusiasm for John. (Sir David Hunter Blair, off serving with the Ayrshire militia, has again left the estate in Hugh Hamilton and Sir Adam's care.) But Ferguson seems a dubious choice from the start. He makes a bizarre error in his very first letter from Rozelle to Sir Adam, before his appointment has even been confirmed. It is a rambling account of the state of the plantation and the people on it. Ferguson finishes by saying how keen he is to be given the manager's job permanently, adding, 'The remuneration it is true is triffling, particularly on this property, but I have no doubt that would be taken into consideration.'

Mocking the promised salary seems foolish for someone still to be confirmed in a job, however well connected they are; though, as George Hamilton had pointed out, it was true that the salary was lower than average. Ferguson is, as the Scots say, mortified by his mistake. He writes twice more to apologise for this 'levity, which I cannot well account for . . . Rather unhappy, a degree of torpidity sometimes overpowers me, that exercise alone gets the better of.' His 'agitated state of mind' looks like depression. But then he again points out that the salary is 'indeed low'.[20]

None of this can have been encouraging. But before Sir Adam receives these letters, he writes to confirm that John has the job, with an Alexander McDonald under him. The 'triffling' salary is put up to £280 (£200 sterling) the following year.

* * *

In a story not short of monstrous people, John Ferguson joins the first rank. He must have been hell to work for. He is quarrelsome, paranoid and hypochondriac, given to mood swings and tantrums while his tone to his employers is nevertheless oleaginous and self-pitying. What troubles Sir Adam most, initially, is his prose: the proprietor prides himself on elegant precision in his writing. Ferguson, by contrast, seems wilfully obscure, incapable of putting his thoughts in reasonable order. Some basic punctuation would help. His first letter set the tone for the next ten years:

> I have suffered much ever since my residence on the Estate & I have been obligd to spend some weeks recently on my brother's Pen [livestock farm] near Bath and use the waters coming down here [Rozelle] once or twice a week since I have been able to ride I am much better altho' I would have staid longer if it were not for the severe continuance of the dry weather and a prevailing influenza among the Negroes which altho' very fatal to many we are as yett without loss but even now four prime people very low in it, yett as the desease is checked I have no doubt they will gett through.[21]

What adds to the annoyance is the minutiae he includes. As if to show his boss how diligent he is, every tedious detail of weeding and hole-digging is laid out in sentences that can wander on for eight or nine pages. Ferguson seems incapable of answering a question straight. Often they have to be asked more than once.

Since letters took two months or more to travel between Britain and Jamaica, a simple query like Sir Adam's 'Why have you not purchased as many females as I asked?' goes backwards and forwards for a year, without much of a resolution. Sir Adam writes to Hugh Hamilton in March 1803 complaining Ferguson is unaware that, in matters of business, 'good writing . . . consists in being as plain and clear as possible'.[22] In 1805, when Ferguson responds to Sir Adam's many complaints about his 'fine writing', the overseer is at his most Uriah Heep-ish: 'The want of simplicity in which recitals I am very sorry you have cause to complain of & by future attention thereto, I hope to evince my inclination to attend to your remarks . . .'

* * *

Despite any doubts about the new manager, Sir Adam and Hugh Hamilton go ahead with the expansion plan that George Hamilton suggested. They buy more newly shipped Africans in an attempt to get the workforce to 200-strong and the sugar crop to the 200 hogsheads much promised but only achieved twice in the previous twenty-five years. Twenty-four new enslaved people arrived at Rozelle in 1800 and 1801.

It was not the right time for these investments. The price of Africans from the Guinea merchants in Kingston was rising higher than ever in history. Between the 1760s and 1807 the quantity of sugar needed to realise the price of one new enslaved person increased by 150 per cent.[23] All the other costs – from shipping to stores from Britain – were rising as well. With the price gap between inputs and output yawning ever wider, the industry was in trouble.

Nonetheless, 1801 is a record year for the sugar crop. But there are outbreaks of diseases. The decade-old plan to increase the enslaved population by natural means is no nearer success. In 1803 only one woman becomes pregnant, and of four pregnancies in 1802 only one child survives.

Meanwhile Ferguson's problems with discipline in the workforce, free and enslaved, continue. His own temper is the cause. He is feuding with influential neighbours while losing workers at Rozelle faster than did Archibald Cameron. Sir Adam chafes: at delays in the arrival of plantation papers, at the failure to produce new babies or more sugar. Ferguson's expenses are extraordinarily high, and some-times silly: in 1803 he orders two dozen knives and forks to be sent out, and in 1804 asks for the same again. 'I should be sorry to suppose this Demand to be owing to want of care of these or other Household Articles',[24] comments Sir Adam, at his driest.

There are much graver problems. The enslaved workers run away or die. Between 1803 and 1810 the mortality rate at Rozelle is more than double what it was under Cameron's regime, and by the time Ferguson leaves the plantation in 1811 the population is 147, its lowest ever.[25] In 1803 one child is born and two die: a child called Debouch, of water on the head, a child called Johnie of dysentery. Adults succumb too: Cato of 'dropsy and rupture', Romeo of 'decay' and Adam from 'eating dirt'.*

Sir Adam, for the first time, starts to suggest his manager may be negligent. On the death of a teenage girl called Amba, he writes to

....
* A common problem among enslaved people on the plantations, often blamed on witchcraft and sometimes savagely punished. Soil-eating is now recognised as a mental health condition and known as pica. It is brought on by stress and emotional trauma.

Ferguson: 'That a person, tho' young, should die, is no wonder. But that a newly purchased Slave should die of Debility and a dreadful sore, does certainly bear the appearance of some oversight in the purchase.'[26] Meanwhile Ferguson is sacking the white staff, for various little-explained reasons.

Escapees

The runaways are another problem. John Ferguson is eager to consign them and other errant enslaved people to the magistrates' courts and the Kingston workhouse. As Sir Adam sourly points out, this is 'a punishment on the Master as well as on the Slave', since he has to pay a sizable weekly fee for their upkeep. Sir Adam's letters may be better expressed than Ferguson's, but they were by this point, especially when on the subject of producing enslaved children, increasingly cross and repetitious.

> The number of runaways so very much exceeding any former experience, as high as six, once eight, and for a considerable time five, is extremely unpleasant. You seem to say that you have hopes of providing a remedy for this evil. It is certainly very desirable to prevent it, if possible; and what I have the more at heart, by attention to pregnant women and proper accomodation for them as well as increased care in the Midwives, to promote the Birth of Children on the Estate a matter which I consider as of the first consequence.[27]

The runaways are extraordinary, as Ferguson had already blithely acknowledged: 'People so addicted to abscond, even though they have never been guilty of crimes either of a felonious or an atrocious nature'.[28] He writes that he has decided to punish all the enslaved people by taking away their weekly day off – the time they use for growing food and mending clothes. Meanwhile five senior enslaved people have been sentenced to a year in the workhouse.

The next news further raised eyebrows in Scotland. John Ferguson's feuding with his white neighbours came to a dramatic and absurd climax in a protracted battle that alienated the most important men in the east end of the island, the powerful plantation tycoon Simon Taylor and his friend, John Scott. They were Jamaica's Creole aristocracy, born to grand and wealthy planter families on the island.

Both men served as justices and members of the governor's council, which allowed them to use the title 'The Honourable'.

With their British connections, Taylor and Scott were key figures among the coalition of planters and merchants busy lobbying against abolition of the slave trade back in London. Scott, like Taylor, an old Etonian, was the owner of large estates and his father, the Rev. John Scott, had been president of the council, the body advising Jamaica's governor.

John Scott junior was notable for just the sort of lavish wealth and 'Creolean' moral licence which ordinary Britons were finding objectionable. He fathered twelve children in Jamaica by four women, three of them enslaved and one his English wife: the name Scott remains very common on the island today. He retired in 1804 and went, with his official wife and their three white children, back to Britain. In 1811, when he died, he left money to free and support those he had left behind: eight or perhaps nine Jamaican children and their mothers, Nanny, Jane and Mary.[29]

Scott and Taylor would have had every reason to dislike John Ferguson, beyond the detail that he was, socially, several rungs beneath them. Traditional plantation overseers and their brutal disciplinary methods were a danger to the West Indian lobby's campaign to disprove the abolitionists' contention that slavery in the British colonies was violent and cruel.

The cause of the row is ugly. It starts with the two senior enslaved women on the plantation who have had long relationships with white workers, the fathers of their children: Annie Cameron and her mother Jeanie.[30] It seems safe to assume that the two women are far from happy. Annie has been stripped of all the privilege – including having a slave of her own – that came with being the senior white man's 'concubine' for fifteen years. You imagine that she chafes under the bad-tempered rule of John Ferguson, and worries for her children's safety too.

Annie has been allowed to 'hire herself' out, paying £20 a year to the estate for this measure of independence. That may have irked Ferguson. They certainly do fall out, perhaps because Annie and Archibald's eldest daughter Jane, thirteen years old when Ferguson arrived, had caught his eye: we learn later that he has been harassing her, and may ultimately have impregnated her. Like his predecessors, he feels free to exploit the enslaved women for sex – he has at least

one child on the Rozelle plantation already. But making advances to
the acknowledged daughter of Archibald Cameron, an aristocratic
Scot, might be considered a step over a line.

Ferguson is at odds with the many other mixed race people on
the estate: he repeatedly asks Sir Adam for permission to sell them
all on the grounds that they cause trouble and do not work adequately.
He proposes using the money a mass sale would raise to buy 'fresh'
– newly shipped from Africa – young men and women between the
ages of eighteen and twenty-two.

In late 1804 Ferguson acts against Jeanie and Annie. They 'never
were corporally punished',[31] as he protests later, but he did imprison
mother and daughter in a room beneath the hospital building at
Rozelle. He also pulled down and burnt a number of the houses
belonging to the oldest enslaved people, whom he considers 'superannuated' and useless.

These events lead to a scandal that nearly brings John Ferguson
down. His long, ranting letter to Sir Adam explains it in a way that
cannot have reassured the owners at all. There has been – between
their manager and the enslaved people – a struggle for power.
Ferguson's account of the 'serious disorders' begins:

> It is of the family so long connected w/ Mr Cameron & Moodie
> whereby they for many years ruled over all with unbounded domi-
> neering sway have been the cause of many victims being shipt off
> & otherwise severely suffering. They viz. Jeanie & *Mulatto Annie*
> under the hopes of freedom for the family remained quiet for a
> time – disappointed however therein – their services called for –
> and power unchecked – villainous machinations were early at
> work . . .

Ferguson's accusations spew out, in no particular order. The women
have defied him, prevented 'harmony & welfare', encouraged the
enslaved workers to run away, harboured an escapee called Hector,
and used estate property to run a needlework business for profit. So
he put them in the underground 'cell', a quarantine room for Rozelle
workers with infected sores.

Ferguson overplays his hand. In a Jamaica tense at the prospect
of a new slave trade abolition bill coming back to the British parliament, such behaviour can only benefit the plantocracy's enemies. John

Scott is quickly told what Ferguson had done and so he goes to see his friend Simon Taylor, who was chief justice and the parish's assembly member, as well as its biggest landowner. Taylor is alarmed, his mind on the fight to keep tales of brutality out of the public eye. He writes to Robert Ferguson, John's brother:

There is a matter come to my ears this morning that gives me a good deal of uneasiness and I sincerely hope is not true. Mr Scott breakfasted with me, and informed me that there is a report in St Thomas in the East that there is a Mulatto woman at Roselle, who has been most severely punished about the loss of some young turkies that she is and has been for a long time confined in a cell or sort of Dungeon highly improper for any human being to be in, and unless the Woman is released that a Public Prosecution will be carried on.

Robert Ferguson is also a magistrate. The first thing he does is send Taylor's letter to his brother. John Ferguson has no difficulty discovering how this embarrassing report got to John Scott and the chief justice. The tell-tale must be a doctor called John Watson Howell, who had dropped in at Rozelle, where he was on contract, and been collared by the estate carpenter, John Moodie. He presumably begged for assistance for the mother of his children, a fifty-eight-year-old, now confined in a 'dark unwholesome cell'.

John Ferguson flies into a spectacular temper. He writes to Howell seeking satisfaction 'for your late active calumnies which you have with so much vindictive avidity propagated maliciously and falsely circulated that you have not even stopt to assert notorious falsehoods without even appearance or foundation'. Clearly Sir Adam's advice to write more succinctly has not got through.

Dr Howell is another member of the Creole elite, a planter in his own right who appears to have had unusually progressive views, for a white person, on the treatment of enslaved people, and his children by enslaved women. In 1799 a mixed race male who was probably Howell's child had been baptised, as was a two-year-old in 1823. Both were named 'John Watson Howell'. The doctor replies mildly to John Ferguson's furious note, saying that he had 'in the most friendly manner in my power' advised Ferguson at Rozelle to release the women he had imprisoned. The burning of the houses was something

John Moodie had told him about on that visit. 'I must say that I have neither maliciously, vindictively nor falsely propagated anything against you', he concludes.

This does nothing to soothe Ferguson. His next letter uses the word 'lie' – a nuclear weapon-like escalation at the time. Howell is forced to retract, partially, and so Ferguson decides to call out John Scott to satisfy his 'honor'. This marks the first step in the formal process that leads to a duel. Ferguson punishes Howell by sacking him as estate doctor.

John Ferguson had all this correspondence copied and dispatched to Scotland for Sir Adam's information. Sir Adam bound the bundle up with a note 'Copies of letters (of little importance) relative to Mr John Fergusson's [sic] dispute with Dr Howell 1805'. What must have mattered to him more was the insight into his employee's paranoia and aggression, laid out in the series of ranting letters. In them Ferguson insults everyone involved: Howell is 'vindictive and iras-cible', John Scott weak and followed 'by a train of sycophants', and everyone else has been 'vilely coerced' into betraying him.

But the matter is now out of John Ferguson's control. Ignoring the challenge, Scott as parish chief magistrate orders the release of Annie and Jeanie from the Rozelle cell. He has them brought to Morant Bay to be tried for the serious crime of harbouring runaways. When the hearing happens, Ferguson calls it 'a collusion of vindictive persecution' – of himself. The jury, he tells Sir Adam, was packed with Scott's 'own people', the enslaved witnesses were deliberately confused under cross-examination, and when the women were found guilty, they were sentenced 'only to a week's labor in the Workhouse'. Ferguson left the court in a rage, 'feeling more like the Culprit myself'.

He goes back to the plantation and vents his fury on the workers, white and enslaved. The issue he lights on is a deficit in the number of piglets. He decides the animals have been stolen and so sacks the junior bookkeeper, a young white man called Henderson, for his failure of oversight while Ferguson was away at court. He accuses the watchman, a senior enslaved man called Quashie,[32] of the actual theft.

Quashie denies the charge and so he is tortured: the only time in all the decades that such an act is retold to Sir Adam by a manager. Ferguson writes that he had Quashie 'put on a pickett'. This military punishment involves suspending the victim from a branch by his arms, with only a narrow peg driven into the earth for a foot to reach and take the body's weight. The word comes from the kind of metal stake the cavalry would drive into the ground to picket – or tether – their horses. Some planters – Thistlewood was one – used a standing bottle instead of a peg.

Quashie endures this until, eventually, he promises that if taken down he will show them 'something' in a hut – presumably the missing pigs. But when he goes off in the charge of another enslaved man Quashie takes his chance and runs off. Then Dr Vick, Howell's replacement, arrives. He is also a magistrate, and he tells Ferguson off for using the picket, which, Ferguson admits to Sir Adam, is not 'a usual method adopted', though he protests that this torture was more for 'intimidation than severity'. Quashie, as far as we can see, escapes and never comes back to Rozelle.

The only reason for John Ferguson telling Sir Adam all this – and at such self-pitying length – is that he must have thought that reports of his errors would get back to Britain by less sympathetic minds than his own. He was right. But Sir Adam, as ever, reacts cautiously to this torrent of disturbing news and refers the matter to Hugh Hamilton, as Sir David Hunter Blair's representative. Hamilton was a veteran of plantation management in Virginia and Jamaica, and knew the island's complex politics. He was a friend of Simon Taylor too. He tells Sir Adam that although he is certainly familiar with the problem 'of bookkeepers Ladies causing mischief and discontent amongst the Slaves', he cannot condone anything this manager has done. He is appalled.

I condemn decidedly Mr Fergusson using any punishment that is not customary, such as the Picket, which I never heard of amongst Slaves. His tedious vindication of his Conduct and the parly made against him, leave an apprehension of his not having acted with that propriety to be wished for, I therefore think it proper to act with Caution in giving him Power to ship of, the meaning of which certainly is a sale to the Spaniards. They may do with their purchase as they please knowing there must be a Crime to cause a Slave being shipped of . . .

I cannot agree to giving Mr Fergusson a power of selling the Mulatos. Their increase upon an Estate may be inconvenient, but selling them would be a Barbarity not to be even thought of. They like the place of their Birth, are attached to their relations and what crime can a Girl of thirteen have committed to be sold as a Felon I cannot allow myself to think John Fergusson means it and I presume it must be the Father who wishes to liberate his Child. . . . Every Master should be the Guardian and Protector of his Slaves. I should deem it dangerous to bring back both the Women mentioned, they might be sent to some other part of the Island without being treated with further severity.[33]

The thirteen-year-old Elizabeth turns out to be an object of Ferguson's own lust. For some time he has been telling Sir Adam that a 'Gentleman' wishes to purchase her, offering a 'Negroe man' in her place from the next ship to arrive from Guinea. Elizabeth has a surname – Stewart – and, unusually at Rozelle, has been baptised. She is presumably the offspring of another former white worker. Sir Adam balks at this cruelty, saying in his clumsy old bachelor's way that surely a teenager can be better looked after than like this.

For selling Elizabeth you do not so much as hint at a reason. I observe that girl to be about 14 and not past the age of being yet cured of such faults as she may have when freed from the bad Advice or bad example of her Mother. As to younger children, it surely may be no difficult task to train them to obedience and regularity if due pains are taken to that purpose.[34]

When Ferguson reveals to Sir Adam that he himself is the mystery 'Gentleman', he permits him to take possession of Elizabeth Stewart for £50.

It is surprising that Hamilton and Sir Adam do not dispense with John Ferguson in 1805. He is told pretty directly by Sir Adam that his account of the dispute with Dr Howell and John Scott is not credible. The letters cause Sir Adam 'real pain', and he refuses all of the measures Ferguson proposes – shipping off Annie and Jeanie 'to the Spaniards', and giving Ferguson blanket approval to sell mixed race people, or the increasing number of dirt-eaters. All this is done in consultation with Hugh Hamilton.

But the owners do not reprimand Ferguson. Rather the opposite: Sir Adam writes to placate him, insisting that he does not wish to 'imply a want of trust' in the manager. Perhaps Sir Adam and Hugh are mollified by the fact that the 1805 sugar crop, being harvested and processed just as all this is going on, is one of the largest ever. Ferguson is rewarded: his salary is increased again, and he is given charge of the Hamilton family's Pemberton Valley estate as well.

* * *

When he hears of Ferguson's imprisonment of Annie Cameron, Sir Adam's first act is to write to Archibald Cameron, to tell him that the mother of his children is now in the Kingston workhouse. Sir Adam points out, somewhat unnecessarily, that if Cameron had gone ahead with the purchase of Annie and the children as discussed in 1800 'this Mischief would have been avoided'. What would Mr Cameron like to do now, given that Ferguson has asked permission to have Annie sold and shipped off the island, as 'the ringleader and chief cause of the Mischief'? He would not wish to urge Cameron to 'an expence that may be inconvenient to you'.[35]

Sir Adam then writes to Hugh Hamilton, still acting for Sir David Hunter Blair, about the 'very unpleasant situation' at Rozelle, enclosing all the letters. He is worried about Annie Cameron: continuing to keep her in the Kingston workhouse is expensive, but the alternative is troubling:

> Mr Fergusson wishes, as you will see, to be allowed to ship off Annie (Cameron's favourite). I will be obliged to you for letting me know what is really meant by shipping her off. I have understood that it meant selling the slave so shipped to the Spaniards to be employed in the mines. If this is its meaning, I confess I could not bring my mind to condemn a woman to so horrible a condition. But perhaps I am mistaken in such a supposition and I wish to be set right by you.[36]

Some doubts are beginning to seed themselves in Sir Adam's mind. In the same letter he tells Hamilton that he does not approve at all of Ferguson's idea of selling all the 'troublesome mulattos', though he agrees to sanction the sale of Elizabeth. Archibald Cameron replies a month later.

I am much obliged to you for the trouble you have taken in acquainting me with this disagreeable business concerning Annie and Jeanie . . . If it is not too late may I request the favour not to ship Annie off the Island but to sell her to me. If she was shiped off her Family would alwise be discontented. This matter makes me really unhappy. I wish it may not originate with Mr Fergusson a friend of mine wrote me he was always plaging Annies daughter. [37]

There is no more correspondence with Cameron in the papers. But we know he did not rescue Annie.

* * *

Like so many others, Annie's story ends in doubt, but not well. Hugh Hamilton and Sir Adam Fergusson deem that the women should not be treated 'with further severity'. So neither she nor Jeanie are 'shipped off', but they are prevented, for the moment, from returning to Rozelle and their children. An agreement is brokered that they should not leave Kingston, and should pay the estate £20 a year – a large sum, nearly equal to the starting salary of young white bookkeepers.

This arrangement appears to have remained in place for a while in Jeanie Moodie's case. In 1811, aged sixty-four, she is listed in the plantation book as absent and 'hired out', but in 1817 she is back at Rozelle.[38] Annie, however, did return to the estate in 1808. She is listed in the books of 1810, a year when many of Rozelle's enslaved people died of a flu-like disease. In January that year she is thirty-nine, 'healthy and able', and her occupation is 'house woman'.

There are only glimpses of the fate of Annie and Archibald Cameron's children. In January 1811 the youngest, Anna, is thirteen, 'healthy and able' and employed in the overseer's house along with her sister Jean, now twenty-one. John, seventeen, is a servant and Bessy Cameron is sixteen and 'weakly, with yaws'. On 28 November 1811 Jean gives birth to a son: it may be that in her mother's absence she was no longer able to resist the 'plaging' of John Ferguson. The child, Annie and Archibald Cameron's grandson, was named John. Cameron remains a common surname in today's Jamaica.

If Ferguson did impregnate Jean Cameron, it may be because he had managed at last to win his long feud with her mother, Annie. He has been trying to get rid of her for six years. In December 1810 he presents Sir Adam and Hugh Hamilton with a fait accompli: Annie has been tried, sentenced and transported off the island. Explaining this act – which they had expressly forbidden five years before – he writes that after her return to the plantation in 1808 she had recommenced her 'usual machinations'.[39]

Ferguson's turgid account does not make clear what these might have been. He accuses Annie and 'Doctor Allan, Her chief instrument and colleague' of having something to do with the deaths of William Brown and Pero, two elderly enslaved men, in the flu epidemic that devastated the people at Rozelle that year. Annie and Allan were tried in the Court of Session in October 1810. There, reports Ferguson, 'it was fully proven to the satisfaction of the Court, that they had spared no pains in creating discontent among the negroes in general and depressing the minds of those unhappily ill, who fell, fatally, under their particular attention, which added to the prevailing epidemic was severe indeed. They were sentenced for Transportation.' He adds that, while in court, Annie admitted her guilt in the 1805 case when she was tried with Jean Moodie, her mother. The magistrate who tried the case was, predictably enough, John Ferguson's brother Robert.

John Ferguson must have enjoyed this victory and may well not have cared too much about his flouting of Sir Adam and Sir David's instructions: he had decided he had had enough of managing Rozelle and Pemberton Valley. In 1812 Ferguson quit both jobs to run his own plantation, bought with his earnings. Jean Cameron, with baby John, was left at Rozelle. She died there in 1821.[40]

CHAPTER 11

THE END OF THE BRITISH TRADE

A superannuated planter

As the nineteenth century began, Sir Adam was ageing. He complains frequently of his gout and bowel afflictions; he has trouble with his teeth and then with the dentures (made by a celebrated physician in Paris) that replace them. Retired from Parliament in 1796, he is still busy, though he seems less certain in his dealings with the plantation and its problems. His concern as his eighth decade begins is to put his Scottish estates in good order for the nephew he has designated his heir – James, his brother Charles's son. Another project is a legal challenge to obtain the title Earl of Glencairn for succeeding Fergusson generations.

Sir Adam writes twice a month or more in this period to 'dear James'. This favoured nephew had returned from Calcutta, aged thirty-two, in 1797, in order to marry and prepare to take over as head of the family. The letters are kindly, full of advice on life, the management of money, health, friendship and so on. There is some political gossip (James's account of the scandal around Lady Hamilton's adultery with Admiral Nelson raises Sir Adam's eyebrows in 1804). Sir Adam's letters often end with 'love to the little ones', about whose health he worries. There is little talk of business and none at all of slavery or sugar.

The letters show a warm side of the man that is not, naturally enough, evident in any of his business correspondence. The family appear to love him back; they can laugh a little at him. In 1803 his sister Helen, Lady Hailes, writes to her nephew and son-in-law James warning that Sir Adam may be lonely: he has invited all the family to visit Kilkerran. Will we 'ever get away?', she wonders: 'Sir Adam seems to wish and expect never to be left alone and certainly it will be the duty of some of us to be always with him.'[1] His sister Jean was indeed always with him until she died in 1804.

Sir Adam can be passionate, too, in pursuing the righting of a perceived wrong, either to the family or to those less fortunate whom he deems worthy. This tendency appears once or twice in the Jamaica letters, but only on behalf of his white workers, such as the ploughman David Dunbar. He died after a few years' work at Rozelle, and left £40 to his mother back in Ayrshire. Sir Adam is furious when he discovers that the Jamaican executors have not paid the sum to 'this poor family' and pesters until that happens. Compassion for the enslaved people is conspicuously lacking, by contrast, beyond the very occasional qualms he expresses about separating families.

Seen through the letters to his family and to friends like George Dempster, it is not easy to square the Sir Adam they knew with the plantation proprietor. He is a man of moral codes, of course, and keen that these should be observed – and imprinted early. Writing about his three-year-old great-nephew, the subsequent fifth Kilkerran baronet Charles Dalrymple Fergusson, an 'uncommonly sensible boy for his years', he warns 'no opportunity should be let slip of impressing upon him the importance of virtuous and honourable conduct, and the meanness of vice and its ruinous consequences'.[2]

He also refers to the Bible and to God, themes that do not appear in the decades of correspondence about Tobago and Jamaica. Here he is, in September 1799, discussing an intimate matter with his heir and nephew, thirty-four-year-old James, whom he describes as his 'friend':

> That you should marry you would naturally have conceived to be my wish, even though I have not said so on the first serious Conversation I had with you at Kilkerran. That your choice should have fallen on one in whom I have such concern and whose Happiness I must naturally have so much at Heart, cannot but be satisfactory to me I have only to pray that it may have God's blessing along with it; and that you may both enjoy all that Happiness which your best Friends can wish you.

The bride-to-be was Sir Adam's niece and James's first cousin, Jean Dalrymple of Newhailes: her father Lord Hailes had married Adam's sister Helen. They were married, and the next heir, another Charles, was born eleven months later.

The letter goes on to address what sum Sir Adam – who is already paying James an allowance of several hundred pounds a year – should 'settle' on Jean should James die before her. James is planning to join Sir David Hunter Blair, Rozelle's co-owner, as an officer in the Ayrshire militia, in charge of southwest Scotland's sea defences as the wars with the French continue. It is an important job, but it pays little. In the event of James's demise, Sir Adam says that he will be very ready to make a 'reasonable' settlement for Jean. Then he goes on to address, delicately, the couple's needs 'while you are both in life'. It all depends, writes the rich uncle, on what he, James, 'can do for Yourself'.

> Do not scruple at speaking openly to me. I shall neither think the less of you for the low state of your Finances, if they are low, persuaded as I am that they did not become so by your own Fault; nor the more on the account of their being otherwise. What I can afford from mine, in consistence with the very considerable load of debt under which I still am . . . is, as in all such cases, much less than you have been led to believe.[3]

Whether this teasing note confounds the hopes of James and his bride is unclear. James's own father, Charles Fergusson, would not have been of much use financially: he had twice gone bankrupt and been bailed out by Sir Adam. Jean Dalrymple's family was wealthy: she had £1,500 settled on her by her father, Lord Hailes. But the marriage contract specified that was to be hers and her children's, not her husband's.

Despite the 'load of debt', within a year Sir Adam increases James's annual allowance to £800.[4] He grants several hundred a year to each of James's two unmarried sisters, as well as £250 for his own brother Charles's maintenance.[5] James and his new wife rent a house in London,[6] and buy one in Charlotte Square, the most gorgeous of those being constructed in Edinburgh's New Town. It is now part of the residence of Scotland's first minister.

* * *

It is not clear that Sir Adam's debts were so large that he was only able to pay off the interest rather than the capital, as he implies to James. It was quite normal at the time to borrow huge sums of money to invest, and many of Sir Adam's acquaintances were operating their colonial enterprises in this way. That was in part inevitable, since promissory notes were the principal way of doing business in a cash-poor economy thousands of miles away.

On average the Rozelle plantation paid rather less in the 1800s than it had in the previous two decades chiefly because of a succession of poor harvests and a drop in the price of sugar. The estate was always in debt to Jamaican merchants. Sir Adam had financial problems, even if just in terms of cash flow. In 1801 he had to borrow £700 at short notice from the Hamilton family's bank, a need he blamed on a shortfall in the expected income from Rozelle, which that year had shipped only thirty-five hogsheads of sugar.

Meanwhile inflation had risen sharply, along with other expenses. Richer Britons paid an income tax from 1800, Sir Adam among them.[7] In 1805 he challenges a tax demand with 'a very mistaken idea of the Income of Rozelle Estate for 1803'.[8] That had been an excellent year in sugar crop: Sir Adam's pre-tax share of the profit was £1,137. In 1805 his share was £1,352. This was the highest it ever reached, but the next year, with sugar prices falling, the share was £532, and in 1807 the proprietors earned nothing.[9]

The novelist William Beckford, son of one of Jamaica's most successful planters, saw his annual income from the island fall from more than £100,000 to £30,000 by 1805.[10] Nevertheless, in 1807 he knocked down Fonthill Splendens, the Palladian mansion his father had built, and replaced it with his own neo-Gothic construction, Fonthill Abbey. In that same year Rozelle made its first overall loss since the 1760s, chiefly because of low sugar prices. The tax records show just how much the British exchequer benefited from the sugar and slave plantations. The duties on sugar and other imports from the West Indian colonies alone provided an eighth of the exchequer's income in 1807: the economic historian Kenneth Morgan believes the assets in the sugar colonies enabled the government to borrow the money necessary to finance its part in the Napoleonic Wars.[11]

Between 1809 and 1811 the value of the sugar processing works on the Rozelle estate were taxed at 2.5 per cent and each enslaved person at 5 per cent, netting the government £2,429 from the plantation in the three years. That is around the cost of building and outfitting a transatlantic merchant ship. The two proprietors' average annual profit in these years after these taxes and the 20 per cent sugar tax was £1,447 – on which they then paid income tax and a 5 per cent West Indies property tax, based on the value of the crop. Thus Sir Adam and Sir David's annual net profit in the 1800s averaged at £608 each – a little less than it had been in the 1780s. But between 1780 and 1810 inflation halved the purchasing power of the pound.

The end of the British slave trade

The reason for the rise in the price of enslaved African workers was the abolition, at last, of the slave trade. On 25 March 1807 the bill for which Wilberforce, Thomas Clarkson, Hannah More, the freed men of the Sons of Africa and thousands of ordinary people had argued, for so long, came into law. It banned the import of slaves to British colonies from Africa and made it illegal for British ships to transport them.

While British people were long taught to see this as an exceptional national triumph – the showing of the way to the rest of the world – a more sober view of the history deflates that claim. The revolutionaries who took over France had stated the equality of all people back in 1789, inspiring the successful uprising in St Domingue, now Haiti. Denmark-Norway had banned the trade in humans in 1792. All the northern states of America had banned not just the trade but slavery itself by 1804. Britain, by contrast, had outlawed only the transatlantic trade. The plantation owners and traders were free to continue it in and between the Caribbean colonies for twenty-seven more years.

Banning the transatlantic trade was expedient. By 1805, no British political administration could have defended it longer and survived. As Sir Adam wrote in February 1807 to Rozelle's manager, John Ferguson, 'the voice of the Country was very much in favour of this Prohibition'. Abolitionist MPs were elected in large numbers in 1806, and the prime minister Lord Grenville, a Tory, led the legislation through Parliament, determined to end a practice he called 'contrary to the principles of justice, humanity and sound policy'. The bill's second reading was passed by 283 votes to 16.

Sir Adam's letter alerting John Ferguson to the likely outcome of the abolition bill puts another light on this move towards emancipation. The establishment had no interest in ending slavery itself, he implies, stating that the government ministers who supported the bill in Parliament had been persuaded that the slave population could be kept up by 'breeding'. 'I have no reason to believe this to be the case', comments Sir Adam, speaking from long experience, in the same letter from February 1807.*

Nevertheless, he goes on, he wishes Ferguson to buy two or three more 'young and healthy' females, in addition to the five they have already agreed to buy annually: 'It is plain that if a West India Estate, as the Law will now stand, is at all to be supported and not, in a very few years, sink to nothing, it must be by breeding; and that cannot be if the Females are not kept up in numbers.'[12]

Ferguson's next letter, in June 1807, told Sir Adam that the price of newly arrived Africans was now up to £120 or £125, but the supply was good because of a lack of money in Jamaica: he thinks he should buy ten or twelve young women for the estate. He had bought seven men in February but by August there is 'a great deficiency of females'.[13] Come December he is fretting over getting no instructions about the proposed purchase from Sir Adam, but it seems the letters telling him to go ahead had gone missing in a ship captured by the French.

* * *

The Abolition of the Slave Trade Act set a deadline of the end of December 1807 for the last importation of enslaved Africans to the Caribbean colonies from Africa. But it was to be some time before the ban was properly enforced. Modern research has shown that many enslaved Africans were still being shipped to Jamaica and other colonies in 1808 and later, while some British slave trading ships simply swapped flags.[14] Trade in enslaved people in and between the British Caribbean colonies continued and it was ten years before the Royal Navy began devoting significant resources to policing the Atlantic between Africa and the Caribbean. Until 1815, the West Africa Squadron had just two small ships devoted to stopping slaving vessels.

....
* He was not wrong. The enslaved population of Jamaica was to decline by 10.8 per cent between 1808 and 1834.

John Ferguson appears to have broken the new law, on his proprietors' behalf. The last legal voyage of a British slave-trading ship,
said to have been the *Kitty's Amelia*, was on 27 July 1807.[15] It landed
a cargo of 233 enslaved Africans in Kingston in January 1808 (forty-
four died en route, along with twenty-three of the crew). Ferguson
paid £830 for some newly arrived Africans – it is not clear how many
– in Kingston sometime between January and May 1808.[16]

It is possible that details of the transaction were removed because
of the illegality of it. In May 1808 Sir Adam writes encouraging
Ferguson once again to buy females. Ferguson responds that he has
waited 'as long as prudence could advocate' for instructions. But now
it is 'really impossible' to buy the three or four extra Sir Adam had
requested.[17] It was of course also against the law, if the newcomers
were directly from Africa: but that is something Jamaican proprietors
– and the island's government – appear to have openly flouted. If
true, the purchase would have been a risk to Sir Adam's reputation
in Britain. As he knew well, gossip made it back from the Caribbean
very quickly.

By 1808 the estate is very short of able workers, a fact Ferguson
has kept back from Sir Adam. The latter was horrified when his copies
of the 1806 and 1807 plantation books, the day-by-day account of
activities, births and deaths, arrived in Scotland in September 1808.
In 1806, seventeen enslaved people had died and fourteen more in
1807, three times the usual toll. 'I have never known the Negroes so
unhealthy', John Ferguson had written in 1806.[18] Sores and venereal
disease were still rife; there had been more runaways.

We only have the names of a few of these dead: Dovetail 'by
worms', Hector in a fit, Leticia after a tree fell on her in a storm,
Eboi after complaining of a pain in the head, Auckie of a 'vermin'-
infected wound on his head, and Cecquin 'in the course of nature'.
An unnamed man and woman drowned after falling in 'the muck
pitt', along with another enslaved man owned by John Ferguson
himself. The only sadness the manager expresses in his letter detailing
this terrible toll is over the loss of one of the white workers, John
McDonald. He died 'of the bottle'.

'It is really painful to read', writes Sir Adam in 1808. Thirty-one
dead in two years, a sixth of all the population as it was at the beginning of 1806. It is like a 'plague or pestilence'. As ever, it is not clear
to what extent his hurt is at the human cost or at the financial pain.

But he is angry, and the scale of the carnage inspires him to comment for the first time about the arguments of the abolitionists, and the unjust fate of the 'poor creatures' he has imported from Africa. He still blames them, though, for the 'scene of Mortality . . . proceeding in great measure, from the vice and irregularity of the poor creatures themselves'. Nevertheless, the death toll makes him 'melancholy'. He comments to Ferguson:

> This state of things, if it had been fully known and attended to by the enemies of the Slave trade, would, in my opinion, have furnished them with a strong additional argument against a Trade, the effect of which was to bring men from a situation in which they probably enjoyed health at least, to such a state of corruption, disease and Death.[19]

CHAPTER 12

DECLINE, DISGUST AND DEATH

BY 1810, SIR ADAM FERGUSSON seems weary of the business of being a West Indian slave owner. The word 'disgust' appears frequently in the letters as he approaches his eightieth year. The death toll from disease and accidents seems now to horrify him. So, of course, does the usual run of disappointing sugar crops.

Perhaps something of the public mood was affecting him. The 'West Indians' had not only lost the vote on the slave trade, they also found their customers turning on them. In most of Britain now, to be a planter or beneficiary of a fortune made in the West Indies was not quite disgraceful, but it was definitely questionable. The country was addicted to sugar – consumption per person had quadrupled since the beginning of the eighteenth century – but some households now bought it from the East Indies, where it was said to be produced without enslaved labour: a forerunner of today's Fairtrade labels.

The promised good effects of abolition of the trade on lives at the plantations were not yet apparent. Reports by visitors – Baptist missionaries and anti-slavery campaigners – told of workers not treated better, but rather worked harder because of financial problems and labour shortages. Unrest continued, not least because many enslaved people could see the signs that their masters' star was falling: emancipation must be achievable. The advance of Christianity in the islands was a threat to the old order, too, since with it came some education and the notion that in the eyes of God white and black were equal. Many planters and overseers were actively hostile: stories of church burnings and harrassment of missionaries made their way back to Britain.

Sir Adam and Sir David Hunter Blair's profit from the plantation was now half, in real terms, what it had been thirty years earlier, not enough even to cover the annual allowance Sir Adam was giving to his nephew James. A thousand pounds a year, as that was by 1810, was not seen as much in terms of what a gentleman and family of the time needed. Jane Austen's *Pride and Prejudice*, published in 1813, features two wealthy men, Mr Bingley and Mr Darcy, who have incomes of £4,000 to £5,000 and £10,000 a year respectively. Sir Adam concedes to James that while the £1,000 is insufficient for the keeping of a coach, horses and coachman, his heir might be able to afford the coach alone and rent horses and a coachman as needed.

In 1810 there occurs the worst disaster in all of the eighty years of Fergusson-Hunter Blair ownership of Rozelle. Twenty-two of the 175 enslaved people living on the plantation in January that year are dead by December, thirteen of them in just three months. The chief cause is described as 'epidemia pleurisy & sore throat': it kills William Brown, the head driver, as well as Quaco, Leah, Jean, Queen, Henry, Matty, Lucretia, Rodney the distiller, Mulatto David the shepherd, Celia the cook, Lucky the washerwoman, and Fema, an elderly woman in charge of 'hogsmeat and children'.

Also among the toll of the dead for 1810 are Felix, who died of a liver complaint, Dick, of lockjaw, Pero the head cooper, and Agnes, a new mother (both of 'burst blood vessels'), Old Pope of 'old age' (he was seventy), Parthenia in childbirth, and the watchman Bacchus after falling into a cistern. Two children died: four-year-old Beck, of 'worms dropsy', and Monimia, thirteen months old, from 'fitts'. In the year just two children are born, to Agnes and Susannah. Agnes died a week after giving birth.

Sir Adam is very distressed when he finds out about the deaths, nearly a year later.

I certainly was not prepared for such a Destruction as this, which has carried off so prodigious a number and among them many that appear to have been valuable Slaves. How the Estate is to go on under such losses I do not know . . . In short, I see the whole matter in so infavourable a light as nearly to disgust me of the business. That Disgust is certainly not lessened by seeing the total disappointment of that hope which I long entertained, if not of keeping up the number by breeding at least of lessening loss by

Deaths. How vain in that hope I was is plain when I see that of 4 only born in 1809, two are since dead, and only two born in 1810, and one of them dead. In short the account seems that of an Infirmary or Hospital rather than that of the ordinary state of human life . . . I have no more to add. The alarming decaying state of the Slaves is so painful that I can hardly submit to write upon anything else.

Nonetheless, he does write a little more: after years of disappointment in the state of the sugar and preserved fruit sent annually to Kilkerran from Rozelle, 'the Ginger now sent home is at last such as I wished, such as I can with pleasure bring to my table'.[1]

Sir Adam and Hugh Hamilton start to discuss dispensing with John Ferguson. They commission contacts in Jamaica to pick up what news they can of him. Ferguson, getting wind of this, is enraged. He writes to Sir Adam complaining of enemies who send false reports of his work and conduct, and wondering if Sir Adam blames him for 1810's death toll. If so, he will quit managing both Rozelle and the Hamiltons' Pemberton Valley. Sir Adam responds meekly, insisting 'I have always been satisfied with your conduct' and begging Ferguson to stay on.[2]

Nevertheless, by November 1811 the proprietors are faced once again with finding a new manager. They dispatch another Hamilton, Alexander West Hamilton – known as Sandy – to take temporary charge since John Ferguson is determined to leave by the next available boat. The charges against him, writes Hugh Hamilton, 'seem to have given him a permanent Disgust to the Island'.[3]

That isn't quite the end of the story of John Ferguson. He was without doubt the most brutal – and, more important to the proprietors, the least productive – of all the managers they employed in these five decades. Sandy Hamilton, who had run the Hamilton plantations in Jamaica in the 1780s and 1790s, knew John and had fallen out with him before quitting Jamaica on health grounds in 1800. He knew Rozelle, too, for it had been owned by his brother Archibald until 1764.[4]

When Sandy Hamilton returns to Jamaica in April 1812, his friends tell him that both plantations are disasters. Hamilton reports 'the most shocking instances of Cruelty to Negroes' at Pemberton Valley and the animals starved. He hears that no white staff remain at

Rozelle: Ferguson has sacked two overseers and his bad temper has caused the others to leave. This has meant spending more than £600 on hired labour to service the sugar canes. More serious offences may have been committed: an acquaintance of Hamilton's had spoken to him on the mass deaths of 1810 at Rozelle: 'I said I was informed that was owing to a particular disorder which had been fatal generally thro' the Parish; he said that this was not the cause of the mortality to the extent that had taken place.'[5] He is referring to venereal diseases, which appear at this time in lists of dead Rozelle enslaved women as 'Lues Venerae'.

Sandy Hamilton writes a full account of what he finds when he gets to Rozelle. He reports on the situation and health of the enslaved workers first. His findings are not good at all – 'twenty or thirty' had run away in the last days of Ferguson's rule, taking shelter with a Mr Graham in Kingston, but since receiving assurances they had all returned, including two consigned by Ferguson to the workhouse. Their complaint was that Ferguson had destroyed their houses in retaliation for them taking straw from the cane fields to repair their roofs. Hamilton believes them and says he has proof they have been 'very ill treated and disatisfied'.

> The greatest neglect however in Mr Fergusson's management was the total want of care and attention to the comforts of the Negroes; his temper is such that he not only deprived [them] of the necessary comforts, by what I have already mentioned respecting their houses, but he had previously pulled down all the fences round their gardens, and ordered the cattle to be driven thro' them. The gardens round their houses I consider to be one of the greatest comforts they have, as they can always have something in them to help to subsist, particularly in time of crop, when they may not find it convenient to go as far as their Provision Grounds. As to the latter, they have been entirely neglected and I was extremely mortified on going thro' them to find they were almost destitute of Provisions.

He goes on to list John Ferguson's other crimes. 'His conduct to [white staff] was such that no decent man could live with him';[6] at the last sugar cane harvest there was no white person at all on the estate, and Ferguson was often absent looking after his brother

Robert's business. So, quite apart from the lack of food, everything is a mess, from the inside of the great house where the manager lives, through to the collapsing walls of the sugar refining works. Though all the 149 enslaved people have returned on the estate, Sandy Hamilton thinks they are too weak from ulcers and want of food to do the work needed to get the cane crop going again. Besides, they need to get their own provision grounds back in order. On top of everything, John Ferguson has taken the estate records and accounts books with him. No one knows where the 1811 sugar crop was dispatched.

Sandy Hamilton hires a new overseer. He gets the buildings repaired and hires gangs of day labour to tackle the crop fields. He orders tools, building materials and ten barrels of herring to be sent out from Scotland. Then, in October 1812, a storm hits the estate. It is severe enough to rip the replanted canes from the ground and blow down the plantain trees.

Sir Adam's response is delayed till the last day of 1812: the ship carrying Hamilton's first letters was taken by the Americans, with whom Britain went to war again in June. The letter is rambling. It compliments Hamilton on as 'complete and satisfactory a detail of business' as he has ever seen – a relief, you imagine, after a decade of John Ferguson's wafflings. He digresses into a long account of what a proprietor expects from a manager – 'good temper, punctual information' – and then gets to the distressing news.

> The account which you give me of the Negroes and the number of them diseased with sores is unpleasant. This is a matter which I have frequently remarked with pain, and that pain is not lessened by your saying that the number in that condition is greater than usual upon Roselle Estate. My wish has always been that every attention should be paid to render the situation of these poor people as comfortable as possible and it pains me to think that there should have been so much inattention to that object from Roselle. One thing that I have more frequently written about than any other to every person successively in the management of the Estate is the care of the young children and their mothers, at those times when care is particularly necessary for them. Not only humanity but attention to the interest of the Proprietor demands a care of this kind; and it has been a constant matter of regret to

me to get a list of Deaths more or less numerous, and to see not above two three or at most four children born, and of these perhaps one half dead before they were a year old, and this out of near to 80 female Slaves. I am afraid that this is an evil for which a cure is not readily to be expected.[7]

This is almost the last letter Sir Adam writes to Jamaica. Not much in him has changed, in the forty-three years he has managed Rozelle. His obsession with increasing the population of the estate by breeding has not abated, despite the failures. While in recent years he has used words like 'pain' and 'disgust' to describe his feelings about the suffering of people enslaved at Rozelle, there is no indicator of any shift in his belief in the morality of the business. His guiding principle of management by balancing 'Humanity and attention to interest of the proprietor' has not been shaken, despite the long succession of years in which its essential impossibility has been brutally revealed.

There is no good proprietor of a farm of enslaved people. There were better ones than Sir Adam and his Hunter Blair partners, and worse. 'Age had not diminished his shrewdness or his realism', wrote my grandfather, who never in any of his writings mentions the Fergussons' Caribbean interests, about his great-great-great-uncle's last years.[8] But, equally, age had not allowed Sir Adam to see more than faintly the devastation and horror his enterprises in the Caribbean had caused, and would continue to cause for many years more.

Sir Adam is now a few months from death. After a life busy with travel, he has done his last 'tour', to Ireland in the summer of 1812 to see the Giant's Causeway. His niece Christian Dalrymple went with him, and shortly afterwards his brother Charles's daughter Kitty moved to Kilkerran to look after the grand old uncle. He paid her an allowance of £800 a year.

His final note to Rozelle and Sandy Hamilton, in August 1813, is dictated. He is too unwell to write. It acknowledges that the year's crop will be 160 hogsheads of sugar, now being shipped to Glasgow. Sir Adam is grateful: 'the prosperous situation of the Estate . . . cannot but be agreeable'.[9] Because of war with the French, the price of sugar was briefly back to the highs of the 1790s, which must have been agreeable too. That was not to last.

Sir Adam's life came to an end as the ultimate decline of the Caribbean sugar economies was just beginning. On 25 September 1813, aged eighty-one, he died at Kilkerran. Most of his famous contemporaries and friends were already gone. 'We have few such men among us', wrote one memorialist. Sir Adam 'almost seemed to belong to another age, and another state of society, more perfect than that we live in'.[10]

* * *

The toll

The cost in human terms of the years that Sir Adam Fergusson ran the Jamaican estate for the Fergussons and Hunter Blairs can only be estimated. There are records of the enslaved people in the form of inventories or lists in the plantation books for twenty of the forty-three years. But we know from the books and from some managers' letters of the deaths of at least 154 enslaved people in that time. The worst casualty rate in one year was twenty-two, in 1810, the year of the flu epidemic. It is rare to find a year with no deaths.

Applying the average of 6.65 people dead per year to the years not covered by the records gives a total of 285 or more enslaved people dying at Rozelle in the period 1769–1813. (Ten free white employees died, as far as the record tells.) Sixty-five per cent of the enslaved people died from disease or 'old age', the rest in accidents or by unspecified causes. This death rate is in the normal range for Jamaican plantations at the time. It is about five times the current death rate in Jamaica and the United Kingdom today.[11]

Infant deaths are rarely noted in the books. Of the deaths of older children that were recorded, 85 per cent died of disease – most often of worms, 'teething' and unspecified fevers. Across Jamaica, fewer than 50 per cent of children born into slavery survived to be adults, which is perhaps twice the mortality rate among children born in early nineteenth-century Britain.[12]

So, leaving the unrecorded dead infants aside, the death toll comes to nearly 300. Beside that account we must put the 319 human beings, 150 of them newly arrived from Africa, bought from slave traders and other plantation owners and put to work at Rozelle. At least ten born on the estate were sold, either to their white parents, or to labour elsewhere. Some were transported as punishment to unknowable fates on other islands. These ruined and anguished lives are the true cost of the modest income – in terms of their overall spending – that came to the Fergusson and Hunter Blair families from their estate in Jamaica.

Some of the people who died are listed below. The names are of course usually those attached by the men who bought and sold them.

The 146 enslaved people of Rozelle estate whose names and deaths are recorded, 1769–1811, in chronological order. Causes of death are from the plantation books or managers' letters.

Women and girls

Luanda, 'Lethargy'

Taditha, 'a smallpox'

Parthia, 'Child bed'

Belinda, 'with Asthma and Age'

Mantunba, aged seventy-seven

Betty, 'fever'

Penelope, 'superannuated'

Amey, child, 'in the Yaws'

Dido

Eve, 'a Pleurisey'

Deborah, 'in Child bed'

Fortuna, (probably Caesar's mother) aged sixty-six. 'She has been useless two years past.'

Violet, child, 'Fever & Worms'

Margaretta, 'Invalid died of a Flux'

Leticia, 'with a tree falling on her in a Storm'

Leonora, 'of the Hydrocephalus'

Belinda, 'of an an Obstructed Viscera'

Monimia, child, 'of Worms'

Juno, 'an inflammation of the bones'

Jean, 'lues venerea' (venereal disease)

Candis, 'a flux'

Mimba, 'an inflammation of the bones'

Catalina, 'of a Dropsy' (an inflammation or swelling)

Lucie, 'an Invalid'

Mary Cameron, child (Annie and Archibald Cameron's daughter), 'in consequence of teething'

Mira, 'a Pluracy'

Bessy

Rose, 'an Invalid'

Juno, 'a Fever'

Jean, 'Lues Venerae'

Candis, 'a Flux'

Bella, 'Old age'

Princess, 'Lues Veneria'

Amba, nineteen, 'the young wench having died after Christmas of a lock jaw, from a bunion on her toe, which the anxiety for enjoying the holidays made her conceal & became fatal'

Deborah, Jessie's child, 'of Water in the head'

Cynthia, 'a fine young valuable Wench, after Child bed, that the operation of taking away the child piecemeal, brought on an inflammatory fever, to which she fell a sacrifice'

Unnamed woman drowned 'in the muck pitt'

Leah, 'pleurisy and sore throat'

Jean, 'pleurisy and sore throat'

Queen, 'pleurisy and sore throat'

Matty, 'pleurisy and sore throat'

Lucretia, 'pleurisy and sore throat'

Celia, 'pleurisy and sore throat'

Lucky, 'pleurisy and sore throat'

Fema, 'pleurisy and sore throat'

Agnes, 'burst blood vessels'

Parthenia, 'child birth'

Monimia, thirteen months old, 'fitts'

Marian, 'sometime sickly and obstructed'

Maria, (baby Sam's mother)

Sophia, Glanders (infection of the lungs)

Celia, 'poverty'

Esther, 'poverty'

Men and boys

Duke, 'with age'

Syley, 'a bloody Flux' (dysentery)

Hamlet of a 'nervous Fever' (probably typhoid)

Towerhill, aged eighty-five

Argyle, 'of a Flux & severe cold'

Dublin, 'of a Flux'

Lawrence, 'being long bad with Cocobah' (leprosy)

Tom

Cooper Dick, 'putrid Fever'

Prince, field worker, 'a Consumption'

William, child, 'in the Yaws'

Jupiter, 'superannuated'

Mars, 'superannuated'

James, a watchman

Hannibal, 'Penkeeper' (animal husbandry), 'a Consumption'

Robin, child, 'a Dropsey'

Milton, fieldworker, 'in a fit'

Jacob, 'of a Lethargy, tho' he was very worthless'

Plato

Debouch, a child, 'of water on the head'

Andrew, three, dropsy

Hope, 'an Old Confirmed Pox'

Elliot, 'a Consumption'

Jim, boy, 'an Obstructed Viscera'

Roselle, 'a decay of Nature'

Hood, 'a Dropsy'

Dicky, a blind child, 'a Fever'

Hazard, 'of an Old Pox'

Sam, 'a Consumption'

Othello, 'a Consumption'
Curtis, 'a Pleurisy'
Duke, 'a Lock Jaw'
Cyrus, 'a Consumption'
Harry, 'a flux'
Jonie, 'a Consumption'
Archibald Cameron, child (Annie
    and Archibald Cameron's son),
    'of the Worms'
Pope
Marquis
Tickales
Barlo
Duke, Nelly's child
Hamlet, 'died of a Dropsy'
Roselle
Tobie
Achilles
Homer
Robert, a child
Colonel, boy, 'an Apoplexy'
Johnie, a child, dysentery
Cato, 'dropsy & rupture'
Romeo, 'decay'
Adam, 'from eating Dirt'
Pompey
Steil
Duke, 'old age'
Dovetail, worms
Hercules, 'in a Fit'
Eboi, 'pain in the head'
Prince, consumption
Smart, 'died of a Rupture'
Peter, 'accidently burnt in a hutt'
Crawford, 'debility and old age'
Sam, one month old, 'severe cold,
    neglected by mother' (Maria)
Achilles

Homer
Duke, 'with age'
Syley, 'a bloody flux'
Hamlet, boy, 'nervous fever'
Unnamed man, drowned 'in the
    muck pitt'
Cecquin, 'in the course of nature'
Auckie, 'vermin infected Wound'
Paul, fell in the mill
William Brown, 'pleurisy and
    sore throat'
Quaco, 'pleurisy and sore throat'
Rodney, 'pleurisy and sore
    throat'
Henry, 'pleurisy and sore throat'
Mulatto David, pleurisy and sore
    throat
Felix, 'liver'
Dick, lockjaw
Pero
Pope, seventy, 'old age'
Bacchus, 'after falling into a
    Cistern'
Beck, four, 'worms dropsy'
Chance, child, 'always pining'
Sammy, 'cocobay' (leprosy)
Sam, from injuries caused by a
    plough
Tommy, a child, worms
Ben, 'Belly ache'
Doctor Hume, 'of Age &
    Poverty'
James, 'of Age & Poverty'
Charles, 'Belly ache'
Sammy, 'shot for the Glanders'
    (infection of the lungs – 'shot'
    means useless)
Prince, consumption

In these forty-two years, only six enslaved people can be said with any certainty to have successfully escaped from Rozelle: Jeanie (1769), Knight (1778), Dr Caesar, who became Augustus Thomson (1779), Fiany (a woman, 1785) and Quashie, tortured by John Ferguson over the loss of piglets (1805).

CHAPTER 13

CLEANSING THE MONEY

I own I am shock'd at the purchase of slaves,
And fear those who buy them and sell them are knaves;
What I hear of their hardships, their tortures, and groans,
Is almost enough to draw pity from stones.
I pity them greatly, but I must be mum,
For how could we do without sugar and rum?

William Cowper, 'Pity for Poor Africans', 1788

WITH THE OLDER GENERATION GONE, the two heirs of the Rozelle estate felt free to spend some money. The fourth baronet of Kilkerran, Sir James Fergusson, was in his late forties when his uncle, Sir Adam, died in 1813; Sir David Hunter Blair, third baronet of Dunskey and Blairquhan, in his mid-thirties. Both were just embarking on new marriages. They had gentlemen's employment, as officers in the Ayrshire militia. But improving their mansions and their estates was the activity that excited them.

Many people across Britain distanced themselves from their slavery-derived wealth by acquiring and developing rural estates. One route was to spend the money necessary to gain a title and establish themselves as landed aristocrats, people very different from the merchants and planters their fathers and uncles had been. Families with 'West Indian interests', the coy formulation of the time, had been doing this since the seventeenth century, long before slave-ownership became a social embarrassment.

The shame then was rather that their money was made through trade, not inherited or gained through marriage as true aristocrats'

wealth should be. But by Sir James and Sir David's time a veiling
of wealth derived from slavery was becoming socially obligatory. At
the same time Britain was tidying its own reputation, cloaking the
story of its exploitation of Africa and Africans with a myth about
the nation's role in the liberation and 'civilisation' of them.

The Hunter Blair Family by David Allan, 1785. David Hunter Blair, third
baronet, is probably the boy with the whip in the centre of the picture. In
1792, aged fourteen, he inherited a half-share of the Rozelle estate in Jamaica.

A building boom was beginning. Grand new houses were sprouting
across the country while older ones were being improved and embel-
lished: capital forged through exploitation transformed into beautiful
architecture and artefacts. More than 130 British estates and mansions
with connections to the story of slavery and other colonial exploitation are items today in the National Trust and English Heritage's
portfolio of historic properties.[1] Many hundreds more are in private
hands. Among the best known are Queen Victoria's Isle of Wight
holiday home, Osborne; Harewood House, the home of the royal
family's relatives, the Lascelles; Alton Towers; West Wycombe Park;
Kenwood House; Fasque Castle, home of the Gladstones; Culzean
Castle; and the Stanhope family's house, Chevening, which is now
the country residence of British foreign secretaries.

    Not all the West Indies fortunes were spent in this way. Hercules
Ross was one of several who came to believe he owed something to

the people who had helped generate his fortune. His story starts as a good example of an ordinary Scot who went out to Jamaica and struck it rich. The ninth son of a Glasgow exciseman, Ross worked his way up from ordinary clerk, at sixteen years old, to slave trader and then plantation owner. By the time he was thirty-four he was an important government official in Jamaica, a wealthy businessman, close friend of Horatio Nelson and the father of six children by an enslaved woman, a 'quadroon' named Elizabeth Foord.

In 1782, after twenty-one years, Ross sold up and went home, as was the practice. He set about turning himself into a Scottish aristocrat, taking a banking heiress for a wife and buying a vast estate in the eastern Highlands. There he built a neo-Gothic mansion, Rossie Castle. This was all quite usual. But then, quite abruptly, Ross changed track. He joined William Wilberforce and Thomas Clarkson, leaders of the abolitionist movement in the 1790s. He became a potent spokesperson, able to talk from direct experience of the 'misery of slavery'. He stated that the slave trade was contrary not only 'to sound policy, but the laws of God & Nature'.[2]

There's no record of what Ross's former friends in Jamaica, such as Simon Taylor, thought of the turncoat. Ross did not divert much of his fortune to the new cause, but his wife and he were among the backers of the new colony in Sierra Leone, West Africa, set up for rescued and liberated Africans. He did free Elizabeth Foord, giving her money to open a boarding house in Kingston, and brought their children to Scotland to live with him and his wife.[3] But, compared with the majority, few of the slavery-wealthy spent anything to improve the lives of those who had worked unpaid for them.

* * *

Both Sir James Fergusson and Sir David Hunter Blair had ample reason to distance themselves from the taint of their uncles' Caribbean ventures. David had much more to spend, however, as heir to both his uncle's and his father's banking fortunes. As a child he lived at his mother's family house, Dunskey in Wigtownshire, but when he reached nineteen his trustees enabled him to buy a proper gentleman's country estate at Blairquhan in Ayrshire.[4] This, at the cost of £34,000 in 1798, set him up in a vast and ancient castle, with farms and woodland totalling 12,000 acres. Blairquhan was deep in the South

Ayrshire heartland, where so many of the old families with West Indies enterprises were rooted.

His co-owners in Rozelle, the Fergussons, were just three miles away at Kilkerran. It was Sir James Fergusson's inheritance. He began great works to improve the house, its parklands and indeed the valley of the Girvan River, shortly after his uncle Sir Adam's death in 1813. With three neighbouring lairds – all connected to wealth from slavery – he began by moving the river and building bridges and a new road connecting their estates and the local towns. All this survives today, and it has 'materially benefited . . . the public', as Sir James promised.[5] In 1818 Kilkerran itself received an elegant new front designed by James Gillespie Graham, one of the architects of Edinburgh's neo-classical New Town. It had a new, semi-circular drawing room, more reception rooms and huge kitchens. He and his two wives already had eleven children, and were to have four more.

Sir David's works up the road at Blairquhan were far grander. He started with a plan to refurbish the crumbling, fire-damaged sixteenth-century castle, hiring a succession of fashionable architects. He then set about landscaping: diverting the river to make it meander more prettily and embellishing his new estate with avenues, ornamental lochs and picturesque walks. He planted nearly a million trees in ten years.

In 1820 Sir David finally settled on an architect, William Burn, and an ambitious project. They took down most of the old castle to build a 'Tudor-Gothic' palace on the site. The works had more than a hundred masons, carpenters and labourers busy on it by 1821: the bill for the job, and a multitude of stables, bridges and lodge-houses, ultimately came to more than £16,000. The cost of the initial purchase and the building of the new house equates to £56 million today. He spent a further £4,000 on fitting out the house, ordering statuary from Italy and furniture from Thomas Chippendale. Sir David was generous. When, on completion of the house in 1824, Burn presented his bill for the agreed sum of £350 and some extras, the satisfied client rounded it up to £500.

Sir David Hunter Blair went on to live happily at Blairquhan for nearly forty years, constructing gardens, walks and parklands. The house had eighteen live-in servants to look after the family – there were two wives and, eventually, thirteen children[6] – and all their many guests. Sir David's old schoolmate, the legal and literary figure – and campaigner against slavery – Henry Cockburn, came to visit in 1844. He wrote in his journal:

> I rose early, I mean at 7 this morning, and surveyed the beauties of Blairquhan. It deserves its usual praises. The most gentleman-like place rich in all sorts of attractions – of wood, lawn, river, gardens, hill, agriculture and pasture. The house (by Burn) is too ostentatious and too large for the place, and, architecturally, it is nothing. But still it proclaims itself the mansion house of a gentleman and a thing that does not intend itself to be taken for a common affair.

Where did all the money for this life come from? Clearly the income from Rozelle would hardly have covered the gardening bills. The Hunter Blair papers lie uncatalogued in a rundown public archive outside the town of Ayr, and no one appears to have asked this question. No account of Sir David's life or of his works at Blairquhan makes any mention of the West Indies or slavery-derived fortunes. Like any respectable landed gentleman of this era, he was not obviously employed, beyond his colonelcy of the Ayrshire militia and later the county's lord lieutenancy. He had inherited the role of King's Printer in Scotland from his father James (who had been procured it in 1785 by Henry Dundas, the great fixer of the time[7]). This gave him the monopoly in printing authorised editions of the Bible, but it is not clear whether that earned much.

The bulk of the Hunter Blair money of the nineteenth century came from the eighteenth-century involvement in trade and banking. The sons of an Ayr merchant, both James and William Hunter enlarged that business, importing everything from Scandinavian timber and Calcutta cloth to wine. The Hunter brothers were involved in lead mining, shipping and sugar refining in Scotland and they were landlords in Edinburgh – one of their tenants was the Duke of Argyll. As was the custom, a successful business of the time necessitated banks and insurance underwriters, which the wise merchant would have on his side by owning them. James worked for and then took over a merchant company with banking interests, Coutts Brothers. With a fellow employee, William Forbes, he lent to Scottish investors with interests in the West Indies and other colonies. Among them were merchants and several plantation owners, including Sir Adam Fergusson.

Sir Willliam Forbes, James Hunter & Co. became one of Scotland's most successful private banks, trusted enough to issue its own notes. A total of £83,000 – £131 million today – of their paper money was in circulation by 1783.[8] Thus Colonel William Hunter – who was the leading partner in another successful bank– and Sir James Hunter Blair (as he became after marriage) go down in history as bankers, not planters and slave owners. James became MP for Edinburgh and then lord provost of the city. He was one of the key people behind late eighteenth-century improvements there, including the New Town.

The income of £500 or so a year from the Jamaica plantation cannot have seemed very significant: it is understandable that Colonel Hunter and then his heir, David, Sir James's son, were happy to leave the direction of the Jamaican estate to Sir Adam and to agents like their step-cousin, Hugh Hamilton.

The Fergussons were as influential, more ancient but far less rich by the beginning of the 1800s. Nonetheless, for a short while Sir James spent nearly as lavishly as his neighbour Sir David. The new front to Kilkerran and other improvements to the estate cost £15,000 in 1814 alone. In the same year he bought a third large house in Edinburgh's New Town.[9] The family owned it until 1851.

Many friends and relatives lived within a short walk of the Fergussons in Charlotte Square, and close cousins lived just east of Edinburgh at the Dalrymple house, Newhailes. The baronet and his new bride, Henrietta Duncan, had 'a gay life' in Edinburgh's New Town. Sir Adam's old friend George Dempster wrote to his godson in December 1813 joking that he might have to step in and restrict Lady Fergusson to 'one dinner, three routs [parties], and two balls, and one supper in the 24 hours'.[10]

But Sir James had nothing like Sir David Hunter Blair's income and little prospect of increasing what he did have from rents in Scotland or from the Jamaica plantation. His best scheme for wealth-making – mining coal at Kilkerran – was ruined by a huge underground fire in the seam that did not go out for decades (the site is still known as the Burning Hill because of the smoke that used to rise from it). Within two years of Sir Adam's death, James was an astonishing £66,910 in debt.

George Fergusson, Lord Hermand, his remaining uncle, aged seventy-two in 1815, stepped in to address this problem, telling off his not-so-young nephew in a manner that must have irked the new head of the family. Uncle George was no kill-joy: he was a witty and hard-drinking judge of the old school, according to his contemporaries. He had built his own mansion, Hermand House, just outside Edinburgh. When in town, while the Court of Session sat, Lord Hermand lived three minutes' walk from Sir James and his family in George Street, in a double-fronted house that is now a very grand branch of Wetherspoon's pub chain.

He dictated that Sir James must devote the bulk of his income to paying off his debts. He must learn to live on just £1,500 a year. This would not allow luxury, a 'great establishment of servants', or the 'erection of buildings and gardens'. But, Uncle George concluded, it would allow Sir James 'to bring up his numerous family as other families just as good have been brought up'.[11]

The notes and calculations that led to this verdict, made by a hired adviser, propose a seven-year plan to put Sir James's finances in order. This includes the sale of Sir Adam's old house in Edinburgh's St Andrew Square and some land worth £15,000 in Galloway, southwest Scotland. The adviser supposes that the Fergusson half of Rozelle estate might fetch £12,000. But it would be hard to sell. Sir James's income, 'after all charges', the adviser put at £10,500 a year – £1,200 of that from the plantation in Jamaica.[12]

A note written in 1819 and titled 'The States of Sir James Fergusson's Affairs' shows that the rein put on the overspending had worked, though not to the extent Uncle George had hoped. The overall debt had been dropping by £1,900 a year. Rozelle had not been sold but it was now valued at only £10,000 'due to borrowing to buy a steam engine [to power the sugar works] and some negroes'.

Sir James's life in Scotland does not seem to have changed much as a result of these economies: the two houses around Charlotte Square remained in family use, as did Kilkerran. There were also, of course, the thirteen children. The oldest, Charles, had just left Harrow School and was studying in Edinburgh to join the old family profession as a lawyer. In addition to inheriting these houses, he was to be made the heir of his unmarried aunt, Christian Dalrymple of Newhailes, the Dalrymple estate outside the city.

CHAPTER 14

EMANCIPATION AT A PRICE

The perpetuation of slavery in our West India colonies is not an abstract question, it is a question in which we are *all* implicated; we are all guilty of supporting and perpetuating slavery. The West Indian planter and the people of this country stand in the same moral relation to each other as the thief and receiver of stolen goods. The planter refuses to set his wretched captive at liberty, treats him as a beast of burden, compels his reluctant, unremunerated labor under the lash of a cart whip, – why? – because WE furnish the stimulant to all this injustice, rapacity and cruelty by PURCHASING ITS PRODUCE.

from Elizabeth Heyrick's much-circulated pamphlet
'Immediate not Gradual Abolition', 1824

There is a frustrating lack of information about Rozelle and Jamaica in the papers of this and following generations of Hunter Blairs and Fergussons. It seems likely that some weeding out has been done: the Hunter Blairs kept the bills for the furnishing of Blairquhan, but very little on their financial dealings of any sort. Sir James, the fourth Fergusson baronet, and his son Charles, the fifth, chiefly kept personal material: accounts books, diaries and correspondence with friends and family.

Was the removal or censoring of documents done because of shame and embarrassment? Or merely because business matters were left in the hands of the family lawyers? As the Victorian age began the public face of a family, its reputation both now and in history, was something to be carefully curated and guarded. This generation of

Fergussons appears to have taken their Christianity more seriously, devoting much time to churchgoing and to the religious politics of the time. Their diaries and letters invoke God, ponder biblical texts and pray for guidance with a fervour that might have surprised their eighteenth-century ancestors. You imagine these spiritual beliefs must have become difficult to reconcile with ownership of enslaved people.

More and more of those around the Fergussons were turning in favour of the abolition of slavery. Some were busy campaigners for it. Their near neighbour at Kilkerran, Thomas Kennedy of Dalquharran, was a Whig MP and a prominent abolitionist. Henry Cockburn, Sir David Hunter Blair's friend from their school days in Edinburgh, was close to Kennedy and a friend of both Lord Hermand and Sir James Fergusson. He was a guest at the wedding of James's son Charles in 1829, and wrote an account of it in his memoirs.

Lord Cockburn – as he became when appointed a judge of the Court of Session – was a celebrity, in the way of the time: famous as an advocate in criminal trials, an intellectual, a reformist politician and most of all as a writer for the popular *Edinburgh Review*. With another Edinburgh lawyer, he restarted the Scottish campaign to abolish slavery, launching petitions and holding a public meeting in July 1814 – a move that, as Cockburn later acknowledged, 'excited great alarm'.[1] With the French wars ending, the British were perhaps exhausted with 'revolutionary' upheaval.

Fierce words and fake news

Nonetheless the abolitionist movement was revived, in Scotland and across Britain. Women were at the heart of it. In Edinburgh in the 1820s my Fergusson ancestors might well have bumped into my Renton great-great-great-grandmother, Agnes. Both would both have been quick to acknowledge they were of very different social classes. But, as the ever-busy do-gooding wife of a prosperous shop-keeping family, I like to imagine Agnes may have pressed one of her leaflets on one of the Fergussons outside church, or around Edinburgh's streets. She might have implored them to join the boycott of any 'blood-sweeten'd beverage'.[2]

Agnes Renton was a founding member of the Edinburgh Ladies' Committee for the 'Total Abolition of Slavery'; the minister of the church she attended was a leader of the men's committee. She can have had no better target than the likes of the Fergussons for pamphlets like 'An Appeal from British Ladies to West India Planters'. These did not hold back: one stated that any sugar-eater was guilty of murder. It went on to insist that sugar's very granules contained effluent from sores on the bodies of enslaved people, while claiming that a merchant had opened a barrel of Jamaican rum to find inside 'the whole body of a roasted Negro'.[3]

Initially the Glasgow and Edinburgh women's committees' call was for 'amelioration' – improvement in the conditions of West Indian enslavement – and women like Agnes worked hard to fund fact-finding visits to Jamaica and other islands. They published and distributed the accounts that came back. By 1833 there were seventy-five Ladies' Associations campaigning across Britain: they delivered a petition to Parliament signed by a total of 187,000 women.

When Agnes was not involved in this work she appears, from the monograph written by her son after her death, to have spent much of her time delivering food and moral advice – including for total abstinence from alcohol – to the poor women of Edinburgh's slums. She visited prisons, too, to deliver 'religious instruction'. She almost became a victim of the Edinburgh murderers and grave-robbers, Burke and Hare. She died in 1863, having supported every liberal cause from the abolition of the Corn Laws to Greek independence. Opposing slavery was a life-long cause: she corresponded with and sent money to campaigners in the United States until her death.[4]

In an age when middle-class entertainment might best be found at church, Agnes, like many liberal-minded Edinburghers, was a fan of the celebrated Church of Scotland minister the Rev. Dr Andrew Thomson. He was another neighbour of the Fergussons in Edinburgh's New Town, and it was from his church, St George's in George Street, that the most powerful abolitionist rhetoric of the era emerged. Not for Thomson any gradual approach to freeing the enslaved in the British colonies – he was an 'immediatist'. Along with campaigners like Elizabeth Heyrick, immediatists attacked the polite, 'gradualist' campaigners, using fierce language to excite a new generation of abolitionists.

At a celebrated meeting in Edinburgh's Assembly Rooms in October 1829, Dr Thomson excoriated those who would merely mitigate and reform an industry 'built on dead men's bones': the institution of slavery must be got rid of, on principle and immediately.

Slavery is the very Upas tree of the moral world, beneath whose
pestiverous shade all intellect languishes and all virtue dies . . . The
foul sepulchre must be taken away. The cup of oppression must
be dashed to the ground. The pestiverous tree must be cut down
and eradicated; it must be, root and branch of it, cast into the
consuming fire and its ashes scattered to the four winds of heaven.
It is thus you must deal with slavery. You must annihilate it – annihilate it now – and annihilate it for ever.[5]

The pro-slavery lobby ramped up its language in turn. 'Those caring
canting hypocritical rascals the Abolitionists', begins a column in the
Jamaica Journal at this time, going on to accuse the campaign's
'purchased rogues' of bribery and corruption.[6] But, rail as the planters
did, Thomson and voices like his were gaining ground in Britain.
The parliamentary campaign abandoned 'amelioration' as its aim,
pivoting to call for complete abolition of slavery in British territories,
and British intervention to prevent the trade in enslaved people
everywhere. Committees like Agnes's, prevented from taking a part
in the male debates in Parliament and church, turned to where they
could have influence: ordinary people.

They revived one of the most effective campaigning tools from
the campaign of the 1790s, the sugar boycott, turning it into a
formalised abstention from the use of any goods produced through
slavery. The abolitionist women can be said to have invented modern
popular campaigning, and found a uniquely powerful role in it, despite
their lack of the right to vote. Further, their arguments chimed with
the growing political interest in 'free trade': both Tory and Whig
voices were questioning the value, moral and economic, of Britain's
massive subsidy of its slave colonies' sugar exports. All this shook the
West Indian lobby, just as the fair trade movement was to scare
multi-national corporations 200 years later. In the pages of newspapers like *John Bull*, the planters and merchants fought back.

In the United States, black anti-slavery activists were becoming
more influential. First-hand accounts of the lives of enslaved people
were being published, and, in 1827, the first African American newspaper. But there is little record of black people in Britain being able
to get their voices heard in the debate. When the Anti Slavery Society
was formed in London in 1823, just one member, Louis Celeste
Lecesne, was black.[7] However, just as the emancipation battle was

reaching its climax, *The History of Mary Prince* was published – the first woman's account of enslavement to appear in Britain.

Prince had been born enslaved in Bermuda around 1788, and worked from early childhood as a domestic servant and as a labourer in the salt pans. She was first sold at the age of one, then at twelve, when her family was split up, and then three more times, to a variety of brutal owners, before she was thirty. She was baptised and married a freed man in Antigua, but her then owner – who sued for libel over the book – separated the couple, horsewhipped Prince and then brought her to England. There she managed to escape and become a campaigner alongside the Anti Slavery Society. Her book quickly sold three editions when it was published in 1831.[8]

* * *

As far as I can see, the Fergussons and the Hunter Blairs did not take part in this debate, on either side. They were not members of any of the West Indies merchants and planters' associations, unlike the Hamiltons, and they do not appear on any lists of subscribers to the abolition campaigns. Both families were involved in the charitable causes of the time. Poverty and lack of education in Scotland concerned them, and they gave generously. The diaries and letters the Dalrymple and Fergusson families kept in the 1820s and 1830s show them to be busy, engaged, Christian and political. Yet I have found only one mention in their papers of the great politico-religious debate of the time, over slavery and its abolition.

It appears in Charles Fergusson's diary on 9 March 1826. He is twenty-five at the time, a busy and social bachelor in Edinburgh, a practising lawyer and also attending chemistry lectures at the university:

> Dined at Maitland's, present William Stirling, Col. Russell, William Clouston, Coventry, Mr and Mrs William Maitland, William McDowall (Greenock). The slave question was discussed after dinner and some facts were stated which I cannot now remember . . .
> N.B. Mr Buxton made his fortune as a slave driver or seller.

This failure of my great-great-great-grandfather's memory calls to mind a passage in Jane Austen's *Mansfield Park*, published twelve years earlier. The heroine's rich uncle, a plantation owner in Antigua, is asked about the 'slave-trade'. The conversation in the drawing room at the Park stops in 'dead silence'.[9] Then the company continues as though nothing has been said.

'Mr Buxton' must be Thomas Fowell Buxton, the MP and leader of the abolitionist movement after William Wilberforce retired in 1825. He founded the Anti Slavery Society and, after British emancipation, raised money for schools in Jamaica and took the fight against slavery to Africa. He is the Buxton after whom the delicious mango that Susan Craig-James gave me in Tobago is named. Buxton was never a 'slave driver or seller', though it was a common accusation made against him by the pro-slavery propagandists.

But it is true – though not mentioned in modern accounts – that he was connected to earnings from slavery. Buxton's grandfather, Osgood Hanbury, made a fortune in Barbados as owner of the Locust Hall estate and his mother had been left part of the money. That fact was made much of by the West Indian lobby in the 1820s, who called their chief antagonist a hypocrite. He was far from the only heir of slavery to become an outspoken opponent of it – Zachary Macaulay, the first governor of Sierra Leone, set up as a colony of freed slaves, is another prominent example.

Both Sir David Hunter Blair and Sir James and then Sir Charles Fergusson left the day-to-day running of their estates in the hands of lawyers and agents in Scotland and Jamaica, so the quotidian correspondence Sir Adam dealt with so painstakingly may never have come to his heirs' desks. A few remaining letters in the Kilkerran archive do provide snapshots from moments at Rozelle, and in the history of Jamaica, over these years. But there is no detail of the enslaved people, no figures for disease, deaths and births, no names.

'Amelioration' was the policy of the planters and merchants' lobby in the face of the resurgent abolitionism. In 1826 a new Jamaican Slave Code brought in further reforms. All enslaved people were to be instructed in Christianity, and their marriages solemnised without fee. There were clearer penalties for mistreating enslaved people, though the planters resisted the notion of the abolition of whipping – to concede that would be to undermine the whole edifice.

Instead earlier rules on a maximum number of lashes were restated: thirty-nine, if the owner or manager was present, ten if an underling handed out the punishment. Legal penalties for mistreatment were reinforced, including for rape and murder. But there was a flaw in the rules. The power to police the planters who abused enslaved people was in the hands of magistrates who were generally planters themselves. This was to prove disastrous in St Thomas-in-the-East, Rozelle estate's parish.

* * *

Nothing in the surviving records shows that the Fergussons or the Hunter Blairs played any part in the slow reforms in Jamaica. Charles Dalrymple Fergusson, Sir James's son and heir, was a member of the Church of Scotland's General Assembly, alongside the ardent abolitionist Dr Thomson. There is no trace of any opinion of his on the religious instruction of the enslaved people he owned. It does appear that by 1832 most people on the estate were baptised, if only by the fact they now have surnames.

In the 1820s the Ayr lawyer Quintin Kennedy, who had worked for Hunters, the bank set up in the 1760s by Sir David Hunter Blair's uncle William, was appointed to oversee the management of the estate in Jamaica from Scotland. His man on the ground in Jamaica was James Whyte, Ayrshire-born, as usual. Whyte had made a career of managing multiple estates with absentee owners. However, in 1827, an extraordinary appeal came directly from the remaining enslaved workers: they urge the proprietors to buy more of them. Quintin Kennedy thought it worth forwarding Whyte's explanation for this to Kilkerran.

> About 30 or 40 good able people, who at the present moment might be obtained for less than £3000 Stg. would greatly tend to the relief of the Negroes and to the maintenance of the crops of this grateful little property. So many hands are necessary during the Crop on the various detached duties of the Estate, that we can only muster eleven able people in the field to cut canes for the supply of a powerful Steam Engine, and the work is distressing where the crop is so large and of course procrastinate.

Whyte points out that lack of workers means he has to spend £350 a year on 'jobbing' – the hire of casual labour. He goes on to say,

'Not one punishment of any kind has been necessary since my arrival, excepting one man who was recently prosecuted at a Slave court for an assault, and most unfairly sentenced to a months imprisonment.'[10]

Fragments of a further discussion about this proposal exist. Rozelle had clearly not been doing well financially. The net returns the previous year were only 'about £1400' (in real terms about a quarter of the earnings in the 1790s), and there were debts to pay off on 'the baneful and injudicious outlay formerly' – the lawyer Quintin Kennedy's phrase.[11] This was presumably the spending on more enslaved workers and the conversion of the sugar-processing works to steam power.

The choice Kennedy put was whether to buy more people or lessen the amount of sugar cane cultivated. This is as good an indication as any of the collapse of the sugar plantation's economic model. Falls in the market price of sugar and increases in the duty paid to the British government on it were chiefly to blame. In 1824 the price per hundredweight of sugar and the tax levied on it on arrival in Britain were the same, at twenty-four shillings, guaranteeing the planters made a loss.

Whyte writes again, in August 1827, begging for some good news to deliver to the enslaved workforce. Using them as leverage with the proprietors seems to be a sign of changing attitudes on the ground in Jamaica. Whyte says he wants £3,000 sterling to buy forty enslaved people, adding that while he hopes he will get good workers, he is likely to have an 'indiscriminate mixture of all ages, character & capability'. That is how it is, he says: 'it is almost impossible to select without enfringing on the rights of kindred or matrimonial selection'.[12] Such concerns would not have occurred to Sir Adam and his generation.

It is indeed the first time that any 'rights' of enslaved workers have been mentioned, in nearly sixty years of correspondence. But this note also puts paid to the idea that British slave trading had been abolished in 1807. Breeding, buying and selling humans was still legal and regularly done in and between the British Caribbean colonies, even as the Royal Navy pursued the ships of other nations attempting to bring people from Africa.*[13]

....
* The historian David Eltis has revealed more than 20,000 such movements of enslaved people between the colonies in the years between 1808 and 1830.

There was another incentive to buy people at this time. As the 1820s progressed, anyone who followed the political debate over abolition in Britain could see the slave owners winning their fall-back argument: enslaved people were their property, in law, so they would have to be compensated if the government freed them. Buying a human being now became a gamble on the outcome of the battle over abolition.

* * *

From 1817 all slave owners in the British Caribbean colonies were obliged to make returns every three years to centrally kept registers. These listed names, ages, deaths, births, 'colour' (negro, quadroon, mulatto or sambo*) and 'African or Creole' – meaning born in Africa or in the West Indies. Many of the registers are now in the British National Archives: the returns for Rozelle plantation for 1817, 1829 and 1832 are there.

So we know that in March 1817 there were 163 enslaved people on the estate, and 101 animals.[14] The 1832 return shows the population higher than ever before, at 203. It may be that Sir James and Sir David had, like others,[15] seen the opportunity in emancipation compensation. Or they were merely responding to James Whyte's pleas for more workers. Whatever the reason, they did make a large purchase of adults and children in 1829 – ninety people. All of them were bought from the River Head estate in the parish of St Ann on Jamaica's northern coast. The sale was organised by the plantation agent, Joseph Gordon. (George William Gordon, his son by an enslaved woman, was to become a martyr for the rights of poor Jamaicans and is now one of the country's official national heroes.)

Forty-seven women and forty-one men arrived at Rozelle, ranging in age from two years old to seventy: an indication of the reluctance to break up families. Most people on the list have surnames, many of them Scottish. The 1832 return also shows that the death rate is as terrible as ever – thirty-nine enslaved people died at Rozelle between 1829 and 1832, nearly a quarter of them all. Sixteen children were born.

....
* The term then used to describe the child of a 'mulatto' and 'black' person.

There are very few names on the 1832 list that figure in the 1817 one. It appears that only one man, seventy-four-year-old David or Davey Hunter, was still alive from the eighteenth century and the early years of the Hunter and Fergusson ownership. Born in Africa around 1758, it is likely that he took – or was given – the surname Hunter at baptism sometime in the nineteenth century, after one of the men who owned him.[16]

The Christmas War

There is no more news from Rozelle until the slow process of emancipation began. The campaign that started eighty years earlier among the Quakers and a few liberally-minded Britons, then spread to hundreds of thousands inspired by the accounts of formerly enslaved people such as Olaudah Equiano and Mary Prince, was coming at last to its conclusion. The efforts of the enslaved and free people of African origin in Jamaica were crucial to winning the final battle and they were helped by the stupidity and brutality of the Jamaican ruling establishment.

At Christmas in 1831 an enslaved man named Samuel Sharpe, a Baptist minister, called on the working population of the island to strike. The mixed race and black population of Jamaica had changed considerably by this time: one in eight of these people were free, thousands were baptised and had had some basic education. They were well-informed. A newspaper aimed at this class, *The Watchman*, had been functioning since 1828, seeking the vote and equal rights for 'free coloureds',[17] and an end to slavery. It also carried news of politics in Britain, and the work of the anti-slavery lobby.

All this must have been encouraging to Sharpe, whose legal owners appear to have permitted his evangelical work: he was deacon of a Baptist church in Montego Bay in the island's northwest. His call for a 'peaceful' sit-down strike for better treatment, wages and a debate with the planters about emancipation was heeded. At the time only 20,000 enslaved people were thought to have been baptised as Christians. But within a few days 50,000 people, a sixth of all the enslaved people in Jamaica, had joined what was called the Christmas Rebellion – and then, when it turned bloody, the Great Baptist War.

The white elite responded in the usual way – with extreme violence.

Though Sharpe's protest began in peace it ended in bullets and mass death. The British commander in chief, Sir Willoughby Cotton, enlisted the help of the Maroons (the communities of free black people who had won rights from the British in the eighteenth century) and he and his forces killed 207 followers of Sharpe in the fighting. Fourteen white people died. It was the biggest, though not the bloodiest, revolt in the history of British slavery.

General Cotton's justification, when accused of overreaction, was that the enslaved protesters were led by educated, politicised revolutionaries – a designation calculated to concern Europeans in an era of radical revolt across the continent. Sam Sharpe's uprising marks the first moment when a rebellion by enslaved people is blamed by the white rulers on something other than the black underclass's essential savagery.

The aftermath of the Christmas Rebellion led directly to the political defeat of the West India lobby, and then to the end of the institution of slavery in the British empire. News of it reached Britain quickly, and caused outrage. An audience already sceptical about justice under slavery was told of cursory court proceedings and the summary executions of people found guilty of even the smallest of crimes. Bodies had piled up outside the courthouses: the death toll through judicial execution was put at more than 300.

The Jamaican establishment appealed to the home country for help and compensation for the losses suffered by the white owners. The British government sent a huge sum, £200,000, to help restore plantations and white property damaged in Jamaica. After the revolt was quelled most of the Baptist chapels were burned down, with no interference from the authorities. White Christian preachers and missionaries were attacked and arrested, charged with sedition and complicity in the insurrection. Their houses were stoned by white mobs and their families threatened.

But this served only to publicise the injustices. After two months one of these ministers, an Englishman called William Knibb, was released from prison. His black congregation voted to send him to Britain to tell of what he had seen. Knibb's addresses, delivered across the country and to both Houses of Parliament, were 'overwhelming', according to a contemporary account. 'Sceptics were convinced, waverers became decided, apathetic people were roused, and great numbers of hearts everywhere kindled to irrepressible support.'[18]

William Knibb was born in 1803, the son of a tailor in the English Midlands. He was a fiery speaker. At a meeting in Westminster attended by 3,000 representatives of dissenting churches he told the story of the Christmas Rebellion, and how in its suppression the Anglican Church (the official one of England and the Crown) had made a union 'with all the fornicators on the island . . . formed to stop the march of mind and religion'. The clergy applauded. Jamaica, Knibb wrote, was a 'land of sin, disease, and death, where Satan reigns'.[19]

In late 1832 Knibb travelled all of Britain. He was heard by tens of thousands; his speeches were reported in newspapers and quickly published in their entirety in book form. In October he was in Edinburgh, a guest of the dissenting churches as well as Charles Fergusson's Church of Scotland. The account of Knibb's speech in Newcastle-upon-Tyne on 30 January 1833 gives an idea of the passion and the certainty of these Christian abolitionists. He speaks of his congregation in Jamaica, free and enslaved, of their kindness and humility; of a poor young black mother passing money through the bars of Knibb's prison cell to help obtain his freedom. The central message is interesting because it addresses an underlying fear then and afterwards: that liberated black people will not just destroy the British West Indies' economy, but threaten white civilisation. Knibb is telling Britain that the people he knows in Jamaica are civilised already.

Knibb energetically – and at great length – rejects the anti-abolitionists' fears, racist and economic. Once freed, 'all will become Christians' – and the Christian black people he has known in his eight years in Jamaica are hard-working and good, far better, indeed, than the whites who tyrannise and exploit them. Most radically of all, he asks the audience to conquer its racism: to consider the enslaved black people of the Caribbean as '800,000 British fellow-subjects'.

Knibb ended his long speech to 'very great applause', according to the *Newcastle Courant*'s report. The meeting passed a motion unanimously. It seems to cover most abolitionist concerns:

Whether we view this most accursed system as a source of misery to the Slave, as a sink of moral corruption and defilement to the Planter, or as a stain of the foulest dye on the national character, sound policy, as well as religion, demands its immediate, utter, and final extinction. [20]

And so it happened. But the end was not immediate, utter or final. When the weight of public pressure forced the government to introduce a bill to outlaw slavery to the House of Commons, the compromising began. The principal argument of the planter and merchant lobby, backed by the financiers, was economic: any swift end to slavery would bankrupt the plantation sugar industry, not merely because paying wages would raise costs but because freed workers might simply abandon their jobs, crippling plantations and causing mayhem in the islands with their tiny ruling white populations. The spectre of the abrupt and violent end of white rule in Haiti in 1791 was still a potent warning of what could happen to an elite when enslaved people took power.

The West Indies lobby proposed another gradualist approach. The enslaved would become free, in name, but would be forced to continue working for their existing owners for another twelve years. These 'apprentices' would have fixed working hours – three-quarters of their time – and holidays, but they would be bonded labourers working only for food and lodging. In addition the owners of the enslaved people should be paid compensation for the loss of these people, their property.

This became the fulcrum on which the last debate about abolition was balanced. It made sense to the more moderate from the abolition side, for whom property rights were an important bulwark in Britain's emerging democracy. Paying compensation to the enslaved people themselves was never seriously considered.

The compensation proposal had been around for nearly a decade. The influential MP John Grosett – a slave-owning Scot with Jamaican connections – wrote in 1824 that recompensing loss of property was a matter of simple justice, and that owners in the colonies must be guaranteed 'indemnity and compensation' by the government. Property was 'sacred', and the right to own slaves authorised by God himself.[21] In 1826 the Jamaican newspaper owner Augustus Beaumont published a pamphlet titled 'An appeal to the commonsense of the people of England'. It put the central, uncomfortably logical argument:

What is their property? Is it the satisfaction of civilising their slaves, and rendering them fit for Emancipation? No, the property in slaves which the British Parliament sold them, is in the rights, the natural – the *born* rights of the Negro – a right to his labour – to all he can acquire, to the possession of him as a mere chattel – destitute of will – subject to absolute power. Cruel as this may be, it is the contract between Parliament and the slave owners.[22]

The British government had sold the owners their plots of land in the Caribbean along with the implied right to use enslaved labour: if the latter were to be withdrawn, the land was blighted and the enslaved people valueless, so compensation had to be paid. The abolitionists saw the dangers in this argument. They tried hard to establish emancipation and compensation as two independent issues. Powerful voices made the point that the British had already spent far too much defending the slave owners and their wealth: £150 million and 50,000 dead in the wars with the French, Americans and Spanish over the Caribbean. Churchmen such as Andrew Thomson railed against the proposal – the people of Britain were to be 'subjected to a kind of poll-tax to uphold their iniquitous system', he said, going on to state that if anyone deserved compensation it was enslaved people, 'before all others'.[23] This point is still being made by Caribbean nations today.

'To the Friends of Negro Emancipation' – a popular print published in 1834 in London. It shows a father pointing to the notice of the end of slavery pinned to a tree. In fact enslaved adults would have to continue working unpaid for four more years.

However, the compensation lobby had conservative and mercantile Britain largely on its side. The origins of much property is in violence and unfairness, argued one submission from the plantation owners and merchants to Parliament: that makes no difference to the law now. Property rights could not be cancelled on moral grounds. Parliament embraced compensation and apprenticeship, not least because they were a solution to the threat of an economic collapse on emancipation that would damage everyone.

Slavery was thus abolished in the British Caribbean by means of British taxpayers and the enslaved themselves paying off the owners.

'Slavery in all but name'

In August 1833 the Slavery Emancipation Act received royal assent, enshrining the principle of 'compensated emancipation'. Today we call it the moment that slavery ended in the British Empire, but that is far from true. The Act did not come into force until the following year and did not apply to substantial British territories including Ceylon (now Sri Lanka) and large parts of India. In the British Caribbean only children under six became fully free on 1 August 1834: all other enslaved people became 'apprentices', bonded to work for three-quarters of their time for their previous owners for a further six years (or four years in the case of domestic servants), in return for food and shelter.

Meanwhile many British people and some British banks continued to profit from slavery, most of all in the Dutch West Indies, where it was not abolished until 1863. The Netherlands also paid compensation to the slave owners, 70 per cent of whom were Scots. But this was less than a twentieth of what the British government handed to the Fergussons, the Hunter Blairs and 46,000 more slave owners, some of them already the wealthiest people in the world.

There is one reference to the events of emancipation in the Fergusson family papers. The man now in charge at Rozelle, Gray Rutherford, sent a letter to Quintin Kennedy, the estate owners' agent in Ayr. It is dated 14 August 1834, two weeks after the historic day.

I have read the new law to the people here some time ago, and then explained in a language suited to their Comprehension with which they seemed all quite satisfied and after enjoying their three holidays, commencing with the 1 August, they returned to work on the 4th without a murmur or a sulky look and have since continued steady and attentive to their duties during the Legal hours of work viz. 48½ hours per Week. On several Estates in the neighbourhood a good deal of passive resistance to the Law was observable for some days and the Stipendiary Magistrates have met with some Clamour and disrespect on their first visits to explain the Law but by a little firmness on their part and by making a few examples we are now all going on smoothly in the district . . .

On the North side of the Island, particularly in the Parish of St Ann's, Negroes on many estates refused to turn out to work, saying the King had made them free, that Lord Mulgrave [Jamaica's outgoing governor] had told them so and they would not work. The Marquis of Sligo [the new governor] however has acted with admirable promptitude. The Militia were called out – the Steamer was sent round with troops and it is rumoured these vigorous measures have already had the effect of bringing the Malcontents pretty generally to a sense of their duty. I have no doubt that after a little while all Classes and Colours will become reconciled in some degree to the changed system but I fear the diminution of Labour and consequently of Crop will be serious felt by all Proprietors, more particularly by those who possess small and laborious sugar Estates, for they cannot long be maintained I fear . . .[24]

Rutherford continues, explaining the terms of the 'bargain' he has proposed to the Rozelle 'apprentices', their food and their hours. They must agree it formally before the stipendiary magistrates.

We do not know how this went down in the Fergusson and Hunter Blair households – there is no record of a response. Rutherford's approving reference to Howe Browne, the Marquess of Sligo, is interesting: he did not get much good press from the white population of Jamaica. Shortly after this letter was written Sligo addressed the island's assembly and told them his objective was to establish a social system 'absolved forever from the reproach of Slavery'. He owned two Jamaican plantations, inherited from his grandmother; but he and his wife Hester de Burgh were both profoundly opposed to the institution. This set them at odds with the planters.

Sligo was determined that the abuses that went with slavery, especially whips and brands, would cease during the apprenticeship period.

'The cruelties are past all idea', he told the Jamaican assembly. 'I call on you to put an end to conduct so repugnant to humanity and so contrary to the law.'[25] He invited any black Jamaican with a problem to visit him in person at Government House. This enraged the planters, as did his appointment as chief of the ninety new 'special magistrates' a man of mixed African and white race, the lawyer Richard Hill. Son of a planter, Hill had led the successful campaign to give 'coloured' free Jamaicans voting rights in 1830. Now his job was to see that the plantations implemented the new laws and the apprenticeship system fairly.

It was to be a fight. Poorer white people were fanatically opposed to the scheme. They had had privilege under the law and commercial advantage: now the free black people would be direct rivals. Troops had to be dispatched to enforce the emancipation edict in outlying parts of Jamaica. Some plantation owners flatly refused to comply. Henry Boucher, a racehorse trainer and owner of Marlborough estate in Manchester, central Jamaica, kept his workers enslaved as ever until the militia marched up to his front door to enforce the new system. Then he went to the stables and 'blew his brains out'. He had a reputation for cruelty: his fellow planters' excuse for this was that his parents had had to flee St Domingue (Haiti) for Jamaica during the revolution in 1792.[26]

The white elite and their supporters in Britain soon managed to get rid of the Marquess of Sligo, whom they accused of 'interpreting the laws in favour of the Negro'. The assembly refused to pass his legislation and when the government of his friend Robert Peel fell his term as governor came to an abrupt end, only two years after his arrival. He left the island in late 1836 bearing a silver candle holder, a present from the 'grateful' enslaved.[27]

Apprenticeship fails

Not for the first time, the planter lobby's overreaction damaged its cause. Back in Britain, Sligo put his weight behind the abolitionists' latest campaign, which was now to end the apprenticeship system and free everyone as soon as possible. In February 1838 he published a pamphlet, 'Jamaica Under the Apprenticeship System', which directly attacked the racism of the planters.

It is treason in Jamaica to talk of a Negro as a freeman. The black and coloured population are viewed by the white inhabitants as little more than semi-human, for the most part a kind of intermediate race, possessing indeed the form of man, but none of his finer attributes.

This added to a pile of evidence coming from visitors to the West Indies that told that apprenticeship was only working in one sense: the economic collapse long predicted had not happened. What partial emancipation had not brought about was any significant change in the lives of ordinary workers on the estates, who were still denied rights and open to many abuses. In many of the colonies the stipendiary magistrates sided with the planters, according to reports from observers who watched the courts in action. Prosecutions were brought by planters against apprentices 'ungratefully undisposed to work'. The old racist slurs about 'natural indolence' and promiscuity come up as well.[28]

From the apprentices' point of view, reluctance to work was hardly an unreasonable reaction to a pseudo-emancipation that left their lives, and those of their older children, in the hands of the old elite. They needed their owners' permission to marry, they could be punished for disobedience, jailed and whipped, and evicted at a week's notice from the estate houses where their families had lived all their lives.

Experiences varied. A report on apprenticeship by Jamaican missionaries for the Methodist Church stated, 'in some instances their bonds have been drawn to the extreme and their yokes rendered more galling than before and in other cases they . . . enjoy advantages hitherto unknown and inexperienced by them'.[29] For the abolitionists the fact that women were still being whipped, and pregnant women and new mothers forced to work in the fields, became a powerful rallying point in the campaign for the genuine end of slavery.

It was possible during apprenticeship to buy freedom. But it was not easy. Records from St Thomas-in-the-East, the parish where Rozelle is, show that it cost an apprentice an average of £35 (£30,000 in equivalent labour value today) to secure their freedom, with higher-skilled people being asked much more. The owner of Green Castle estate demanded £111 of a man called Thomas McDermot. Since the apprentices had to work for their masters for forty-five hours a week, earning the money was hard: it took McDermot more than a year.[30]

The most effective spokespeople among white Britons for the completion of emancipation were the missionaries. The fiery William Knibb and his family had returned from his campaign tour of Britain in 1832 to his parish in Jamaica. Thence he offered legal advice to apprentices and started schools while raising funds that helped thousands of formerly enslaved people to buy land. Then, in 1838, the Marquess of Sligo announced in the House of Lords that he was now going to free all the apprentices on his two plantations immediately. This, from so eminent a servant of the Empire, bounced the government into action. It was decided to end apprenticeship two years early.

Thus, on 1 August 1838, slavery finally ended in the British West Indies. At Knibb's church in Falmouth, Jamaica, a service was held and a coffin containing a whip, chains and an iron punishment collar was buried. An inscription read: 'Colonial Slavery died 31st July 1838 aged 276.'[31]

CHAPTER 15

FREEDOM'S DEBT

The emancipation of that race was the brightest page in our history . . . It was that conduct regulated by moral and religious feelings which was the source of England's greatness.

Whig MP Henry Labouchere to the
House of Commons (1844)

The British historians wrote almost as if Britain had introduced Negro slavery solely for the satisfaction of abolishing it.

Eric Williams, *British Historians & the West Indies*, 1964

The great pay-off

Early in 1836 Sir James Fergusson and Sir David Hunter Blair received some excellent news from the British government. The Slave Compensation Commission had awarded them £3,591, eight shillings and eightpence for the 198 formerly enslaved people at Rozelle on 1 July 1835, valuing them on average at a little over £18 each. Today this amounts to slightly more than £3 million. There is no information on how the two men split the sum.

Compensation to owners was based on the slave market prices of the 1820s. Amounts varied from colony to colony. In Jamaica, a child was valued at £6, a field worker £50 and a valuable artisan like a sugar-boiler might be £100. A Scottish artisan then earned around £1.25 a week, a junior bank clerk about £1, so the compensation shared by the two baronets was enough to pay the annual wages of sixty-five skilled workers.[1]

Many British slave owners were paid far more in compensation, especially in more out of the way colonies where prices of enslaved people had been higher. The Gladstone family tops the list. Sir John Gladstone received £106,769, more than £90 million today. The sum was for 2,508 enslaved people working on nine different plantations in Jamaica and Demerara (now part of Guyana).

Gladstone's life had begun as one of the sixteen children of a small-time merchant in the port of Leith. By the 1830s his Scottish home was Fasque, in Kincardineshire, a vast red sandstone pile in the Elizabethan style, built in 1809 by the Ramsays of Balmain, who also had slavery connections.[2] Sir John had paid £80,000 for the house and estate in 1829. His son William Ewart Gladstone had entered Parliament, after Eton and Oxford, in time to speak against abolition in 1832. He would come to be regarded as the Victorian age's greatest liberal prime minister.

Parliament agreed to pay a total of £20 million to the slave owners, perhaps £17 billion today, though some calculations put it much higher. It went to 46,000 different claimants, half of them in the UK, and a disproportionate number in Scotland. It was a vast sum: 40 per cent of the government's national annual budget of the time, and the Crown's largest loan of the entire nineteenth century – enough, as one economic historian has said, to carry on a 'medium-sized war'.[3]

The bankers Nathan Mayer Rothschild and Moses Montefiore lent the government £15 million at a generously low interest. This was seen as a charitable act on their part, at the time, in that it enabled emancipation to happen. Rothschild got a little of the money back quite quickly: he held a mortgage on an estate in Antigua and was paid compensation of £1,750 and eighteen shillings for the sixty-five enslaved people on it.[4]

This blatant pay-off, an essential part of the story of the ending of slavery in the British Empire, was swiftly obscured by Victorian and twentieth-century myth-making about the benevolence of British colonialism. In 2015 the British Treasury announced that the loan had at last been paid off. Most people had known nothing of the deal that brought about the end of slavery. The Treasury – the British government's ministry of finance – saw the repayment as a feat of which to be proud. On 9 February 2018, under the hashtag 'surprisingFridayFact', the department's third of a million Twitter followers were told this:

> Millions of you helped end the slave trade through your taxes. Did you know? In 1833, Britain used £20 million, 40% of its national budget, to buy freedom for all slaves in the Empire. The amount of money borrowed for the Slavery Abolition Act was so large that it wasn't paid off until 2015. Which means that living British citizens helped pay to end the slave trade.

The historian David Olusoga wrote that this statement had 'the unctuous feel of a pat on the back': should we really be boasting about a policy that made humans property, and rewarded those who held them as such? The Treasury's Twitter followers were pretty sure what the answer to that was. One woman replied: 'So basically, my father and his children and grandchildren have been paying taxes to compensate those who enslaved our ancestors, and you want me to be proud of that fact. Are you f**king insane??'[5]

* * *

'Compensated emancipation' was an astonishing final coup by the plantocracy and the merchants and bankers who supported and backed them. It marked the end of 250 years of governmental support for them, with the devotion of millions in military and naval resources to securing the colonies and their trade routes. Britain itself had been enriched by the slavery-fuelled industries that were such a significant part of its economy – responsible for 12 per cent of GDP in 1800[6] – for more than a century. As we've seen, the British Treasury made more money in most years from the Fergusson-Hunter Blair plantation than the owners did. Nonetheless, one generation's investment of time and money in slavery and its spin-off industries was sufficient for many families, such as the Harewoods and the Gladstones, to set up the succeeding three or four generations to live in comfort to rival that of any civilisation the world has known. The power and influence such wealth generated is not measurable.

It is hard to imagine any Briton, from the poorest to the richest of the nineteenth century, who did not in some way benefit from slavery. Jobs and wealth were created by industries exporting goods to the slave colonies: that in turned fuelled Britain's Industrial Revolution and the huge growth in living standards of the nineteenth century. Until 1860 most of the American cotton crop, grown and picked by enslaved people, was shipped to British mills to produce textiles for export throughout the world. The only set of people to lose in every way were the Africans bought and exploited to enrich Britain and the other European countries. Their children were sold. They died prematurely for our profit. And, at slavery's end, they too paid the planters for their freedom; not in cash, as the British taxpayer did, but with their bodies and their labour over the following years.[7]

* * *

The list of the 46,000 awardees has been placed by University College London on a website called Legacies of British Slave-ownership. This contains names and records of some of Britain's richest families, many still powerful today. More than a few still benefit from the wealth generated by investing the profits of slavery – and the compensation windfall – in Britain's nineteenth-century industrial boom. 'Out of slaves and into railway shares' was the potted explanation used of some wealthy Scottish families. The Ayrshire railway lines were indeed funded by the local wealthy, many of them with fortunes made or augmented in the Caribbean. One successful railway company, the Edinburgh & Northern, sold 40 per cent of its initial subscription to slave owners and their heirs.[8] Today its track is part of the British East Coast Main Line.

Three thousand people in Britain owned 50 per cent of all the enslaved people of the British Caribbean.[9] But as analyses of the data show, there were also many less grand and wealthy people among the compensees. Of 25,000 awards of less than £500, some indeed went to 'widows and orphans' in Britain, as the pro-compensation lobby had argued they would.[10] Some also went to slave owners outside Britain, and a few to people who were themselves descendants of African enslaved people.

One of the most famous of these was the man called the first mixed race MP in Britain's parliament, John Stewart. His father, also called John and also an MP, owned multiple plantations in the Caribbean. He fathered John, a 'natural son', by a woman in Demerara called Mary Duncan. He then inherited the estates and managed them through emancipation and beyond, using his position in Parliament to defend both slavery and apprenticeship. The compensation scheme gave him a huge award – more than £25,000.

Another appears to have been James Graham, my great-great-great-grandfather on my father's side. He was born in Jamaica in 1789 to Elizabeth Delaroche, a 'free mulatto', and a Scottish merchant, John Graham. In Jamaica James would have been considered a 'free coloured' or 'quadroon'. He is listed as owning two enslaved women in Manchester parish in Jamaica in 1817 – one was Nancy, Jamaica-born and seventeen years old, the other Sarah, twenty-six, who had been born in Africa. It seems likely that they were house servants. In 1835 Margaret Reid, James's first wife, was awarded compensation of £46 for enslaved people in Jamaica, probably two adults and a child.[11]

Thus people from the super-rich to the quite ordinary were among those who shared the great slave owners' pay-off. There was confusion and fraud as people began to realise how accessible this great money gusher was, and how complex a job the Compensation Commissioners had been set. A former planter, Frederick Martiny, wrote to the Commission from Marylebone in London asking if he could take his daughter's beloved nanny, bought as a gift by the girl's grandmother for £215, back to Honduras in order to claim the compensation due on her.[12] He was refused.

The powerful and titled had a major share of the large claims, though the compensation frequently ended up in the hands of mortgagees and banks to whom the owners were indebted. At least fifty Members of Parliament were directly affected by the compensation provisions of the Abolition Act. Three dukes, one marquess, forty-two viscounts, barons and earls, and seventy-five baronets (among them Sir James Fergusson and Sir David Hunter Blair) are on the list of recipients.[13] Over the coming decades many British people enriched by slavery and the businesses that fed on it obtained titles: for some, it remains a time-honoured way to offset any taint in the origin of one's wealth.

All sorts of people and professions received compensation: the records reveal much that eminent institutions, from universities to international banking corporations, would prefer was hidden even now. Forty London banks are there, many surviving in different forms today.[14] Christian institutions appear. The Bishop of Exeter, Henry Phillpotts, obtained, as an executor of the Earl of Dudley, £12,000 compensation for 665 enslaved people in Jamaica. One hundred and eighteen other Church of England clergy are named in the compensation records, most of them direct beneficiaries.

Only half a dozen ministers of Scottish churches appear, though 20 per cent of all claims for compensation were from Scots. The 'Elders and Ministers' of Kilmadock in Perthshire lodged a claim for £332, for fifty-two slaves on an estate in Trelawny parish in Jamaica, part of which they had been left in the will of its owner, Thomas Paterson. The well-known Anglican missionary body, the Society for the Propagation of the Gospel in Foreign Parts, received the huge sum of £8,558, two shillings and tuppence for the 410 enslaved people on the estate it had owned in Barbados since 1710. For a time the enslaved people who worked on the Codrington plantation (three years was their average life-span after arrival, according to a report from the 1790s) had the word 'Society' branded on their chests.[15]

It is only very recently that, mainly through the historians working on the UCL project, research has begun into where the compensation money went and how it was spent. Many people in the West Indies then and today believed that the money was earmarked so that the planters would use it to educate and 'civilise' – the word used at the time – the newly freed people. But that was not set into the law, though the British government did recognise that there was need to help the people of the Caribbean emerge from enslavement.

However, the government was far from generous. Only £60,000 was granted by Parliament for the setting up of schools in Jamaica. This was less than 1 per cent of the sum paid in compensation to owners of slaves in Jamaica;[16] not lavish, with a largely uneducated population of 350,000 to address. Only five years earlier the British government had given £200,000 to help the Jamaica planters get over the damage done during the few days of Sam Sharpe's Christmas uprising.

Some retired and absentee owners spent money from compensation or from their profits on good works for the poor. But not for their former slaves. Archibald Kerr left his entire Jamaican estate to the Edinburgh Royal Infirmary, then and now the city's principal public hospital.[17] Others used slavery-derived money to create further misery back at home. George Rainy made one of the greatest fortunes of all in Demerara (Guyana). He returned to Scotland in 1837 and spent £36,750 on buying the Hebridean island of Raasay. (Scottish islands were trinkets that attracted several tycoons of the slavery industry.[18])

After the potato famine of the early 1840s, he decided to get rid of Raasay's people. He banned marriage, and then forced several hundred of them off their land. Most had to migrate to Australia.

A few owners did spend the money, or a part of it, on improving the lives of their newly freed workers in the Caribbean. The most striking example in Jamaica is Howe Browne, the Marquess of Sligo, the former governor. Sligo's compensation was £5,526, nine shillings and a penny, for 386 slaves in St Dorothy parish.[19] He built two schools for freed workers and is said to have been the first planter to pay wages. Eventually he divided the land into smallholdings which were leased or sold to emancipated locals.

The first village of freed people was named Sligoville, after him. He built a school and church there and it became a model for other 'free villages' across the island. Sligoville is now famous as the place where the pan-Africanist preacher Len Howell bought land and set up a co-operative community that became the beginning of Rastafarianism. The great house at the Pinnacle, a former slave estate notorious for ill-treatment of the workers during apprenticeship, became the Howell family's home.

But there are very few Sligos in the records. One third of the £6 million paid in compensation in Jamaica went to merchants and financiers, often reclaiming mortgages and outstanding loans made to planters. A small group of merchant bankers in Glasgow received more than £400,000 (perhaps a third of a billion today) through compensation, according to research done by the historian Stephen Mullen. None of them directly owned more than a handful of people, but they held the loans and mortgages on the slave estates.[20] One Glasgow family, the Smiths of Jordanhill, and their associates took nearly £70,000 in 1836 in compensation, mainly on repayment of mortgages. Not one of these people appears to have returned any of the money to the islands and their people. The Glasgow Smiths, according to Mullen, put their money into yachts for pleasure and railways for profit.

A moral triumph

By the middle of the nineteenth century the deal done to buy off the West Indies businessmen for the loss of their property had been fully rebranded. It was now a sacred act of philanthropy, typical of the enlightened British approach to the world's wrongs. The Whig politician Henry Vassall-Fox, Lord Holland, was another conflicted member of the political establishment – a beneficiary of slavery, and of compensation, and a supporter of the abolitionist Charles James Fox, his uncle.

Nevertheless, Holland stated in his popular history of the party that the Whigs had 'put an end to one of the greatest evils to which the human race has ever been exposed, or at least to our share in the guilt of it'.[21] Even the Conservative leader of the 1830s and 1840s, Robert Peel, agreed. Abolition was a 'moral triumph' that would outshine even England's naval victories and the defeat of Napoleon, he stated in 1841.[22]

But the reality remains that the families and the banks swiftly deserted the people and the places which had served them. A report on poverty in Jamaica published in 1858 quotes an unnamed clergyman on the effect, after 1831, when 'capital had fled the country':

> Half the productive land in the island was thrown out of cultivation. Consequently a whole class disappeared i.e. the wealthy absentee proprietor . . . some few are holding on in poverty. Capital had fled the country . . . advances from English mercantile houses bought estates at less than the value of the works on them. No country can prosper with an upper class of foreigners. Something better is wanted for Jamaica than this.[23]

* * *

In 1838 Sir James Fergusson died, passing the baronetcy, Kilkerran and the family possessions to his son Charles, my great-great-great-grandfather. The fifth baronet was a member of various committees of the Church of Scotland – a Kirk elder and commissioner in its parliament, the General Assembly. He devoted himself to intellectual and religious affairs in Edinburgh, the usual and proper after-work entertainment of an educated gentleman. He was a friend of the dominant figure of the time, Sir Walter Scott (who died in 1832), and a member of the Royal Society, the Speculative Society, the Bannatyne Club and all the others that met to discuss matters from scientific discoveries to moral and educational questions.

Sir Charles's diaries record dinnertime debates on whether the 'lower classes' should be educated (yes, 'for their morals', but only in religious knowledge) and whether children's early education should include Hebrew. He delivered talks on the history of painting and on the development of criminal law, and he published a very dry book about the early history of the Church of Scotland. When not talking, dining, or in the courts, he was doing charitable works around Edinburgh: schools for the children of poor fishermen in the villages beside the Forth, for example. His diaries record every penny spent in charity – a shilling every Sunday in the kirk collection, 2/6 for 'an appeal for distressed seamen', a shilling to a begging woman, a pound for the Society for the Suppression of Begging and another one for missionary work in India. There was some entertainment. He played backgammon for small amounts and he had subscriptions to magazines like *The Spectator*. On 20 January 1831 he paid ten shillings for tickets to a concert given by the soprano Margarethe Stockhausen.

He was the picture of an early Victorian gentleman and the last member of the family to acknowledge the source of a part of its wealth: his entry in the 1889 edition of the *Dictionary of National Biography* calls him, coyly, a 'colonial proprietor'. He inherited Kilkerran and the Dalrymple estates in Lothian, including Newhailes, a beautiful Palladian mansion outside Musselburgh, and took the name Sir Charles Dalrymple Fergusson. The *DNB* states: 'He initiated the Ayrshire Educational Association, and at his own expense built schools and churches'. But none were in Jamaica.

By the 1840s the earnings from Rozelle were nothing like the sums Sir Charles's father and his great-uncle had known. In February 1841 he received news from Rozelle via the lawyer Quintin Kennedy: 'The prospect for this year is quite as bad as could be but after that there seems to be a reasonable ground for anticipating a fair return. It is quite evident that the cause of the deficient crops was nothing but the grossest negligence and management.' Only thirty-four hogsheads of sugar were made in 1840, by which time sixty was more normal, albeit less than half what was usually produced forty years earlier.

This was 'disastrous', said Kennedy, apologising. Now elderly, the lawyer was shortly to hand over management to the Glasgow-based merchant and banking company Stirling, Gordon & Co. The Rozelle estate was carrying £3,580 of debts and earned a mere £1,072 from sugar in 1840, a result as bad as the worst years of the 1770s, when a pound sterling was worth three times as much. Kennedy arranged for a new sugar-boiler to be constructed and sent out. He concluded the letter by suggesting various ways Sir Charles could pay off his debts with Kennedy's employers, the Ayrshire Bank.[24]

In 1842, the last year for which we have a financial record, Sir David Hunter Blair and Sir Charles Fergusson shared a net profit from Rozelle, before tax, of £2,182. That may have been their last of any size. Most historians agree that the sugar estate economy on the Caribbean islands was essentially bankrupt by this time. The value of the core property – the works, the land and the workers' houses – was in steep decline. The export prices of sugar and rum in the late 1830s were a quarter, in real terms, of what they were in the 1790s.[25]

Coffee was becoming nearly as valuable an export crop as sugar: more alert landowners such as the Hamiltons had adjusted their Jamaica plantations accordingly.[26] A plan drawn up for them in 1843 suggested planting coffee and selling marginal land to the emancipated ('it will calm their quarrels and make them eager to labour'). The Hamiltons wanted to encourage more people from Africa to migrate and work as indentured labour, a common idea across the Caribbean as planters addressed the plain fact that the freed people did not wish to work as had their enslaved fathers and mothers.

The great political changes in Britain during the 1840s hastened the decline in the Caribbean exporting colonies. One of the sweeteners promised to the planters at emancipation was that their crop should continue to enjoy less tax in Britain than sugar from elsewhere in the world. But sugar got dragged into the great trade reform battles of the time, and in 1846 tariffs on sugar from outside the British colonies were dropped. From now on Jamaican and other British islands' sugar had to compete on equal terms with cheaper product from Brazil and Cuba. Ironically, this liberal reform had the effect of putting slave-grown sugar back on the British market. Forty years later 12 per cent of sugar arriving at British ports was still grown by plantations using enslaved people, and this continued until Brazil abolished slavery in 1888.

With the tariff change, many Jamaican sugar plantations went bust overnight. Some were abandoned: in 1847 the Jamaica assembly was told that that 140 of the 653 sugar plantations that had existed at emancipation were gone, 'the works broken up'. Many coffee plantations had failed too. The assembly relayed this report to London, stating that the destruction of the plantations had meant the loss of nearly 50,000 labouring jobs since 1832 – perhaps one fifth of the island's total workforce. Nevertheless, it was impossible to find enough casual labour to harvest the crops. Exports had dropped 40 per cent, and Cuba was – with enslaved labour – able to produce sugar at less than half the minimum price necessary to cover costs in Jamaica. The following year the assembly sent a memorial directly to Queen Victoria, saying that her government must choose between 'protection or destruction' of Jamaica's sugar industry.[27] It chose the latter.

During this unsettled and impoverished time the planters' lobby and their many supporters raised the old slurs about people of African descent being lazy or unwilling to work, no matter the wages. John Candler, a wealthy draper from Essex who had been prominent in the Quaker campaign for abolition, toured Jamaica in 1850 and kept an interesting diary of his inquisitive conversations with planters, clergy and ordinary workers, from plantation day-labourers to urban washerwomen. Moral standards and low wages are his principal concerns: on the latter, he found a shilling (£0.05) a day was the wage for men on Lord Howard de Walden's estate of Montpelier; ninepence a day (£0.0375) for a female on Lord Airlie's estate, the Ferry, though there they had free housing so long as they continued to work.[28]

Candler interviews a group of 'strong Creole women' working on the estate. They were 'very cheerful', had enough to eat and had no complaint about the work or their 'master', though since Candler was Lord Airlie's house guest, they might have been a little hesitant. He repays their friendliness with some finger-wagging about their casual marital arrangements.[29]

The lack of workers led to the indenture on many estates of new immigrant Africans. These were ex-captives who had been freed by the British Navy when it intercepted slave traders' ships and temporarily housed in Sierra Leone or the island of St Helena. Taking them back home was never considered, it appears. In St Thomas parish in Jamaica there are still villages populated by these peoples' descendants who proudly remember their origins.

An island abandoned

The West India lobby's muscle had withered. The smart money had left the Caribbean, more interested in trade with the east, or financing the factories of industrial Britain. The former slave colonies were economic backwaters, their history an embarrassment to a nation reimagining itself as a global moral leader. The British parliament, partly reformed, was no longer quite as dominated by the traditional alliance of colonial money and landed aristocrats.

The Chancellor of the Exchequer who began the debate that led to the Sugar Duties Act 1846, Henry Goulburn, was himself still a planter in Jamaica, and had received £5,000 in compensation in 1836. But his political devotion to the principle of 'free trade' all but killed off the Caribbean sugar plantation system, damaging rich and poor. The planters and merchants campaigned shrilly for a restoration of the preferential tariff regime, saying that the promises of the emancipation period were being betrayed. They had a point. But the betrayal was of both black and, for the first time, white. It began a century of exploitation and neglect that kept Jamaica and many other colonies in debt and bound to Britain.

By 1848, with plantations closing and jobs disappearing, the British government's statistical survey reported that only some 12,000 children were going to school daily – less than 20 per cent of those eligible. John Candler found, in the 'delapidated houses and neglected streets' of Kingston, schools whose pupils had simply stopped attending. 'Much complaint is made of the carelessness of Black Parents in not sending their children to school; some say that they are very poor and can neither clothe their children nor pay the weekly pittance for them', he writes.[30]

Other visitors saw clearly that the white rulers of the island were wilfully averse to educating the masses. They were shocked: the policy or lack of it was in huge contrast to America, where baptism and education were the tonics that the anti-slavery states prescribed for the emancipated. In 1860 the Canadian journalist W. G. Sewell wrote in the *New York Times*: 'Of the 320,000 slaves that were liberated [in Jamaica], only the tradesmen and head people, numbering not more than 45,000, had ever picked up the merest waifs of knowledge. The balance – field-laborers and domestics – were almost as savage and untutored as their fathers were when they were dragged from their homes on the African coast'.[31] His point was that Jamaica needed a productive middle class, and yet the white plantocracy had no notion that educating the emancipated people was in their economic best interest.

It was clear to Sewell that the planters would rather their former slaves remained labourers dependent on the plantation system. He dismisses the common racist contention that education was pointless because of 'African' mental backwardness and immorality, citing the freed people he met who had managed to set up as small merchants and farmers. 'The change they have undergone, within twenty-two years, is assuredly no sign of incapacity, no proof of indolence, no indication of unconquerable vice . . . I think that the position of the Jamaica peasant, in 1860, is a standing rebuke to those who, wittingly or unwittingly, encourage the vulgar lie that the African cannot possibly be elevated.'[32]

* * *

Sir Charles Dalrymple Fergusson had not quite forgotten Rozelle, or the hope of gaining from it financially. He was convinced that the British government would listen to the complaints from the Caribbean colonies, backtrack and restore the protective tariffs. So, in 1848, in the middle of an international banking crisis, he made one of the most bizarre decisions in all the history of the family's financial dealings.

The agent for his Jamaican business was a friend, the Edinburgh businessman James Hope. He told Sir Charles to get rid of his half of the Rozelle estate while he still could: it was said that British bankers were lending money to buy estates for less than the value of the sugar works on them.[33] Hope thought Charles might be able to get £2,500 for his half of Rozelle – a valuation of the land and buildings that amounted to 12.5 per cent of their worth in real terms half a century earlier. At that price his share would be £2 million today.

Nevertheless, he decided to ignore Hope's wise counsel. Instead of selling up he bought out Sir David Hunter Blair's half-share, for £2,500. Sir David, now seventy, must have been pleased. On the envelope of one of these letters Sir Charles scribbled: 'I declined to take [Hope's] advice believing that a change in House Policy, by the repeal of [the tariff Act] of 1846, wd. Make all right, and that if the Country is to be saved, that must take place soon.'[34] He was wrong. Far from restoring the Caribbean colonies' preferential tariff, in 1851 a further Act made duties on all sugar imports equal, no matter whence they came.

It was a catastrophe for all the sugar-exporting colonies. In Rozelle's St Thomas parish, the eighty-four sugar estates of 1804 were reduced to just twenty-one by 1851. The poorer inhabitants suffered outbreaks of cholera, smallpox and measles in the early 1850s, all exacerbated by this new poverty. The Fergussons were now saddled with all of the 1,500 acres of unproductive land in Jamaica, along with its decayed sugar works and dwelling houses, and an unknown number of resident people without obvious rights.

Sir Charles died in 1849, aged forty-eight. He was succeeded by his oldest son, James, who had just turned eighteen. The baronetcy, Kilkerran, Rozelle and the other Scottish land and houses were now his. James had just left Rugby School, determined to skip Oxford and join the army. Sir Charles's younger son, David, inherited Newhailes, the Dalrymple house and estate outside Edinburgh, where his father had died.

* * *

At this point Rozelle disappears from the family papers for more than a century, until my grandmother and grandfather, Frances and Sir James Fergusson (the eighth baronet), went to visit Jamaica in 1973. The basic facts of the last decades of Fergusson ownership are to be found in Jamaica's Island Records Office. They show that, with his mother Helen's 'express counsel', as required by his father's will, the young Sir James ended eighty-two years of control of the plantation from Scotland. In 1850 he leased the Rozelle land and all the buildings on it for seven years, at £250 sterling a year. It was a paltry amount compared with earlier times. But as a 5 per cent return on the £5,000 at which the estate was valued in 1848, it cannot have seemed so bad a deal.

The terms of the lease ask the new tenant, a doctor called John Graham Delancy,[35] to pay the taxes, keep the place in good order and repair hurricane damage. There is nothing about any sitting tenants. The young Sir James Fergusson must have given little thought to Rozelle. He had joined the Grenadier Guards as an officer and, at twenty years old, was off to fight against the Russians in the Crimean War alongside Sir David Hunter Blair's son and heir, also called James. In 1851 both the armies around Sebastopol and the people of Jamaica were fighting a worldwide cholera epidemic: 40,000 died in Jamaica, a tenth of the population. The disease was brought to the island from Panama, it was believed, by an American steamboat.

In 1858 a City of London firm, Cottam, Morton & Co., takes

over the Rozelle lease at the same rent in partnership with a local planter, Samuel Shortridge, employing some 140 people from the nearby village of White Horses. Shortridge owns the nearby Plantain Garden River estate too. His involvement is remarkable for one thing: for the first time in its near 200-year history as a sugar plantation, the land is now managed by someone of mixed race. Shortridge is descended from a line of white male planters, and on his mother's side from freed African women.

Sir James Fergusson is by now a Member of Parliament for the Conservative Party, beginning a career that will take him to seats of power across the British Empire. He becomes a minister in the governments of Lord Derby, Benjamin Disraeli and finally of Lord Salisbury. In between stints in the House of Commons and the Foreign and Colonial offices, he goes overseas to serve as governor of South Australia, New Zealand and then Bombay. These jobs were seen as an honour more than a means of enrichment: Sir James's finances, according to family lore, were precarious. He kept afloat by selling off land in Ayrshire, the last Edinburgh house and other family assets, eventually renting out Kilkerran House itself.

In 1875, after 106 years of family ownership, the Rozelle estate is sold. The buyers are the tenants, Cottam, Morton & Co. They pay just £4,000, a thousand pounds less than its valuation when Sir James's father bought the Hunter Blair half nearly thirty years earlier, and 6.25 per cent of its value in 1792. It is, nonetheless, a good move financially. The sugar plantation industry in the Caribbean is in crisis again, with prices collapsing as a result of a new rival in the market: sugar made from the roots of the beet plant grown in northern Europe. Three years later, in October 1878, Cottam, Morton go bust, sacking all the workers on nineteen Jamaica plantations. It had employed 6,000 'labourers', most of them in St Thomas-in-the-East. A newspaper reports that the collapse 'seriously affected this Island'.[36]

CHAPTER 16

BETRAYAL: ABSENTEE LANDLORDS AND PLANTER-MAGISTRATES

I know of no country in the world where prosperity, wealth, and a commanding position have been so strangely subverted and destroyed, as they have been in Jamaica, within the brief space of sixty years. I know of no country in the world where so little trouble has been taken to investigate the causes of this decline, or to remedy the evils that have depressed the colony.

W. G. Sewell, *New York Times*,
27 January 1860

THE TENSIONS OF POWER AND race in Jamaica were no nearer resolution by the 1860s than they had been at emancipation: if anything, the island was poorer, more volatile and primed for conflict. Many of the owners of plantations still behaved as though the era of slavery had not ended. But resisting reform was not a battle they could possibly win. From the economics of the plantation export business to the changing attitudes in an increasingly liberal Britain, everything was against them. So were the demographics.

By the 1850s white people in Jamaica were a declining minority, less than 3 per cent of a population of 450,000.[1] 'The consequence is that in the course of time the black people must get their proper position in the country', pointed out George William Gordon, businessman, Jamaican assembly member at the age of twenty-seven, and a freed mixed race slave himself.

People like Gordon were the future. Yet his reforming zeal was to be rejected in the most brutal way. The white minority, with very few exceptions, were determined to cling to their privilege and their power. We have to rely on the reports of men sent as Christian missionaries to hear what this meant for Jamaicans living and working, as many still were, on the plantations. From them come stories that echo those of the slavery period: humiliation, poverty, continued use of the whip, and – told in the most veiled way – overseers and book-keepers exploiting women on the plantations for sexual purposes. Picking on workers who were Christians, and thus troublemakers, is a common story.

Absentee ownership, like that of the Fergussons, was one of the problems that held Jamaica back in the years after emancipation. When sugar became hardly profitable, many proprietors simply milked the island and its people for the little that could still be had in rents. They put nothing back, and the returns – £250 a year from Rozelle to the Fergussons after they let it to tenants in 1850 – were tiny. But their tenants continued a regime over the black working class that was tyrannical and illegal: there is no record of the Fergussons' noticing, let alone intervening.

The merchant bankers who bought up the broke estates were just as neglectful. Most acquired the land as speculation, devalued prop-erties that might one day go back into use and repay the investment. Few did until the late nineteenth century, when growing bananas and other fruit for export became viable. The world had turned elsewhere for its sugar, not least Cuba and Brazil, where it was still produced through slave labour.

The *New York Times*'s correspondent W. G. Sewell visited the island in late 1859. He wrote of a 'stupendous' decline from wealthy colony to poverty. Over the next six months the newspaper published five of his lengthy reports under the title 'Emancipation in Jamaica', well-timed as the United States fought its own way towards the end of slavery (which came in December 1865). What Sewell, who had also visited Trinidad, discovered was deeply discouraging.

Of Kingston, the 'godforsaken' capital of Jamaica, he wrote in disdain that 'there is not a house in the city in decent repair; not one that looks as though it could withstand a respectable breeze; not a wharf in good order; not a street that can exhibit a square yard of pavement; no sidewalks; no drainage; scanty water; no light. The same picture of neglect and apathy greets one everywhere . . . The people, like their horses, their houses, and all that belongs to them, look old and worn.' Failed policy since emancipation had brought the island to 'hopeless ruin', Sewell concluded.[2]

Four years later another American journalist, John Willis Menard, who had settled in Jamaica, wrote acidly in response to reports like Sewell's that Jamaica was not in fact destroyed: 'The ruin of the slave owner has been taken for the ruin of Jamaica.' He blamed foreign speculators for Jamaica's economic misery.[3] But Menard – who was black and had worked as an emissary for the US government – would naturally have agreed with Sewell's firm rebuttal of the notion that the answer was a return to slavery. This issue needed addressing: powerful planters and businessmen had floated the idea of Jamaica seceding from Britain and joining the United States as a slave state.[4]

In his book on the Caribbean, published in 1861, Sewell stated that the medicine Jamaica needed was policy that encouraged black participation in the economy and loosened the white elite's grip on power. Most of all, he advocated foreign investment in what was still a 'fresh and fair, and abundantly fertile' island with a small population.[5]

But farming was not what excited the venture capitalists of the nineteenth century. Poking around the remains of colonial-era Jamaica today, you are struck by how pieces of old ironwork and even bricks are embossed with the names of British companies in British cities. As economic historians have pointed out, there was little point developing Jamaican industry or educating the workforce when the island was most useful as a captive market for British goods.

Rigging the vote

Jamaicans, of course, were not content with this. Slowly, education was beginning to turn the children and grandchildren of the enslaved into citizens informed of their rights, and, to an extent, about what other subject peoples across the British Empire were demanding. Most of the planter class, still almost entirely white, saw any attempt by the black working class to improve their lives as a direct threat to their power. 'The planters' policy has been to keep the people uninstructed, and the Government has never even encouraged education, much less insisted upon it as one of the most important of reciprocal duties between a free State and its citizens', thundered Sewell.[6]

This was no exaggeration: the assembly had more than once

rejected bills to set up not just basic schools, but also training colleges for doctors and lawyers. One of George William Gordon's campaigns was to raise funds for a college on the island, providing further education in trades for all Jamaicans.

The ruling elite would not tolerate this sort of project. Attempts to set up co-operative farms and 'mercantile associations' were branded as sedition in the white newspapers and forcibly stopped.[7] The ideology behind this was clear. As Sewell found, planters and officials had a common theme: freedom was damaging to the minds of black people, and it led to wrongdoing. William Carr, a magistrate and large-scale plantation proprietor, summed the view up in 1866, when he told a government inquiry: 'Their very independence is an evil'.[8]

White people, though a tiny minority, were most of the electorate: only tax-paying male 'freeholders', with a certain income or amount of property, were allowed to vote. These rules were similar to those in Britain, where until 1867 only some 5 per cent of the population had the right to vote. But the franchise policy for Jamaica came straight from a racially biased government in London, with a colour bar built in. One of the stated fears of senior British ministers such as Earl Grey was of the 'negro population obtaining a preponderating influence' in the Jamaica assembly.[9]

Black people were too 'excitable' to be encouraged to vote and allowing them to do so 'does mischief', stated the Jamaican attorney general, Alexander Heslop, in 1866. He was himself of mixed race.[10] So poorer Jamaicans were given an added hurdle between them and the ballot box: in addition to having to own land worth at least £6, there was a tax of ten shillings – a month's wages for a labourer – to get your name onto the voting register.

As a result, of an estimated 50,000 freeholders in 1859, only 3,000 were registered to vote. By 1864 that had dropped to 1,903: only 1,457 cast a ballot in that year's election.[11] But determined organisation did succeed in getting a few supporters of the poor – such as George William Gordon in St Thomas-in-the-East – elected.

* * *

Myself was born free, but my mother and father was slaved; but now I am still a slave by working from days to days. I cannot get

money to feed my family, and I working at Coley estate for 1s.,
and after five day's working I get 2s. 6d for my family. Is that able
to sustain a family?

                        James McLaren, campaigner for access to abandoned land
                                                     in St Thomas-in-the-East

Land brought freedoms, both social and economic. What use was
personal liberty if the conditions of your work as hired labour, living
in a rented house, were little different from those of apprenticeship?
Even today, as the sociologist Clinton Hutton writes, Jamaicans still
refer to such work as 'going to slave'.[12] James McLaren and others like
him made the point that if the unused land of the many abandoned
sugar plantations was given to them they could make a living, 'pay
taxes to the Queen and . . . not want anything from the white people'.[13]

But this kind of liberation was a double challenge to the whites,
a threat to their status as well as depriving them of a needy workforce
on call. And so land and the opportunity to acquire it were tightly
controlled: McLaren and many others of the village of Stony Gut
were to die trying to obtain it. An American missionary in Jamaica,
Henry Garnet – who was of African origin – wrote in 1854 of what
he had seen to anti-slavery campaigners in Britain. One telling story
was of a neighbour in Westmoreland parish who owned a cane field
and decided to build a still and a boiling house to make sugar. The
proprietor of the next-door sugar estate came to see him. The conversation went like this:

So you are going to turn planter.
    How so master?
    Well, I hear that you are going to grind your canes and boil
your sugar?
    Yes master. I was intending to do so.
    Well, I should like to see you doing anything of the kind. You must
remember that you have no title for the land you occupied, and I
doubt if you will ever get one if you persist in your undertaking.[14]

Garnet concludes: 'I am informed that the poor man has been
completely overawed by the threat, and will proceed no further.'[15]
Sewell of the *New York Times* found in 1859 that agricultural land
could be bought for '£2 or £3 an acre'[16] – not much more than it

cost to lease. He calculated that a fully employed labourer could earn just over £10 a year, though few labourers living on plantations got work year-round. So the financial barriers to owning land reinforced the social and racial ones.

The policy of controlling the black working class through economic means took many forms. Vicious taxes were imposed that appeared to target the black population as people attempting to set up the means to make a living. An individual who owned a horse, ox or mule had to pay a tax approaching a month's wages for a labourer. Cartwheels were taxed at six shillings each, carts at eighteen shillings. But 'estates' were exempt from these taxes.

Meanwhile tariffs on imported goods that the Jamaican wealthy required, from fine timber to foods, were lowered. Sewell found this astonishing. The planters had 'schemed to deprive the independent settlers of their means of livelihood, to destroy their market, and compel them to accept again the shilling a day and the Slavery of plantation work that the master condescendingly offered'. This, he concluded, was a 'strange and fatal misunderstanding of their true interests'.[17]

Income from taxation went largely to benefit the white elite. Their Anglican church received £40,000 in subsidy in 1865, 10 per cent of the Jamaican government's budget. The non-denominational churches, used by poorer people and responsible for most of the schools, received nothing. The education budget that year was only £3,000, the same as it had been in 1859, and two-thirds of that went via the Anglican church.

The result was an uneducated population that was convinced of its inferiority. John Willis Menard wrote: 'In Jamaica, I am afraid, the greater portion of the people have been made to believe that they are not susceptible of attaining a high degree of civilisation . . . Reform should be organised before this dangerous belief germinates in the young mind.'

In October 1865, nine months after writing this in Jamaica's *Sentinel* newspaper, Menard was arrested and banished from the island by the governor, Edward Eyre, without trial or charges.[18] He never returned: in 1868 he was elected to the US Congress to represent Louisiana. But he never took his seat, because the US Congress voted against it: 'it was too early to admit a Negro', it was said.[19]

* * *

You can have no idea of the number of people turned back from different estates every Monday morning because there is no work for them. The poor people often go away with tears in their eyes for the want of employment. These planters who are from time to time complaining that the people are lazy and won't work must know they are uttering a downright falsehood. The truth is they cannot afford to employ the people. It is money they want, and not labour. Besides, many of them treat the people like brutes, especially those that are living upon the estates and who rent provision grounds. If they do not submit to the bad treatment they are turned off the properties . . . and they dare not say a word, for, as to *justice*, there is none of it in this parish.

> From a letter published in the *Anti-Slavery Reporter*,
> by a correspondent in St Thomas-in-the-East,
> dispatched 12 March 1859[20]

Reports like this were written for a less than impartial audience: the *Anti-Slavery Reporter* was a popular monthly publication for an audience committed to ending slavery worldwide. The 120 pages of its May 1859 edition contain reports from Cuba, Brazil, Liberia and of a 'grand auction' of 436 enslaved people in the American state of Georgia. But the charge that there was no justice in the parish of St Thomas-in-the-East is provable. The evidence comes from an impeccable source, the inquiry of a Royal Commission on Jamaica's unrest – which led to hundreds of deaths in 1865 – held in early 1866.

The magistrates in St Thomas were largely plantation owners, unqualified beyond being members of the ruling elite. They regularly sat in judgement on cases in which they were personally involved. Samuel Shortridge, co-tenant of Sir James Fergusson's Rozelle estate, was one of the busiest of those magistrates. In the years 1862 to 1865, 661 cases were heard at Bath, the parish capital. In 161 of them, one of the two magistrates presiding was also the complainant. Most of the cases were against men and women described as 'labourers' and were for petty crimes arising from friction between a workforce and its employer-landlords: larceny, trespass, breach of contract and 'neglect of duty as a servant'. But the penalties often seem grotesquely large – ninety days in jail for stealing a pig, a month's wages for 'verbal abuse'.[21]

Shortridge sat on dozens of cases in these three years, and he was accustomed to judging those who had fallen foul of him. In 1864 Frederick, 'an African' – presumably one of the migrants from Sierra Leone now living in St Thomas-in-the-East – was in court for stealing sugar canes from Samuel Shortridge. The latter was the magistrate: he gave Frederick a fine and costs totalling thirteen shillings. If he did not pay, he would face ten days in jail.

In 1865 Shortridge had two labourers, Margaret Brown and Sophia Blackwood, arrested for disorderly conduct, and went on to fine them fifteen and twenty shillings respectively, with a sentence of thirty days in jail if they were unable to pay the sum, which amounted to at least three weeks' wages. On the same day William McKay, a planter who frequently sat with his friend Shortridge on the bench, gave a worker, John Warren, six months in jail for stealing coconuts from his co-magistrate.

In more than 98 per cent of these cases, those who ended up in court were found guilty. Very occasionally 'planters' were in the dock, usually for failure to pay taxes, but the outcome was rarely a guilty verdict. If found against, the fines they paid were far less than those levied against black people.[22] In a rare case Augustus Hire, another St Thomas parish magistrate and the manager of a large local estate called Amity Hall, was successfully sued by an Alexander Scott for £8 and nine shillings in unpaid wages. Scott, a black labourer, had to pay a lawyer £4 to represent him. But though found against, three years on Hire had still not paid up.[23] The resentment caused by the patent injustice of the local court system was to have terrible consequences for Hire along with everyone in the parish.

* * *

Poverty increased in Jamaica in the early 1860s, chiefly because of the continuing depression in the sugar export market. Cholera had been endemic for a decade, and a drought in 1865 brought more hardship, including reports of famine. An explosion was perhaps inevitable. When it came, St Thomas-in-the-East parish was the focus of it.

What was initially dubbed the Morant Bay rebellion became a civil war between the black majority of working-class Jamaica and the white ruling class. The British government's armed forces acted to enforce the oligarchy's will. The war was brutal but that is put into the shade by its aftermath. This was astonishingly unjust, as many people in Britain recognised. It has had a lasting effect in Jamaica, as it did throughout the British colonies, though today few beyond Jamaica know of the Morant Bay war.

One of the story's principal villains was Samuel Shortridge. For all his mixed race heritage, Shortridge was as tyrannical a planter as existed. He was very tall, 'stout' and famously handsome: this went with a reputation for arrogance and severity. The local people called him 'Mash'. In 1930, an eighty-six-year-old man, William Hinson, who had lived on one of Shortridge's plantations recalled being horsewhipped as a boy by Mash for getting in the way of his carriage at night.[24]

By 1865 Shortridge was among the most powerful landowners in eastern Jamaica, with control of more than 10,000 acres of sugar and coffee in St Thomas-in-the-East, all of it dependent on the labour of local black communities. Shortridge owned two plantations, and called himself 'attorney', or manager, for six more, including Rozelle, where he was one of the lessees. He and his wife, Eleanor, lived with their children on one of the largest and wealthiest, the Plantain Garden River estate. This multiple-ownership system was the model for the late-nineteenth-century planter, if they were to have any success.

But agriculture was not the only income. Shortridge rented out land and houses on the plantations. He told the Royal Commission of 1866 that he charged £1.04 to £1.25 a year to people for 'provision grounds', and £3.12 to £3.90 for a house with an acre of land. Given that he and his London partners were paying only £250 a year for Rozelle's 1,500 acres, they would have done well from these sub-lettings. Many of the tenants also worked for them, so Shortridge was able to dip into their wages if they failed to come up with the rent, or the fines he imposed as a magistrate.

His casual labourers, mostly women and children, earned between a shilling and a shilling and sixpence a day (£0.05 to £0.075), depending on the season and how much they did. Digging eighty holes for planting cane was judged a decent day's labour. 'Africans' got more, for harder work. In busy weeks, 400 or 500 people were on his pay-roll.[25]

Also among the magistrates for St Thomas parish was George William Gordon, a local figure even better known than Shortridge.

Gordon was a merchant and successful planter. He was one of the parish's two members of the Jamaican House of Assembly (by 1860 there were seventeen people with African heritage among the forty-seven members). His father, a successful Scottish planter called Joseph Gordon, had had eight children by an enslaved woman, Ann Rattray.

G. S. Gordon
Hung at Morant Bay
28th October 1865

The only known (undated) picture of George William Gordon, 1820–1865.

George, born around 1820, was the second-eldest child. Joseph Gordon freed him and possibly all his children by Ann, but in the 1850s he sold up and retired to the island of Jersey with his legal wife Sarah and their six legitimate children. Joseph died two years after his son became famous in Jamaica and across the world as – depending on your sensibility as an educated Victorian – either a treacherous revolutionary or a martyr for justice.

Ann was listed as a 'mulatto', so George William Gordon was a 'quadroon': three-quarters white. This would have meant higher status, as the lighter the skin, the more socially acceptable a person was deemed. The good financial standing of his white planter father would confer advantage too. Gordon first went to work for a white godfather, a merchant, and then opened a shop in Kingston when he was only sixteen. This was a success and he started to buy land and property. He also founded an insurance company and was successful enough to send his sisters to England and France for their education, the usual course for the island's wealthy ruling class.

Gordon married two white Jamaican heiresses in succession, and by the 1860s he and his family were comfortably established – as much as any of mixed race could be – among the planters in St Thomas-in-the-East, still one of the island's predominant sugar-growing areas. Gordon owned two plantations there himself and was attorney, or manager, for several others. But integrating with the white elite was not his ambition. As he grew more successful, he became more involved in the campaigns for rights and equality. He gave or sold his own land to help the rural poor become farmers. By the early 1860s he was seen as a spokesman for Jamaica's working class and a leader in the movement for a fairer judicial process: to the white elite, he was a troublemaker and a threat.

Gordon left his middle-class Protestant church and joined the Native Baptists in 1861, sitting down to worship with the poorest of the island. He helped set up Baptist missions in the St Thomas-in-the-East towns of Spring Garden and Bath, and he became a lay preacher. Doing this work he became a friend and ally of a Native Baptist minister called Paul Bogle, a small farmer in the St Thomas village of Stony Gut, where he was deacon of the church. Born free, Bogle was one of only 106 people in St Thomas parish who had the vote: many would have been white planters, but Bogle managed to get Gordon elected and back into the Jamaica assembly.

There Gordon spoke up for the disenfranchised of the island. He was naturally at loggerheads with the latest governor, Edward Eyre, who had arrived in 1862. Eyre was an Englishman who had spent most of his career in Australia, raising sheep and exploring the outback. He then served as a governor for some of the smaller British colonies. It is hard to see why the Colonial Office chose him to take charge of Jamaica at a time of economic crisis and poisonous unrest.

The two fell out soon enough. In 1862 Gordon, in his role as a magistrate, raised the case of a pauper in the Port Morant jail who had been locked up in a latrine by the town's Anglican parson. The man had died there. Gordon sent a report to London, and the British government ordered an investigation. Eyre reacted by sacking Gordon both as a magistrate and as one of the parish vestrymen, church officials in charge of schools. But that did not silence the trouble-maker: in 1863, re-elected to the assembly, Gordon made speeches about Eyre's failures, pointing to poor people dying in the streets of Kingston.

Eyre's dislike of him was no doubt fuelled by the fact that Gordon had already gone over the governor's head. He had written to the Colonial Secretary, Edward Cardwell, to raise issues about conditions and the use of compulsory labour in Jamaica's prison. This undermined Eyre, two years into his job as governor.

Cardwell had more than Gordon's information to assess. He was also dealing with concerns passed to him by the senior Baptist churchmen in England, who had been reporting their Jamaica minis-ters' accounts of poverty and injustice in their parishes. Cardwell's request for more information from the colony was widely circulated in early 1865: meetings were held in Jamaican villages so that ordinary people could transmit their views straight to the British government via the Baptists.

This infuriated Governor Eyre and the elite. He publicly denounced the Baptist campaign as 'sedition', an encouragement of 'resistance to the laws and constituted authorities'.[26] Eyre decided a display of power was needed: he put a bill through the assembly to bring back the use of whipping and the treadmill, the disciplinary tools of the slavery era, as punishment for criminals. A further law was enacted to bring back apprenticeship as a punishment for minors convicted of 'petty larceny'. On the say-so of two magistrates, children under sixteen convicted of theft or damage to goods worth less than ten shillings could be apprenticed to a planter, merchant or artisan for five years.

It is unsurprising that these moves horrified ordinary Jamaicans. Under the new apprenticeship law, boys from a reformatory were soon sent to work for five years on a sugar estate in St Elizabeth: the local church minister reported that the population was in 'great excitement', afraid that slavery was coming back.[27] Across the island during the early part of 1865 planters complained that labourers were disrespectful and unwilling to work. Parish custos – the government-appointed chief magistrates – wrote to Governor Eyre warning of 'disturbances' and 'preparations for worse'. One said that the 'chat' among the people was 'Buckra has gun, negro has firestick' – if shot at, the labourers would respond with arson, always a fear in a land of dry cane fields and wooden houses.[28]

As the year wore on, tension built. From all over the island came stories of political meetings, demonstrations and outbreaks of violence. A planter was stabbed in the eye by a labourer whom he had caught eating his sugar canes. In Kingston a British naval officer, Captain Thomas Stephen, kicked a boy to death. The *Colonial Standard* reported that the boy and others had teased him for being drunk. Captain Stephen was arrested but, not unusually, there does not appear to have been any trial or punishment.[29]

In St Thomas-in-the-East, where more than in most of the island people worked on estates rather than for themselves, trouble seemed inevitable. One planter and government official, Wellwood Anderson, said he was so alarmed by the 'evident change in manners' that he took a loaded and cocked revolver wherever he went. Samuel

Shortridge said, 'For two or three months before the massacre at Morant Bay [black people] were sulky and sullen – they would not perform their usual tasks, and then of course they did not get their usual amount of wages on pay day, and they quarrelled and kicked up a great noise'. Shortridge was a hard employer. As he told the Commission, he held back his day-workers' wages if they were rude, or lacked 'a sense of discipline': he boasted that his policy was to keep labourers '*in terrorem*' of not being paid. Soon Mash Shortridge was to experience terror himself.[30]

CHAPTER 17

THE EMPIRE STRIKES BACK

The cruelties of property and privilege are always more ferocious than the revenges of poverty and oppression. For the one aims at perpetuating resented injustice, the other is merely a momentary passion soon appeased.

C. L. R. James, *The Black Jacobins*, 1938

Blood for blood – the Morant Bay War

The trouble, long expected, started with a peaceful protest by the poor of St Thomas-in-the-East. It escalated into the only civil war of the colonial-era British Caribbean. In September 1865 Paul Bogle, George William Gordon's friend and fellow Native Baptist, led a march of poor farmers from his village of Stony Gut, just two miles from Rozelle, to see Jamaica's governor, Edward Eyre. The group travelled the forty-five miles to Spanish Town on foot. They hoped to tell of their problems with poverty and the unfair magistracy in St Thomas-in-the-East. A particular grievance was over a parcel of unused land the villagers believed they had bought from the Middleton and Amity Hall estates. The owners and their representatives – led by the magistrate Augustus Hire – were backtracking on the deal.

Governor Eyre refused to see Bogle and the delegation from Stony Gut, sending a message that they should seek redress through the legal system. This cannot have been inspiring. The magistrates of St Thomas-in-the-East were at best compromised, if not entirely corrupt. The magistrate who had issued warrants for arrest for trespass over the disputed land was none other than Hire, who lived at Amity Hall and managed the estate.

South-east Jamaica, 1865

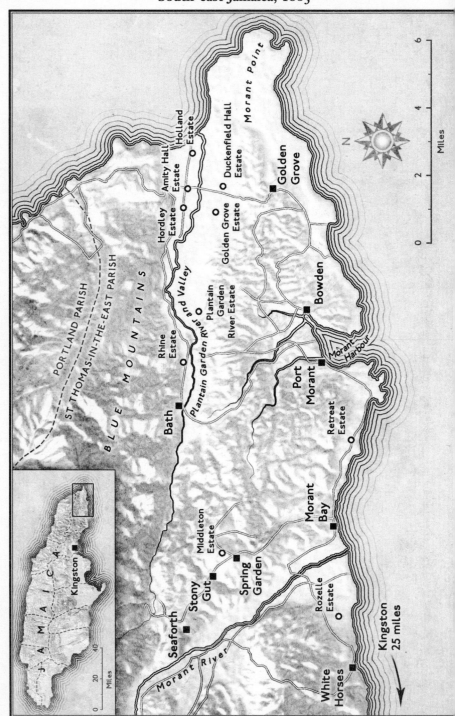

A few weeks later, on Saturday 7 October, a crowd gathered in the centre of the little town of Morant Bay, three miles east of Rozelle. It was market day, but there was a greater draw. Samuel Shortridge and another magistrate-planter, Thomas Walton of the Retreat estate,[1] were due to hear a series of cases involving allegations of trespass on the estates near Stony Gut. Paul Bogle, his son and others from the village crowded into the courthouse.

There are differing accounts of what happened next. But it is clear that the two magistrates handed down a series of harsh fines – Alick White of Stony Gut was told to pay sixteen shillings and sixpence for an assault. That was the equivalent of two or three weeks' labourer's pay, but what incensed White and the onlookers was that the fine was just four shillings: the costs made up the rest of the bill. The excessive court fees levied in St Thomas were one of many complaints made by the locals against the magistrates. The crowd in the little courtroom started objecting, more and more noisily. The magistrates were losing control.

A farmer named James Geoghegan, from Stony Gut, shouted to White that he should not pay the costs, only the fine. A policeman pushed Geoghegan down, and he was thrown out of the courthouse. Paul Bogle tried to calm the crowd, saying they should not interfere with the court. But then the magistrates ordered a policeman to arrest Geoghegan, who was brought back and sentenced to ten days in prison. In the street, as the police tried to take him to the jail, the crowd intervened and amid the shouts and scuffles Geoghegan got away. Retreating, the police took all the names they could of the men and women who had opposed them. The court went on to hear the trespass cases, finding a man named Lewis Miller guilty. Bogle stood bail for him.[2]

On the Monday, 9 October, arrest warrants for Bogle and twenty-four other people in Stony Gut were issued by the Morant Bay magistrates. When the police, eight strong, arrived at the village the following day, they went first to Bogle's chapel, where they read the warrant. Bogle said he would not give himself up to them. The villagers then overpowered and disarmed the policemen. Three of them were told to swear on the Bible to 'desert the whites'[3] – Governor Eyre's phrase in his report to the British government – and join the protesters' cause. They were made to drink rum laced with gunpowder, an obeah ritual. Then they were released.

Paul Bogle told the policemen as they left that he would come to

Morant Bay police station the following day to prove his innocence. Then the villagers sat down to write another petition to Governor Eyre, protesting at how they had been treated by police and magistrates and asking for his protection. It contained a warning. If the governor did not act, the villagers of Stony Gut would be 'compelled to put our shoulders to the wheel, as we have been imposed upon for a period of 27 years [since the end of apprenticeship] with due obeisance to the laws of our Queen and country, and we can no longer endure the same'. The petition was signed by Bogle's son and brother, by James McLaren and fifteen others. It was later used as evidence against them.[4]

On Wednesday, 11 October, Bogle walked the three miles to Morant Bay with other men from Stony Gut, including James Henry and Alick White, whose argument with the magistrates on Saturday had lit the fuse. They may have been intending to give themselves up. But Bogle's message via the police had provided a warning and the parish's head justice of the peace, the planter Baron Maximilian von Ketelhodt, tried to take advantage of it. He called out the parish volunteer militia, eighteen men, and sent a message to Kingston for regular troops. That was received too late.

Hundreds of people joined the march. It is not clear what Bogle's intentions were: he had, in previous weeks, warned people that violence might occur soon in the parish, and that they should be prepared. When the crowd arrived at the police station around lunch-time a riot started. The Morant Bay courthouse, just next door, was holding a meeting of magistrates and parish officials, including von Ketelhodt. The crowd, now five hundred people or more, were beating drums and blowing shell-horns – illegal acts – and shouting. They surrounded the building.

From the courthouse balcony von Ketelhodt read out the Riot Act, and the militia then opened fire on the protestors, downing at least five. The crowd fought back by throwing stones and then stormed the courthouse and set it on fire. Groups went through the streets attacking and looting shops. Meanwhile Bogle and his closest supporters went to the district prison and persuaded the officer in charge, Sligo Campbell, to free all fifty-one prisoners.[5]

As this happened, a slaughter was taking place round the burning courthouse. By the evening, von Ketelhodt, the much disliked Anglican curate Victor Herschell, Thomas Walton and two other magistrates, the captain of the militia and the police inspector were dead, either in the fire or hacked to death with cutlasses and harpoons. Newspapers later reported – incorrectly – that Herschell's tongue was cut out while he was still alive and von Ketelhodt's fingers taken as trophies.[6]

One of the casualties of the riot that bloody afternoon in Morant Bay was an eminent black man, the building contractor Charles Price. He had been the second black member of the Jamaican assembly. The Royal Commission held the following year heard that when he was seized by protesters someone said, 'Don't kill him; we have orders to kill no black, only white.' Someone else said, 'He has a black skin but a white heart.' British newspapers reported, untruly, that Price was 'eviscerated'.

The rioters set about burning the houses of other prominent people, of all colours, in Morant Bay along with the schoolhouse. Having taken weapons from the police station, some set off for the towns of Bath and Port Antonio, and the valley of the Plantain Garden River, where several of the magistrates involved in the land dispute lived on some of the island's grandest sugar estates. By nightfall on the Saturday the whites had lost control of the parish, and all across it protesters were marching on the plantations.

It is not known how many died in Morant Bay between three p.m. and midnight that Wednesday. The Royal Commission's report listed seven dead militia volunteers and eight white civilians, along with Charles Price and three old men – 'pauper negroes, burnt in the courthouse'.[7] But there is no record of deaths of protesters or other black people. Many on both sides were injured: this would prove fatal to some, since a bullet wound was seen as sufficient grounds for summary execution as the militia and army took revenge the following week.

* * *

Samuel Shortridge was lucky not to be in the courthouse at Morant Bay with his fellow magistrates and landowners. He had gone to Kingston to buy cattle. On his way home to his family at the Plantain Garden River estate, he stopped in the village of White Horses, which borders Rozelle estate. Many people who worked for him lived there, and many had gone to the town to protest. They told him of the events in Morant Bay, three miles further down the road. People 'black and also brown' said the rioters 'had been swearing they would have my life', Shortridge said later. So he spent that night at Rozelle.

The following morning he sent his servant William Smith, 'a sambo-coloured man',* down the road towards the town to see what was happening. Smith returned and told his master it was impossible to get through: 'I could not get to my wife without rushing into certain death', Shortridge said later. (All these remarks are from evidence given to the Royal Commission's inquiry six months later.)

The two of them went on by horse, taking the back roads towards Plantain Garden River and home, passing groups of men with newly sharpened cane-field tools. They were, Smith said, looking to kill his master and Alexander Chisholm, Shortridge's manager at the Golden Grove estate. Shortridge told of one man at the roadside with a 'perfectly bright cutlass' and a 'sort of swagger', who said as he saw Shortridge: 'Ah, ah, my friend! They before you and we come too.'

The pair were now quite close to home. But at the Retreat, the magistrate John Walton's estate, some elderly workers told Shortridge it was not safe to go any further. He and Smith fled back to the relative safety of Rozelle. Earlier, 'rebels' had arrived there seeking the overseer, a Mr Whiteman. They 'wanted his head'. But the estate bookkeepers and Whiteman had taken horses and fled into the bush. No damage had been done to the property.

The first Eleanor Shortridge and her household heard of the events in Morant Bay was early in the morning of Friday, 12 October, while her husband was trying to ride across the hills to his family. The alarm was raised when news came of the burning of the courthouse in Bath, two miles away. A crowd was looking for her husband, Eleanor was told. Still in her nightdress, she saw estate workers carrying flags made of coloured handkerchiefs tied to bamboo; she was told they were going to burn the great house. 'All the people were leaving their work, and there was a dead silence all about the estate', she told the Royal Commission.

Alexander Chisholm of the Golden Grove estate arrived to take the Shortridge family to nearby Hordley, where James Harrison, the estate's manager, was organising white workers to protect the great house and its occupants. Eleanor Shortridge, the governess Miss Jones, 'a coloured girl named Jane Baxter' who was the nurse, and six children

---

* Every witness's skin colour is noted in the Jamaica Royal Commission's report. 'Sambo' was used to describe the child of a mixed race person and a black person.

left in a carriage. One child who was seriously ill was carried wrapped in a sheet. As they drove, 'negroes' watched them, holding up their hands. 'Where do you run to? It is the bush you must run to', the family were told. Behind them, the house was looted and burnt.

* * *

There are no first-hand accounts of what happened that night beyond those of the surviving white people and a few second-hand fragments from black locals who helped them. The contemporary newspaper reports are inaccurate and biased. But it seems clear that a large crowd, inflamed by the events at Morant Bay, made its way in the afternoon and night of 12 October from estate to estate along the river valley at Jamaica's eastern tip, site of some of the grandest sugar plantations. They had looted in the town of Bath and then stopped at Hordley estate, where a force of special constables opened fire. Two 'rebels' were shot.[8]

The crowd then went to Duckenfield Hall estate's great house, and 'plundered' it. The next-door estate was Amity Hall, home of the hated magistrate Augustus Hire, who earlier in the year had played a part in evicting smallholders from the ground up the valley known as Smoothland. The farmers believed they had fairly purchased it: Hire and the other planters in the valley called them squatters.

According to his son Henry, Hire ordered the senior workers to defend the house and the five white men inside it, one of whom was the judge and owner of Mount Pleasant estate, Thomas Witter Jackson. Hire told the staff that the army would arrive and shoot them if they were found to have helped the rebels. At midnight, the crowd arrived at Amity Hall. To shouts of 'Colour for colour!' and 'Buckra's [white man's] blood we want', they surrounded the house and forced the front door.[9]

Augustus Hire's hand was severed during the fighting at the door and he was dead before dawn. 'Hip hurrah,' shouted the rioters as they entered the house, 'Sebastopol is taken!' – a reference to the Crimean city that the British army had besieged ten years before. Henry Hire, carrying a cutlass wound that would scar his forehead until his death in 1903, escaped with the other three white men, all of them injured. They hid in the bush and then made their way to the sea.

This same crowd that attacked and destroyed the great house at

Amity Hall next arrived at midnight in Hordley, three-quarters of a mile away and the home of another magistrate, James Harrison. He was, with Shortridge and Hire, one of the five most busy magistrates sitting in judgement at Bath and Morant Bay; there are five cases on record against labourers in which he sat as both complainant and judge. During the day and evening as many as twenty-four white women and children from other estates had sought refuge at Hordley, a dangerous move since, with Harrison's reputation, it was sure to be a focus of the mob's anger. But events worked out differently there.

The Shortridge household made it to Hordley by evening. The estate had one of the grandest of all the plantation mansions, featuring a vast double staircase: it had been the possession of the popular novelist Matthew 'Monk' Lewis,* friend of the poets Shelley and Byron. Now the house was crowded with white people and their mixed race servants, all gathered from various estates in the Plantain Garden River valley. The men were preparing their weapons and barricading doors. At midnight when the rebel crowd appeared James Harrison told Eleanor Shortridge 'it is no use, they are too many', and gave her a revolver. The London *Daily News* account says that fifty of the 'black labourers' of the Hordley estate refused to let the mob pass. [10] While the argument went on, the white women, nursemaids and children were smuggled out of the building by a 'coloured' bookkeeper, Joseph Wood, and the house's head female servant, a young black woman named Diana Blackwood. The rebels then got into the house and started to destroy it while the white men escaped.

Mrs Shortridge and all the other women and children were taken to the sugar works, to hide behind the trash house – a store for drying used cane to make fuel. Some ten adult women and as many children spent the night huddled in the roots of a bamboo, trying to dry their rain-soaked clothes. They listened to the screams of the female servants in the Hordley great house as the 'rebels' arrived. 'The most awful yells I have ever heard in my life', said the Shortridges' governess Ann Jones later. 'Most dreadful, I never wish to hear such again.' But

---

* In 1818 Lewis, who owned more than 500 people in Jamaica, stayed at Hordley for five days. He described his overseer's treatment of the enslaved people as making a 'perfect hell'. Lewis died of yellow fever on the ship carrying him home. His journals, in which he deplores slavery, were not published until 1834, rather too late to influence the debate.

the crowd left eventually for Holland, the estate of the great tycoon of the eighteenth century, Simon Taylor.

The account of the refugees' next hours is grim. But it is remarkable that the women and children's escape and survival was only possible because of the help of a succession of black people who put their own lives at risk. Early in the morning of Friday 13 October Diana Blackwood and another house servant came to the group hidden in the bamboo and told them, 'Don't be frightened, we come to save you.'

The first plan was that the women and children should shelter in Blackwood's own house, half a mile away. But as soon as they got there, noises were heard and the place judged at risk. Blackwood's brother Patrick ran up from the great house, saying, 'Sister, clear the ladies, make haste, for mercy sake, otherwise all of them murder.'

'Run, mistress, for your life,' said Blackwood, who then also fled into the bush, aware she would be a target for having helped them. So the Shortridge household, James Harrison's wife, nanny, two ladies named McKay and all the children, wearing their nightgowns, were carried deeper into the forest, their party led by Joseph Wood, the bookkeeper from Hordley. More than anyone else, he seems to have been responsible for saving these lives.

The Shortridges were found by two men sent by Samuel Shortridge's servant William Smith with a message that they should go and find a ship in Morant Harbour, a few miles south. Eleanor Shortridge, Ann Jones and the children spent the night wandering the countryside in the rain. Kindly people warned them of the whereabouts of the rebels and helped carry the children as they dodged from one hiding place to another. One old man sheltered them in his hut while his wife fed the children roast breadfruit, the first food they had had in two days. 'In my excitement I kissed the old woman,' Eleanor said. Her name was Cypron. She gave Eleanor her 'common negro mat' to sleep on, saying, 'Missis, you done for; you tired till you can't walk.'

At dawn on Saturday the 14th, Cypron brought news that British troops had arrived in the valley and more were expected. Then Joseph Wood arrived and the Shortridge household were taken by carriage to the Rhine estate, where Dr Edward Major and his wife lived as tenants of George William Gordon. Dr Major was well-liked in the community, and the Gordon connection may have made him and his

house a safer option: the doctor had been at the Morant Bay courthouse when it was set alight, and many of the details of the killings
there come from him. As the fire burnt, Paul Bogle had ordered the
rioters not to harm the doctor.

Later on Saturday Samuel Shortridge arrived at the Rhine estate.
He had ridden into Morant Bay from Rozelle the previous morning
to find Captain Henry Luke of the West India Regiment and a
hundred men. They had come overnight by steamer from Kingston.
Dr Major and Shortridge begged Captain Luke to go to the Plantain
Garden River valley to rescue their families. A detachment set off.
On the way they met Governor Eyre and Brigadier-General Alexander
Nelson, who had sailed from Kingston to Port Morant with fifty
more soldiers: they confirmed the plan for Luke to go to Bath and
the valley estates to rescue the white women and children.

Shortridge accompanied the soldiers – most of whom were black
men from the West India Regiment – and Captain Luke. On their
way they surveyed the town of Bath and the looted great houses of
the estates. Luke said they engaged and killed some rebels they found
on Shortridge's land. When the Royal Commission looked into the
events of Saturday's march they heard that the troops with Shortridge
had killed unarmed villagers at a plantation called Winchester just a
mile from his home: a man, John Williams, was shot out of a fruit
tree, and when two old ladies ran for their houses at the sight of the
soldiers, one, Jessy Barrett, was shot in the hip, probably by Shortridge
himself.

At Rhine, Shortridge saw his wife and children arrive 'in the most
pitiable condition', along with several wounded white men from the
various estates. Later that day the soldiers escorted them down to the
sea at Bowden where they boarded a small navy gunboat, the *Onyx*.
About a hundred refugees, all white people or their personal servants,
were taken to Kingston. Among them were Victor Herschell's widow,
Henry Hire and the three surviving men from Amity Hall. The rain
kept falling, and the *Onyx* could provide neither food nor shelter. 'I
came into Kingston in a miserable plight', said Eleanor Shortridge. 'I
had not a hat on my head.' But, it turned out, in the forty-eight hours
of mayhem not one white woman or child had been hurt.

* * *

The retribution has been so prompt and so terrible that it is never likely to be forgotten.

Governor Eyre to Secretary of State for
the Colonies Edward Cardwell,
22 November 1865

The punishment had already begun. Governor Eyre, who had declared martial law on the Thursday, was overseeing the first courts martial in Morant Bay on the Saturday morning as the *Onyx* with its load of refugees steamed past the town. A 'principal' of the insurrection, named Edward Fleming, was hanged and another young man flogged. A woman arrested with them was released. By the end of Saturday four more men were hanging from the arched door of the burnt-out courthouse where von Ketelhodt and the others had died three days earlier. This spot was to see much more death.

A dispatch was sent straight back to London, where the *Daily News* published it, praising the governor's swift action. Eyre's first report concluded:

> We had indeed accomplished some most important results in a singularly brief space of time. A military post was established at Morant Bay, and another at Port Antonio, whilst the centre of a line connecting the two was occupied by the friendly Maroons. The greater portion of the rebels were therefore hemmed in within the country east of this line. The spread of the rebellion westward was stopped, and if no independent outbreak occurs in any other part of the island we shall have the disturbed districts under control, and can at leisure deal with and punish the insurgents, At the same time, all the helpless and unprotected ladies, children, and other refugees, have been got in and saved. All our most important work being thus done, and the troops comfortably established in their barracks, we had for the first time a night of quiet and rest, on the night of Sunday, the 15th of October.[11]

Eyre and his soldiers were soon to be busy again. A second, much greater massacre was just beginning.

* * *

Samuel Shortridge did not follow his wife and children to Kingston.
Instead he set up house at the estate of Golden Grove, a mile down
the road from his wrecked home at Plantain Garden River estate and
eight miles from Rozelle. The army commanders told a Captain Hole
to billet his men there and take advice and instructions from
Shortridge. The latter had already recruited a young merchant from
Kingston, Henry Ford, and invited him to organise an informal squad
of volunteers – mainly young white men, the bookkeepers and overseers of the devastated estates in the valley. They combined with
Hole's regular troops, white and black, and there then followed a
month of mayhem, murder and pillage.

The stories were vividly told by both victim and perpetrator at
the inquiry the British government held in Jamaica the following
year. They call to mind the scorched earth atrocities carried out
against civilians in eastern Europe in the 1940s. Historians agree that
the reprisals carried out by the army and volunteer militias, at Eyre's
orders, were more savage than any seen in the Caribbean in the
nineteenth century. They were also illegal, going far beyond the
provisions of martial law. That seems not to have bothered Governor
Eyre at all. He must have known that one of his first acts, the most
notorious of all, was completely beyond the law, yet he boasted at its
accomplishment.

This was the arrest, court martial and execution of the assembly
member, and campaigner for rights for the poor, George William
Gordon, who had been nowhere near St Thomas parish before or
during the riots. Eyre had arrested Gordon himself in Kingston,
after he had given himself up as requested at the offices of Major-
General O'Connor. But martial law was not in force in the capital,
so Eyre had Gordon dispatched to Morant Bay where he could
be swiftly and summarily dealt with. On his arrival Gordon was
beaten and perhaps tortured. The following day Brigadier-General
Nelson appointed two navy lieutenants – one the commander of
the *Onyx* – and a cavalry ensign to try Gordon for high treason
and sedition.

It was all done in a few hours. Gordon was not permitted to consult
counsel and was convicted on all charges and sentenced to death. He
wrote a brief and moving final letter[12] to his wife before he was
hanged, along with seventeen others, from the entrance arch of the
ruined courthouse early in the morning of Monday 23 October.

Paul Bogle and other Stony Gut villagers were hanged the following day. Within a few months campaigners in Britain were calling for Edward Eyre to be prosecuted for Gordon's murder.

* * *

The stories of the suffering of ordinary black people during martial law in St Thomas-in-the-East excited less public outrage. But they are horrifying. 'Mr Shortridge's Volunteers',[13] as they became known, and Captain Luke and Captain Hole's soldiers of the 1st and 6th West India regiments roamed the valleys, taking animals and goods to feed themselves, arresting people and flogging or executing them, and killing others at random. This was all told to the following year's inquiry and published in its long report.

Reading the testimony, you are struck by the lack of shame among the perpetrators – indeed Shortridge's recruit Henry Ford protests at the negative way his actions have been portrayed in some English newspapers. Captain Hole seems delighted, with his long accounts of operations in the Plantain Garden River Valley. He tells how his men go off to search for looted goods, returning with 'two wagon loads of plunder' from Augustus Hire and Samuel Shortridge's houses. (Shortridge's crest was on the silver-plate teapots.) The soldiers said that in retrieving the goods they had shot around ten 'rebels'. Hole says his policy was that every house with unaccountable goods found in it should be burnt down, and that anyone who ran away should be shot. His soldiers are mentioned in dispatches for this feat.[14]

Ford was a civilian, though he awarded himself the title Captain after Shortridge told him to organise the young white men in the valley into a fighting force. He reads to the inquiry a letter to his brother, telling how hard he has been working as a leader of Volunteers. The job is 'exciting, pleasant, though to some fatiguing'. Their pay is only in food, though they are allowed to take what they please from the farms, including pigs, turkeys and horses. Every morning the 'gentlemen', as many as thirty-nine of them, ride off on 'raids' with their muskets and whips, arresting suspected 'rebels' and burning houses. Finding goods that must have come from a store, like some cinnamon, is enough for an arrest. People refusing to work on the estates are arrested too. The preacher John Anderson was flogged simply because he admitted taking part in the Underhill meetings held earlier in the year. They had been organised to report to the Baptist church in England problems faced by the poor in Jamaica.

Anyone suspected of involvement in the violence earlier in the month – for example, a man found 'wounded and eight miles from his house'– is deemed deserving of immediate execution. So are people who try to escape. 'This is a picture of martial law; the soldiers enjoy it, the inhabitants have to dread it: if they run at their approach they are shot for running away', Henry Ford sums up to his brother, signing off 'with love to Victoria and the girls'.

Questioned by the Royal Commission's counsel, Ford fills in a bit more about the Shortridge Volunteers' activities. Some army officers were present at first, but for much of the time Ford was in charge of the squad. After their daily raids, in the evening at the Golden Grove headquarters Ford and his friends question the prisoners they have taken and then carry out the hangings, shootings or floggings decided upon. Over eight days at the estate, fifteen or twenty a day were flogged: on one day as many as forty. One in five of them are women.

Men get fifty to a hundred lashes, the women thirty. The whips, or 'cats', have twelve or more tails, made of window-sash cord and stiffened with piano wire. (A witness to the inquiry is one of the black artisans who was ordered to make dozens of them.) The cats cut a person's back and behind to 'raw meat' very quickly. Mr Stewart, manager of a nearby estate, likes to help with the flogging, while Samuel Shortridge, you assume, merely oversees it all. He is a stout man.

Some prisoners, men and women, plead to be whipped. They take off their shirts and say, 'Massa I ready for flog.' 'They rather liked it?' asks the inquiry's counsel – facetiously, you imagine. 'No – they begged me to flog them rather than send them to Court-martial', says Ford, the implication being that the men already know that a court martial in St Thomas-in-the-East leads straight to the gallows. There is no questioning on the legality of all this.

It is frustrating to read in the Royal Commission's report of the counsel's repeated failures to follow up on the obvious. There's lots of detail: the punishment of women and the exact numbers of strokes of the cat-whip are closely examined. Most non-white witnesses are asked how and where they work, what they are paid and what rent they pay. But startling admissions from witnesses – white civilians and soldiers who carried out extra-judicial punishments and executions, for a start – go unremarked.

One of Ford's victims appeared before the inquiry in February 1866. Inarticulate and clearly frightened, Alexander Paul manages to tell how he and his neighbour Lydia Francis were arrested in her house on 24 October, tied together and dragged to Shortridge and Ford's headquarters at Golden Grove. There they were flogged with the cat. Paul got 150 strokes – as the court was told, that was equivalent to 1,500 individual lashes, given the number of tails to the cat. Lydia Francis got fifteen strokes. Paul was questioned by 'two officers' but told of no charge or witnesses against him – 'nobody don't swear against me that I do anything', said Paul. He was told the flogging was done on the orders of Mr Stewart, overseer of Holland estate, where Paul worked as a labourer cutting canes.

On the same day in October five men were convicted – there's no information on the nature of the trial – of the murder of Augustus Hire at Hordley on 12 September. Isaac Burke, Henry Aldgate, William Wilson, William Chambers and an 'African' named Luce were executed the same day.

Another of Stewart's workers, Robert Johnson, stated that he was arrested and tied up at the mill at Golden Grove for two days, until Stewart himself arrived and joined in with the Volunteers as he got fifty strokes with the cat. Johnson said he understood the punishment was nothing to do with the uprising, but just because he had owed a week's rent to Stewart.

As the squads of soldiers and volunteers spread across the parish in the month after the massacre, the ordinary people living at Rozelle estate suffered along with the rest. Several told the Royal Commission of being taken to Morant Bay police station and flogged without being told a reason. Agnes Stewart Davis, a woman who lived at Rozelle (the Commission's report notes she is 'black'), said that white soldiers arrived on the Sunday after the riot and set her two houses alight. Agnes was heavily pregnant, and she and her four children fled into the bush, where, hiding in a broken hut, she gave birth.

A 'coloured' groom named Richard Scott was accused of stealing the axle from a ruined cart belonging to Samuel Shortridge. He denied it – 'If I had, I know Mr Shortridge and I would have taken it up to him.' This did no good: he was given twenty lashes. A week later, four Maroons sent by John Woodrow, a 'white' friend and employee of Shortridge, came and set light to Scott's house. Scott was arrested again and taken to see Woodrow at Morant Bay. 'It is a lucky thing I have not burnt you in it and shot you too,' said Woodrow, a civilian volunteer.

Woodrow sent Scott to be hanged, saying, 'You are all a parcel of vagabonds. The governor has ordered me to shoot, burn, and hang, and flog every one of you.' Scott survived after a Maroon who knew his father released him on the way to execution. Woodrow was an engineer who lived in Bath: his store had been looted in October. The sadism and savagery with which he worked during the reprisals struck the Royal Commission as extraordinary.

* * *

When martial law ended a month later, it was clear that the whole parish had been punished for the events of the weekend of 11–13 October: more than a thousand people were dead, according to estimates in the Jamaica press,[15] a similar number of homes burnt – the entire village of Stony Gut was razed – and thousands of floggings carried out on black men and women. Just twenty-one white men were killed, all in the first twenty-four hours,

In a previous time this might have gone with little notice in Britain. But communications by telegram were now in use. Newspapers in Britain and throughout the world took up the story – excited initially by the reports of white women in peril. Within two months of the massacre, grave questions about the mayhem wreaked at Eyre's behest were being asked in the press and high up in the British government. On 6 December 1865 Edward Cardwell, the minister responsible for the colonies, told the British cabinet: 'It seems hardly credible that the governor of a colony should have allowed such terrible numbers of the inhabitants to be put to death by military court-martial without giving any report whatever of the circumstances to the Secretary of State.' William Gladstone, the slave owner's son and future prime minister said: 'Eyre must have lost his head'.[16]

A reckoning was inevitable. But powerful forces were marshalling on both sides of the debate. An Eyre Defence and Aid Fund was set up, in response to suggestions that his prosecution might follow. Britain's most eminent historian, Thomas Carlyle,[17] an avid supporter of theories of white racial superiority, headed it, supported by Lord Tennyson, Charles Dickens and John Ruskin.

By December the British newspapers had divided along traditional lines. 'The nobs and snobs [including the *Times* and *Telegraph*] all champion the butchery, while on the side of coloured humanity are the *Daily News*, *The Star*, the *Morning Advertiser* . . . and nearly all the weeklies.' So reported the liberal-minded *New York Daily Tribune* in December 1865.[18]

One British weekly, the *Spectator* magazine, was of the second camp. In February 1866 an article declared Governor Eyre, who was still in place, wrong to call the black people 'savages'. The real savages, the magazine said, were the white men in charge of reprisals. It named 'Captain' Henry Ford, and a Captain Hobbs.[19]

In March 1866 a *Spectator* column on the evidence given to the Royal Commission's inquiry concluded that Eyre's defence was worthless. It was nonsense that there had been a 'general insurrection deliberately planned'. Furthermore, stories of black men mutilating white corpses were untrue, and the government's assurance that 'comparative safety was speedily restored to all persons, of whatever race or colour' were belied by the stories now emerging of black people being summarily hung or flogged 'with whips made of piano wire' during the month after the Morant Bay events.[20]

Conservative against progressive

The furious debate over Eyre's responsibility for the massacres and the justice, or lack of it, of his reprisals has been called the most intense ideological battle of the latter part of the nineteenth century. It was rooted in race and class: the Tories, backed by the aristocracy, were supporters of Eyre. Many members of the Carlyle defence committee and fund were inheritors of slavery fortunes or compensation payouts from 1836.[21] The intellectual left joined an anti-Eyre committee headed by the political philosopher John Stuart Mill. It numbered many of the celebrity liberals of the age: Charles Darwin,

Thomas (*Tom Brown's Schooldays*) Hughes, Henry Fawcett, John Bright and so on. There was popular support too: in early 1866 a large crowd of 'working class radicals' gathered in London in support of the Jamaican poor and burnt Eyre in effigy.[22]

The right-wing press retold, and invented, stories of barbarous atrocities committed by Paul Bogle's 'gang', picturing them in racial terms: 'Not New Zealanders or Indians could have shown more cruel ferocity than the insurgents', reported the *New York Times* in a fantastical account of the assault on the courthouse.[23] Carlyle blamed the 'half-brutish' George William Gordon and his supporters for all that had happened and said Eyre deserved honours for 'saving the West Indies and hanging one incendiary mulatto [Gordon]'. His committee swiftly raised £10,000 for Eyre's defence. He dismissed Mill's committee as a group of 'rabid Nigger-philanthropists, barking in the gutter'.[24]

It is a depressingly familiar discourse. The Eyre controversy divided people along lines we would recognise today: conservative versus progressive. Those who were sceptical of the imperial project, in favour of extending the vote and improving the condition of factory workers supported a prosecution of Eyre and compensation for the abused poor in Jamaica. One of John Stuart Mill's supporters, the scientist Thomas Huxley, recognised this polarisation. In a letter to the pro-Eyre novelist Charles Kingsley, he said: 'Men take sides on this question, not so much by looking at the mere facts of the case, but rather as their deepest political convictions lead them. And the great use of the prosecution [of Eyre], and one of my reasons for joining it, is that it will help a great many people to find out what their profoundest political beliefs are.'[25]

Even the caricatures of Mill's Jamaica Committee supporters are recognisable – stiff, top-hatted, humourless, they have evolved from earlier satirical depictions of abolitionists. They would be dubbed woke metropolitan elitists today. Anti-slavery campaigners were among the supporters and members of Mill's Jamaica Committee, just as former slave owners joined the pro-Eyre campaign.

For Mill the core principle was that the rule of law should be put above all other concerns, even 'the maintenance of the social order'[26] – the latter a code for the race and class concerns of his opponents. But for conservatives like Charles Kingsley, author of *The Water Babies*

(1863), a wildly popular novel inspired by the awful exploitation of child chimney sweeps in Britain, defending Eyre was equally a moral cause. He replied to Huxley:

> I have been cursed for [supporting Eyre], as if I had been a dog . . . and imperilled my own prospects in life in behalf of freedom and justice. Now, men insult me because I stand up for a man whom I believe ill-used, calumniated, and hunted to death by fanatics.

Kingsley nodded along with Carlyle's fierce beliefs regarding the racial inferiority of black people, the underpinning of all the historian's writing about the Eyre case.[27]

Published in *Punch* magazine two months after the Morant Bay massacres, the 'White Planter' is asking the top-hatted liberal 'Am not *I* a man and brother too, Mr Stiggins?', parodying the famous abolitionist slogan.

* * *

A theme for all these defenders of Eyre is his feat in saving white women from 'fates worse than death' at the hands of black men: rape was much discussed in the reporting of the Indian Mutiny too. Eyre, said the scientist John Tyndall, had protected the honour of 7,000 British women from the 'murder and lust of black savages'.[28] First among the many ironies here is that it seems that in Jamaica in 1865 the only rapes, or indeed assaults of any kind on women, were carried out by Eyre's own troops and militiamen.

But as powerful as these voices were, others were horrified at what had happened: the MP and philosopher John Stuart Mill considered it a blow to the moral soul of Britain. The echoes of the savage reprisals after the Indian Mutiny were still fresh, and they were what impelled Mill to make the 'Jamaica business' his cause.

For a while, the progressives were winning. Lord Russell, the new Liberal prime minister, told the House of Lords on 6 February 1866 that the Conservatives' support of Eyre, and their opposition to an inquiry, was a dereliction of duty. In effect, he said, the Eyre lobby was saying: 'We do not care whether 500 persons have been put to death without necessity, but we will support the governor whether he was right or wrong, and we care nothing about those persons' lives because they happened to be black.'[29]

Mill's committee concluded that the British government must 'uphold the obligation of justice and humanity towards all races beneath the Queen's sway'. Not to prosecute Eyre for murder, Mill wrote, was to give 'impunity to the crime which is the most dangerous of all to the community – the crime of a public functionary who abuses the power entrusted to him to compass, under the forms of justice, the death of a citizen obnoxious to the government'.[30] It seemed that Eyre might well have to face the courts.

There is no record that my great-great-grandfather Sir James Fergusson involved himself in this question. He was an active MP in the Tory opposition, a Jamaica landowner whose own tenant Samuel Shortridge (though we have no evidence that Sir James knew of him) was at the heart of the reprisals. Sir James was busy in Parliament in 1865 and 1866, mainly occupied with a bill about controlling disease in cattle; there is no record of him speaking about the Morant Bay rebellion, or on the Eyre case as it dragged on. In June 1866, when Lord Russell's government fell, Sir James joined Lord Derby's Conservative administration as under-secretary of state for India.

Meanwhile his colleagues in the Colonial Office set about getting Eyre off the hook.

* * *

Questions about race, and the right to justice of the subjugate nations of the British Empire, were at the heart of this debate and so there was much interest in the official inquiry. It was ordered in December 1865 by the Liberal British government and set up by Governor Eyre, still nominally in place in Jamaica. The Jamaica Royal Commission was headed by another imperial governor, Lieutenant-General Sir Henry Storks, of Malta. He was supported by some fairly eminent British legal figures.

The inquiry began in late January 1866 and worked with astonishing speed to find and hear witnesses from all sides, visiting Morant Bay, Bath and Stony Gut to enable 'poorer people' to come forward. Seven hundred witnesses were heard in less than two months and its report, of nearly 1,200 pages, was delivered to the British government on 9 April 1866, just six months after the first protest at Morant Bay courthouse. (The inquiry into the 2017 fire at Grenfell Tower in London had been sitting, off and on, for more than two and a half years when it was suspended again in January 2021, due to the coronavirus pandemic.)

The Commission's report totted up the bill of that terrible month in St Thomas-in-the-East: 439 black Jamaicans were stated to have died, half of them executed under martial law, the rest extra-judicially. At least 600 people had been flogged, many of them women. A total of 1,008 dwellings had been burned. Many people had been given prison terms, some as long as twelve years. The point was not made, though it must have been obvious, that nearly twenty times as many people had died in the reprisals as were murdered in Morant Bay on 11 October.

The inquiry heard that martial law had been interpreted, from the top, as the right of the island forces and irregular groups of volunteers to do pretty much as they pleased. 'Rebels' (words like 'loyal' and 'rebel' or 'traitor' is the language used of this entirely civilian population in the military reports) were shot on the spot by the army if there was any evidence at all of involvement. People were executed if their houses were found to contain what was considered 'plunder'

– no court martial was deemed necessary. The houses were razed too. The commanding officer Brigadier-General Nelson's first dispatch noted that he considered it 'temperate and judicious' of his officers to have executed rebels on the spot even if they had surrendered, a fact that the Royal Commission 'noted'.

In the long columns of the Commission's report we have extraordinary first-hand descriptions from the heart of a race and class war in Jamaica. It lets us hear the voices of the black underclass. But while clearly interested in the injustices and poverty that caused the initial protests, the inquiry process fails to follow through in questioning the men behind the failure of governance in St Thomas-in-the-East.

Samuel Shortridge is named seventy-nine times in the report. The counsel of the Commission clearly suspected that he and other planters had taken advantage of martial law and the fog of the revenge frenzy to punish many black people for issues that had nothing to do with the rebellion, including failure to 'attend to their work'. Shortridge was asked whether he had been present, as alleged, when the troops shot two women in St Thomas – he denied it. Counsel knew that Adam Smith, a man who was owed money by Shortridge for work mending fences at Plantain Garden River, had been executed without trial by the army. But while the inquiry heard from Shortridge twice, and Eleanor his wife once, there were no questions about Smith.

Not much at all was explored in the long but friendly questioning of Samuel Shortridge; he was not even asked about the activities of Henry Ford, John Woodrow and 'Mr Shortridge's Volunteers'. The counsel for the inquiry was far more interested in the details of Eleanor and the family's escape, down to what clothes they wore as they ran through the bush.

Nor was he cross-examined about his activities as a magistrate. That seems an extraordinary omission. The Commission's report shows that it knew just how Shortridge and the other planter-magistrates had failed to provide justice in the St Thomas courts – the key issue that had enraged the local people. The appendix to the report contains a lengthy analysis of the court records from St Thomas for 1863 to 1865. This is clearly designed to show the corruption of the magistrates, including Shortridge: it lists how often they appeared as both complainant and judge in the same case. It also shows the racial bias in terms of guilty findings and the amounts of the fines. That this evidence was published, but never used, may argue towards there having been some degree of political interference.

Nonetheless, the Royal Commission's ultimate conclusions were enough to end Edward Eyre's career. They stopped short of castigating the governor, though the paragraph praising the 'skill promptitude and vigour' of his actions is damningly short. And it is entirely condemnatory about his part in what is called the 'suppression', particularly on the grotesque failures to hear cases fairly. George William Gordon's trial had been illegal, on various grounds, and there had not been any conspiracy to begin a rebellion, the report stated. Martial law had gone on too long, the punishments were excessive, the floggings 'positively barbarous', and the house burnings 'wanton and cruel'.

This was devastating for Governor Eyre, who was now recalled. That was a disgrace, but he was safe from official prosecution, covered by an Indemnity Act that the Jamaica assembly had swiftly passed at the end of martial law. This had been approved in London, though privately government ministers decided Eyre was indeed directly responsible for George William Gordon's illegal court martial and – more serious, in their view – the excessive period of martial law.[31]

Several of Eyre's direct subordinates faced criminal proceedings, including the provost marshal, Gordon Ramsay, a senior policeman who had been put in charge of punishments by Eyre. He was accused of murder. John Woodrow, the Bath engineer, was charged with excessive flogging of women. Two military officers – a surgeon and the ensign who had been one of George William Gordon's judges – were tried for shooting prisoners without trial. But the Jamaican juries threw all the cases out.

A Conservative government took over from the Liberals just as the Commission's report was published, in June 1866. By now, party allegiances fixed the position politicians took on the 'Jamaica affair'. So when John Stuart Mill demanded in the House of Commons that thirteen British military and civil officers be prosecuted for acts committed during the aftermath of Morant Bay, he was 'fluently, lengthily, and assiduously'[32] put down by the greatest Conservative orator of the time, Benjamin Disraeli, then Chancellor of the Exchequer. Eyre dodged prosecution and was eventually granted a government pension for life, reduced to second grade because of his foreshortened tenure as governor-general of Jamaica. This annoyed his supporters once again.

All the others got away scot-free. The shopkeeper Woodrow was the only white civilian involved in the reprisals to face prosecution, singled out perhaps because he was of lower social rank. Samuel Shortridge's career as a planter continued. He was still listed as a magistrate in St Thomas-in-the-East in 1870,[33] and in 1875 he added Golden Grove, where his Volunteers had murdered and flogged so many people, to his portfolio of plantations. In 1891 he was a member of the organising committee of the Jamaica International Exhibition, a showcase of Jamaican products and industry designed to attract foreign investors. The organisers clearly had in mind similar events in London and Paris. It made a loss of £30,000.

* * *

The Empire's darkest slum.

> Colonial Secretary Joseph Chamberlain on the
> 'sugar colonies' of the Caribbean, 1902

Morant Bay and its aftermath were a turning point in the imperial story. The Victorians recognised this when they called the events the West Indian Mutiny, echoing the huge and bloody uprising in India eight years earlier, now more justly named India's first war for independence.

Quite apart from marking an end of the first high, confident age of the British Empire, the story brings doubt to notions of the benevolent paternalism of nineteenth-century British imperial rule, or that British law treated all imperial subjects equally. It also confirms race, and discrimination on account of it, as being a keystone of the ideology and the culture of imperialism.

The events of 1865 have been seen as Jamaica's Amritsar, the island's equivalent of the massacre of innocent protesters carried out in 1919 by repressive British authorities in India. The Morant Bay martyrs were vilified for a century by the British. But after independence in 1962 they became official national heroes of the new country, with their faces on Jamaican coins and banknotes.

In the little town of Morant Bay the courthouse was swiftly rebuilt on the same spot – it stands there now, stolidly British, made of square-cut limestone and redbrick from England. The eighteenth-century cannons stand around it, facing the sea, as they did in 1865. It is evocative, not least because, once again, it is a roofless shell, burnt-out in a fire started by vandals in 2007.

There are plans to put this right. But for now the site of the mass graves where the victims of the courts martial were buried is waste ground. The proud statue of Paul Bogle clutching a cutlass, erected in front of the building after independence, has been removed for safe-keeping. Morant Bay town is sleepy, grubby and poor: there are homeless people camped in the locked doorways of the Anglican church.

After 1865 the parish changed utterly, everyone agrees. From the beginning of plantation farming in the seventeenth century St Thomas-in-the-East was the richest corner of Jamaica: now it became the poorest. The smallholder class was destroyed in the reprisals. Many people left, including all the many Bogles. As Jamaica tried to align itself with the power that was Britain, any association with Morant Bay or St Thomas-in-the-East became a matter of shame.

The events of 1865 are still potent for many Jamaicans today. Lloyd Phillips, a taxi driver who drove me around Kingston, told me his great-grandmother had escaped St Thomas-in-the-East in the aftermath of the massacres. 'Her father was a Bogle. It was not safe, so they moved away and changed their name.' We had started talking about this because that day's *Daily Gleaner* had a headline – 'Bitter downward spiral of the sugar industry'. It was over a story about Golden Grove, Samuel Shortfield and Henry Ford's headquarters in October and November 1865. The sugar plantation was to be closed by Seprod, the last big sugar company on the island, with the loss of 150 jobs. 'Ah, St Thomas,' said Lloyd. 'People there, they never get it easy.'

In 1883 a commission appointed to look into Jamaica's problems declared that the parish's population and teachers were forty or fifty years behind the rest of Jamaica – singling out the Plantain Garden River district, where the worst of the reprisals of 1865 had happened, as the most backward of all. The same report notes that many people had left the parish and that there was a labour shortage: even the unemployed did not want to work on plantations.[34] In 1895 the British colonial power at last started selling unused land in plots to the small farmers of St Thomas[35] – thirty years after Paul Bogle and the villagers of Stony Gut had died for the same.

A fighting spirit remained in St Thomas-in-the-East. In the late 1930s sugar workers on those same plantations went on strike for better wages and conditions from the sugar corporations: once again the police were called out, shots fired at peaceful protesters and harsh prison sentences imposed. The battle was the beginning of a labour movement in Jamaica that eventually would improve workers' conditions and coalesce into the movement for independence.

Today's St Thomas seems a thousand miles from the resort hotels of Montego Bay, or the business and embassy suburb of New Kingston: it is a byword for backwardness across the island, known mainly for crime and illegal marijuana plantations. It has the worst poverty statistics outside the barrios of downtown Kingston. Shells of failed factories dot the flat lands around Morant Bay town while the swell from the Atlantic endlessly grinds at the rubble-strewn coast: there are no luxury hotels in St Thomas parish, no markets selling rasta wigs and Bob Marley T-shirts, no tropical paradise beaches.

* * *

Morant Bay and its aftermath did have an effect on Victorian Britain. It shook the belief of the liberal intelligentsia in the imperial mission, though not much happened that was of use to the people who suffered most in Jamaica. There were changes, though. The reporting of the massacres, and the inquiry, let British people see clearly the brutal stupidity of Jamaica's white elite. The British government realised that it could not trust the planter class to run the island's affairs. So Jamaica's independence was removed in 1866: the cowed assembly voted itself out of existence and the island become a Crown colony, administered directly from London.

But this of course prevented Jamaicans from having a direct role in running the island for another century: the elected 'legislative council', as in other colonial nations, was merely advisory. The moment when progressives like George William Gordon might have been able to take charge on behalf of the descendants of enslaved people had passed. It was not until 1944 that all Jamaicans got the vote.

The return to direct rule on the island entrenched– as it did across the Caribbean colonies – a hierarchy based on race and 'colourism'.

In the white colonial administrators' minds, the black people were the unreliable, potentially rebellious, underclass whereas the brown or mixed race middle class were a caste to be relied upon. Esther Chapman, a white English author based in Jamaica, wrote in 1938: 'It is obvious that the man within whose veins flows the blood of two races cannot openly set himself to preach hatred against either. The coloured people of Jamaica are in a special sense its hope and its safeguard'.[36] Using lighter-skinned ethnic groups as a buffer between the white elite and the darker working class became policy across the empire. It was a policy as unashamedly racist as it was pragmatic. Its divisive effects are still felt today.

The 1866 Royal Commission, with the work of Mill's Jamaica Committee, did establish a principle that would eventually provide some help to people all over the British Empire – that British law applied equally to them all, regardless of colour. The exercise of this was, of course, not perfect. Martial law obliterated such principles. It was declared many times more in order to crush insurrection and popular rebellions against British imperial injustice – in India, Ireland, Egypt, Palestine, Malaya (as it then was), Nigeria, South Africa and Kenya, among others. The author Richard Gott has written that martial law was used regularly in the twentieth century by British colonial governors to crush legitimate dissent: 'Normal judicial procedures were replaced by rule through terror; resistance was crushed, rebellion suffocated . . . It means the absence of law.'[37]

Like so many stories of insurgency and protest in the imperial world, the Morant Bay uprising was nothing as simple as protest against the colonial power. It was named a 'war' almost immediately, but it was never any kind of military engagement. George William Gordon and many others went to execution in 1865 proclaiming their loyalty to the Queen. Jamaicans then and for a century more felt proud of their connection to Britain, and trusted its institutions. Fifty years later they would volunteer in their thousands to fight for the empire in the trenches of Flanders. Morant Bay was a rebellion not against the sovereign or Britain, but against the corruption and cruelty of the Britons put in charge. It was a desperate cry for the justice that the British had promised, but not delivered.

CHAPTER 18

JAMAICA TODAY

To the editor, Sir,

Recently, I had the opportunity with my family to visit one of Jamaica's historical sites, a former sugar plantation in Trelawny, where in 2019 we continue to perpetuate the emotional distress found in the history written for us, as was evidenced in the well-rehearsed, regurgitative pain of the young lady giving the tour in outlining the benevolence of the plantation owner or overseer.

There was nary a sentence on how the slaves, maybe a direct ancestor of the tour guide from the same community, survived the daily drudge of work without pay, what they ate, where they slept, how they cared for their children, how many died over the years of enslavement on the plantation, where are they buried, what were the punishments meted out, what medicines did they use, what was their house like.

Instead, the focus was on the benefits of the ill-gotten gains and prestige housed in the majestic plantation buildings, where the oppressors entertained, how they got the land from the Crown, how well-constructed the plantation great house was, how cool it was, and where the various spouses came from.

We are left pondering why a lot of our young men in the Jamaican society today pursue a dishonest path via a different medium. Maybe in 200 years it's them that will be glorified in Jamaican history as we subconsciously, or deliberately, validate that crime pays.

Gary Watson, Captain (Retd)

Letter published in Jamaica's *Daily Gleaner*,
21 October 2019

Dozens of fat jets from North America and Europe land every day at Montego Bay airport. They disgorge – or they did, until the coronavirus pandemic – most of the 2.7 million tourists who visit Jamaica annually, shuttling them straight to the beach resorts of the country's western end. If they get bored of the sun and sand, there are a host of family-friendly outings nearby: souvenir markets, zip wires and snorkelling trips, 'James Bond Beach', Bob Marley's birthplace at Nine Miles and a chance to 'chill in a real Rasta village' near Negril. Tourists tend to keep out of Montego Bay's downtown, which is considered unsafe.

On the old sugar plantations on this coast there are not yet any re-enactments of escapes from enslavement, which are popular now in the States. But you can tour the planters' houses and gardens. High on TripAdvisor's 'Best Things to Do in Montego Bay' is the Rose Hall Great House. If you take the night tour you're warned you may see the white witch, a planter's wife said to have taken enslaved men as lovers and who murdered her husbands with voodoo. Johnny Cash, who owned a villa nearby, had a minor hit with a song about her.

Not far away in Trelawny is Good Hope plantation, once the family home of John Tharp. He was an English planter and sugar trader, Eton and Cambridge educated, and one of the most successful of all of them. Tharp owned 3,000 enslaved people on his various plantations in the area; in 1805 he shipped home 2,500 hogsheads of sugar, fifteen times as much as Rozelle produced in its most successful years.* The hill-top house was built a few decades earlier by a descendant of one of the first English settlers in Jamaica. It is a lovely thing, an airy structure of wild orange wood on squared limestone blocks, with a view across the green undulations of Jamaica's Cockpit Country. The drive up to it, along three miles of gravelled road between low stone walls and tidy fields, shaded by great trees, could be to a country house in Hampshire at the height of a particularly lush summer.

It is the off-season when I go. There are only me and a group of middle-aged African American women from Macon, Alabama, doing the tour. Our guide, whom I'll call Mike, a young farmer from a

---

* Tharp retired to Chippenham Park in Cambridgeshire, where his white children's descendants live today. Tharp's daughter by an enslaved woman was left £600 a year. She married an Englishman.

nearby village, is knowledgeable and enthusiastic: he is proud of the place and he enjoys this part-time job. He seems keen to play down any unsavoury past. He shows us a barred cell under the counting house. The prison, he says. 'I thought most often the slaves got whipped,' says one of the American ladies. 'Only if they misbehaved,' says Mike.

He tells us that this had been a 'good' plantation. 'There were no uprisings. They were good masters, built a hospital and a school. We know they sheltered the slaves in times of trouble.' The Americans wander off to explore in the breeze-filled living rooms. So I take the moment and tell Mike why I am in Jamaica, asking what he thinks.

'You know,' he says, after a pause, 'it can't be changed. It is what it is. It wasn't you.' He has young children, and one of the reasons he is working two jobs is to pay for their education. The government school should be free, but you have to buy extras, books and clothes. His girlfriend is jobless: she never obtained her school diploma because her mother could not find the money for her to finish the year.

Would he tell his children what he knows about the plantation and the chattel slavery time? 'I'm not going to tell my kids. I don't want to put traumatic things in their brain. They've got to learn "one love".'

I wonder if he thinks people like me, and my country, have some responsibility today. For the wrong we did. 'Well, slavery is what God meant to be. I have to ask, where would I be without? Back in Africa squeezing mud to get water?' He isn't the only young Jamaican I meet who says something along these lines.

I say to Mike I think that every European tourist getting off a plane in Montego Bay should be sat down for a lecture on what happened here before being allowed to get their bags. He laughs. 'Yeah, well, the teachers could certainly use the extra income.'

To Rozelle

My hotel in Kingston is uptown, opposite the British High Commission. This is 'New Kingston', the suburb formed when business and the middle class fled the decay and violence of the old city centre thirty years ago. In the hotel café a group of white English businessmen banter between their meetings, or shout into their phones. When they sit down with two Jamaican lawyers, I eavesdrop, pretending to watch football on the big-screen TV. The talk is of bad debts, foreclosure and court orders to sequester assets.

In the dining room, at the breakfast buffet, American tourists in shorts and sports tops sniff sceptically at the chafing dishes of local food – fried plantain, salt fish and ackee. Most settle for bacon and eggs. Some are the children and grandchildren of Jamaicans who emigrated to the States in the mid-twentieth century, in Kingston to visit relations for a couple of nights and take in the Bob Marley museum. Then it's off to the other end of the island for a week in the international beach hotels. 'That's the real vacation,' some Chicagoans tell me. 'This city is kinda . . . well, it's historic but it's real dirty.'

Not many tourists head further east than Kingston. The beaches of the last corner of the island are sharp black stones and the surf pounds through the jumbled reefs with frightening energy. Great dykes of boulders have been dumped to shield the coast road from the bullying of hurricanes. This is where they hit most often.

The A4 road turns through the roots of the Blue Mountains and then winds across boggy river plains: it is potholed and scary with heavy trucks. The south coast route is one of the country's oldest, built between the richest districts and the capital when it was still Spanish Town: it is a journey into the country's history. It begins at the old Kingston Penitentiary, on the edge of the capital. Built in the decade after emancipation, it is still a working prison and its horrors have a worldwide reputation. The road then ducks round a vast cement works and past the dust-clad fort that once guarded the causeway to Port Royal, the first colonial city. Then, dodging through the foothills, weaving from the sea and back again into the plains, it pushes into St Thomas (the 'in-the-East' has been dropped) parish.

My ancestors' employees knew this road. The Africans they bought would have been transported along it from the Guinea merchants' warehouses in Kingston. Down the coast road marched the British redcoats under Brigadier-General Alexander Nelson to put down the Morant Bay rebellion of 1865, burn houses and murder hundreds of poor residents of St Thomas-in-the-East. Along it came eighteenth- and nineteenth-century planters and their families in search of social life and relief from the heat of summer, finding it in the valley of the

Blue Mountains above Morant Bay, where there were breezes to enjoy and balls to attend in plantation mansions. The old road ended at a little town with a cooling spring whose water was thought to have healing properties. The plantation gentry built houses there, as well as botanical gardens, and with the usual expatriate whimsy they called the place Bath. It is still there, though unfashionable for 200 years: 'sadly decayed', says the guidebook.

No Fergusson of my family came to Jamaica during the slavery era. Sir James Fergusson – my great-great-grandfather who sold the Rozelle plantation in 1875 for a pittance – died in Kingston in the devastating earthquake of 1907, crushed when the lintel of a tobacconist's shop doorway fell on him. It was said that 'it took an earthquake to kill him' – he had after all survived a wounding in the Crimean War and a career that took him all over the British Empire, losing two wives to cholera. Sir James appears to have been in Jamaica on holiday at the time of his death, guest of a transatlantic steamship business of which he was a director. Nothing remains in his papers to indicate that he visited Rozelle. I have no idea if he had any thoughts about the people who lived and died there, or the mess he and his forefathers left behind.

* * *

Names from the eighteenth-century records pop up on road signs – Bull Bay, Yallah's, Grant's Pen, Danvers' Pen – most of them shabby shack-towns not yet recovered from the destruction brought by Hurricane Ivan in 2004. Churches, chapels and temples, Pentecostal, Baptist and many more, seem to be the main business of these hamlets; those and jerk places, tin-roof cafés with ranks of half-barrel barbecues on stands. It's Sunday and so it is not busy. Apart from the diesel fume-farting trucks, most of the traffic is bicycles. Middle-aged ladies in church dresses and smart hats make their way on foot in the dust.

Lloyd Phillips, who has been driving me round Kingston, was born and brought up in St Thomas. He still has a small farm there, on land where his family have been 'since slavery time', around the old sugar estates called Prospect and Arcadia. (There are many people with the surname Phillips in St Thomas, perhaps connected to Nathaniel Phillips, a notoriously brutal owner of four estates in the parish who fathered many offspring.[1]) Lloyd tells a story of the decline he has seen over his long life: the closing of the port at Bowden, the failure of the garment factories and of a Goodyear tyre plant that once served all the Caribbean. These disasters sent the young people to Kingston, seeking work. They didn't come back.

Like that of so many Jamaicans, the Phillips family's twentieth-century history is of migration to find work: Lloyd's grandfather went off with thousands of others to dig the Panama Canal. Many of them died but he survived and brought back money to buy land at Arcadia. But it turned out that he couldn't earn enough to keep the family. Lloyd's father, a tailor, spent half his life in England, and Lloyd's sister lives there now. Of his class at Morant Bay High School in the 1950s, only Lloyd and one other live in Jamaica. Lloyd would much rather be a farmer but, now in his seventies, he will work as a driver in Kingston until he can no longer.

* * *

When we pass the little hamlet of White Horses, I start peering at Google Earth on my phone: both it and my photo of an early nineteenth-century Rozelle estate map show a curve in the coastline, after a small river. Directly inland stood the great house and the sugar works. I don't know what to expect: Chris Thompson, a Jamaican friend who has come along to show me around the parish, has never heard of Rozelle, or any grand buildings this side of the Morant River. But the road into the old estate is where it should be, just before the coast juts out. There is a sign announcing the police department's sponsorship of the local football team, and then the Rozelle vehicle testing station. A few yards away from the main road is a busy primary school, bubbling with break-time noise. And then, moving inland and uphill a bit, a couple of conversations with people working on vegetable patches beside their concrete bungalows lead us quite swiftly to the two-storey building that people still call the Great House.

The building is much more modest than its name. From a window upstairs Aston 'Bull' Smith calls a friendly hello. This is his home. He, his wife and son live in the upper storey of the four-square building: it is made of concrete and tin, planted on old solid stone. You might pass by without a second glance – it is no more than eight or nine rooms in total – if it were not for the remains of a grand brick staircase that rises from the ground to his front door above. The ground floor is derelict, but the walls are solid: cut-limestone blocks, mangy with ancient plaster. Spaced around the house are the traces of circular stone pillars, some shoulder-high, some cut off at ground level.

'Must have been the supports of a veranda, right around the building,' says Bull. He is a burly, smiling sixty-one-year-old. He grew up in St Thomas. Recently retired, he spent his career working in land management with the parish council. One of his roles was assisting the small farmers who were granted land plots on Rozelle after the Jamaican government bought the remains of the plantation in the 1970s. It was a project to help the rural poor.

He shows me things he has found in the debris of the old house. There is an oblong piece of iron that he says was part of a window, with a cord on it to pull the window up and down: it is a sash weight. A grand window, once, I say. Yes, says Bull. Now it's just a hole into a room filled with builders' rubbish. Bull says he's planning to do it up. He is proud of the place, how the walls have stood up to 300 years of hurricanes. He's going to use the old pillars to support a water tank – maybe a new veranda? 'You can sit out there with a cocktail,' I say. He laughs. 'I'm thinking about it.'

He digs a finger into the old mortar between the stones – sand, lime from the kiln and a black substance he says is charcoal mixed with molasses. 'That's what they used from the sugar furnace, to bind the stonework. Best mortar they made, as strong as can be. This is a relic – the bottom section is all slavery construction. The house for the bucky massa – the slavemaster's house.'

On my phone I pull up the maps from the eighteenth and nine-teenth century that I found in Scotland, and in Kingston's National Library. They are precise and pretty things, finely inked and coloured: one has scrolls and an elaborate shield topped with an ibis around the words 'A Plan of Rozell Estate'. On another, whimsical sailing ships indicate the sea. The neatly squared fields, each one labelled, the ranks of 'negro houses' and the cluster of buildings labelled 'works' don't make much sense to me. Today's landscape is a confusion of secondary jungle dotted with mature trees. Once it must have been as neat as the industrialised farmlands of England.

But Bull is gripped by the maps. 'This is all just right. There's lots of the remains of buildings down there' – he points to the river –

'where they must have had the boiling for the sugar. And you can see what was the water mill. There was a heavy metal wheel, broken, but some guys took it for scrap. All the development is here, in a half-mile radius.' The 'Queen's Road' from Kingston to Bath that the earlier maps indicate, bisecting the estate and running just down the hill from the 'Dwelling House and Offices', was long ago replaced by the coast road up which we drove. But the old road is now a track, solid and stone-founded under loose earth and leaves. It places Bull's house exactly, and shows that it was indeed the 'great house'.

I promise to email him the maps. 'I don't want to know too much, Alex,' he says. 'I'll read what you write, maybe. But I would like to have it in case I want to look, one day.' Bull's son, Desian, has shinned up the huge mango tree beside the house: he comes down with a bucket full of fruit and gives us each one to try. It's small, a rich apricot colour and fabulously sweet, with a sharp back-taste that makes it delicious. It dribbles down my shirt. It is the best I've tasted since Susan Craig-James's Buxton mango in Tobago.

On the slope above the house there are more stone foundations. I pick an intricate piece of metal out of some dead leaves under a mango tree. Bull nods when I show it to him: bits and pieces like that are quite common. There are hoops of iron that once were the rim of cart or carriage wheels, bits of heavy chain, tackle for animals. He once found half the jaw of a big, toothed trap. 'There is stuff everywhere: this land, it holds a lot of history,' he says.

I scrape the caked yellow mud from the device. It is three links of metal bent into curves, each of them bonded to the other by a neat twist. It has the surprising heaviness of very old iron, hardly rusted, a quality metal hand-forged long ago. On my phone I find some images of Swedish ironmongery sold to British slave plantations – manacles, leg irons and instruments of torture. I show these to Bull. 'Yes,' he says. 'Maybe. Or it could be a horse's bit.'

Bull says he will show me the 'mass grave'. It's just a few yards above the house. There is a slab of modern-looking concrete, about ten metres long and a couple wide. Some years ago staff from Jamaica's National Heritage Trust visited Rozelle and had a look under it. 'I don't think it's to do with slavery. They asked me to preserve it, they said it was the grave of white people. Quite a number of persons. A continued interment over many years.'

I mention the shocking death toll on the plantation. Bull says: 'It bothers me so much, Alex, you wouldn't believe – when I watch some of those TV programmes, movies, etc, how blacks were treated in America, and the Middle Passage, it really, really bothers me. I put it aside. I don't want to know more about it.'

I feel I'm behaving just like a tourist. Gushing about the mangoes. Spicing my visit with a bit of grim history. 'Me and lots of people like me, in Britain,' I say to Bull, 'now, we also feel appalled by what happened. And we know it was our ancestors who did it.'

He takes a big breath. 'I don't know. I don't know that you can feel the way I do. In Jamaica we have a saying – "It's na de man weh shit de road remember it, but de man weh walk in it cyan forget." Meaning, it is not the person who created the mess who remembers the mess, but the person who the mess affects. So you're just telling me that you really feel bad because your ancestors orchestrated all of the shit. Really?

'We feel worse, because we're the ones who paid, physically. We felt it, *felt* it. Beaten, scourged, rejected. Even in recent time, twentieth century, in Alabama, in America, it's going on. You get me emotional, man. You name it, I don't even want to remember it, I want to get rid of it out of my mind, go drink some rum – you laugh, Chris?'

'Give respect to him for acknowledging it, Bull, man,' says Chris Thompson.

But, ashamed, I say, 'You're quite right, Bull. I can't possibly begin to feel the pain your ancestors went through. But I am angry at the denial of it. I live in a city in Scotland built on the blood of slaves, and people don't much know or care.'

'If you go resurrect those things, you might have a thing you can't handle, Alex,' says Bull calmly. 'But it's crazy if you people aren't interested. You look at Jamaica's economics – it's like that because nobody cares. You failed completely. We can't stand upon our feet. We don't have to be as rich as you, but we need to be self-sufficient, have enough reserves for when catastrophic things happen, like a major hurricane.

'If that happens, then we have to go beg. I lost my roof when we had Hurricane Gilbert in '88 and I got nothing. No help, no compensation, nothing. The soldiers were here, and I asked, but they said no, this is a quality house. You mend it yourself.'

We talk a little about the realities of being a small farmer here. Most people, like Bull, have three acres under the National Land

Agency's scheme to re-purpose under-used land. There are some ninety-five plot holders, with more titles being granted as more sections of the old plantation are released. Two of Bull's daughters and their families are living on plots on the other side of the river.

This explains why the once-squared fields that were the Rozelle plantation are now the jumble of a spread-out village, with gardens, woods, scrub and small farms. There are many shacks of tin and wood, but several two-storey villas are being built, grey concrete soon to be painted in creams and pinks. On this sunny Sunday afternoon it seems a happy place, laughter and talk rising from behind the fences.

Bull shows me what he is growing. 'I have ackees, breadfruit, a few mangoes and some goats. I intend to do some chickens – there's my coop, behind you, and some apiculture. Listen, I've got some of the best honey you ever tasted.' He sells to higglers, middlemen who take the ackee and mangoes from locals and sell them at the markets in Kingston. 'I'd like to do my own marketing. That's how you get the real money. The higglers take too much.'

His best crop is the heavy wax from the beehives, which sells for US$800 a pound to the cosmetics industry. 'But it's not enough to keep us. People living on just that, I don't know how they get by. They depend on their little parcel [of land] for all their income, clothing, school costs.' Bull, with his council pension, has an income of less than US$400 a month. As a result his wife has had to go back to Trinidad, where she was born, to support the family by working in a hotel.

As we talk Bull's stepson works around us, carefully touching-in little seedlings in the flower pots that cluster around the house. They're cannabis, he tells me. Growing the plant for personal use is legal now, and industrial production of it for the health-products market in the States is an idea being discussed in St Thomas. The white plantation owners made fortunes from this land, of course, I say. 'Yes, man, but they had no competition, and they had free labour. And then Jamaica was a market for your goods. Look at these bricks' – he waves at the neat old blocks that make the grand staircase – 'they came from England. You sent us your bricks, you didn't want us to make our own. You wouldn't release us, man. You kept us dependent.'

But Bull seems content. 'I like the place. I love it, man.' What about the things that happened here? 'Ghosts?' he says. 'They're all about the place. I know there's blood spilt here. This was a slave community, slaves would have died from punishments. I know that they're here, but they're not interfering with me. I don't hear them crying.'

I ask Bull what is the root of his happiness here. 'I like it because it's semi-remote and it's close to the town, it's historic, it's comfy. My wife, when I brought her here, prior to getting married, she was just all over the place, loving it. When I came here first we didn't have the trees, I could sit on the steps and see the ships going west. That's why they built it here, elevated. The master could sit here and see right around him, with the enormous veranda right around him. See what's going on. I'm not going anywhere, going to live here the rest of my time.'

We say our goodbyes, and I offer again to send him the material I have on Rozelle. He shakes his head. 'I don't want to revisit the past. In Jamaica we say let bygones be bygones. Bury the hatchet. Live for today, don't live in the past. Live in the past and you live in problems. I want to stay young by going forward.'

At a wooden stall on a slow corner on the coast road an old lady is selling Rozelle honey in used bottles of Wray & Nephew rum. Chris rolls down his window and we buy three of them, for twenty US dollars. He insists I taste it now, here, where it was made. It is warm from the sun, brown-gold and liquid with a deep, woody taste. 'Oh man, that's good,' I say. He nods, dreaming. 'Every time I come down here, I just don't want to go back to Kingston. This life, here, in the country, it's right.'

* * *

I want this next generation to do better than us. I'm very hopeful. I don't want those things from the past to hold me down: I want optimism for my children and my grandchildren.

Aston 'Bull' Smith at the great house at Rozelle,
his family home

I asked Bull Smith at Rozelle what he thought we, the descendants of the exploiters, should be doing today. 'Let bygones be bygones' is his core belief, but that need not end the matter. 'I know somebody's lobbying for reparation,' he says, 'and I think Britain and whosoever is liable should think hard about it and should do their best.'

He talks about the *Windrush* and how West Indians helped rebuild Britain after the Second World War. 'We'd like to see that you are sincere and you want to give back. There are ways: you can see how the Chinese are helping us improve the country, the road network infrastructure.' This is true: Chinese state investment is revolutionising the island's rickety road network, though no one is very clear on what the cost to Jamaica will be.

Every Jamaican and Tobagan I have spoken to backs the call for reparations, though for many that is just a detail in a much bigger process of acknowledgement and reconciliation: if the reparations issue can work as a lever to open the doors for a frank debate with Europe, then that is a good tactic. Many are sceptical about the likelihood of any former slaving nation actually reaching for its chequebook, and then about their governments' ability to spend any funds that might come through fairly or productively.

Similarly, not many people I meet are much impressed by the official reparations campaign. 'Lots of talk over recent years, and no progress,' grumbles Chris Thompson. The fact that it is now state-backed doesn't help: like most of us, ordinary Jamaicans do not have much faith in the processes of modern government. 'The academics up there,' says one veteran Jamaican media commentator (who asked not to be named) waving from the café of my Kingston hotel up at Mona and the University of the West Indies campus, 'are very good at high-level conferences. But that's not worth much if nothing comes of them.'

But in these conversations I suspect that this cynicism comes as much from an awareness that asking for things from Europe in the name of justice has always met with disappointment. 'The last time Britain promised us more aid, all we got was some money for a new prison. Good for putting away all the criminals that you send us, in return for taking our doctors and nurses and teachers,' the journalist continued.

That statement is no exaggeration. When David Cameron visited Jamaica as British prime minister in September 2015, he did pledge new aid money for the Caribbean, including £25 million to help build a new, 'human rights compliant' prison in Jamaica. This was practical: government lawyers were worried that Jamaicans in British jails could not be deported to serve out sentences because conditions in Jamaica were so poor. But sending home Jamaican long-term prisoners would save the British government £10 million a year. The ironies of this new traffic from Britain – still going on in 2021 – were noted in Jamaica.

Many Jamaicans had expected Cameron to address the reparations claim on his visit, and even make the long-expected apology. After all, University College London's compensation database had revealed an ancestral relation, Sir James Duff, son of the Earl of Fife, who owned a plantation with 202 enslaved Africans in Jamaica.[2] There is no evidence that Cameron's direct family benefited, however.

Cameron made no apology for the colonial era, of course, or any commitment to reparations. Instead, he recalled Britain's 'work to wipe slavery off the face of the planet' and said, in a speech to the Jamaican parliament, that he wished both countries to 'move on from this painful legacy'. Some parliamentarians in his audience shook their heads at this.[3]

Since 2015 hundreds of Jamaicans – no one seems to have a reliable figure – who had right of residence in Britain have been deported to Jamaica after completing sentences. British newspapers characterised the passengers on the charter flights as murderers and rapists, following the Home Office line. But a typical charter flight's load of 'serious foreign criminals' in February 2019 contained one murderer and rapist: nearly half were drug dealers and one was a hairdresser deported after serving a fourteen-month sentence for a driving offence in which no one was injured. He, like most of the deportees, had left Jamaica as a child and been granted 'indefinite leave to remain' in the UK.[4]

There's human traffic in the other direction too. Despite a crackdown on visas for academics and others, Jamaican health and education professionals continue to migrate as they have since independence, much to the despair of those services in the country. In 2018 the NHS announced a huge new scheme to bring nurses over (disguised as a 'three-year educational secondment'), while British school academy trusts and commercial agencies regularly hold job fairs for teachers in Kingston. Eighty-eight nurses quit the University of the West Indies hospital in 2019.[5]

British schools pay six times what a teacher can earn in Jamaica and many, especially science and maths teachers, leave for the UK and North America.[6] I visited three schools in Kingston and St Thomas. The headteachers' story was the same: salaries declining, class sizes increasing, staff having to work second jobs, maths teachers unobtainable. All of the heads knew teachers who had migrated: one said she was considering doing so herself.

Underfunding education in Jamaica is a story that starts at emancipation. A century later, in 1943, less than 1 per cent of black people and 9 per cent of mixed race people attended secondary school. In Britain in 1951 nearly 50 per cent of children attended secondary school. When British rule in Jamaica ended in 1962, 25 to 30 per cent of the country was illiterate.[7]

Cameron's vaunted promise of increased aid spending was empty: the UK's aid and development spending in the Caribbean was set at £41 million in 2020–21, down from £49 million ten years earlier.[8] The former sugar and slavery colonies are still transferring their wealth in people to Britain and getting ever less in return.

'Does reparations fix my pain, heal my country? How about mere fair treatment?' asks a young Jamaican sociology student I met at a discussion on the reparations movement in Kingston. 'We have people dying in hospital while the UK poaches our nurses. We have people uneducated in our schools while the UK poaches our teachers. These dynamics started in the slavery era. I'm interested in ending them.'

'Soul murder' and the future

Frederick Hickling had to cancel our meeting in Jamaica, and in May 2020 he died, aged seventy-four. He was retired, much bemedalled and hugely respected across the world, Professor Emeritus of Psychiatry at the UWI. He was not just the Caribbean's most eminent psychiatrist but, as he was fond of saying, a third-generation one. His most recent book, *Owning Our Madness: Facing Reality in Post-colonial Jamaica*, is part memoir, part call to arms.

In it he draws on years spent at the receiving end of racism in his profession (he trained in psychiatry in London and Edinburgh in the 1970s) and as a black man in Britain – he was caught 'driving while black' in London in 1992 when researching at the Maudsley Hospital. The police stopped Hickling in his rental car and accused him of having stolen it. He told the story to his peers in an article in the

British Medical Journal that went on to address the psychological trauma that can result from racist discrimination.

Forty-five years of clinical experience in Britain and Jamaica left Hickling profoundly pessimistic. He believed that personality disorders affected Jamaicans at three to six times world average rates, and in 2016 he stated that mental illness prevalence in Jamaica was at 70 per cent of the population.[9] He was sure of the root cause. The legacy of slavery and colonialism had left Jamaicans with unequalled problems over the management of identity and power: these affected individuals and thus the whole society. He wrote in his book, *Owning Our Madness*:

> This often manifests as difficulties in managing their own impulses and in managing interpersonal relationships. The resulting transgressive behaviour, defiance, conflict, power struggles, drug abuse, hyper sexuality, other sexual problems and male/female relationship problems are as common in the Jamaican society as 'ackee and saltfish'.

Hickling had come to believe that European culture, with all its duplicity and racism, is in itself psychotic. He quotes Bob Marley's famous description of Babylon – the corrupted, colonialist world – as the vampire. 'When it is all behind us,' Hickling writes, 'the human race will look back at major aspects of European civilisation as monstrously evil constructions of a dangerously deranged people, totally concerned by their narcissistic egotism, and dominated by delusions of power and control.' European colonialism protected white people from schizophrenia while engendering it in the 'coloured'. The culture of the colonialists must be rejected, their psychosis negated, he goes on, if black people are to flourish and black mental health is ever to be restored.

You sense, though, that he doubts that the descendants of the enslaved can be saved from the ongoing damage of the 'psychological ravishment' done to Africa and its people, and the 'soul murder' of enslavement. Hickling's conclusion, in this, the last major work of a lifetime spent addressing the endless mental health crisis in the Caribbean countries, is stark: 'If we are to develop as an independent and free people . . . we must own our own madness.'[10]

'Justice repairs all crimes'

Tucked into the foothills of the Blue Mountains, a half-hour's taxi-ride from downtown Kingston, are the remains of an old sugar estate called Mona. Its owners in the eighteenth and nineteenth century, the Bond family of Croydon, just south of London, kept more than 360 enslaved Africans on their three estates: it is good to imagine the look on their faces if they were to see how their property is now used.[11]

Mona today is the primary campus of the University of the West Indies. The cane fields are lawns. A former rum warehouse, severe and symmetrical in white limestone, is now a chapel. A long aqueduct curves across the lawns: it once carried water from the Hope River to power the sugar mills. The hand-cut stones and brick-lined arches tell you what work once was for the young of Jamaica: the lecture halls and libraries proclaim what it now can be.

When I arrive, at lunchtime, the place hums with the chatter of young people from all over the Caribbean and beyond. It is a relief to duck out of the hard June heat into the cool of the main administration building. Here is the Centre for Reparations Research, its rooms next to the office of the university vice-chancellor. He is Sir Hilary Beckles and his work on the social economics of slavery and its legacy led to the founding of the centre. In 2013 the heads of government of Caricom, the regional bloc of nations, came together to call for reparations for damage done and ongoing as a result of the transatlantic slave trade and chattel slavery. This was addressed to the European nations responsible. The centre was set up to lead research to underpin that campaign. It gathers academics, lawyers and activists under the hopeful motto 'Justice repairs all crimes'.

Beckles and his long-time collaborator Professor Verene Shepherd follow an honourable line of Caribbean academics, radical chroniclers of slavery and the African diaspora who turned, sooner or later, to working in politics to redress the wrongs of the colonial era. These historian-economist-politicians begin with C. L. R. James, the great historian who chronicled the Haitian revolution in *The Black Jacobins*, and with Eric Williams. His *Slavery and Capitalism*, published in 1944, is the foundational text for the generations who came to doubt that British colonialism was the benevolent machine for dispensing civilisation and democracy about which they had been taught at school.

Williams served twice as prime minister of Trinidad and Tobago. After getting a first at Oxford in 1938, his career in England was blighted by racism: he could not get grants. This is a story you hear even now from senior Caribbean academics who have worked in the UK.

Williams's twin theses electrified modern historians of the period and its aftermath, and they still resound today. These are, first, that financial benefits of the slave trade and plantation enslavement were the source of Britain's economic growth in the nineteenth century: slavery was the engine of the Industrial Revolution, of British capitalism itself. And, second, that Britain's pride in ending the transatlantic slave trade in 1807,* and plantation slavery twenty-six years later, is arrogant and misplaced: abolition came about because the British industrial machine no longer needed slavery and could profit more without it.

Since 1944 there have been many critics of Williams, and particularly of this economic analysis. But they have come and gone: Williams's theses live on, not least because of his charisma, his fiery, witty prose and, most important, the work he does to counter a dominating historical theory that sought to diminish the failures of the British colonial powers and blame instead the enslaved people and their descendants.

'Slavery was not born of racism: rather, racism was the consequence of slavery,' Williams wrote in *Slavery and Capitalism*. Today that is as influential a principle as his economic arguments. It has been challenged too. There are historians who argue that Europeans considered Africans inferior before the period of enslavement began. But there is a higher truth in Williams's statement, and it serves to energise all of us who want a rational explanation of modern racism. It fires the campaign for reparations, too, because if you believe that slavery was a wrong that can be righted, then Williams's precept also argues that racism and racial discrimination can be ended.

* * *

....
* 'Transatlantic' is important. Williams was the first modern historian to make the point that the British carried on trading slaves for twenty-five years after 1807, between their colonies in the Caribbean islands and on the South American mainland.

There is a press conference today at the Centre for Reparations Research. It will announce new data on the involvement of different European nations in the slave trade. In a lecture hall some forty people have gathered – a couple of TV cameras, some reporters with dictaphones and notebooks. There's only one other obvious white European in the audience: a tall young man with yellow-grey skin, wearing a dingy suit, tie and a bushy mat of black beard.

There are dreadlocks and robes too: among the guests are representatives of the Maroon community, including one of their leaders, Colonel Rudolph Pink of Scott's Hall. He is a former builder returned to the island after many years in the UK: his title 'Colonel' harks back to the Maroons' history as a militia of free Africans. Because of their eighteenth-century treaty with the British colonial regime, the Maroons consider themselves independent of the Jamaican state – indeed, they were the first sovereign African people in the Americas. It is more than a courtesy to treat them as a separate interest group.

Half a dozen people, most of them elderly, are wearing pendant images of the Lion of Judah and of Haile Selassie. One young man, sleek in gold silk trousers, matching shirt and fez, carries a ceremonial fly whisk. Later he introduces himself as a prince from Nigeria, representing the African Union.

Professor Shepherd – regal in gold and green from head to foot – leads the event as director of the centre. We are here, she explains, to announce the updating of a twenty-year-old database that attempts to list every one of more than 36,000 voyages from Africa to the Americas carrying enslaved Africans.[12] The new research has lengthened the list of European states that 'contributed to the sale, exploitation, torture and death of millions of enslaved Africans':[13] 12.5 million people forcibly removed from Africa and transported across the Atlantic between 1514 and 1866.

It is a shock, as Professor Shepherd runs through the bullet points, to realise how much of this is utterly unknown in Britain. First, that we are second only to Portugal in terms of the number of Africans transported – more than 3.75 million people were taken in British ships, largely to British colonies. France and Spain, in third and fourth place, are each responsible for a third as many, and the USA, post-independence in 1776, a mere 305,000.

Professor Shepherd then lists the new additions to the list of European countries involved in the trade and plantation slavery. Most have not been cited before. She quotes a Swiss historian's analysis of wealth that derives from profits made by Swiss plantation investors, insurers and the Swiss merchants who provided supplies to the ships and the sugar colonies. There is the Duchy of Courland, now in Latvia, which established a settlement in Tobago using enslaved people they transported from Africa in one single voyage. Denmark, Sweden, Sardinia, Genoa and some states that are part of modern Germany are also on the new database. So is Russia.

'This trading in black bodies, this dastardly act that saw babies as young as one year old, men as old as seventy, captured and sold away from their homeland . . . this digital memorial aggregates that information and holds these countries accountable and makes them aware of their responsibility.' Though some countries, as Shepherd remarks, are still in denial.

Then there are the enslaved people's real names. The database lists 94,191 of them. Most enslaved Africans lost their birth names, and for 300 years there were no original African names in the slave records at all. You might well argue that the lack of names and places of origin, of the things that give us our identity, helped dehumanise the victims of the trade. It has made it easier to turn them into statistics.

So these original names are to be treasured. The database is able to list them now because, as nations abolished the slave trade, navies were licensed to capture and impound slave trading ships. In the records of these engagements the names of the Africans found aboard were listed, chiefly by the British Royal Navy.

Professor Shepherd reads some of them out, slowly, as at a service of memorial.

'Ekhusumee, a girl, aged two. Maloah, a girl, aged two. Captured from Lagos, both of them. Kangah, a girl aged five, captured from Lagos. Peekah, a girl aged four, captured from Lagos. Coulta, a girl aged three, captured from Lagos. Torquah, a girl aged six from Bonny. Ajameh, aged one, a boy, captured from Lagos. Asemah, a boy, aged one, from Porto Novo . . .'

All these names were recorded in Freetown, Sierra Leone, where many captured trading ships were first taken by the Royal Navy. But most of these Africans, though free, did not get home – that was not part of the rescue service. Many ended up in the Caribbean anyway: nearly 15,000 of the freed West Africans who were first landed on the remote Atlantic island of St Helena eventually arrived in Jamaica, after emancipation. A trace of their community still can be seen at the furthermost tip of St Thomas, where freed people of the Kroo ethnic group built the lighthouse that marks Jamaica's easternmost point, the place closest to Africa.

* * *

The press conference continues long beyond the normal span of such things. Professor Shepherd's colleague Dr Ahmed Reid gives a presentation expanding on the new data. He spent some time on the discovery of a Russian-owned and -flagged ship trading slaves to Cuba in 1838. This revelation has already attracted an angry letter of denial from the Russian ambassador to Jamaica, published in the *Daily Gleaner.*

There are other European slaving countries hitherto under-examined. Swedes from their monarchs downwards were small but enthusiastic slave traders, principally via the island of St Barthélemy, which they used as a marketplace for Africans. The country was also for two centuries the principal supplier of iron ore for making the necessary kit – chains, shackles, handcuffs, collars and so on – for the British slave ships, Swedish iron being particularly pure (it supplied Germany's munitions factories in both world wars). Lists of stores shipped from Sibbald's of Leith and Houston's of Glasgow to the plantation at Rozelle sometimes note that the ironware is 'Swedish'[14] – a sign of quality.

Dr Reid's point is that all over Europe a huge number of people, of very different sorts, were implicated in the slave trade: 'It was not only the wealthy. The carpenters would have benefited. Whoever did the laundry benefited. Whoever made the bread benefited. These voyages pervaded the entire fabric of these European societies.'

When we get to the Q&A the bearded young European bounces up. He tells us he is Aleksei Sazonov, a senior official with the Russian embassy. 'So,' he begins, 'I would like to say that in Russia we condemn the very fact of the slave trading and we believe such a horrible thing should never have happened and should never happen again. But I believe we should not mix [the database] with vaguely supported allegations. Any fact should be properly checked. As for the ship that in 1838 allegedly had the flag of the Russian empire on it, it is a well-supported historic fact that Russia never had colonies in the Caribbean and never was involved in transatlantic slave trading.'

Mr Sazonov takes a deep breath and looks round at all of us. 'If there was documented that a ship with a Russian flag supposedly entered the port then we should double-check. There's not enough details. I didn't see the name of the captain. We all know that a flag can be changed in a split-second . . .' At this some gentle laughter begins, but he presses on: it's like someone forging a passport. Or someone with a British passport supporting Isis. 'That doesn't mean Britain is a terrorist-supporting country,' he says.

And there is one more thing: 'In Russia there was a tradition of a very equal approach to those who came from beyond Russia. For example, there is one of the most-known Russian poets, surname Pushkin, who was originally from Ethiopia. So we should double-check all the facts.' At this point the muttering – 'What about the serfs?' – and the laughter get too much. Sazonov says thank you very much and sits down.[15]

Dr Reid answers that the database is clear that the ship, listed as the *Goliubchik*, was carrying the Russian flag and had a captain called Barnadas. There is multiple sourcing of the information, which the database lists. It can be easily inspected. 'We're not in the business of calling out states without evidence,' says Professor Shepherd, adding that allegations about Russian slave trading are not new. Which is true: they were first made in a protest to Russia by Viscount Palmerston, then British foreign minister, reporting the evidence of the Royal Navy when it arrested the *Goliubchik* and found three other Russian slave trading vessels in the Atlantic in 1839.

* * *

The afternoon wears on in the Mona conference room. More questions, and statements, follow: they are a good reflection of the various debates that run through the reparations movement today. Several of the Rastafarians want reassurance that repatriation 'to the homeland' is still on the campaign's agenda. 'It has been forgotten in all the talk of money,' says one. The desire to return to Africa is a central tenet of every branch of the religion: it will be 'the ultimate justice', as one woman, Empress Pethrona, puts it. She has a soft English accent and long grey dreadlocks. She runs a blog titled International

Repatriation Movement – subheaded 'Let us begin our journey home to Africa'.

The principle of a right of return has been a key theme of political activism among people of African descent in the Americas since the Jamaican Marcus Garvey first promoted it along with pan-Africanism in the 1920s. '[Repatriation] has never dropped out of focus,' says Professor Shepherd in reply to the questions. 'It's high up on the agenda, deliberately so. There's no dichotomy between having a conversation about development and one about repatriation.'

Professor Shepherd is punctilious in according respect to the Rastafari elders and the Maroon representatives. But she is less so when dealing with the young, silk-clad man with the fly whisk. He introduces himself as His Majesty Chief Sumako of Nigeria, finance minister of a Nigerian state, and a representative to the African Union's diaspora division.[16] 'Given the four- or five-hundred-year journey our people have gone through, the topic of return is no small topic. Our ancestors have fought for generations on generations just to catch a snippet of that dream of return,' he states.

When returning to Africa next week he promises to report to the president of Ghana and all African heads of states that the topic of return must be addressed. And not just of return – 'What land and money will returning Africans be given? The United States promised forty acres and a mule [to freed Africans after the Civil War], and failed on that. What is the continent prepared to give to the diaspora?' Ghana is marking the 400th anniversary of the arrival of the first West African, as a slave, in Virginia with a Year of Return and has, he says, commemorated it by granting citizenship to 200 Jamaicans.

Professor Shepherd points out that Jamaicans will still need to find money for the travel and they need to get visas. Ghanaians don't need visas to visit Jamaica. 'We're not talking about deporting people and leaving them at the airport. We're not talking about tourism.'

* * *

After the conference I sit down to talk with Verene Shepherd. Six years on from the Caricom nations' formal call for talks to begin with Europe on reparations, not much seems to be happening, I say. The idea is not on the political agenda in Britain, beyond a mention in the 2019 Labour Party manifesto.

'You're right,' she agrees, 'it's not high up on the agenda for the British government. For governments to act there has to be a ground-swell. There's none at the moment. You can go to see Rastafari, and have a grounding with them, but generally even intellectuals are not engaged. But though you may not hear it, the work is going on. For the moment we have to focus on public education, in the communities.

'So we are doing the work. When you think about enslavement and how these wars of resistance were planned, sometimes you never heard about them and until something happened. When I think about the war led by Sam Sharpe [the Baptist church leader who led the 1831 uprising], I remember that while Sharpe was talking a peaceful sit-down strike, he had also lined up all his generals, in every parish. Sometimes you have to retreat from the public eye and do the groundwork.'

There has been discussion in France of paying reparations to Haiti, but that is over a specific incident, the transfer of what today would be twenty-one billion dollars' worth of gold bullion from the Haitian exchequer in 1825 after France bullied the Haitians into paying compensation to planters for damage done in the Haitian revolution in 1791.* Does Verene get a sense that the broader principle of reparations is getting support in the other complicit European nations?

'Sweden has said it is open to discussion. No other country has said that. The responses from the governments have been, "Yes, it was wrong, but it was a long time ago, and we need to move forward . . . Forget about that and let's have a modern relationship." So now another round of letters is being written, taking in the new countries.

'I think many states do not understand the dynamics of the period of enslavement and the transatlantic trade, of the actual involvement of states, rather than individuals. We're mining the documents to tailor each letter to each country, to say to Portugal, to Germany, and so on – this is how you were involved.' The Jamaican parliament, she points out, has now mandated the government to pursue a repa-rations claim. Things are moving ahead.

Verene and I are the same sort of age, and at university we had

---

* Haiti had to borrow to pay compensation to the French. Paying off the loan took until 1947.

similar causes. 'Anti-apartheid was our thing,' she agrees. 'Remember how music and cricket became a focus for mobilising against apartheid. It was actually very fast, in the end, the change. I always tell people, remember: the emancipation fight took 350 years.' The key to the anti-apartheid movement's spread across the world, it seems to me, was about the offer of hope for a better future for all of us. She agrees. Reparative justice is not just about recompensing the heirs of enslaved people, but a decisive move towards ending racism.

But there are steps that must come first. 'No one has apologised to the African-descended people of the Caribbean. There have been statements of regret. That is different from a statement of apology, which has three dimensions. An apology accepts blame and responsibility, an apology commits to no repetition, an apology commits to repair. That has not been done for the Caribbean.

'An apology from a church, or a family, or conversations about reparatory justice with universities – they are all great. But it does not take away the responsibility of the state. The state created the superstructure for this system and the state has to take responsibility.'

Verene has to go: she needs to catch a plane for a conference in Brussels. We say goodbye. I step out onto the lawns of Mona. In the late afternoon sun, students play softball where the sugar canes once stood.

APPENDIX: WHAT HAPPENED
NEXT? AND WHAT TO DO?

What happened next?

Researching a family's involvement in the industries of the slavery era used to be harder: scrubbing away the plaster applied by ashamed and embarrassed Victorians was difficult and time-consuming. It was and is particularly hard for researchers working in the Caribbean countries, where only part of British colonial-era records are held: they not only have to fund the trip to Britain and its archives but also get a visa out of an increasingly unfriendly system.

Some of this is beginning to change, however, as more data becomes available online. Thanks to the work of the Centre for the Study of the Legacies of British Slave-ownership centre at University College London, it is now easier at least to research the slave owners at the time of emancipation in the British Caribbean. The centre has digitised all the records of the Commission for Compensation of the 1830s, so a simple search can bring up an extraordinary amount of information. Research continues to examine plantation histories and what happened to the compensation money after it was handed to the slave owners.

What follows below is a summary of what is known about what happened to some of the places and people who appear in this book.

Ballantine, Fairlie & Co. were slave merchants, bankers and lawyers, Ayrshire men based in Kingston, Jamaica. They acted for the Fergussons and many other planters in Jamaica and made a considerable fortune from the seizure of plantation estates whose owners went bankrupt. Patrick Ballantine came back from Jamaica and built a mansion at Castlehill in Ayrshire. James Fairlie built one at Bellfield outside the town of Kilmarnock. The site of the latter is now a rundown council estate. James's nephew, Colonel James Ogilvy Fairlie (1809–1870), was a friend of Lord Eglinton and took part in his tournament. But he is now best known as the inventor of modern competitive golf, as founder of the 'Open' (which was actually closed).

Blairquhan Castle, Sir David Hunter Blair's Ayrshire mansion, built in 1821, was sold by the family in 2012. It appeared as a stand-in for Balmoral in the Oscar-winning film *The Queen* (2006), starring Helen Mirren. The castle is now owned and run as a wedding and corporate meeting venue by a Chinese investment company. In October 2020 Shenzhen Ganten Food & Beverage told the *Financial Times* it was worried that Blairquhan's history, of which it had not been aware, would damage the company's 'hard-earned business reputation'.[1]

Paul Bogle, the farmer and Baptist deacon whose protest in 1865 sparked the Morant Bay uprising, is now a National Hero of Jamaica: his head is on the country's ten-cent coin. The Scottish Bogle family, on whose Jamaican plantations Paul's mother Cecelia Bogle may have been enslaved, were one of the wealthiest: they shared £55,798 (£48.6 million today) in compensation at emancipation in 1835 for enslaved people on their estates in Trinidad, British Guiana and Jamaica.[2] Gilmorehill, their nineteenth-century estate, is now part of Glasgow University.

William Bruce of Stenhouse befriended my distant uncle James Fergusson, and it was at Bruce's Tobago estate that he died. In 1836 his descendant Sir Michael Bruce of Stenhouse claimed £30,000 in compensation money, but lost to a counter-claim by a London banker, Nathaniel Mason, who held a mortgage on Shirvan and many other Tobago estates.[3]

Edward Colston, a Bristol slave trader and Member of Parliament, was responsible through the Royal Africa Company for the shipping of more than 80,000 enslaved Africans to the Americas. In June 2020 a crowd took down his statue and threw it into the River Avon. A man claiming to be Colston's direct descendant, Alex Colston, tweeted (in response to Sajid Javid MP's objections to the toppling): 'Naw, man, as the singular heir of this family, I declare it's cool'[4] He posted links for people wishing to donate in support of the Black Lives Matter movement in the United States.

Culzean Castle and the Kennedys of Cassillis The ancient Ayrshire family invested in the slave trade in the eighteenth century: there were four slave ships called *Lord Cassillis* (the family's title) in the time of Thomas, the 9th Earl of Cassillis and owner of Culzean Castle and a 250,000-acre estate. Archibald, the 12th Earl (and Marquess of Ailsa), married Eleanor Allardyce, daughter of a Jamaica slave trader and factor named Alexander Allardyce in 1814. He had given Eleanor £30,000 (£23.7 million) and a Scottish estate.

Later generations intermarried with the Oswald and Montgomerie/Eglinton families. The family gave Culzean Castle to the National Trust for Scotland in lieu of taxes in 1949, and sold their other home, the fourteenth-century Cassillis House, in 2009 to the founder of confused.com.

Deacon, Labouchere & Co. The bank that handled the compensation payments to most of the Scottish slave owners in 1835–40 became a part of the Royal Bank of Scotland.

Dundas/Melville In August 2020 the City of Edinburgh Council put a new plaque beside the column and statue of Henry Dundas, 1st Viscount Melville, in St Andrew Square. This records the fact that by introducing the principle of 'gradual' abolition of the slave trade, Dundas brought about the enslavement and shipping to British colonies of 500,000 more Africans between 1792 and 1808. His descendant, Bobby Dundas, 10th Viscount Melville, is campaigning for its removal as unjust and an 'assault on our history'.

Eglinton Castle and the Eglintons The Montgomerie/Eglinton family intermarried with the Scottish plantation-owning families the Lindsays (Balcarres), Fergussons and the Hamiltons. Archibald, the 13th Earl of Eglinton, was said by his granddaughter to have spent 'most of the estate' on his washed-out medieval tournament in 1839.

In 1925 Eglinton Castle had the lead stripped from its roof and was abandoned by the family. They moved to a more modest Gothic mansion in Perthshire. For 250 years, the Earls of Eglinton have been, like many inheritors of slavery wealth, among Britain's pre-eminent Freemasons.

John Gladstones (the 's' was dropped when John got his knighthood) rose from humble beginnings in Leith to own nine Caribbean plantations and, with them, 2,508 enslaved African people. They were valued at £336,000 in 1833 (£290 million today). Sir John received a record £106,769 in compensation for 'giving up' the enslaved people. Some of the wealth was spent on Aberdeenshire's Fasque Castle and an 80,000-acre estate next door to Queen Victoria at Balmoral. His son William was to become prime minister, and lived at another mock-Gothic castle, Hawarden in Wales, which had been built by his wife Catherine Glynne's slave-trading father.

Gladstone's great-great-grandson, Charles, has said that he would not oppose any democratic decision to take down or re-plaque the statues of slavers. He believes that his forebear, as a democrat committed to liberty, would support his view. 'Liberty today means countering racism, sexism and intolerance wherever we see it. That is where our energy should be exerted. That would be truly Gladstonian.'[5]

In 2019 **Glasgow University** completed an audit of its benefactors whose wealth derived from slavery, and of the material benefits it gained (see the Bogles, above). It announced a programme of reparative spending worth £20 million. A partnership with the University of the West Indies will bring students to both universities to study the history of slavery and 'reparatory justice'.

George William Gordon, illegally executed in the aftermath of the Morant Bay uprising of 1865, is one of Jamaica's official National Heroes: the country's parliament building is named after him. There is little trace of his descendants, and though he owned several plantations none of his wealth appears to have survived him. One of his children, Thomas, was a small farmer near Morant Bay: he and his wife Marie Ducat had ten children, of whom only six survived. Most of them migrated. Thomas's daughter Edna Mae became a nurse in New Jersey, and died in 2013 aged a hundred.[6]

Harewood House and the Lascelles The Lascelles family began trading with the Caribbean in the seventeenth century, and eventually owned enslaved people and 27,000 acres of plantations in Jamaica, Grenada, Tobago and Barbados. They campaigned in parliament against abolition of the trade and of slavery itself. The second Earl of Harewood received more than £21,000 in compensation in 1835–36: at his death in 1841 he is said to have left £300,000, or more than a quarter of a billion pounds today. The family still owns Harewood House in Yorkshire, built in 1759.

In June 2020 **David Lascelles**, 8th Earl of Harewood, issued a statement on behalf of the family and the Harewood Trust acknowledging the source of the wealth that built the house and enriched the family. 'Today, Harewood House is an educational charity set up to share Harewood's story, to listen, to learn, and to enrich people's lives using our collections, surroundings, and our history as means of creating a better society today. We condemn racism in all its forms, we believe that black lives matter, and we commit to tackling how Harewood shares and confronts the past, and to question what that means for communities today. Harewood cannot change its past, but we can use it.'[7] The Lascelles Slavery Archive is now at York University.

Lloyds Banking Group The fortune that enabled Sir David Hunter Blair to build Blairquhan came chiefly from his uncle William and his father Sir James's banking enterprises, in which their relations the Hamiltons were also involved. They were eventually absorbed into the Bank of Scotland, now part of Lloyds Banking Group. One of these was Hunters and Company of Ayr, another was Sir William Forbes, James Hunter & Co., which Lloyds describes as one of 'Scotland's most successful private banks'. The success of that bank, originally called Coutts, was in part because of its involvement in financing of plantation ownership in Tobago, Jamaica and elsewhere in the Caribbean. Lloyds' history of the Bank of Scotland on its website names Sir William Forbes, James Hunter & Co. in a list of twenty Scottish banks and businesses that became part of Lloyds. All of them funded and profited from the slave trade and plantation slavery.

Newhailes House The last of the Dalrymple family, who intermarried with the Kilkerran Fergussons, gave the house, outside Musselburgh, to the National Trust for Scotland in 1997.

Royal Bank of Scotland The bank has many connections to the slavery industries of the eighteenth and nineteenth century, through smaller banks that it absorbed. General John Hope, 4th Earl of Hopetoun, was a governor of RBS in the 1820s. His second wife, Louisa Wedderburn, was the daughter of the planter Sir John Wedderburn, the biggest landowner in Jamaica at the end of the eighteenth century. In October 2020 RBS's new owners NatWest group re-plaqued Hopetoun's statue in St Andrew Square to acknowledge this history.

Rozelle House The mansion built in 1760 by the Hamilton family and named after the estate in Jamaica that they sold in 1765 is now owned by Ayr Town Council. It is an art gallery and a museum of the Ayrshire Yeomanry. The council literature does not mention that the Hamilton family's fortunes were made in part in Jamaica through slavery.

James Whyte/The Canadian Imperial Bank Yet another migrant from south Ayrshire, he and his brother John made a career, and a fortune, out of managing the plantations of absentee owners in Jamaica in the 1820s and 1830s, including Rozelle. As abolition loomed, James Whyte sold his own plantation and the 110 enslaved workers and took himself to Canada. There he became a landowner in Hamilton, Ontario. He helped found and became president of the Gore Bank, whose descendant, the Canadian Imperial Bank of Commerce, is today one of the country's biggest.[8]

WHAT TO DO?

We who inherited the material goods or the privilege and opportunity that derived from exploitation of the enslaved are the luckiest people in this story. Those of us who are able to acknowledge that millions of people are still marked, or limited, by the damage our ancestors did are debating what we can do now.

In Britain in the summer of 2020, as this book was nearing completion, this conversation was hugely energised. The Black Lives Matter protests that followed the killing of George Floyd in the United States, and then the toppling of a slavery tycoon's statue in England, caught the attention of the mainstream media. For a few weeks my country, so long complacent in denial and ignorance of this history, discussed the ongoing legacy of transatlantic slavery.

Whether the shock of this awakened white Britain to the challenges offered by the Black Lives Matter campaign remains to be seen. But things have happened since: there are signs of a new openness. Institutions are auditing their history and proposing ways to address what they find. People are questioning their beliefs and attitudes to race and to our colonial history.

Most important, another generation – my own children included – are now involved in a constructive debate that is, in the end, about the task of making Britain a fairer and more honest place. They may already be freer of the dishonest past: David Olusoga has spoken about a generation with no need to believe in the 'magical exceptionalism' notion of Britain as the only country that has done good.[9] Nearly two centuries after the botched and self-serving act of emancipation in the Caribbean, it seems about time.

The furious counter-reaction after Colston's statue toppled was a shock too. But it was useful because it showed, to many of us who were blithely unaware, how deeply embedded racism is in Britain, in its structures and particularly in its elites. Just one example: the Conservative-leaning *Times* published a belated obituary of George Floyd at the end of 2020. One reader wrote that running the article was 'outrageous', an endorsement of the 'Marxist' BLM movement. The number of racist comments on the online version 'kept the moderators busy for days', wrote the paper's archive editor.[10]

After June 2020 I spoke to several people who are heirs or descendants of those who profited from slavery. Some felt under attack: at least two had seen demonstrations outside their homes as the Black Lives Matter movement gathered steam. Some had been contacted by people asking them to explain their history. None felt they or their property had been physically threatened.

Their reactions differed. One man, the titled head of a family famous in slavery history, told me he was going to enlist a historian to audit the family past and the origins of the wealth that built the house and bought the land where he still lives. Then he was going to consider how he might best act to acknowledge the story. He said he had been in contact with several others in a position like his. Unlike him, they were all minded to tough it out.

Some members of other families who feature in this book have been to the Caribbean to see the places where they exploited people, and talk to those who live there now. One told me he had decided to 'sell all the silver' and donate it to organisations doing work with disadvantaged young people in London and Jamaica. A number of people with similar stories are already donating to educational charities and other bodies in the Caribbean and in Britain. A list of some such organisations is on this book's website at bloodlegacybook.com.

These small steps are less than inadequate. This enormous, neverending wrong can never be put right. At the very least the inequalities, social and financial, between Britain's former colonies and Britain itself must be addressed. The discussion over the possibility of that has hardly begun, yet it is clear that we heirs of the wealth of slavery, more influential than most in the world, can put our privilege to work. Asking European governments to consider the Caricom countries' call for a debate on reparations would be a start.

I asked Colson Whitehead, the American novelist who has addressed slavery in the USA and its legacy in books such as *The Underground Railroad* and *The Nickel Boys*, when he thought racism would end. 'When the aliens land,' he said. The undoubted truth of that is a challenge to those of us lucky enough never to have suffered racism, to have been privileged because of the colour of our skin. The story of transatlantic slavery is not over: we have it in us to change its consequences.

ACKNOWLEDGEMENTS

Some of the people who helped and encouraged me with this project are acknowledged in the text. Among the many who are not are . . .

In Jamaica
Ainsley Henriques, Justine Henzell, Chris Thompson, Donald Reynolds, Kimberly Robinson-Walcott, Jon Earle Spence, Dr Swithin Wilmot, the staff of the National Library of Jamaica and of the library at the University of the West Indies, Mona.

In Trinidad and Tobago
Muli Amaye, Professor Bridget Brereton, Greg Fitzgerald, Ancle George, Anthony de Verteuil, the Paper Based Bookshop and the Fergusson family of Port of Spain.

In the UK
Graham Campbell, Vahni Capildeo, Eric Graham, Dr Miranda Kauffman, Caroline Kean and Jack Kennedy of Wiggin, Sian Loftus, Lorraine McCann, Geordie Milne, Dr Stephen Mullen, Ruaridh Nicoll, Sir Geoff Palmer, Bethany Parsons, Professor Diana Paton, Rida Vaquas and everyone at Canongate Books.

Special thanks to
My editor, Hannah Knowles; my agent, Jenny Brown; my wife, Ruth Burnett; my children, Adam and Lulu; and many members of the Fergusson, Renton and related families who have been helpful, tolerant and generous throughout.

SELECT BIBLIOGRAPHY

These books and websites have been particularly important in my education about this history. References are separately listed in the Notes section.

Transatlantic and plantation enslavement

Beckles, Hilary McD. and Verene Shepherd. *Liberties Lost: The Indigenous Caribbean and Slave Systems*. Cambridge: Cambridge University Press, 2004

Burnard, Trevor. *Mastery, Tyranny, and Desire*. Chapel Hill, NC: University of North Carolina Press, 2004 – and many other papers and essays

Donington, Katie. *The Bonds of Family: Slavery, Commerce and Culture in the British Atlantic World*. Manchester: Manchester University Press, 2019

James, Marlon. *The Book of Night Women*. London: One World, 2009 (fiction)

Parker, Matthew. *The Sugar Barons*. London: Hutchinson, 2011

The Trans-Atlantic Slave Trade Database website: slavevoyages.org (Data and details of 36,000 voyages between 1514 and 1866)

University College London's Legacies of British Slave-ownership website: ucl.ac.uk/lbs/ (Data and analysis of the 1830s compensation records and details on earlier ownership of plantations)

Williams, Eric. *Capitalism and Slavery*. Jamaica: Ian Randle Publishers, 2005 (first published 1944)

Emancipation and the legacy of British slavery

Draper, Nicholas. *The Price of Emancipation: Slave-Ownership, Compensation and British Society at the End of Slavery.* Cambridge: Cambridge University Press, 2010

Hall, Catherine et al *Legacies of British Slave-ownership: Colonial Slavery and the Formation of Victorian Britain.* Cambridge: Cambridge University Press, 2014

Hickling, Frederick W. *Owning Our Madness: Facing Reality in Post-colonial Jamaica.* Jamaica: Caribbean Institute of Mental Health and Substance Abuse, UWI, 2016

Olusoga, David. *Black and British: A Forgotten History.* London: Pan Books, 2017

Palmer, Geoff. *The Enlightenment Abolished: Citizens of Britishness.* Penicuik: Henry Publishing, 2007

Jamaica – history

Anonymous, *Marly: Or, a Planter's Life in Jamaica.* Glasgow: Griffin & Co., 1828 (fiction)

Craton, Michael. *Searching for the Invisible Man: Slaves and Plantation Life in Jamaica.* Cambridge, MA: Harvard University Press, 1978

Hutton, Clinton A., *Colour for Colour, Skin for Skin: Marching with the Ancestral Spirits into War Oh at Morant Bay.* Jamaica: Ian Randle Publishers, 2015

jamaicanfamilysearch.com/ (Archival records from Jamaica Almanac and other sources)

Paton, Diana. *No Bond but the Law: Punishment, Race, and Gender in Jamaican State Formation 1780–1870.* Durham, NC: Duke University Press, 2004

Petley, Christer. *White Fury: A Jamaican Slaveholder and the Age of Revolution.* Oxford: Oxford University Press, 2018 (On the planter Simon Taylor)

Thomson, Ian. *The Dead Yard: A Story of Modern Jamaica,* London: Faber, 2009 (History and travelogue of modern Jamaica)

Turner, Sasha. *Contested Bodies: Pregnancy, Childbearing and Slavery in Jamaica.* Philadelphia, PA: University of Pennsylvania, 2017

Scotland – history

Devine, T. M. (ed.) *Recovering Scotland's Slavery Past: The Caribbean Connection*. Edinburgh: Edinburgh University Press, 2015

electricscotland.com (Vast archive on the history of Scotland, notable people and the Scottish diaspora)

Fergusson, Sir James. *Lowland Lairds*. London: Faber, 1949

Graham, Eric. *Burns & the Sugar Plantocracy of Ayrshire*. Edinburgh: MDPD, 2014

Whyte, Iain. *Scotland and the Abolition of Black Slavery 1756–1838*. Edinburgh: Edinburgh University Press, 2006

Trinidad and Tobago – history

Archibald, Douglas. *Tobago, 'Melancholy Isle'*. Trinidad: Westindiana Books, 1987

Craig-James, Susan E. *The Changing Society of Tobago 1838–1938* (two volumes). Stevens Point, WI: Cornerstone Press, 2008

Phillips, David. *La Magdalena: The Story of Tobago 1498 to 1898*. iUniverse, 2004

NOTES

Abbreviations used

AC – Archibald Cameron, manager of Rozelle estate 1785–1799

AF – Sir Adam Fergusson of Kilkerran (1733–1813), 3rd Baronet, co-proprietor of Carrick and Rozelle plantations in Tobago and Jamaica

AM – Andrew Murdoch, manager of Rozelle estate 1777–1785

AWH – Alexander (Sandy) West Hamilton, manager of Rozelle estate 1812–?

CF – Charles Fergusson (1740-1804), AF and JF's brother

F of K – Fergusson of Kilkerran papers

GH – George Hamilton, manager of Rozelle estate 1799–1801, 1812

GP – Gilbert Petrie, proprietor of Englishman's Bay estate, Tobago

HH – Hugh Hamilton (1746–1816), lawyer and trustee for Hunter Blair family

JF – James Fergusson (1746–1777), CF and JF's brother

JF – John Ferguson, Rozelle estate manager 1801–1812

JP – John Paterson, manager of Rozelle estate to 1777

JRC – the report of the Jamaica Royal Commission of 1866, available via Google Books

WH – Colonel William Hunter (1739–1792), co-proprietor of Rozelle estate

UCL/LBS – The database of the Legacies of British Slave-ownership project at University College London (ucl.ac.uk/lbs)

NOTES – INTRODUCTION

1   Knight Frank website June 2018: 'Scottish farmland average price £4,285 an acre'.

2   Since the records, especially before 1817, are incomplete the number 950 is an estimate based on average totals and a death rate (excluding perinatal infants) at the Rozelle plantation of 6.3 per cent a year.

3   Draper, Nicholas reported remarks in Guthrie, Jonathan. 'Lex in depth: Examining the slave trade – "Britain has a debt to repay"', *Financial Times*, 27 June 2020. Also: Rönnbäck, Klas. 'On the economic importance of the slave plantation complex to the British economy during the eighteenth century: a value-added approach'. *Journal of Global History*, 13(03), November 2018, pp. 309–327.

4   Academic consensus in 2020 was that British ships trafficked 3.25 million Africans in total between 1600 and 1808 – 2.6 million went to the Caribbean colonies and more than 300,000 to North America. See: slavevoyages.org. At least 14% died during the voyages.

5   Schama, Simon. *A History of Britain: The British Wars, 1603–1776*. London: Random House, 2003, p. 324.

6   Twenty-seven years later, if you take the true end of British enslavement in the Caribbean as 1838. The British Slavery Abolition Act became law in August 1834, but apprenticeship continued for four more years.

7   Williams, Eric. *British Historians & the West Indies*. Trinidad: PNM Books, 1964, p. 182.

8   Bhui, Kamaldeep S. and Kwame McKenzie. 'Rates and risk factors by ethnic group for suicides within a year of contact with mental health services in England and Wales'. *Psychiatric Services*, 59(4), April 2008, pp. 414–420.

9   Johnson, Boris. 'Rather than tear some people down we should build others up'. *Daily Telegraph*, 14 June 2020.

10   ONS data published 7 May 2020, quoted by the Health Foundation in 'Emerging findings on the impact of COVID-19 on black and minority ethnic people' at health.org.uk, 20 May 2020, and in Haroon, Siddique. 'BAME Britons still lack protection from Covid, says doctors' chief'. *Guardian*, 20 September 2020.

11   'COVID-19 Hospitalization by Death and Race/Ethnicity'. Centers for Disease Control and Prevention, November 2020.

12   Olusoga in conversation with Lewis Hamilton, BBC Radio 4 *Today*, 26 December 2020.

CHAPTER 1 – IN THE FAMILY PAPERS

1   £40,000 is £3.5 million by RPW, £33.3 million by RWI (see note on 'Relative value' at the beginning of this book). More likely that this figure was Eglinton's total debts at his death. His granddaughter wrote that he had spent 'most of the wealth of the estate' on the tournament (Montgomerie, Viva Seton, *My Scrapbook of Memories*. Privately published, 1955).

2   *Spectator*, no. 584 (for the week ending 7 September 1839), vol. 12, p. 848.

3   Queen Victoria's personal diary, 2 September 1839, quoted in Shaw, Karl. *Mad, Bad and Dangerous to Know: The Extraordinary Exploits of the British and European Aristocracy*. London: Hachette, 2017.

4   measuringworth.com RPW (2019) – see note 'Relative value' at the beginning of this book.

5   Sir James Fairlie of Bellfield/Coodham, Ayrshire – see Centre for the Study of the Legacies of British Slave-ownership database at www.ucl. ac.uk/lbs/ (henceforth UCL/LBS) and his biography at historicalportraits. com. For some other families mentioned in this section, see UCL/LBS entries for 'John Wedderburn of Balindean' (for the Dundas family), 'Viscount Gage', 'John de la Poer Beresford', 'Dame Mary Kent (née Wordsworth)', 'Edward Jerningham' and 'Matilda Jerningham (née Waterton)' (Staffords).

6   RWI (2019), as in all such calculations unless otherwise stated – see note on 'relative value' at the beginning of this book.

7   £17 billion to £23 billion in 2020 money are the figures generally used in academic studies. The *Financial Times* (Guthrie, 'Lex in depth: Examining the slave trade') looked at the value in labour today. Adding in the value of the years of unpaid labour most of the 'freed' enslaved were forced to do until 1838, it comes up with £6 billion as a 2020 equivalent. But, Guthrie points out, £10 million invested in corporate bonds in 1836 would be worth £250 billion today. Seeing the £20 million in the context of overall government spending, the historian Michael Taylor puts the figure at £340 billion today (*The Interest: How the British Establishment Resisted the Abolition of Slavery*. London: Bodley Head, 2020).

CHAPTER 2 – ACQUIRING A FORTUNE

1   12 August 1773, CF to AF. These attributions refer to transcripts of the F of K papers organised by date of sending. For more information on access to these sources see bloodlegacybook.com.

2   From his *A Descriptive Account of the Island of Jamaica*, published 1790. Quoted in Parker, Matthew. *The Sugar Barons*. London: Hutchinson, 2011, p. 334.

3   5 May 1773, JF to CF

4   Scots appear in disproportionate numbers among British landowners, particularly in the ceded islands of Grenada, Tobago, St Vincent and in British Guiana. See Devine, T.M. (ed.) *Recovering Scotland's Slavery Past: The Caribbean Connection*. Edinburgh: Edinburgh University Press, 2015, p. 175.

5   Morgan, Philip D., edited Devine, T.M. *Recovering Scotland's Slavery Past*, foreword, p. iv.

6   14 June 1773, JF to AF

6b Bridenbaugh, Carl and Bridenbaugh, Roberta. *No Peace Beyond the Line: The English in the Caribbean 1624–1690*. New York: Oxford University Press, 1972, pp. 123–124.

7   14 June 1773, JF to AF

8   A decade earlier Grenada had 1,225 Europeans, 455 'free coloured' and 13,680 enslaved Africans. Both sets of statistics are from Quintanilla, Mark. 'The World of Alexander Campbell: An Eighteenth-Century Grenadian Planter'. *Albion: A Quarterly Journal Concerned with British Studies*, 35(2), summer 2003, pp. 229–256.

9   20 June 1773, JF to AF

10 For example, *Marly: Or, a Planter's Life in Jamaica* published in 1828.

11 20 June 1773, JF to AF

12 9 October 1773, JF to CF

13 The story of Colonel Patrick Ferguson's extraordinary career is told in Ferguson, James. *Two Scottish Soldiers*. Aberdeen: D. Wylie and Son, 1888, pp. 55–94. On the plantation at Castara, see Phillips, David. *La Magdalena: The Story of Tobago 1498 to 1898*. iUniverse, 2004, p. 157.

14 7 February 1774, JF to AF

15 19 February 1774, JF to CF

16 Craig-James, Susan E. *The Changing Society of Tobago 1838–1938*. Stevens Point, WI: Cornerstone Press, 2008, vol. 1, p. 7.

17 11 February 1774, JF to CF

18 *Abridgment of the Minutes of the evidence taken before a committee of the whole House, to whom it was referred to consider of the slave-trade*. Publisher unknown, 1789, vol. 1, pp. 91–97.

19 By 1777 two other 300-acre lots at Bloody Bay were being actively used. Nine sites at Bloody Bay, totalling 1,900 acres, were sold to investors between 1768 and 1769. By 1774 all had changed hands. Most were owned by men with Scottish surnames. (Source: documents in the Tobago Historical Museum, Fort King George, Tobago.) JF refers to a Campbell who had adjoining land.

20 The family were from Auchenskeoch, in modern Dumfries and Galloway, where they had a castle, and one of their Tobago plantations was called that. Young was governor from 1771–77.

21 Phillips, *La Magdalena*, p. 157.

22 Craig-James, *Changing Society of Tobago*, vol. 1, p. 56.

23 Notes to display in Tobago Museum, Scarborough.

24 Ottley, C. R. *The Story of Tobago*. Longman Caribbean, 1973, p. 34.

25 Notes to display of uniforms in the Tobago Museum.

26 *Abridgment of the Minutes of the evidence . . .*, pp. 92–94.

27 O'Shaughnessy, Andrew Jackson. *An Empire Divided: The American Revolution and the British Caribbean*. Philadelphia, PA: University of Pennsylvania Press, 2015, p. 146.

28 Phillips, *La Magdalena*, p. 155. In other respects Phillips is inaccurate on James Fergusson, confusing him with the Pitfour Fergusons at Castara and with JF's own father.

29 27 May 1777, JF to AF

30 26 May 1774, JF to AF

31 Simon Taylor and Nathaniel Phillips in Jamaica, quoted in Turner, Sasha. *Contested Bodies: Pregnancy, Childbearing and Slavery in Jamaica*. Philadelphia, PA: University of Pennsylvania, 2017, p. 59.

32 Long, Edward. *The History of Jamaica*. London: T. Lowndes, 1774, p. 403.

33 Long, *The History of Jamaica*, p. 470.

34 Sherrard, O. A. *Freedom from Fear: The Slave and his Emancipation*. London: The Bodley Head, 1959, pp. 79–80.

35 Long and Codrington quoted in Krug, Jessica. 'Constructs of Freedom and Identity: The Ethnogenesis of the Jamaican Maroons and the Treaties of 1739'. *PSU McNair Scholars Online Journal*, 1(1), 2004, Article 6.

36 27 May 1777, 17 February 1776, 12 March 1775, etc., all JF to AF

37 14 per cent on average.

38 29 June 1774, JF to AF

39 29 June 1774, JF to AF

40 The beef for the enslaved people was the cheapest – 'skirt and head', according to the bills of lading for supplies sent to James in Tobago. The quantities of salt herring he orders, 15 barrels (89 kg of contents each, if flour barrels were used) on this occasion, suggest they were for all the people at Carrick. (29 July 1776, JF to CF)

41 30 May 1774, CF to AF

42 25 July 1774, JF to CF

43 'Tho not without difficulty', Sir Adam adds. (16 June 1774, AF to CF)

44 2 December 1774, JF to AF

45 As described in the inventory made in November 1777 (Fergusson papers).

46 Quintanilla, Mark. 'Mercantile Communities in the Ceded Islands: The Alexander Bartlet & George Campbell Company'. *International Social Science Review*, 79(1/2), 2004, pp. 14–26.

47 12 March 1775, JF to AF

48 20 April 1775, JF to AF

49 Bissessarsingh, Angelo. 'Panchoo Campbell The Last Living Former Slave'. *Trinidad & Tobago Guardian*, 3 August 2014.

CHAPTER 3 – PEOPLE AS PROPERTY

1 John Newton (1725–1807) looking back on his time as a slave ship captain in the mid-eighteenth century. He became a campaigner against slavery and wrote the hymn 'Amazing Grace'.

2 27 June 1775, CF to AF

3 Grant's letter of 3 May 1775 to CF, quoted in 27 June 1775, CF to AF

4 28 April 1775, JF to CF

5 14 July 1775, JF to AF

6 14 July 1775, JF to AF

7 17 February 1776, JF to AF

8 27 May 1777, JF to AF. In this letter James mentions taking fourteen of the Los group, having recently bought three other 'prime seasoned slaves'.

9 22 September 1780, Gilbert Petrie to AF

10 24 May 1776, JF to AF

11 22 September 1780, GP to AF. Gilbert Petrie's Englishman's Bay estate expanded from 68 to 212 enslaved people between August 1772 and August 1780.

12 2 December 1774, JF to AF

13 Copied in 27 June 1775, CF to AF

14 28 April 1775, JF to AF

15 3 July 1775, AF to JF

16 The brand is mentioned in the list of possessions stolen by an American privateer in 1777. Silver was used because it was thought to lessen the chance of infection.

17 He had been born in Jamaica, but was sent home at ten for his education. His brother lasted just two years in Jamaica before emigrating to the United States where he became a politician, his son George becoming vice-president in 1845. The city of Dallas is named for the latter.

18 Quoted in Parker, *Sugar Barons*, pp. 336–338. Dallas published several books about Jamaica, though the one quoted here, 1790's *A Short Journey in the West Indies*, was anonymous.

19 And 8,643 enslaved black people (Phillips, *La Magdalena*, p. 153).

20 24 May 1776, JF to AF

21 Carrington, Selwyn H. H. 'The American Revolution and the British West Indies' Economy'. *The Journal of Interdisciplinary History*, 17(4), Spring 1987, pp. 823–850.

22 More recent historical consensus is that the British West Indian economies were still thriving perhaps as late as the 1820s. Tobago seems unusual, especially as control went back and forth amongst the French and British. (Author's correspondence with Dr Stephen Mullen, 2020)

23 27 June 1776, JF to CF

24 28 May 1777, JF to AF

25 A vessel, or vessels, called the *Charming Nancy*, appear in several accounts of eighteenth-century transatlantic shipping, first taking German Amish settlers from Holland to Philadelphia in the late 1730s and then shipping Scots to Jamaica in the 1770s. A thirty-ton schooner of the same name was sold by its London owners in Philadelphia in 1778 (and then played a part in the story of the American traitor Arnold Bennett). See Murdoch, Richard K. 'Benedict Arnold and the Owners of the *Charming*

Nancy'. *Pennsylvania Magazine of History and Biography*, 84(1), January 1960, p. 22.

26 Gilbert Petrie, James's neighbour in Tobago, had been governor of Cape Castle on the Gold Coast (now in Ghana) from 1766 to 1769.

27 29 July 1776, JF to CF

28 22 September 1780, GP to AF

29 This detail from 1 August 1777, JF to AF. Eighteenth-century medicine made distinctions between bilious, putrid and bloody flux, all forms of diarrhoea.

30 29 July 1776, JF to CF

31 Analysis of records continues: in 2020 the figure used by the Caricom Centre for Reparations Research was 14.2 per cent deaths on passage.

32 Turner, *Contested Bodies*, p. 11.

33 Between 1.75 and two enslaved Africans per ton was the usual rule on British ships, though the ratio on the *Zong* was four per ton. See slave-voyages.org

34 Dobson, David. *American Data from the Aberdeen Journal 1748-1783*. Baltimore, MD: Clearfield, 1988, p. 72. In some records Craik is called 'Craige'.

35 Or so it seems (20 September 1790, GP to CF)

36 James paid his share of these costs on top of the £93.

37 An account from a few years later of a deal done at Elmina says the price per adult man was 'twelve dozen knives' (Richardson, D. 'The Slave Trade, Sugar, and British Economic Growth, 1748–1776'. *Journal of Interdisciplinary History*, 17(4), spring 1987, pp. 739–769). Also see Lovejoy, Paul E. and D. Richardson. 'British Abolition and its Impact on Slave Prices Along the Atlantic Coast of Africa, 1783–1850'. *Journal of Economic History*, 55(1), March 1995, pp. 98–119.

38 Information from slaveyoyages.org and British National Archives' Treasury Board papers T70/32, p. 55; T70/1541.

39 Richardson, 'Slave Trade, Sugar, and British Economic Growth', footnote, p. 744.

40 8 March 1788, GP to AF

41 20 September 1780, GP to CF

CHAPTER 4 – PEOPLE AS PROPERTY

1 Raw cotton prices at sixteen pence a pound from Broadberry, Stephen and Bishnupriya Gupta. 'Lancashire, India, and Shifting Competitive Advantage in Cotton Textiles, 1700–1850'. *Economic History Review*, 62(2), May 2009, pp. 279–305.

2 8 January 1777, JF to AF

3 Quoted in Phillips, *La Magdalena*, p. 170.

4 This quote and other details are from the website American War of Independence At Sea (awiatsea.com).

5 'Extract of a letter from Tobago, July 28th'. *Caledonian Mercury*, 22 November 1777.

6 At the end of May he reported it all harvested, but not yet 'gined and cleaned', guessing there was eight thousandweight (27 May 1777, JF to AF).

7 25 July 1777, JF to AF

8 8 October 1777, William Bruce to AF

9 Inventory, November 1777

10 AF notes, 'Carrick settlement 1777'.

11 14 February 1788, George Fergusson to AF

12 30 March 1778, GP to AF

13 'Inventory of loss', attached to unknown letter, GP to AF, 1778

14 This does not definitively happen until 1814.

15 10 December 1785, AF to GP

16 25 May 1784, GP to AF

17 De Bouillé appears to have left the island in 1783, to take up governmental jobs in France, so must have had representatives in Tobago.

18 10 December 1785, AF to GP

19 26 February 1785, GP to AF. The sale appears to have been done as a mortgage, perhaps in settlement of debts to the Petries.

20 Ottley, *Story of Tobago*, p. 55.

21 Gilbert Petrie's will – see UCL/LBS entry for 'Gilbert Petrie'.

22 10 December 1785, AF to GP

CHAPTER 5 – TOBAGO TODAY

1 Maggie Harris is Guyanese writer living in the UK. She has won The Guyana Prize twice for her poetry and was Regional Winner of the Commonwealth Short Story Prize. www.maggieharris.co.uk

2 14 July 1775, JF to AF

3 14 July 1775, JF to AF

4 Craig-James, *Changing Face of Tobago*, vol. 1, p. 7.

5 Susan Craig-James's curriculum vitae published by parliament of Trinidad and Tobago, 27 April 2018.

6 Craig-James, *Changing Society of Tobago*, vol. 1, p. 128.

7 The 1790 census recorded 14,170 enslaved people in Tobago. By 1797 the slave population rose to 16,190 and reached 18,153 in 1807, the year the slave trade was abolished.

8 Hickling, F. W. and G. Hutchinson. 'The Roast Breadfruit Psychosis – Disturbed Racial Identification in African Caribbeans'. *Psychiatric Bulletin*, 23(3), March 1999, pp. 132-134.

9 The Adult Psychiatric Morbidity Survey (APMS). Available at mental-health.org.uk – 'Black, Asian and minority ethnic (BAME) communities'.

10 See, for example, Kevin Mitchell's blog Wiring the Brain, 'Grandma's trauma – a critical appraisal of the evidence for transgenerational epigenetic inheritance in humans', 29 May 2018.

11 Quoted in Carey, Benedict. 'Can We Really Inherit Trauma?' *New York Times*, 10 December 2018.

12 Martin Amis cites this in *Inside Story* (London: Vintage, 2020), presumably referring to Snyder's *Black Earth: The Holocaust as History and Warning* (London: Tim Duggan Books, 2015).

13 For example, Morgan, Craig, Gemma Knowles and Gerard Hutchinson. 'Migration, ethnicity and psychoses: evidence, models and future directions.' *World Psychiatry*, 18(3), October 2019, pp. 247–258.

14 Hutchinson, Gerard. 'The Brutal Impact of Crime on Public Health'. *UWI Today*, January 2012.

15 Published by the Caribbean Institute of Mental Health and Substance Abuse, 2016.

16 Zimmer, Carl. 'Tales of African-American History Found in DNA'. *New York Times*, 27 May 2016.

17 Zimmer, 'Tales of African-American History found in DNA'.

18 According to the 1783 and 1784 inventories of Carrick estate, where he is listed as a house servant.

19 Buchan, A. R. *Pitfour: 'The Blenheim of the North'*. Buchan: The Buchan Field Club, 2008. This and other sources used available via 'George Ferguson: Lt-Governor of Tobago' at engole.info.

20 From *Anti-Slavery Reporter*, November 1832, quoted in Draper, Nicholas. *The Price of Emancipation: Slave Ownership, Compensation and British Society at the End of Slavery*. Cambridge: Cambridge University Press, 2010, pp. 65–67.

CHAPTER 6 – A FINE PROPERTY IN JAMAICA

1 For modern (post Eric Williams) economic analysis of exports to the West Indies and the UK, see Richardson, 'Slave Trade, Sugar, and British Economic Growth'. Also, Devine, T. M. 'Did Slavery Make Scotia Great?' *Britain and the World*, 4(1), March 2011, pp. 40–64.

2 Campbell subsequently became a colonial administrator in Georgia.

3 See multiple letters, CF to AF and AF to CF, 1764.

4 What is now Lloyds Banking Group eventually absorbed both the successful banks in which the Hunter brothers and other Ayrshire families connected to slavery (Ballantines, Hamiltons, Kennedys) were involved. See Lloyds Bank archives: 'Hunters and Company, Bankers, Ayr' and 'Sir William Forbes, James Hunter and Company' at archiveshub.jisc.ac.uk.

5 It isn't clear how the £4,000 loan from Charles Fergusson to Charles Montgomery in 1764 was counted into the sale price.

6 In the late eighteenth century 30 per cent of plantation owners in Jamaica were Scots. In St Thomas-in-the-East the proportion seems higher: 40 per cent of the white population of St Thomas was Scottish in 1804 (see Whyte, Iain. *Scotland and the Abolition of Black Slavery 1756–1838*. Edinburgh: Edinburgh University Press, 2006, p. 42).

7 In 1768. By 1823, 24,000 enslaved people were in St Thomas-in-the-East (Craton, Michael. *Searching for the Invisible Man: Slaves and Plantation Life in Jamaica*. Cambridge, MA: Harvard University Press, 1978, pp. 36–39).

8 Indicators – an adult enslaved African cost around £50 sterling, a plantation manager's salary was £150 a year, an indentured white ploughman's £20 to £30, passage from Scotland £5. For more detail, see Karras, Alan L. *Sojourners in the Sun: Scottish Migrants in Jamaica and the Chesapeake*,

1740–1800. Ithaca, NY: Cornell University Press, 1992, *passim*.

9 For example, see *The British and Foreign Anti-slavery Reporter*, 19 February 1845, p. 32.

10 See UCL/LBS entry for 'Robert Hamilton of Bourtreehill' and other Hamilton entries.

11 See Graham, E. 'Scots Penetration of the Jamaican Plantation Business' in Devine (ed.), *Recovering Scotland's Slavery Past*, p. 92.

12 Sometimes called Eleanora. There are no details of her dowry, but she inherited half of Pemberton Valley estate in Jamaica, and Bourtreehill and Rozelle in Ayrshire, some of which passed to the Eglintons on her death in 1812. See Graham, Eric. *Burns & the Sugar Plantocracy of Ayrshire*. Edinburgh: MDPD, 2014, pp. 29 and 46–47.

13 Charles Fergusson agreed to pay interest direct to Robert Hamilton on the money Charles Montgomery owed from the purchase – see 26 February 1765, RH to James Hunter.

14 Or so Sir Adam told George Dempster of Dunnichen after Charles's death, see 12 February 1805, AF to George Dempster (F of K).

15 Rozelle estate was owned by Graham and then Clement Richardson before the Mitchells. See Grant, W. L. and James Munro (eds). *Acts of the Privy Council of England: Colonial series Volume 3, A.D. 1720–1745*. London: HMSO, 1910, pp. 782–783.

16 Lindsay, Andrew O. '"Negro-driver" or "Illustrious Exile": Revisiting *Illustrious Exile: Journal of my Sojourn in the West Indies*'. *International Journal of Scottish Literature*, issue 4, spring/summer 2008.

17 Lindsay, '"Negro-driver" or "Illustrious Exile"' and Graham, *Burns & the Sugar Plantocracy*, p. xiii. By 1786 James Hunter had become Sir James Hunter Blair, lord provost of Edinburgh and an important patron of Burns. See *Blairquhan*, brochure privately published for visitors to the house by James Hunter Blair, 1970s, p. 33. Burns wrote an elegy for Sir James on his death in 1787.

18 1771, John Paterson's plan for years 1771–1777 at 'Rozell Plantation' (F of K papers)

19 24 July 1777, JP to AF

20 AF's notes, 'Sketch of Produce of Roselle', 1773

21 'An Inventory of Slaves Cattle Mules & Buildings upon Rozell Estate . . .', 14 July 1773 (F of K). In a note AF corrects the auditors' total of 160 to 164.

22 18 July 1775, JP to AF

23 Descriptions of causes of death are all from the Rozelle plantation books, and their lists of increase and decrease in people and animals.

24 By 1775 Sir Adam had lent Charles at least £2,000, and had to rescue him again a few years later. In 1800 he wrote to Charles declining to lend more (see 12 February 1805, AF to George Dempster). Charles liked a party: he appears as a hard-drinking gentleman in John Macdonald's *Memoirs of an Eighteenth Century Footman* (1927).

25 See the dire victim torn from social life,
   See the sacred infant, hear the shrieking wife!
   She, wretch forlorn! is dragged by hostile hands,
   To distant tyrants sold, in distant lands:
   Transmitted miseries, and successive chains,
   The sole sad heritage her child obtains.
   E'en this last wretched boon their foes deny,
   To weep together, or together die.
                    (From Hannah More's 'Slavery – a Poem', 1788)

26 10 March 1777, AM to AF

27 9 July 1777, AM to AF

28 14 December 1777, AF to AM

29 From Sir Adam Fergusson's entry on the official History of Parliament website, histparl.ac.uk.

30 18 November 1779, AM to AF and WH

31 The ships were the *Eleanor* under Captain Ballantine and the *Friendship* under Captain Thomson. No more details exist than that they were lost near Jamaica.

32 15.5 hundredweight to the hogshead, price assumed as forty-three shillings (£2.15) per hundredweight. Shipping in 1778 cost nine shillings a hundredweight, and the duty payable was perhaps nine shillings and sixpence (see Colquhoun, Patrick. *A Treatise of the Wealth, Power, and Resources of the British Empire*. London: Joseph Mawman, 1814). Sugar prices and freight costs in the 1770s: Carrington, Selwyn H. H. 'The American Revolution and the British West Indies' Economy'. *Journal of Interdisciplinary History*, 17(4), 1987, pp. 823–850.

CHAPTER 7 – ENLIGHTENMENT GENTLEMEN AND RUNAWAY SLAVES

1 Boswell, James. *Life of Johnson*. London: John Murray, 1876, p. 276.

2 13 August 1797, AF to Henry Melville, NRS GD1/1/527. The role was governor-general of Fort William in Bengal, but historians refer to it as

governor-general of India. Richard Wellesley, Earl of Mornington, got the post. Henry Dundas was president of the Board of Control for India from 1793 to 1804.

3 Diary of Margaret Hope, unpublished, partially quoted in Fergusson, Sir James. *Lowland Lairds*. London: Faber & Faber, 1949, p. 36.

4 'The Author's Earnest Cry and Prayer', a poem addressed to Scotsmen sitting in the London parliament.

5 Boswell, James in Harris, Mark (ed.). *The Heart of Boswell*. New York: McGraw-Hill, 1981, p. 259.

6 See Graham, *Burns & the Sugar Plantocracy*, pp. 80–81, and Whyte, *Scotland and the Abolition of Black Slavery*, pp. 50–57.

7 By the lawyer James Stephen, William Wilberforce's brother-in-law, consisting of his letters to the then prime minister Henry Addington.

8 *The Interesting Narrative of the Life of Olaudah Equiano; or, Gustavus Vassa, the African, Written by Himself* (1789) – widely available online.

9 Chambers, Douglas B. *Runaway Slaves in Jamaica (1): Eighteenth Century*. University of Southern Florida, November 2013. (Texts of advertisements from Jamaican newspapers. Document stored digitally at udfc.ufl.edu)

10 No other female name of a likely age appears in the list of names in the 1771 inventory of Rozelle made by John Paterson; in 1783 Murdoch writes of intercepting a letter to 'Caesar's mother'.

11 Ukawsaw Gronniosaw's *A Narrative of the Most Remarkable Particulars in the Life of James Albert Ukawsaw Gronniosaw, an African Prince, as Related by Himself* (1772) is thought to be the first account of all, but its anti-slavery message is muted.

12 18 February 1781, AF to AM

13 Long, *History of Jamaica*, p. 402.

14 Most notably in 'Of National Characters,' in Hume's *Essays, Moral, Political, and Literary*. 'Consistently' is taken from the abstract to Garrett, Aaron and Silvia Sebastiani. *The Oxford Handbook of Philosophy and Race*. Oxford: Oxford University Press, 2017.

15 Long, *History of Jamaica*, p. 4.

16 Thistlewood and Long corresponded on botanical matters after Long's return to Britain in the 1770s. See Burnard, Trevor. *Mastery, Tyranny, and Desire*. Chapel Hill, NC: University of North Carolina Press, 2004, pp. 121–126.

17 Long, *History of Jamaica*, vol. 2, p. 270.

18 From the Court of Session's judgment: 'the dominion assumed over this

Negro, under the law of Jamaica, being unjust, could not be supported in this country to any extent: That, therefore, the defender had no right to the Negro's service for any space of time, nor to send him out of the country against his consent: That the Negro was likewise protected under the act 1701, c.6. from being sent out of the country against his consent.'

19 Quoted in Edwards, Paul. 'The History of Black People in Britain'. *History Today*, 31(9), September 1981.

20 See Whyte, *Scotland and the Abolition of Black Slavery*, p. 17.

21 Olusoga, David. *Black and British: A Forgotten History*. London: Pan Books, 2017, p. 73. He is said to have been the inspiration for the anti-slavery poem 'The Dying Negro' by Thomas Day and John Bicknall, 1775.

22 Serju, Christopher. 'The Legend of Jack Mansong'. *Daily Gleaner* (Jamaica), 4 June 2011.

23 Paton, Diana. 'The afterlives of Three-Fingered Jack'. *Essays and Studies*, vol. 60, 2007, p. 42ff.

24 24 April 1781, AM to AF

25 6 June 1781, AM to AF

26 25 June 1781, AM to AF

27 30 June 1781, AF to AM

28 Petley, Christer. *White Fury: A Jamaican Slaveholder and the Age of Revolution*. Oxford: Oxford University Press, 2018, p. 103, quoting Richard Sheridan.

29 7 December 1781, AF to AM

30 13 May 1782, AM to AF

31 Sivapragasam, Michael. 'After the treaties: a social, economic and demographic history of Maroon society in Jamaica, 1739–1842'. Doctoral thesis, University of Southampton, June 2018.

32 26 February 1783, AM to AF and WH

33 3 February 1784, AF and WH to AM

34 14 April 1784, AM to AF and WH

35 9 August 1784, AM to AF and WH

36 16 September 1785, Ballantine and Kennedy to AF and WH. But plantation book for 1785 says Murdoch died on the 18th.

37 16 September 1785, Ballantine and Kennedy to AF and WH

38 7 December 1785, AF to Peter Ballantine

39 11 December 1785, Peter Ballantine to AF and WH

40 Pybus, Cassandra. *Black Founders: The Unknown Story of Australia's First Black Settlers*. Sydney: UNSW Press, 2006, p. 46.

41 Chambers, *Runaway Slaves in Jamaica*. Twenty-six people called Caesar appear in these texts of advertisements of runaways.

CHAPTER 8 – GOATISH EMBRACES

1 6 July 1786, Peter Ballantine to AF and WH. There must also be a white man for every 150 head of stock animals.

2 For being two white men short (12 September 1789, AC to AF and WH)

3 An Archibald Cameron was manager at Long Pond in Trelawney parish in 1779 and 1780.

4 The spelling appears as McDermot and McDermit, but this appears to be the same man.

5 Petley, *White Fury*, pp. 215–216.

6 Letter quoted by Meleisa Ono-George in '"Washing the Blackamoor White": Interracial Intimacy and Coloured Women's Agency in Jamaica'. In: Jackson, Will and Emily Manktelow (eds). *Subverting Empire: Deviance and Disorder in the British Colonial World*. London: Palgrave Macmillan, 2015, Chapter 3.

7 Long, *History of Jamaica*, p. 328.

8 Burnard and others have calculated the figures as 167 women and older girls and 4,000 sex acts.

9 Turner (*Contested Bodies*, p. 215): the new felony came into the 1826 Slave Code because in 1822 a white man, Thomas Simpson, was tried in Jamaica under British law and sentenced to death for the rape of an enslaved nine-year-old. (The girl was not his property, which may explain how he came to be prosecuted in the first place.) The sentence was not carried out because it was ruled the law only applied when the victim was a free person.

10 For example, in the diaries of Maria Nugent, wife of a governor-general of Jamaica who arrived in 1801. Quoted in Parker, *Sugar Barons*, pp. 347–348.

11 William Beckford of Somerley, *A Descriptive Account of the Island of Jamaica*, 1790.

12 Evidence given by a plantation doctor to the 1789 parliamentary committee, quoted in Turner, *Contested Bodies*, p. 91.

13 Burnard, *Mastery, Tyranny and Desire*, pp. 85–87.

14 From *A poetical Epistle from the Island of Jamaica to a gentleman of the Middle-Temple*, published as an addendum to *Jamaica, a Poem in three parts* (Burnard, *Mastery, Tyranny and Desire*, p. 262). The two poems echo James Grainger's well-known verse epic *The Sugar-cane*, which pictured an idyllic Jamaica. 'The Muse thinks it disgraceful of a Briton to sing of the Sugar Cane, since to it is owing the Slavery of Negros', writes this anonymous author in his 'argument'.

15 He is sometimes referred to as James, but they are clearly one man.

16 1 June 1789, AF to AC

17 2 May 1788 AF to AC (and see 1 June 1789). By 1789 the estate is in debt to its shipping company, Alexander Houston & Co. of Glasgow, by over £1,000.

18 'Disappointment and sickness' are probably the causes of Moodie's laziness, Cameron writes (15 December 1787). He had come out from Scotland in 1774, his passage paid by AF, as a millwright, at an annual salary of just £35.

19 8 May 1790, AF to AC

20 5 May 1788, AC to AF and WH

21 12 September 1789, AC to AF and WH

22 Turner, *Contested Bodies*, pp. 11 and 12.

23 Morgan, Kenneth. 'Slave Women and Reproduction in Jamaica, c.1776–1834'. *History*, 91(302), March 2006, pp. 231–253. Slavevoyages.org has 2.63 million people shipped by the British directly from Africa, and a further 78,000 via what became the United States. For 'free coloured' populations in the West Indies, see Green, William. *British Slave Emancipation*. London: Oxford University Press, 1976, p. 13.

24 Paton, Diana. 'Enslaved women and slavery before and after 1807'. *History in Focus*, 12, 2007.

25 Sheridan, Richard B. *Doctors and Slaves: A Medical and Demographic History of Slavery in the British West Indies, 1680–1834*. Cambridge: Cambridge University Press, 1985, p. 229.

26 Golden Grove is an example (Turner, *Contested Bodies*, p. 107).

27 Turner, *Contested Bodies*, p. 51.

28 'Report of the Commissioners for Trade and Plantations on the Slave Trade', 1789.

29 28 May 1789, AF to AC

30 Sheridan, *Doctors and Slaves*, pp. 200–201 and 238–240. See also Turner, *Contested Bodies*, pp. 152–153.

31 12 September 1789, AC to AF and WH

32 Simon Taylor quoted in Petley, *White Fury*, pp. 152–157.

33 Letter to Chaloner Arcedeckne, quoted in Petley, *White Fury*, p. 147.

34 Letter to the multiple plantation owner Nathaniel Phillips, a stalwart of the Society of West India Planters and Merchants after his retirement to London in 1789. Quoted in Donington, Katie. *The Bonds of Family: Slavery, Commerce and Culture in the British Atlantic World*, Manchester: Manchester University Press, 2019, p. 126.

35 Sheridan, Richard B. *Sugar and Slavery: An Economic History of the British West Indies, 1623–1775*. Baltimore, MD: Johns Hopkins Press, 1974, pp. 62-65.

36 *The Code of Laws for the Government of Negroe Slaves in the Island of Jamaica* (1789), p. vi.

37 27 May 1788, Cameron to AF and WH.

38 Stephen Fuller, quoted in Newman, Brooke N. *A Dark Inheritance: Blood, Race, and Sex in Colonial Jamaica*. New Haven, CT: Yale University Press, 2018, pp. 247 and 249.

CHAPTER 9 – THE MONEY AND THE POX

1 On 27 January 1785 Sir Adam notes a letter written at Rozelle by Murdoch on 24 September 1784 has just been received from Glasgow 'after a tedious passage of 16 weeks and five days' on the ship *Martha*.

2 As in all measures of volume at the time, there was no reliable standard. The figure of 1,550lb/700kg is an average using various sources, including two quoted in Hancock, David. *Citizens of the World: London Merchants and the Integration of the British Atlantic Community 1735–1785*. Cambridge: Cambridge University Press, 1995, p. 418. The fixed duty on imported sugar was 3s. 4d. a hundredweight in 1746, a little 6s. 4d in 1776, a little over 11s. 11d. in 1781, 15s. in 1791, £1 by 1799, then £1 and 7s. and briefly thirty £1 and 10s. by 1812. In the years 1807–1812 it amounted to 68 to 78 per cent of the London wholesale price. Part of the duty was passed on to the consumer (Colquhoun, *Treatise of the Wealth*, pp. 324–325. Sugar prices, see Sheridan, *Sugar and Slavery*, pp. 496–499).

3 This calculation is an estimate. It is complicated by insurance payouts received later on lost cargoes – for example, in 1781 a £1,349 claim from loss of sugar on the *Trecothick* and the *Adventure* (one 'lost', the other's cargo taken by the French). But four of the underwriters had

gone bankrupt and could not pay up: it is unclear what was actually paid.

4   18 January 1810, AF to JF

5   Trevor Burnard estimates 13.5 per cent was the average net return between 1763 and 1776. He quotes David Ryden, who puts the average annual gross returns on slavery economy investment between 1752 and 1807 at 17.8 per cent (a figure which should be halved to account for expenses and taxes). See Burnard, Trevor. 'A Serious Business: Slave Prices in Jamaica, 1674–1784'. Presentation available on University of Paris website, 2011.

6   6 January 1789, AF to AC

7   1792 Valuation at the order of the Colonial Secretary. The 178 enslaved people at Rozelle were worth £12,955 (Jamaican currency), the buildings £5,000, and the animals £2,415. The Jamaican pound was 1.4 x 1 pound sterling.

8   Hunters and Co. and Sir William Forbes, James Hunter & Co., both serving West Indies merchants and slavery-related activities. They were eventually absorbed into what is now Lloyds Banking Group. Forbes & Hunter was, according to the LBG website, one of the most successful of all the Scottish banks of the late eighteenth and nineteenth centuries.

9   Quoted in Geggus, David. 'The Enigma of Jamaica in the 1790s: New Light on the Causes of Slave Rebellions'. *William and Mary Quarterly*, 44(2), 1987, pp. 274–299.

10 14 December 1791, AF and WH to AC

11 Geggus, 'Enigma of Jamaica', p 275.

12 18 May 1792, AC to AF

13 Quoting letter from a John Cartland, Greenock, to William Hunter, Newark, near Ayr (1789).

14 15 May 1790, AC to AF

15 11 September 1790, AC to AF

16 14 December 1790, AF to AC

17 19 March 1791, AC to AF

18 17 March 1794, John Hunter to HH enclosing AC to AF

19 17 July 1790, AC to AF

20 'Mercure. Calcinat.' causes infertility. Cantharides is also listed: a sexual stimulant probably for livestock but also used in the eighteenth century as an aphrodisiac.

21 Burnard, Trevor and Richard Follett. 'Caribbean Slavery, British Anti-slavery, and the Cultural Politics of Venereal Disease'. *Historical Journal*, 55(2), June 2012, p. 429.

22 Burnard and Follett, 'Caribbean Slavery', p. 432.

23 30 August 1791, AF and WH to AC

24 14 April 1792, AF to AC

25 Quoted in Donington, *Bonds of Family*, p. 117.

26 Long quoted in Lewis, Gordon K. 'Main Currents in Caribbean Thought: The Historical Evolution of Caribbean Society in Its Ideological Aspects, 1492–1900'. Lincoln, NE: University of Nebraska Press, 2004, pp. 110–111.

27 Quoted in Newman, *Dark Inheritance*, p. 243.

28 Quoted in Newman, *Dark Inheritance*, p. 249.

29 31 December 1795, AF to AC

30 This plantation book is missing but Sir Adam quotes from it in 29 August 1797, AF to AC

31 Burnard and Follett, 'Caribbean Slavery', p. 439.

32 Quoted in Newman, *Dark Inheritance*, p. 250.

33 20 March 1792 according to 21 March 1792, AF to AC. Also reported in London by the *Scots Magazine*, vol. 54, March 1792.

34 Becomes Sir David Hunter Blair, 3rd Baronet of Dunskey, in 1800. Colonel Hunter's will (National Archives PROB 11/1217/93) appears to leave everything to David, via his trustees, except a £500 payment to a niece.

35 AF corresponded with William Dalrymple about legislation on religious matters.

36 Whyte, *Scotland and the Abolition of Black Slavery*, p. 88 and 'Significant Scots: Sir William Forbes' available at electricscotland.com. See UCL/LBS on plantations in which the bank's partners were involved.

37 In 2020 Bobby Dundas, 10th Viscount Melville, and others started a campaign to stop a new plaque being erected next to a statue to Henry Dundas in central Edinburgh (Leask, David. 'Descendant fights claims that Henry Dundas prolonged slave trade', *The Times*, 18 July 2020).

38 Thomas, Hugh. *The Slave Trade: The Story of the Atlantic Slave Trade: 1440–1870*. New York: Simon & Schuster, 1997, pp. 529–530. Thomas writes that by 1799 Dundas's position had turned to 'outright opposition' to abolition of the trade. The academic research site slaveryvoyages.org uses the figure 583,000 for Africans shipped by British ships between 1791 and 1807.

39 One of the rare occasions in the period that names of MPs who voted were recorded – see Sir Adam Fergusson's entry at histparl.ac.uk.

40 Williams, Eric. *The Economic Aspect of the Abolition of the West Indian Slave Trade and Slavery* Lanham, MD: Rowman & Littlefield, 2014, p. 87.

41 21 March 1792, AF to AC

42 18 May 1792, AC to AF AF

43 11 October 1794, AC to AF

44 26 December 1795, AC to AF

45 Or Cassillis. All of them are Ayrshire names. 10 June 1796, AC to AF

46 19 August 1797, AC to AF

47 2 February 1798, AF to AC

48 29 June 1798, AF to AC

49 25 June 1799, AF to HH

50 25 June 1799, AF to HH

51 27 February 1800, AF to GH

CHAPTER 10 – SLAVERY MODERNISED

1 Death figures are very poorly recorded: Cameron does not often mention them, and we only have plantation books for nine of the years 1785 to 1799. There are twenty deaths known. The total comes from an average of 3.5 deaths per hundred people per year in Cameron's time.

2 Precise birth dates only for Archie, Mary, Anna and John – the others may be up to one year out.

3 Inheriting the baronetcy on the death of his uncle, Sir John Hunter Blair, 2nd Baronet of Dunskey.

4 Prices quoted in correspondence and referring to Eltis, David et al. 'Slave Prices, the African Slave Trade and Productivity in the Caribbean, 1674–1807'. *Economic History Review*, 58(4), 2005, pp. 673–700.

5 George Hamilton in June 1800 wrote to Hugh Hamilton that 'a good seasoned slave' was at present £160 to £200 Jamaican currency (£114 to £143 sterling), but this is the highest price that any records note.

6 GH letter of 1801 indicates Cameron was paid less than £200 Jamaican currency (£142).

7 Dallas, Robert. *The History of the Maroons*. London: A. Strahan, 1803, vol. 1, p. 127.

8 19 May 1800, AF to AC

9 2 June 1800, AC to AF

10 Possibly David Alexander, a merchant who arrived on the Isabella plantation in Jamaica in 1775.

11 18 June 1800, HH to AF

12 20 June 1800, AF to AC

13 10 September 1800, AF to GH

14 12 September 1800, GH to AF

15 6 January 1800, AF to HH

16 12 September 1800, GH to AF

17 12 September 1800, GH to AF

18 10 July 1801, GH to AF

19 15 August 1801, Hugh Fergusson to AF

20 7 August, 15 August and 4 September 1801, JF to AF

21 4 June 1802, JF to AF, including 28 March 1802, JF to AF

22 4 March 1803, AF to HH

23 Burnard, 'A Serious Business'

24 29 September 1804, AF to JF

25 Between 1803 and 1810 the annual death rate was 8.11 per cent and the number of enslaved people on the estate dropped by 12.1 per cent (calculations from Charles McKelvey's unpublished thesis on the Rozelle Estate plantation books, Edinburgh University, 2018. For discussion of the hugely increased death rate, see letter dated 28 September 1811, AF to JF).

26 3 December 1803, AF to JF

27 3 December 1803, AF to JF

28 17 July 1803, JF to AF

29 Details of the Scott family from UCL/LBS and from the 'Ballingarry' page at aparcelofribbons.co.uk, a website examining Jamaican history through family archives.

30 'Favourite' is Sir Adam's word, 23 June 1805, AF to HH. Moodie died at some point in 1805.

31 Note attached to bundle sent by JF dated 1805 by AF. All subsequent material on the row over Jeanie, Annie and Quashie is from that, unless stated.

32 Quashie's name doesn't appear in plantation books, but was very

commonly used. It may be a nickname – it is of West African origin. Or he may have been temporary hired labour.

33 25 June 1805, HH to AF

34 29 June 1805, AF to JF – and to the end of this section

35 17 June 1805, AF to AC

36 23 June 1805, AF to HH

37 20 July 1805, AC to AF

38 1817 Slave Register, held by British National Archives/ancestry.co.uk

39 21 December 1811, JF to AF, but misdated at the top – actually 1810.

40 Rozelle estate Slave Register, held by British National Archives/ancestry.co.uk

CHAPTER 11 – THE END OF THE BRITISH SLAVE TRADE

1 12 August 1803, Lady Hailes to James Fergusson (subsequent 4th Baronet of Kilkerran)

2 1803 (date unknown), AF to James Fergusson

3 20 September 1799, AF to James Fergusson

4 Increased further to £1,000 in 1808 and £2,000 in 1810.

5 12 October 1799, AF to James Fergusson

6 In Wimpole Street. Fergusson, James (ed.). *Letters of George Dalrymple to Sir Adam Fergusson.* London: Macmillan, 1934, p. 324.

7 First set at a top rate of 10 per cent, for incomes over £200, then lowered to 5 per cent from 1803. It remained at 10 per cent for income from West India property.

8 17 May 1805, AF to HH

9 Rozelle income statements, 1805–1807 (F of K)

10 Parker, *Sugar Barons*, p. 352.

11 Morgan, Kenneth. *Slavery, Atlantic Trade and the British Economy, 1660–1800.* Cambridge: Cambridge University Press, 2001, p. 52.

12 28 February 1807, AF to JF

13 10 June and 27 October 1807, JF to AF

14 See Shapiro, Steven. 'Review: After Abolition: Britain and the Slave Trade since 1807'. *Origins: Current Events in Historical Perspective*, Ohio State and Florida Universities, July 2008.

15 The *Kitty's Amelia* had received clearance to sail on 27 April: its actual voyage was delayed till July.

16 28 May 1808, JF to AF – it implies twelve were bought, but the price seems very low. There is confusion in historical accounts – and perhaps in the colonies at the time – over whether the hard stop on importation of enslaved people from Africa under the abolition Act was 31 December 1807 or 31 March 1808.

17 28 July 1808, JF to AF

18 9 December 1806, JF to AF

19 3 September 1808, AF to JF

CHAPTER 12 – DECLINE, DISGUST AND DEATH

1 28 September 1811, AF to JF. 'Two are since dead' in 1809 is only partially legible.

2 29 November 1811, AF to JF

3 9 December 1811, HH to AF

4 Graham, *Burns & the Sugar Plantocracy*, p. 104. Archibald Hamilton of Carcluie married into the Eglinton family, via a daughter of the 11th Earl. Sandy was to marry Hamilla Montgomerie, a niece of Hugh, the 12th Earl of Eglinton.

5 10 June 1812, HH to AF, with partial copy of Sandy Hamilton (AWH) letter of 12 April 1812 to HH

6 4 September 1812, AWH to AF

7 31 December 1812, AF to AWH

8 Fergusson, *Lowland Lairds*, p. 42.

9 28 August 1813, AF to AWH

10 Robert Jamieson, the antiquary, to Grímur Thorkelin, quoted in Fergusson, Sir James (ed.) *Letters of George Dempster to Sir Adam Fergusson*. Glasgow: The Grimsay Press, 2004, p.43.

11 Crude death rates: 7.6 per cent in Jamaica, 9.4 per cent in UK, 2019. Death rates and mortality rates are different things. Source: United Nations/macrotrends.net

12 Turner, in *Contested Bodies*, and others have different figures: 25 per cent as the child death rate in urban Britain in the early nineteenth century is the highest I have seen.

CHAPTER 13 – CLEANSING THE MONEY

1   A few were homes to people who opposed slavery, for instance the Quaker Peckover family's house in Cambridgeshire. Preliminary audits (2020) of properties managed by the National Trust have identified ninety-three in England and Wales, and eighteen in Scotland, linked to 'slavery and colonialism' – a third of the total in the NT's control. Data in UCL/ LBS indicates many hundreds or thousands more in private hands. Dr Miranda Kaufmann's report for English Heritage in 2007 examined thirty-three properties in its care, all built between 1600 and 1830, and identified links to slavery in twenty-six of them.

2   Ross quoted in Clarkson, Thomas. *The History of the Rise, Progress, and Accomplishment of the Abolition of the African Slave-Trade by the British Parliament.* London: John Parker, 1839, pp. 232 and 234. (First published 1808).

3   Ross, Anne. 'The Jamaican Diaspora' at aparcelofribbons.co.uk

4   *Blairquhan* brochure, pp. 3–5. It had been most recently owned by the Kilkerran Fergusson relatives the Whitefoords, whose role in the collapsed Douglas, Heron bank of Ayr led to them selling it to the Hunters, whose own banking enterprises profited by the bank's failure.

5   Fergusson, *Lowland Lairds*, p. 44.

6   1st Dorothea Hay Mackenzie, 2nd Elizabeth Hay, daughter of Sir John Hay, another partner in the Forbes, Hunter bank. Thirteen children according to *Blairquhan* brochure, p. 39. Peerage.com lists only eight who survived to adulthood.

7   *Blairquhan* brochure, p. 5.

8   Lloyds Banking Group website, 'Our Heritage' page.

9   Sir Adam owned a house in St Andrew Square: it was sold around 1815. Sir James owned a house in Charlotte Square and one nearby at Glenfinlas Street, which was sold in 1845 by his son Sir Charles Dalrymple Fergusson, the fifth baronet, for £1,600. Number 5 Charlotte Square was sold in 1851. Kilkerran was in use by the family for most of the century, apart from a period in the 1880s when it was rented out.

10 Quoted in Fergusson, *Lowland Lairds*, p. 46.

11 23 October 1815, George Fergusson, Lord Hermand, to Sir James Fergusson

12 Undated notes, F of K papers, NRAS 3572/5/34

CHAPTER 14 – EMANICIPATION AT A PRICE

1   Whyte, *Scotland and the Abolition of Black Slavery*, p. 45.

2   Phrase popularised by the poet Robert Southey, in Sonnet 3 of his *Poems Concerning the Slave Trade* (1797).

3   Quoted in Parker, *Sugar Barons*, p. 343. Origin unclear.

4   *Memorial of Mrs Agnes Renton, for the Private Use of her Family*. Kelso, 1866.

5   Whyte, *Scotland and the Abolition of Black Slavery*, p. 195. The upas is a tropical tree famous for its deadly toxicity.

6   Quoted in Jennings, Judith. 'Alexander Barclay'. *Jamaica Historical Journal*, p. 374 (edition date/number missing).

7   Lecesne was the son of two refugees (his mother had been enslaved) from St Domingue/Haiti, and was deported from Jamaica to London as a leader of the 'free coloured' political movement in 1824.

8   There were two libel cases over the book. Thomas Pringle, who arranged for Mary Prince to dictate her story and published it, was successfully sued by John Adams Wood, who had owned her. But Pringle won a second case against two pro-slavery campaigners. Prince gave evidence in both cases but she disappears from history in 1833. She may have returned to Antigua and her husband.

9   Edward Said wrote in his *Culture and Imperialism* (London: Vintage, 1994, p. 115) that this moment suggests 'that one world could not be connected with the other since there simply is no common language for both'.

10   Extract of Whyte letter copied in 2 May 1827, Quintin Kennedy to Sir James Fergusson

11   15 October 1827, Quintin Kennedy to Sir James Fergusson

12   Extract of 21 August 1827 Whyte letter copied in 15 October letter Quintin Kennedy to Sir James Fergusson

13   Most of this trade was to Trinidad and the British colonies on the South American coast. In the period stated, Jamaica imported 1,910 enslaved people and exported 1,772 (Eltis, D. 'The Traffic in Slaves between the British West Indian Colonies, 1807–1833'. *Economic History Review*, 25(1), 1972, pp. 55–64).

14   Return for March quarter, county of Surrey, parish of St Thomas, Morant divison, downloaded via ancestry.com

15   For example, the Hervey family's Plantain Garden River estate, near Rozelle, bought a hundred more enslaved people two years before emancipation, increasing its population to 275.

16 Davey, Davie or David appears in all the plantation lists from 1773 (when he would have been around fifteen, and is valued at £40). He was head cooper in the 1790s and 1800s.

17 In the British Caribbean, as in other parts of the empire, designations of people as 'coloured' (of mixed African and white European heritage), 'black' and 'white' carried distinct legal, administrative and social meanings. For this reason, these terms are used here.

18 Quoted in Masters, Peter. *Missionary Triumph Over Slavery: William Knibb and Jamaican Emancipation*. London: Wakeman Trust, 2006, p. 29.

19 Letter, William Knibb to S. Nicholls, Kingston, March 1825. Quoted in Hinton, John Howard. *Memoir of William Knibb, Missionary in Jamaica*. London: Houlston & Stoneman, 1849, p. 46.

20 *Newcastle Courant*, 9 February 1833.

21 Draper, *Price of Emancipation*, pp. 37 and 75.

22 Beaumont, Augustus Hardin. *Compensation to Slave Owners Fairly Considered*. London: Effingham Wilson, 1826, p. 8.

23 Whyte, *Scotland and the Abolition of Black Slavery*, p. 195.

24 14 August 1834, Gray Rutherford to Quintin Kennedy, forwarded to Sir James Fergusson. The 48½ hours he mentions appears to have in fact been 45 hours under the law.

25 See Paton, Diana. *No Bond but the Law: Punishment, Race, and Gender in Jamaican State Formation 1780–1870*. Durham, NC: Duke University Press, 2004, p. 86-88.

26 *Jamaican Historical Review*, 2(3), 1953, p. 103. Author unknown. Richard Boucher, a brother or son, is mentioned in UCL/LBS.

27 For Howe Brown details, see Chambers, Ann. 'The Irish Lord who freed Jamaica's slaves'. *Irish Times*, 15 December 2017; and Finn, Clodagh. 'The Irish champion of slaves'. *Irish Independent*, 4 March 2014.

28 Reports from the British Caribbean in *The Anti-Slavery Examiner*, published by the American Anti-Slavery Society, 1836.

29 Quoted in Robinson, Pansy. *Jamaican Reflections: a look at St Thomas parish*. Unpublished and undated manuscript, p. 127.

30 Robinson, *Jamaican Reflections*, p. 126.

31 Reddie, Richard S. *Abolition! The Struggle to Abolish Slavery in the British Colonies* Oxford: Lion Hudson, 2007, p. 229.

CHAPTER 15 – FREEDOM'S PRICE

1 Figures from Eric Graham, quoted in Leadbetter, Russell. 'Secret Shame: The Scots who made a fortune from abolition of slavery'. *Herald*, 28 February 2013. See also 'Victorian Money – How much did things cost?' at victorianlondon.org/finance/.

2 Thomson, Heather and pupils of Finzean Primary School. *Aye, It Was Aabody: A story of Scotland's Role in the Slave Trade*. Magic Torch Comics, 2019, available on the Issuu publishing platform. A historical book published by the Birse Community Trust to acknowledge the continued effect of the money spent in their community by the enslaver Gilbert Ramsay.

3 R. J. Barro, quoted in Draper, *Price of Emancipation*, p. 107 (footnote). See also HM Treasury statement about the loan released, 31 January 2018 – available online as FOI2018-00186.

4 Draper, *Price of Emancipation*, p. 247.

5 Olusoga, David. 'The Treasury's tweet shows slavery is still misunderstood'. *Guardian*, 12 February 2018. Author of response tweet was @OohhhBam. The Treasury's tweet was incorrect in speaking of the 'slave trade' rather than slavery itself.

6 Guthrie, Jonathan. 'Lex in depth: Examining the slave trade – "Britain has a debt to repay"', *Financial Times*, 27 June 2020.

7 Draper writes that enslaved people paid between 20 and 50 per cent of the cost of their freedom in labour under apprenticeship (*Price of Emancipation*, p. 106).

8 Draper, Nicholas. 'Slavery and Britain's Architecture', UCL/LBS blog, 13 May 2019.

9 David Olusoga in *Britain's Forgotten Slave-Owners, Episode 1: Profit and Loss*, BBC 2, first broadcast 15 July 2015.

10 Draper, *Price of Emancipation*, p. 230.

11 Six people in Jamaica called James Graham and one called Margaret Reid were awarded compensation in 1835 for small numbers of enslaved people – it seems likely that one of these, or Margaret Reid, is my ancestor.

12 Draper, *Price of Emancipation*, p. 226.

13 Draper, *Price of Emancipation*, pp. 230–238.

14 Draper, *Price of Emancipation*, Appendix 16, p. 347.

15 Hochschild, Adam. *Bury the Chains: Prophets and Rebels in the Fight to Free an Empire's Slaves*. London: Macmillan, 2006, pp. 67 and 68.

16 By 1840, when the commission's work was complete, the owners of 311,455 enslaved people on Jamaica had been given £6,121,446 of the total £20 million – more by far than any other British colony.

17 In 1750, when Kerr's estate provided £218 income annually. It enabled the charitable hospital to start paying doctors (*Scottish Journal*, vol. 1, 1848, p. 38).

18 Leadbetter, 'Secret shame'.

19 Draper, *Price of Emancipation*, p. 169.

20 Examples are the Glasgow houses J. & A. Smith & Co., Kirk & Todd, Smith & Brown and John McCall & Co. (Mullen, Stephen. 'A Glasgow-West India merchant house and the imperial dividend, 1779–1867. *Journal of Scottish Historical Studies*, 33(2), November 2013, pp. 196–233 and Mullen, Stephen. 'The great Glasgow West India house of John Campbell, Senior and Co.'. In Devine (ed.), *Recovering Scotland's Slavery Past*.

21 *Memoir of the Whig Party* quoted in Hall, Catherine. 'Reconfiguring race: the stories the slave owners told'. In Hall et al. *Legacies of British Slave-ownership: Colonial Slavery and the Formation of Victorian Britain*. Cambridge: Cambridge University Press, 2014, p. 171.

22 1841, Tamworth manifesto, quoted by Keith McLelland. See 'Redefining the West India interest' in Hall et al. *Legacies of British Slave-ownership*, p. 149.

23 Quoted in *Jamaica Historical Review*, 1(1), 1945, p. 97 (author unknown).

24 15 February 1841, Quintin Kennedy to Sir Charles Dalrymple Fergusson

25 Based on twenty-one shillings per hundredweight in 1836 from Martin, Robert Montgomery. *Statistics of the Colonies of the British Empire . . .: From the Official Records of the Colonial Office*. London: W. H. Allen and Company, 1839.

26 Martin, *Statistics of the Colonies* – sugar exports £1.5 million, rum £1 million, coffee £1 million.

27 See 'Appendix to Seventh Report of the Select Committee on Sugar and Coffee Planting'. *Parliamentary Papers*, HMSO 1848, 25(3), pp. 154–155.

28 It is unclear whether these sums are Jamaican currency or sterling: a labourer's wage in rural Britain in 1850 was around £1 a month.

29 Candler quoted in Jacobs, H. P. 'The Parish of St Thomas on the Eve of the Morant Bay Rebellion'. *Jamaica Historical Society Bulletin*, 4, September 1966, p. 138.

30 Candler's diary, quoting the British Colonial Office's statistics for 1848, *Jamaica Historical Review*, 3(1), March 1959, p. 33.

31 Sewell's dispatches from Jamaica were published in the *New York Times* in 1860 and subsequently collected as a book, *The Ordeal of Free Labor in the British West Indies*. New York: Harper, 1861.

32 Sewell, W. G. 'Emancipation in Jamaica'. *New York Times*, 27 January 1860.

33 Jacobs, 'Parish of St Thomas', p. 83.

34 2 October 1848, James Hope to Sir Charles Dalrymple Fergusson

35 Or De Vancy, or Delaney. No other record of him exists.

36 *The Patriot* (Canada), 25 October 1878.

CHAPTER 16 – BETRAYAL

1 The 1861 census has 360,000 black, 81,000 coloured and 13,000 whites, using those terms.

2 WGS, 'Emancipation in Jamaica', 1860.

3 J.W. Menard, quoted in Heuman, Gad. *'The Killing Time': The Morant Bay Rebellion in Jamaica*. Knoxville, TN: University of Tennessee Press, 1994, p. 158.

4 Heuman, *'The Killing Time'*, pp. 38 and 39.

5 Sewell, *Ordeal of Free Labor*, p. 176.

6 Sewell, *Ordeal of Free Labor*, p. 255.

7 Hutton, Clinton A. *Colour for Colour, Skin for Skin: Marching with the Ancestral Spirits into War Oh at Morant Bay*. Jamaica: Ian Randle Publishers, 2015.

8 *Report of the Jamaica Royal Commission 1866, Part Two: Minutes of Evidence* (*JRC2*). London: Eyre & Spottiswoode, 1866, p. 508.

9 Letter from Grey, then Colonial Secretary, to Sir Charles Grey, Governor of Jamaica, 1 June 1847, quoted in Hart, Richard. *From Occupation to Independence*. London: Pluto Press, 1998, p. 66.

10 *JRC2*, p. 331.

11 Hutton, *Colour for Colour*, p. 26.

12 Hutton, C., review of *'The Killing Time': The Morant Bay Rebellion in Jamaica* by Gad Heuman in *Social and Economic Studies*, 44(1), 1995, p. 202.

13 *JRC2*, p. 165.

14 Ofari, Earl. *'Let Your Motto Be Resistance': The Life and Thought of Henry Highland Garnet*. Boston: Beacon Press, 1972, p. 158.

15 Letter to Louis Chamverow, chairman of the British and Foreign Anti-Slavery Society, October 1854. Quoted in Hutton, *Colour for Colour*, p. 8.

16 Sewell, 'Emancipation in Jamaica' and subsequent articles

17 Sewell, *Ordeal of Free Labour*, pp. 248–249.

18 Hutton, *Colour for Colour*, pp. 84–86.

19 Remark attributed to Congressman James Garfield.

20 Published in the *Anti-Slavery Reporter* of 2 May 1859, p. 100.

21 Magistrates' judgments and duties are all from Appendix to *JRC2*. Accounts of wages differ. Multiple evidence to the 1866 Commission has female and child labourers earning between one shilling and sixpence and three shillings (£0.075–£0.15) a week and males earning from two shillings to an 'average' of five shillings (£0.10–£0.25) a week. Provision grounds rented at twenty-six shillings (£1.30) an acre a year (*JRC2*, pp. 344, 889 and 111).

22 Hutton (*Colour for Colour*, p. 68) shows five labourers who had not paid taxes being fined more than the sum owed (one of them 170 per cent more), while five planters on the same charge were fined on average two-thirds of the tax owed.

23 National Museum of Jamaica Facebook post, 16 November 2015.

24 William Hinson was born at Golden Grove estate in 1843. His memoir quoted in Jacobs, 'Parish of St Thomas'.

25 *JRC2*, pp. 538–539.

26 Heuman, '*The Killing Time*', pp. 48–50.

27 Hutton, *Colour for Colour*, p. 23–25.

28 *JRC2*, p. 857.

29 Hutton, *Colour for Colour*, p. 34.

30 Shortridge, *JRC2*, pp. 22 and 439. Unless otherwise stated all quotes and details in my account of the Morant Bay uprising and aftermath are from the Jamaica Royal Commission report, available online via Google Books and searchable.

CHAPTER 17 – THE EMPIRE STRIKES BACK

1 According to Jane Edwards, *JRC2*, p. 235. Other accounts name Bowen as the magistrate who sat with Walton that day. The complaining man in the body of the court who is mentioned later is named as James Miller by Edwards, but more accounts name him Geoghegan.

2 Most of the events in the courthouse come from Sergeant John Burnett's account, *JRC2*, p. 329.

3   Quoted in 'The Negro Insurrection in Jamaica', *Illustrated London News*, 25 November 1865.

4   The Stony Gut villagers' petition, Governor Eyre's (and other official correspondence relating to the Morant Bay 'disturbances') are in *Accounts and Papers of the House of Commons, 1866*, vol. 13, pp. 160–161, available online through Google Books.

5   Some detail in this section is from the excellent account in Winter, Sarah. 'On the Morant Bay Rebellion in Jamaica and the Governor Eyre–George William Gordon Controversy, 1865–70'. *BRANCH: Britain, Representation and Nineteenth-Century History*, May 2012 (branchcollective.org).

6   Newspaper accounts reprinted in *Anti-Slavery Reporter*, 13(12), 1 December 1865, p. 282. These put the deaths at eight 'civilians' and six 'volunteers'. Other accounts have eighteen dead.

7   *JRC2*, Appendix 1.1.A, has a list of fifteen civilians, most of them government officials, killed at Morant Bay on 11 October. But that includes three white men (Dunn, Cochrane, Hire) who died elsewhere and later. The six officials and twenty-five militia injured at Morant Bay that afternoon give an idea of the extent of the violence. Various sources estimate that six black people died.

8   Eyewitness account printed in the *Colonial Standard*, 21 October 1865, reprinted in *Anti-Slavery Reporter*, 1 December 1865, p. 383.

9   From oral and other accounts, quoted in 'Uprising', National Museum of Jamaica Facebook post, 16 November 2015.

10 A summary of events of 11 and 12 October published 14 December 1865. Quoted in the Jamaica Committee's *Facts and documents relating to the alleged rebellion in Jamaica*. London: Jamaica Committee, 1866, pp. 14 and 15, available online through Google Books.

11 Jamaica Committee, *Facts and documents*, p. 88.

12 Gordon's final letter: 'All I ever did was to recommend the people who complained, to seek redress in a legitimate way; and if in this I erred, or have been misrepresented, I do not think I deserve the extreme sentence. It is, however, the will of my Heavenly Father that I should thus suffer in obeying His command, to relieve the poor and needy, and to protect, as far as I was able, the oppressed.' Gordon attempts to console his wife: 'Comfort your heart. I little expected this. You must do the best you can, and the Lord will help you; and do not be ashamed of the death your poor husband will have suffered.' Quoted in Winter, 'On the Morant Bay Rebellion'.

13 Hutton, *Colour for Colour*, Chapter 9.

14 Ellis, A. B. *The History of the First West India Regiment*. London: Chapman & Hall, 1885, p. 288.

15 Clinton Hutton follows others in estimating 1,013 dead. The Jamaica Royal Commission concluded only 439 deaths were proven (Hutton, *Colour for Colour*, p. 173).

16 This section draws from Knox, B. A. 'The British Government and the Governor Eyre Controversy, 1865–1875'. *Historical Journal*, 19(4), December 1976, pp. 877–900.

17 Carlyle was author of the controversial *Occasional Discourse on the Nigger Question* (1853).

18 Hutton, review of *'The Killing Time'*, p. 191.

19 *Spectator*, 3 February 1866. Henry Ford was never officially given the military title.

20 *Spectator*, 3 March 1866.

21 McLelland, 'Redefining the West India interest', p. 156.

22 Thompson, Andrew S. *The Empire Strikes Back?: The Impact of Imperialism on Britain from the Mid-Nineteenth Century*. London: Routledge, 2005, p. 131.

23 'Affars [sic] in Jamaica'. *New York Times*, 6 November 1865, p. 1.

24 *Works of Thomas Carlyle*, vol. 30. London: Chapman & Hall, 1869, p. 12.

25 12 April 1866, T. H. Huxley to Charles Kingsley (collected at mathcs. clark.edu/huxley)

26 Quoted in Winter, 'On the Morant Bay Rebellion'.

27 *The Water Babies* contains damning stereotypes: 'poor Paddies' become the Doasyoulikes, a people de-evolved due to their lack of moral structures.

28 Quoted in Kent, Susan Kingsley. *Gender and Power in Britain 1640–1990*. London, Routledge, 2002, p. 220.

29 Hansard – House of Lords, volume 181, column 102 (available at hansard. parliament.uk).

30 Mill, J. S. *Essays on Equality, Law, and Education*. Toronto: University of Toronto Press, 1963, p. 461.

31 Knox, 'Governor Eyre Controversy', pp. 877–900.

32 Knox, 'Governor Eyre Controversy', p. 887.

33 1870 Jamaica Almanac, list of magistrates.

34 Quoting the Crossman Commission in *Jamaican Reflections – a look at St Thomas Parish, 1494–1962*, unpublished.

35 St Thomas in 1883 and the 1930s: Jemmott, Jenny. *A History of St Thomas Parish*. Pdf at parishhistoriesofjamaica.org/st-thomas, p. 120.

36 Chapman, Esther. 'The Truth About Jamaica'. *West Indian Review*, July 1938.

37 Gott, Richard. 'Let's end the myths of Britain's imperial past'. *Guardian*, 19 October 2011.

CHAPTER 18 – JAMAICA TODAY

1 Nathaniel Phillips began life in poverty, the illegitimate son of an East London sugar merchant. Until recently his descendants lived at Slebech Park, the estate he bought in Wales when he retired wealthy from Jamaica. See UCL/LBS entry for 'Nathaniel Phillips of Slebech'.

2 As the son of a great-uncle of Cameron, Duff was technically a first cousin six times removed (Davies, Caroline. 'How do we know David Cameron has slave owners in family background?' *Guardian*, 29 September 2015).

3 Doyle, Jack. '"Move on": David Cameron tells Jamaican anti-slavery campaigners that billions in compensation is NOT the answer and the time has come to "build for the future"'. *Daily Mail*, 30 September 2015; and 'David Cameron rules out slavery reparation during Jamaica visit', BBC News online, 30 September 2015. But there is a discrepancy with the actual transcript (see 'PM's speech to the Jamaican Parliament' at gov.uk, 30 September 2015), indicating that remarks on abolition and reparations were toned down for delivery.

4 See Freeman-Powell, Shamaan. 'Windrush row over criminal deportation flight to Jamaica' and '"Living in fear" after being deported from the UK'. BBC News online, 6 February 2019 and 13 May 2019.

5 Ford, Steve. 'UK Government does deal with Jamaica to recruit nurses for NHS'. *Nursing Times*, 20 April 2018; and Francis, Kimone. 'Almost 100 nurses resign from University Hospital in 2019'. *Jamaica Observer*, 20 January 2020. See also 'UK to establish global nursing partnership with Jamaica', Department of Health and Social Care press release, 20 April 2018.

6 I have failed to find up-to-date statistics. Sives, Amanda et al ('Teacher Migration from Jamaica: assessing the short term impact'. *Caribbean Journal of Education*, 27(1), 2006, pp. 85–111) cite the Planning Institute of Jamaica in 2003: in twenty years Jamaica had lost 54,288 highly skilled professionals to North America alone, representing 30.2 per cent of the output of Jamaica's education system.

7 Education statistics: Meditz, Sandra W. and Dennis M. Hanratty (eds). *Islands of the Commonwealth Caribbean Islands: a regional study*. Washington, DC: GPO for the Library of Congress, 1987; and Statistics on International Development 2013 (Department for International Development (DfID)) for 2011 figure, p. 43. British historical statistics (UK Parliament) are calculated from 4.8 million primary and 2 million secondary pupils in 1951. See also *World Illiteracy at Mid-century: A Statistical Study*, Unesco, 1957.

8 'Profile of Development – Caribbean', DfID, file 723125, July 2018.

9 Quoted in 'Respected Jamaican professor Freddie Hickling has died'. *Daily Gleaner*, 8 May 2020.

10 Hickling, Frederick W. *Owning Our Madness: Facing Reality in Post-colonial Jamaica*. Kingston: Caribbean Institute of Mental Health and Substance Abuse, 2016, pp. 8 and 201-202.

11 'Evidence grows of Croydon's slavery links'. *Croydon Citizen*, July 2020. Two nieces inherited from William Bond, who owned two other estates in Jamaica – Cardiff estate and Spring estate in St Thomas (see UCL/ LBS entry for 'William Bond').

12 The database is at slavevoyages.com. It is sometimes known as the Eltis database, after David Eltis, the Anglo-American historian who started it. It has always been 'live', a work-in-progress with many contributors: in 1999 it listed 27,000 voyages, by 2021 the number had increased to over 36,000.

13 Centre for Reparations Research (CRR) presentation, University of the West Indies, 10 June 2019. Figures cited correct at the time of writing.

14 See Sibbald's of Leith invoice dated 19 November 1807 (F of K papers)

15 I asked Aleksandr Sazonov if his research into the evidence provided by the CRR, most of which is from the records of British Royal Navy ships that encountered the Russian slavers off West Africa, has supported his rejection of the claim. He promised to get back to me.

16 No trace of him on the internet.

APPENDIX

1 Mance, Henry. 'How UK heritage is coming to terms with its links to slavery'. *Financial Times*, 25 September 2020.

2 Paul Bogle was free at his birth. The fortune was made chiefly through the family merchant business, Robert Bogle & Co., of Glasgow – see UCL/LBS entry for 'Archibald Bogle'.

3 See UCL/LBS entry for 'William Bond'.

4 @re_colston, Twitter, 7 June 2020. I have not been able to verify if Alex Colston is a direct descendant of William Colston.

5 Statement on Black Lives Matter on gladstoneslibrary.org.

6 The family literature only says that she was a 'direct descendant' of George William Gordon – see 'After "A Wonderful Life" Edna Mae Gordon is laid to rest'. *Jamaica Observer*, 29 December 2013.

7 Marano, Rebecca. 'Harewood House acknowledges slave trade history and speaks in solidarity with Black Lives Matter'. *Yorkshire Evening Post*, 10 June 2020.

8 See Whyte's entry in the Canadian *Dictionary of National Biography*.

9 David Olusoga interviewed by Lewis Hamilton. *Today*, BBC Radio 4, 26 December 2020.

10 Wild, Rose. 'Feedback: What connects Jane Austen and George Floyd?'. *Times*, 16 January 2021.

IMAGE CREDITS

p.13 'A Knight Enters The Lists at The Eglinton Tournament' by Edward Henry Corbauld. England, 1840 © Victoria and Albert Museum, London.

p.71 Blue road sign, 'Welcome to Bloody Bay'. Reprinted by permission of Alex Renton.

p.79 'West India Luxury!!' print © The Trustees of the British Museum.

p.83 Photo of naval cannon above Bloody Bay. Reprinted by permission of Alex Renton.

p.100 Portrait of James Graham, 1789–1860. Reprinted by permission of Alex Renton.

p.110 Map of the Rozelle estate. Reprinted courtesy of the National Library of Jamaica.

p.137 Mr. Wood as Three Fingered Jack, published by E. Skelt. London, England, nineteenth century © Victoria and Albert Museum, London.

p.161 Rozelle estate plantation book, 1872, from the Fergusson of Kilkerran papers. Reprinted by permission of Alex Renton.

p.173 'Adventures of Johnny Newcombe', plate 1, print © The Trustees of the British Museum.

p.243 'To the Friends of Negro Emancipation' print © The Trustees of the British Museum.

p.295 'The Jamaica Question', 1865. The Cartoon Collector / Heritage-Images / TopFoto.

INDEX